Peasant Cooperation and Capitalist Expansion
in Central Peru

Latin American Monographs No. 46
Institute of Latin American Studies
The University of Texas at Austin

Peasant Cooperation and Capitalist Expansion in Central Peru

Edited by Norman Long
and Bryan R. Roberts

Institute of Latin American Studies
The University of Texas at Austin

International Standard Book Number 0-292-76451-0 (cloth)
0-292-76452-9 (paper)

Library of Congress Catalog Card Number 78-54292

The Latin American Monographs Series
is distributed for the Institute of
Latin American Studies by:
  University of Texas Press
  P.O. Box 7819
  Austin, Texas 78712

Contents

Maps

Preface

This volume is one of two that bring together the main findings of research carried out in the Mantaro region of central Peru from August 1970 until December 1972. The project was financed by a British Social Science Research Council grant made to Norman Long and Bryan Roberts at the University of Manchester. Its aim was to undertake a regional study of social change and development in an economically diversified area of highland Peru. We selected the Mantaro region with the help of Carlos Samaniego, who, at the time, was a member of the National Agrarian University in Lima and registered for a doctorate at the University of Manchester. Carlos Samaniego's family had migrated from the Mantaro Valley to Lima but maintained contacts in their area of origin. Carlos, who is both agronomist and anthropologist, convinced us that the changes occurring in the area were especially interesting to those concerned with the general problems of agrarian change and regional development.

Since the area was relatively well documented in the literature, we were able to begin our work by choosing two rural locations from which to explore regional interrelationships: the villages of Matahuasi and Pucará. We were lucky to recruit two Peruvian researchers who already were well acquainted with the region and its problems. These two, Teófilo Altamirano, now of the Catholic University, Lima, and Juan Solano, of the Central University, Huancayo, worked with us for the duration of the project, living both in the villages and in Huancayo. Both of these researchers played a crucial role in shaping the field research and took major responsibility for particular case studies. Their help and enthusiasm were major factors contributing to the success of the project.

Our manner of working, in both village and city settings, was to start with detailed case studies of households and of economic enterprises of various kinds, and to use these studies to identify interesting dimensions for further research, including large-scale sample surveys.

This procedure opened up possibilities of collaboration with other researchers, both Peruvian and foreign. Thus, Julian Laite, who was supported independently by a British Social Science Research Council studentship, undertook the study of the relationship between the mining sector and the village economy of the valley. Gavin Smith, who had Canada Council support, decided to join us from Sussex University and became interested in the case of Huasicancha. Huasicancha was interesting not only because of successful peasant political action but also because it represented a type of highland village with close connections with the valley and with Lima. Our contacts with the Mexican anthropological research institute, CISINAH, resulted in Marcelo Grondin's cooperating with us to undertake a "restudy" of Muquiyauyo. Richard N. Adams had traveled with us on our first trip to see the Mantaro Valley and had encouraged us to think of looking at the changes that had taken place in Muquiyauyo since he had finished his field study almost twenty years earlier. Carlos Samaniego had by this time come back to teach in the National Agrarian University, and he also began to work with us, carrying out, with the help of his students, an intensive study of the microregion of Chupaca. Part of his support came from the Ford Foundation and the rest from his university's research funds. Finally, David Winder, of the Department of Overseas Administrative Studies, Manchester University, joined us with the support of the British Ministry of Overseas Development to document community reform and to study the possibilities of communal enterprise.

These research relationships were loosely structured, but they led to a considerable interchange of ideas and data and to enduring friendships. For our part, we gained a great deal from these relationships, both in the work context and in terms of personal support. Our own writing has been influenced deeply by the data and ideas contributed by each of these other researchers.

Our research base in Peru was the Instituto de Estudios Peruanos, whose director, Dr. José Matos Mar, helped us by providing useful contacts and a stimulating intellectual environment. At the time we were affiliated with the Instituto, Giorgio Alberti and Rodrigo Sánchez were completing a study focused mainly on the Jauja end of the Mantaro Valley. Both of them became our good friends and helped considerably in orientating us to the special features of the Mantaro area. We would especially like to thank them for their generosity in making available the preliminary results of their own work. Another important link for us was that with the Catholic University in Lima, through Fernando Fuenzalida and Enrique Mayer. Fernando had spent a period at Manchester and throughout our stay in Peru was a lively critic and conversationalist as well as an additional source of academic support. Enrique Mayer, who was also familiar with the peculiarities of the British academic scene, was equally supportive of our efforts and, in addition, introduced us to his parents. The Mayer family, who lived in Huancayo, proved invaluable to us, as friends and as knowledgeable local people, throughout the research. Indeed, much of our information on the development of Huancayo was obtained through the help and insight of Guillermo Mayer.

In Huancayo, we received considerable help and support from researchers and teachers in the Central University and in the Technical Institute, Mariscal Cáceres. At the University, first Ramiro Matos and, subsequently, César Fonseca and Jesús Véliz Lizárraga helped us by recruiting students, by sharing their considerable local expertise, and by giving us what, at times, was crucial institutional backing.

One of the most pleasant and rewarding associations during the work was with the anthropology and sociology students of the Central University in Huancayo. They conscientiously carried out a series of important case studies and interviews in the communities of the valley and in Huancayo. They also did the interviewing for the large-scale survey of Huancayo in 1971. We cannot name them all individually, but the following helped over the longest period: César Palacios, Raúl Santana, Germán Matos, Rosa Benavides, Manuel Ortiz, Julio Olivera, Pedro Cano, Sergio Gamarra, Herly Deza, Marcial Segovia, Flora Ruiz, Isabel Rodríguez, Carmen Rojas, Roy Rosada, José Zavala, and D. Mesa, and Máximo Castañeda S., who also carried out an individual study of the cooperative of the *Margen Derecha* of the Mantaro. In addition, Padre José Atalaya of the Catholic University helped us with his detailed study of Sicaya. He continued this study independently and has collected a considerable body of field data.

Naturally, given the nature of our work, some of our most lasting memories are of the villages, fiestas, and people of the Mantaro area. It was a beautiful and invigorating place to live and, more important, it was a friendly milieu for both participation and observation. Of the very many people who invited us into their homes and to their celebrations, we would like especially to mention the Carmelo Indigoyen and Julio Oré families, who were the first to offer us accommodation and good counsel. The other researchers have their own individual debts of gratitude in the villages of Matahuasi, Pucará, Ataura, Sicaya, Muquiyauyo, Ahuac, Chupaca, Hualhuas, Chongos Bajo, Cacchi, Huasicancha, Yanacancha, and Concepción. Even in the more "impersonal" research locations of La Oroya, Huancayo, and

Lima, many friendships developed. We should also add that throughout the research we received the cooperation and interest of local and
central government officials whenever we requested it: we encountered
no difficulties in obtaining access to official materials.

As we write these acknowledgments, we realize just how fortunate
we were in our research. In both our experiences, this Mantaro research has been one of the most rewarding and trouble-free of projects.
We were undoubtedly lucky in undertaking the study at a particularly
favorable period for research in Peru, when there was considerable
intellectual excitement about the possibilities of major social reform.
Our experiences have given both of us a deep affection for Peru and
an enduring interest in Peruvian affairs.

Norman Long was also supported by a postdoctoral Foreign Area
Fellowship. Furthermore, when in Peru both of us received useful
assistance from the local representatives of the Ford Foundation. We
would like to mention, in particular, Richard Dye, Abraham Lowenthal, Bob Drysdale, and Peter Cleaves. They were especially helpful
with, and sympathetic to, the further training of Peruvian anthropologists and sociologists. Some of our own collaborators were able to
complete advanced degrees as a result.

In preparing this manuscript and in its final typing, we are grateful
to Mrs. C. Dowson, Mrs. D. Robinson, and Mrs. B. Elvin, of Durham,
and Miss Jane Connah, of Manchester. Their help was the more valuable since neither editor has legible handwriting. Naturally, we
reserve until last our gratitude to our respective families. They enjoyed living in the Mantaro Valley with us. We are grateful for their
patience with us as overly enthusiastic field workers in fiestas and other
celebrations. In many ways, the worst period for our families has been
that of preparing this manuscript. Since we are now teaching at different universities, it has been difficult to organize our work together
without encroaching on time that we would otherwise spend with our
families.

Norman Long and Bryan R. Roberts

Peasant Cooperation and Capitalist Expansion
in Central Peru

1. Introduction

NORMAN LONG AND BRYAN R. ROBERTS

In this volume we present a series of case studies analyzing the different ways in which groups of peasants* and other inhabitants of the central highlands of Peru have cooperated in the face of major economic and political transformations. These transformations involved the development of small-scale commercial farming, a marked increase in migration and forms of wage labor, the extension of a more intricate market and transport system linking villages directly to the large urban centers and Lima, the capital, and the increasing political integration of the area into the national system. A major stimulus for this process, and for the direction it was to take, was provided in the late nineteenth century and early twentieth century by the establishment of large-scale capitalist enterprise, often under foreign ownership. In the central highlands, this enterprise was mainly concentrated in the mining sector, but it also included large livestock haciendas and, on the coast, cotton plantations dependent on migrant labor from the highlands. In recent years, this penetration of external forces has been accelerated by more permanent migration to Lima and other urban centers and by the extension of government programs of agrarian reform that have led to the growing presence of different government agencies in even the remoter areas of the region.[1]

The theme of this collection thus centers on the interplay of local-level processes and the centralizing tendencies of modern economic and political development. We view this process primarily from the perspective of provincial groups and actors in order to show that the

*We use the term *peasant* in a broad sense to characterize a rural population that owns and works land but that may also receive income from other, non-agricultural occupations, including wage labor. These matters are discussed in the concluding chapter.

organization and activities of local people are not simply responses to externally initiated change but contribute to and modify the pattern of regional and even national development.

The central highlands of Peru have attracted considerable attention as an area in which community-based forms of cooperation have long flourished.[2] Commentators have stressed, for example, the vitality of such customary modes of mutual aid as communal work parties (*faenas*) and various forms of interhousehold exchange and reciprocity. They have also emphasized that the region has been exceptionally successful in adapting traditions of community self-help to meet modern necessities. A large proportion of the public services, including schools, in the villages of the area have been constructed utilizing communal labor and community land and often have had the financial assistance of resident and migrant members of the community. In one such village (see Grondin in this volume) members collaborated to build a hydroelectric plant that eventually provided the first electricity service to the nearby provincial capital of Jauja. There are numerous migrant associations in the mines, in other work centers, and in Lima-Callao, representing villages of the area. Some of these associations date from the beginning of this century; over time, they have contributed to local developments by lobbying national government departments, raising funds, and providing various forms of technical and organizational expertise. The interest of migrants in their villages of origin is evident in their active participation in villages fiestas, in their retaining rights to land and other productive resources, and in their frequent return visits to see family and friends.

The region has the highest density of legally recognized *comunidades indígenas* (now called peasant communities, *comunidades campesinas*) in the country. These are official organizations, found at village or hamlet level, that control and exploit communal land resources and labor; they are governed, as Winder describes in chapter 8, by a specific body of legislation dating from the Peruvian Constitution of 1920. According to a report of 1967, some 144 villages of the central highlands were officially recognized as *comunidades* and a further 25 had applied for recognition.[3] This left only about 30 villages in the area that were not registered as such. In contrast, in Puno, one of the poorest and most solidly Indian departments of Peru, there were, in 1968, only 152 recognized *comunidades indígenas* out of a total of 705 villages.[4]

These communal traditions and patterns of community organization, however, flourished in a region that was one of the earliest and most thoroughly exposed to the effects of modern capitalism. From the end of the nineteenth century, mining developed rapidly in the central highlands, employing at its height some twenty thousand workers; in the same period, the coastal cotton plantations recruited thousands of workers from the region for seasonal employment. By 1908, the Lima-Huancayo railroad had been constructed, and an all-weather road linking the area to the coast was completed by 1939 using labor from the *comunidades indigenas*. These developments stimulated the growth of Huancayo city as a commercial, transport, and, ultimately, industrial and administrative center.

Improved communications and new work opportunities led to considerable out-migration from the villages and small towns of the region: though much of this migration was temporary, an increasing number of households settled permanently in Lima, Huancayo, or one of the mine towns. By 1940, for example, the department of Junín in the central highlands was among the three departments in the nation that contributed most migrants to Lima-Callao.[5] In this period, village agriculture became increasingly commercialized through a small-scale, household-based entrepreneurship and was accompanied by the growth of craft industry, transport, and retail businesses. Most of these economic enterprises remained under local control and were relatively small-scale. Hence, the region also became noted for an exceptionally active class of local entrepreneurs. This vitality of the village economy has long antecedents and was noted by mid-nineteenth-century commentators also.[6]

The area has also been noted for its high level of political activity. APRA (American Popular Revolutionary Alliance) had a strong basis of support in the region through the mining and textile unions and particularly among the richer small-holding farmers and small businessmen. In the 1960s Junín became one of the strongholds of Acción Popular, the party of President Fernando Belaúnde, which came to power with an ideology of community participation and self-help.[7] Some of the most vigorous peasant federations of Peru, such as the Movimiento Comunal del Centro, also originated in this area.[8] As Smith and Cano describe in this volume, a history of conflict with neighboring haciendas that spanned several centuries led in the case of the community of Huasicancha to a serious weakening of one of the largest of these haciendas. This history of peasant protest was in part reflected in an active guerrilla movement and a spate of land occupations in the central highlands in the early 1960s, and it became an important precipitant of the present government's land-reform program. The first major livestock estate to be converted, in 1969, into an agrarian cooperative (or sociedad agraria de interés social, SAIS) under the agrarian reform was that owned by the Cerro de Pasco Corporation, the principal mining company of the central region. This was followed, in 1971, by the expropriation of the haciendas of the Sociedad Ganadera del Centro, which were grouped together to form SAIS Cahuide, benefiting twenty-nine communities at the southern end of the Mantaro Valley.[9]

The main analytic interest, therefore, of the central highlands of Peru is the coexistence of three different responses to the increasing integration of the region into the national structure: the revitalization of communal and cooperative institutions; the development and diversification of a predominantly household-based economy allowing for considerable local entrepreneurship; and the emergence at the local and regional levels of organized political action. The papers in this volume concentrate on cases of collective economic and political action. They argue that the development of a household-based economy, along with the patterns of economic and social differentiation associated with it, provides an important key to understanding the persistence of cooperative institutions and collective action. Another dimension explored is the way in which state policies and the development of the national economy itself have shaped the nature and evolution of community-based forms of cooperation.

The General Setting

The material for this volume was collected in the Mantaro region of the central highlands of Peru during 1970–1972. The Mantaro region is situated about three hundred kilometers due east of the capital city of Lima (see map 1). The population of the area is mainly concentrated in the valley zone, which is approximately seventy kilometers long and varies between seven and twenty kilometers in width, and which lies at between 3,100 and 3,500 meters above sea level. The bulk of the region's agricultural (as against livestock) production comes from the valley itself: the Mantaro Valley, together with the nearby provinces of Tarma and Satipo, provides some 25 percent of the vegetables and cereals sold on the Lima market. Surrounding the valley is a high plateau (*puna alta*), some 800 to 1,200 meters above the valley, that is dominated by large cattle estates[10] (now made up of the cooperatives of the SAIS of central Peru), but where there are also small independent villages and hamlets specializing in pastoral activities.

The high plateau and the valley (which together make up the Mantaro region) have been interconnected historically through the political control originally exercised by valley towns and villages over the scattered peasant populations of the plateau, and through barter and marketing. In recent years the towns of the valley (particularly Huan-

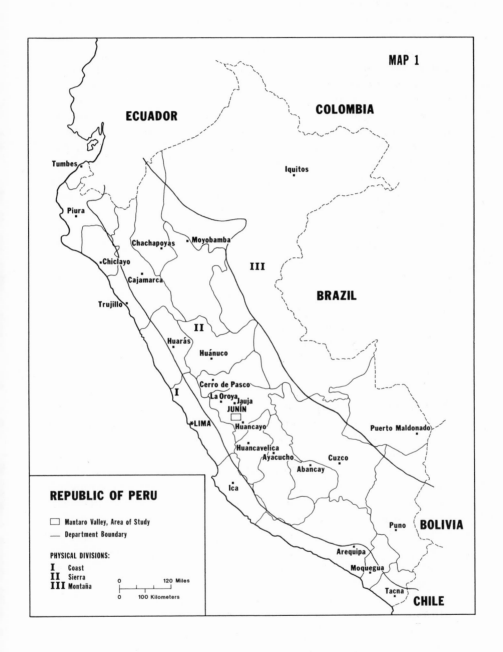

MAP 1

ECUADOR

COLOMBIA

Tumbes

Iquitos

Piura

Chachapoyas • Moyobamba

•Chiclayo

Cajamarca

III

Trujillo

BRAZIL

II

Huarás

Huánuco

Cerro de Pasco

La Oroya Jauja

I

JUNÍN

•LIMA   Huancayo

Puerto Maldonado

Huancavelica

Ayacucho

Cuzco

Abancay

Ica

Puno   BOLIVIA

Arequipa

Moquegua

Tacna

CHILE

REPUBLIC OF PERU

☐ Mantaro Valley, Area of Study
— Department Boundary

PHYSICAL DIVISIONS:
I   Coast
II   Sierra
III Montaña

0   120 Miles

0   100 Kilometers

cayo, Jauja, Concepción, and Chupaca) have become focuses for both permanent and temporary migrants from the highland villages, including students seeking secondary and higher education. We found, for example, that in 1971 the majority of migrants from one highland village (Cacchi) were resident either in Huancayo or other valley towns for reasons of education.

The Mantaro region lies 12° south of the equator and consequently suffers only slight seasonal differences in temperature. In winter (October to April) temperatures range from 1°C. to 21°C. (average 10°C. to 12°C.), while in summer (May to September) the range is from 6°C. to 23°C. (average 8°C. to 11°C.). Almost all the rain (about 30 inches per annum is the average for the central valley zone) falls in winter, particularly in January, February, and March. July, August, and September are months of very low rainfall when maximum demands are placed on irrigation supplies. They are also months when the phenomenon of temperature inversion can cause sudden local frosts and considerable damage to crops. For example, in 1972 almost the entire maize crop was destroyed by frost. These climatic uncertainties, together with market fluctuations, mean that there is considerable uncertainty in agricultural production, and crops vary in any given year in different parts of the region.

Soil conditions vary greatly within short distances, due primarily to the effect of the three glacial epochs of the quaternary that radically modified the geomorphology of the valley. Most of the agriculture is carried out on three sets of natural river terraces located between two and one hundred meters above the river bed.[11] Soils on these terraces range from coarse gravels to rich loams. Land close to the river is badly drained and subject to flooding in winter; the soil on the steep slopes of the valley sides tends to be thin and infertile. The most productive agricultural land is that which is irrigated by the two major canals, one on each side of the valley. The longest one (sixty-four kilometers in length), which runs down the eastern margin of the valley, was completed in 1942 and now irrigates 4,200 hectares.

The region falls within the boundaries of three of the provinces of the department of Junín (see map 2). These three provinces, Huancayo, Concepción, and Jauja, are further subdivided into eighty-four districts, sixty-four of which are located in the valley and the remaining twenty on the surrounding plateau. Total population for this zone is 410,740, of which 115,000 live in the city of Huancayo, the provincial and departmental capital and the main commercial center of the central highlands.[12] The remainder live in about two hundred towns and villages scattered throughout the area. Outside the urban areas of

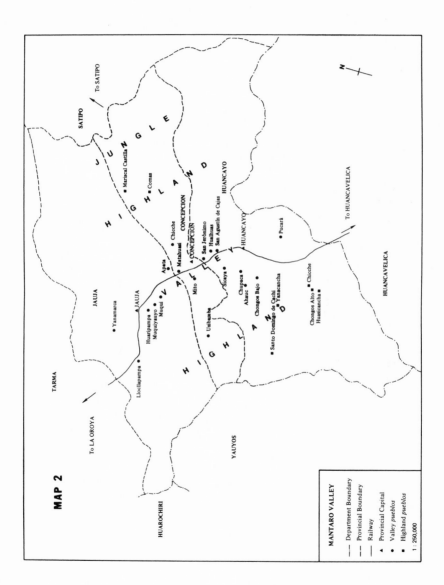

MAP 2

TARMA

To LA OROYA

HUAROCHIRI

YAUYOS

SATIPO

To SATIPO

Mariscal Castilla

Comas

JUNGLE

HIGHLAND

CONCEPCION

HUANCAYO

To HUANCAVELICA

HUANCAVELICA

Chicche

San Jerónimo

Hualhuas

San Agustín de Cajas

CONCEPCION

Apata

Metahuasi

JAUJA

Yanamarca

Huaripampa

Muquiyauyo

Muqui

Llocllapampa

JAUJA

VALLEY

Mito

Usibamba

Sicaya

Chupaca

Ahauc

Chongos Bajo

Santo Domingo de Cachi

Chongos Alto

Huasicancha

Chicche

Yanacancha

Pucará

HIGHLAND

HUANCAYO

MANTARO VALLEY

---- Department Boundary

— Provincial Boundary

— Railway

▲ Provincial Capital

• Valley *pueblos*

■ Highland *pueblos*

1 : 250,000

Huancayo and Jauja (the capital of the province of Jauja, population 13,936), districts vary in population from as few as 817 people to as many as 10,000. The average district has between 2,000 and 3,000 inhabitants. The valley itself is one of the most densely populated regions of Peru, with about 150 inhabitants per square kilometer for the districts located on the *puna* pasture lands.

The most common form of landholding in the Mantaro area is the privately owned *minifundio* (microholding). In all three provinces, farms of five hectares or less make up at least 80 percent of the total number of agricultural holdings (see table 1). The provisional results of the 1972 census show that 41 percent of the farms in Huancayo province were less than half a hectare in extent, as against 25 percent for Concepción province and 34 percent for Jauja province (see table 2).

TABLE 1

NUMBER, SIZE, AND EXTENSION OF AGRICULTURAL
UNITS AND OF THOSE IN PRIVATE OWNERSHIP,
BY PROVINCE

A. Agricultural Units

Province	Size of Units	Number	% of Total	Extension (Hectares)	% of Total
Huancayo	Under 1 hectare	13,051	57.9	6,567.9	2.1
	1 to under 5 hectares	8,484	37.7	17,574.9	5.6
	More than 5 hectares	999	4.4	288,872.2	92.3
Concepción	Under 1 hectare	2,576	35.9	1,490.3	1.1
	1 to under 5 hectares	3,700	51.6	8,623.4	6.4
	More than 5 hectares	900	12.5	124,344.6	92.5
Jauja	Less than 1 hectare	5,830	48.5	3,048.5	1.4
	1 to under 5 hectares	4,579	38.1	9,663.6	4.4
	More than 5 hectares	1,616	13.4	207,914.9	94.2

B. Private Property

Province	Size of Units	Number	% of Total	Extension (Hectares)	% of Total
Huancayo	Under 1 hectare	11,199	85.8	5,627.7	85.7
	1 to under 5 hectares	7,264	85.6	15,101.6	85.9
	More than 5 hectares	815	81.6	185,857.7	64.3
Concepción	Under 1 hectare	2,291	88.9	1,321.4	88.7
	1 to under 5 hectares	3,203	86.6	7,444.0	86.3
	More than 5 hectares	795	88.3	92,173.9	74.1
Jauja	Under 1 hectare	4,961	85.1	2,542.8	83.4
	1 to under 5 hectares	3,620	79.1	7,499.5	77.6
	More than 5 hectares	1,446	89.5	146,830.3	70.6

Source: 1961 Census, Department of Junín.

Although the larger landholdings (more than five hectares) constituted a small percentage of the total number of arable holdings, in all three provinces they included more than 90 percent of the available land.

TABLE 2
NUMBER AND SIZE OF AGRICULTURAL UNITS

Province	Size of Units	Number	% of Total
Huancayo	Under ½ hectare	16,801	40.6
	½ hectare and more	23,583	59.4
	Total	39,644	100.0
Concepción	Under ½ hectare	3,303	25.0
	½ hectare and more	9,937	75.0
	Total	13,240	100.0
Juaja	Under ½ hectare	8,253	38.8
	½ hectare and more	13,044	61.2
	Total	21,297	100.0

SOURCE: 1972 Census, Provisional Results, Department of Junín.

This structure of landholding is broadly similar to that found elsewhere in the highlands of Peru. In the neighboring department of Huancavelica, for example, 95 percent of landholdings in 1961 were less than ten hectares in size, while those landholdings of more than ten hectares held 88 percent of the land. Indeed, landholdings of more than five hundred hectares accounted for 72 percent of the land in use.[13] Nationally, 83.2 percent of landholdings are five hectares or less, but these include only 5.5 percent of the land in use; in contrast, landholdings of over five hundred hectares make up 76 percent of the total area.[14]

In the Mantaro region, small holdings are concentrated in the valley, while large landholdings or estates predominate on the high plateau. This pattern is characteristic of much of highland Peru and reflects the ecological division between lands devoted largely to pastoral activity and those more suited to arable farming. Nevertheless, the Mantaro Valley is somewhat exceptional in that it is the second largest of the inter-Andean valleys, is well irrigated, and thus supports a large population.

There has been a tendency in much writing on Peru to overemphasize the economic and political significance of the concentration of land in large estates. The "hacienda system" has, in this way, been seen to characterize the agrarian structure of Peru prior to the implementation of the recent land reform, with peasant communities being viewed as marginal to this system. In fact, the large landholdings in the highlands, despite their control over the vast majority of land, employed directly or indirectly only a small proportion of the rural population. Even when the large coastal sugar and cotton estates are included, medium- and large-scale landholdings employed in 1961 less than 30 percent of the rural labor force.[15] In the highlands, the pastoral estates continue to employ a very small permanent labor force, one that, even for the largest of them, is unlikely to exceed one hundred workers. The 269,115 hectares of the SAIS Cahuide, made of seven former haciendas, employ a total of about five hundred workers.[16]

The importance of peasant farming is evident from the national statistics on agricultural production. About half of Peru's production of potatoes, wheat, barley, and bananas and more than a third of maize production come from farms of less than five hectares;[17] and in the 1960s, potatoes were as important in total value of production as such export crops as cotton and sugar.[18] Even more surprising is the contribution of peasant production to livestock farming. In 1961, well before agrarian reform, 74 percent of cattle and 76 percent of sheep were raised on farms of less than five hectares.[19]

This economic structure is also apparent even in those situations where large-scale capitalist livestock enterprises have predominated. Thus in the Mantaro region we find that at the time of the dissolution of the Sociedad Ganadera del Centro hacienda complex, the company controlled 95 percent of the *puna* pasture land but only a maximum of 59 percent of the sheep. In contrast, twenty-nine adjacent peasant communities controlled only 5 percent of the land but possessed 41 percent of the sheep.[20] The figures imply the overgrazing of community land, which is documented by Samaniego and Roberts in chapter 9, and there is no doubt that the quality of the sheep was considerably lower among peasant owners. However, the sheer number of sheep being produced in peasant communities leads Horton to argue in his recent survey of land reform enterprises that, even if hacienda production was three times greater in carcass and wool weight per animal, "we cannot be sure that total production per unit of land was significantly higher in the modern enterprise than in the backward neighboring communities."[21] Though peasant production has not played a major part in Peru's export economy during this century, it has nevertheless been a mainstay of the domestic agricultural market, providing foodstuffs for the mines and urban centers, and primary materials (wool, leather, and timber) for local industrial production. Expanding peasant production provided the basis for the internal economic differentiation of peasant villages and led to the development of indigenous entrepreneurial activity in the fields of trade and transport.

The reasons for what appears to be the relative lack of dynamism of the highland hacienda require more extensive investigation. Evidence suggests that the hacienda was unable to control production on its own land effectively, though this varied from region to region and from hacienda to hacienda.[22] In some cases, "tied" peasants were able to build up considerable amounts of livestock and commercialize them on their own account; likewise, on arable haciendas, peasant *colonos* often had effective control over their production that could equal that of the hacienda itself.[23] Given poor pasturage, low quality soils, and harsh climatic conditions, large-scale commercial farming in the Andes is a risky and, probably, not highly profitable enterprise. Under these conditions, there were low levels of investment in most haciendas and a reluctance to invest in fencing, supervision, and general infrastructure.

Background Themes and Literature

The case studies presented in the chapters that follow form part of a team project that studied social aspects of regional development in the central highlands of Peru. Our aim in undertaking the original study was to examine the processes of social change in a provincial region, viewing this change as a product of internal economic trans- formations and not simply as responses to external economic and political forces. Such an orientation would enable us, we hoped, to document and explain variations in the growth of village and town economies and provide some understanding of how provincial develop- ments might influence change at the national level. Part of our interest was in the familiar problem of how "traditional" village-based forms of social organization were affected by the expansion of a modern capi- talist economy. We aimed, for example, to study small-scale entrepre- neurs operating in the towns and villages of the area so as to explore how local initiatives contributed both to the internal articulation of the region and to its incorporation into the wider economy and polity. By studying the existing interrelationships of localities and social groups within and outside the region we hoped to avoid making arbitrary cultural distinctions between rural and urban milieu or between mod- ern industrial locations (in our case, the large smelting plant of Cerro de Pasco at Oroya) and peasant villages. Such distinctions, we felt, had contributed to the misleading opposition of "traditional" and "modern" patterns of social organization and to the equally misleading view that the main obstacle to economic progress was the presence, in countries like Peru, of a mass of supposedly conservative peasant farmers.

Although we have tried to build on previous studies, our perspective and conclusions differ from many of them in the importance we place on the internal differentiation of the village economy in explaining the nature and evolution of communal and cooperative institutions, and in the way we account for land invasions, conflicts with other villages, and conflicts with the haciendas. We also stress changes in the Peruvian state.

Following recent interpretations by economic historians, we view the process of differentiation as existing from at least early in the colonial period and as being characteristic of highland Peru as a whole. Fluctuations in national and regional economies, warfare, large-scale migrations, and the development of distinctive class interests at the village level produced changes in local society. Though the pace of change may have increased with the development of modern communications, it is a mistake to contrast, as some have done, changes in the contemporary period with an unchanging traditional society prior to the Second World War.[24] In the concluding chapter of this volume, we elaborate this criticism and discuss the interconnections between local-level processes and developments in the national and international economy. Related to this is our contention that the peasantry has been a major and relatively independent force in the economic and political development of highland Peru. We reject the view that, for much of its history, highland Peru was characterized by a monolithic power structure in which peasant populations were subordinated economically and politically to a hacienda system and to its associated urban elites. We argue instead that the power domain was much more fragmented and that in certain critical periods, and especially in areas like the Mantaro region, the crucial focus of economic and political power was the village and small town, not the hacienda or provincial capital.

We also eschew explanations of regional development that give weight to the contribution of specific cultural and historical factors—such as, in the Mantaro case, the special nature of Huanca social organization and conquest experience—to the evolution of provincial society. Such an emphasis, we believe, on the one hand tends to obscure the broad regularities of social change occurring throughout highland Peru, while on the other it fails to account for the diversity of responses shown by different villages and peasant groups within the same cultural region. Likewise we do not attempt to isolate the special characteristics of so-called Andean forms of social and cultural organization found in the Mantaro area. This, we argue, is a task more appropriate to those specifically interested in exploring the idea that there exist certain broad cultural patterns and themes underlying contemporary forms of social organization that have persisted in the face of major economic and political change.[25] Nevertheless, in order to develop our analysis, it is necessary to examine several institutions and cultural practices characteristically associated with the Mantaro area, such as the elaborate system of religious fiestas, institutionalized patterns of reciprocity, exchange, and redistribution, and the high degree of intervillage competitiveness. These and other customary practices are briefly dealt with in the chapters by Samaniego, Winder, and Grondin and are discussed in our conclusions.

We can best clarify our own position by relating it to literature that deals with the same themes and geographical area of study. Much of the research on Indian communities, especially in the years immediately following the Second World War, can be seen as a response to the writings of Mariátegui in the 1920s.[26] Mariátegui's theoretical analysis was complemented in the same period by the ethnographic and historical work of Hildebrando Castro Pozo, who resided for a time at Jauja in the Mantaro Valley and who wrote about the village of Muquiyauyo (see Grondin in this volume) and about other peasant communities.[27]

Faced by an increasing foreign penetration of the Peruvian economy and evident inequalities in the distribution of wealth, Mariátegui emphasized the merits of a socialist reorganization of the national economy based in great part on the revitalized Indian community. Likewise, Castro Pozo emphasized the ways in which the Indian community served to stimulate indigenous, communal enterprise that could contribute substantially to national economic and social development. The enemies of progress were the large landowners who kept the Indian population in a state of semiserfdom and the "liberal" bourgeoisie who wished to destroy communal land tenure in order to encourage capitalist accumulation in agriculture. One of the most interesting points in Mariátegui's analysis is his belief in the persistence of communal patterns of cooperation, despite the continuing attempts by government and landowners to individualize ownership of community property. He also stresses the flexibility of communal organization and its ability to adapt to economic change. He writes: "But in the sierra the latifundium has preserved its feudal character intact and has put up a much stronger resistance than the 'community' to the development of a capitalist economy. In fact, when a 'community' is connected by railway to commerce and central transportation, it spontaneously changes into a cooperative."[28] To Mariátegui, then, the Indian community represented the "progressive" force in the agrarian structure, in contrast to the failure of the majority of large highland estates to modernize in a capitalist direction. Both he and Castro Pozo stressed that the *latifundio* compared unfavorably with the "community" as an enterprise for agricultural production.[29]

These themes of the social and economic "progressiveness" of Indian communities and their articulation with the national economy are taken up, after the Second World War, by anthropologists who initiated intensive field work in the highlands. Escobar, who in 1945 began the first detailed anthropological study of a Mantaro community (Sicaya), points out that it had been recognized even in earlier studies that highland Indian culture was not homogeneous and had been affected, to different degrees, by the penetration of the national economic and political system.[30] Thus, Tschopik, who worked among the Aymara Indians in the southern highlands of Peru and completed a regional survey of highland communities in the central area in early 1945, concluded:

> It is hoped that the data presented . . . will serve in some measure to correct the widespread misconception that the entire Sierra of Peru is "Indian" and that its peoples are uniformly primitive, backward, and non-progressive. Indeed, our survey can claim to have revealed a diversity of patterns and an essential lack of cultural unity in the Central Peruvian Highlands. Marked differences from one community to the next have been described with reference to economic adaptations, trade and marketing, social and political organization, religious practices and material culture. . . . Without any intention of postulating a unilinear evolution of Central Sierra culture through a fixed series of stages, the range of adaptations represented by the contemporary Highland communities does, in a very general way, seem to mirror the post-Conquest development of Highland Peru.[31]

Tschopik's survey included several of the communities that are the subject of the present volume, and the data he provided on migration, economic exchanges, and social differentiation have proved very useful in our own analysis of subsequent changes. Tschopik also pointed out that, in comparison with other communities surveyed in Junín, Huancavelica, Pasco, and Ayacucho, those of the Mantaro Valley showed an unusual degree of economic progressiveness and assimilation to mestizo and Spanish culture. To explain such community differences, he suggested that research should focus on ecology, prehispanic social organization, and the degree of penetration of the modern economy through the impact of the mines, railways, et cetera.

As a direct outcome of this survey two studies were carried out in the Mantaro valley of communities apparently exhibiting a high degree of cultural assimilation and "progressiveness." In his study of Sicaya (see also Winder in this volume), Escobar concentrated on the cultural and social changes occurring in the village as a result of its increasing integration into the national economy through trade and migration. A major preoccupation of his work is the cultural significance of the process of *mestizaje* (i.e., becoming assimilated to mestizo culture), which he documents by reference to changes in family organization, religious observance and fiestas, dress, and patterns of speech. On the basis of this, he argues that the people of Sicaya were experiencing an increasing individualization of their social and economic interests and aspirations. Considerable emphasis was placed on the idea of progress, often interpreted in competitive terms and measured by the social mobility of the individual family through education, investment in business, and so on. In this context, Escobar claims that the concept of "community" constitutes an ideological orientation and does not reflect actual cooperative practice. Hence the ideals of progress and community provide an ideological framework within which social and economic tensions could be interpreted and partially resolved without destroying social relationships within the village. Moreover, the increasing incorporation of local families into the national society had made village relationships and village identity an important means of personal security and mobility: migrants, faced by the competitiveness and uncertainties of Lima, formed associations identified with and named after the village and continued to take an active interest in the affairs of the village. A similar interpretation of the significance of village and regional associations for highland migrants is found in the work of Mangin and Doughty, who studied peasant communities in Ancash and their migrants in Lima.[32] Throughout this volume we extend the work of Escobar and others by examining, in relation to the specific economic transformations that have occurred in the Mantaro area, the changing definitions of community and concepts of cooperation and progress.

The second major field study carried out in the Mantaro Valley was Adams's study of Muquiyauyo (see Grondin in this volume), a village noted for its progressive spirit and record of community achievements.[33] Adams's book also focuses on the issue of ethnicity, though, more explicitly than Escobar, he identifies the main direction of social change as the movement from a caste-stratified community (Indian-mestizo-*blanco*) to one structured by differences of social class. This change he attributes, first, to the ethnic homogenization produced by the breakup of the separate *comunidad* institutions at the turn of the century and by increasing land fragmentation; and, second, to the emergence of new occupational status divisions within the community resulting from migration, work in the mines, and the expansion of trade. Grondin's study in this volume reexamines specific aspects of Adams's study using new data and extending the analysis into the contemporary period. One important theoretical implication of Adams's study is that he questions the analytical usefulness of viewing the community as a "natural" corporate grouping that persists in the face of threats from outside. Rejecting the community-study approach of the Redfield tradition, Adams stresses the ways in which the internal developments in Muquiyauyo were intimately connected with external economic and political changes. Thus, although his study concentrates on village-level data, it indicates the necessity of developing a more specific regional and national focus to account for changes in local society.

One of the most important issues in the integration of the highlands into the national economy is the significance of highland labor for the development of modern capitalism. Arguedas described the evolution of Mantaro Valley communities, stressing their economic prosperity when compared to communities elsewhere in highland Peru, which he saw as generally subjugated to the hacienda system.[34] He emphasized the significance of this "free" peasantry for the development of enclave mining and plantation agriculture, since they provided a readily available and mainly temporary labor force. He also stressed that their status as small, independent property owners gave them the incentive to return and invest some of their earnings locally, thus contributing to the prosperity of the valley and at the same time inhibiting the emergence of an industrial or agricultural proletariat. Later Hutchinson, in a detailed study of Acolla, situated in the adjacent Yanamarca valley, shows that even those communities that had been regarded as most "Indian" and economically undifferentiated in the Mantaro area were heavily involved in migration to the mines from the beginning of the twentieth century.[35] The impact of this migration was to accelerate economic differentiation and diversification into new locally based occupations. In Acolla's case, this led to specialization in musical activities: the village provided musicians and bands for religious fiestas and celebrations throughout the valley area—a demand that itself reflected increasing levels of prosperity in the region.

This concern for developing more systematic comparisons of peasant communities within the national economy characterized many of the anthropological and sociological studies undertaken in the late 1950s and 1960s. Some of these continued in the ethnographic survey tradition and were sponsored by official Peruvian agencies: for example, Schaedel directed surveys of land tenure, household economies, migration, education, and religious practices in the villages and towns of the southern departments of Peru.[36] These surveys provided a valuable framework for subsequent case studies of specific communities, haciendas, and forms

of political organization, such as Dew's study of the increasing participation of peasant groups in regional politics in Puno.[37] Such studies
made clear that, even in the more solidly "Indian" regions of Peru,
there was considerable diversity in social and economic organization,
that villages were internally differentiated, and that even the poorest
peasantry were integrated into the market economy. Referring to the
department of Puno, Schaedel shows the concentration of wealth and
power, estimating that the lowest social class, which was mainly composed of Indian small holders, constituted 85 percent of the population.[38] The better-off social groups were mainly resident in the larger
towns and ranged from craftsmen, factory workers, and small traders
to the larger landowners and merchants. However, he also stresses the
chain of exploitation linking the poorest peasant to the international
market through local traders, middlemen, and the large exporting
houses. But he points out that the regional elite generally has little
direct economic control over most of the population, since the incorporation of the poor peasant into the wider economy takes place through
the activities of relatively small-scale, local entrepreneurs who are often
in competition with the larger operators. Schaedel sees this rising class,
which he labels *cholo*, becoming numerically dominant and gradually
displacing the large landed and commercial groups, a process that, as
he and Karen Spalding have indicated, has considerable historical
depth.

Spalding argues that the hacienda system in the southern highlands
was relatively weak until the late nineteenth century.[39] Up until this
time, the economic structure of the region was fragmented and based
on small-scale productive and commercial activity. According to her,
even the development of the wool trade with Britain in the nineteenth
century was not initially monopolized by the larger landowners but
provided opportunities for smaller producers and traders, who marketed their produce through regional fairs that were also attended by
large foreign merchants. Indeed, as Piel points out, from at least the
nineteenth century the major part of the state's revenues came from
the peasantry, both through taxation and through their contribution
to agricultural exports, particularly wool. Next to guano, wool was from
the early 1840s until the end of the century Peru's most important
export product.[40]

Studies such as these show the differentiated nature of the highland
peasantry and the continuing importance of small-scale capital accumulation alongside the development of large "semi-feudal" or capitalist
enterprise. They also imply that agrarian reform intending to secure
a more equitable distribution of wealth and aimed at a stimulating

agricultural production is unlikely to be achieved simply by removing the large landed and commercial elites.

The latter point is well illustrated by the findings of the Cornell-Peru Vicos Project.[41] This project originally aimed to demonstrate the social and economic benefits to be gained by replacing the existing authoritarian hacienda structure and by encouraging the hacienda workers to gradually take over the running of the enterprise. As Holmberg put it, "The major lesson of Vicos, or Peru as a whole, is that its serf and suppressed peasant populations, once freed and given encouragement, technical assistance, and learning, can pull themselves up by their own bootstraps and become productive citizens of the nation."[42] These ideals, however, were constantly thwarted in practice by the complexity of the regional economy and power structure. Stein points out that the hacienda system as it existed in the Vicos area thrived on a fine balance of interests between the hacienda and the residents of the nearby valley towns.[43] The hacienda in fact was the instrument by which town-based traders and richer peasant farmers exploited the rural sector, obtaining gratuitous service for public works, cheap labor and products, and so on. In addition, there was a relatively wealthy group among the hacienda *peones* who rented lands from the hacienda, employed other *peones*, and acted as brokers between the poorer peasants and the townsmen and hacienda authorities. According to Stein, "The ties between Vicosinos and townsmen were among the most salient limiting factors with which the Cornell-Peru Project had to cope in its efforts to promote Vicos autonomy . . . occasional 'outside' renters (i.e., previous administrators of the hacienda) brought disaster on themselves by limiting contacts between Vicosinos and the *mestizos* of the valley towns, under which circumstances these townsmen aided the Vicosinos in fomenting protest movements."[44]

During the course of the Vicos research, further evidence emerged on the importance of peasant differentiation and of the complex pattern of interdependence between haciendas, small towns, and villages. These findings seriously question any categorization of highland social organization as a simple opposition between exploitative haciendas and a dependent peasantry. In reviewing the materials from the Vicos project, Stein, who had been associated with the project from 1951, compares the Callejón de Huaylas area (where Vicos is located) with Huánuco, where a similar pattern of regional organization was described by Fonseca. According to Fonseca, "Even in the most remote towns there emerged sectors of 'powerful' *campesinos* dedicated to the monopoly of agricultural and pastoral products and the sale of manufactured articles in small stores and bars. Communities favored by their proximity to mining centers and big cities were transformed several decades ago into veritable armies of intermediaries. From that time, they began to derive great personal advantages based on the manipulation of the traditional rules of barter." [45]

It also became clear that ethnic distinctions were not fixed status attributes but rather were situationally used to justify exploitation or to reinforce collective solidarity. [46] The ethnic attributes of individuals and even of social groups could change dramatically with alterations in their place of residence or economic fortunes or as a result of the increasing importance of their town in the regional economy. Thus Doughty, in his study of the economically progressive town of Huaylas, describes how its "Indian" population had all but vanished by 1940 due to changing attitudes in the community toward the significance of ethnic status: "Indians" ceased to be recorded as such and were labeled by the authorities, by other townspeople, and by themselves as *mestizos*. [47]

Readers will find many similarities between the patterns of regional organization for Puno and Callejón de Huaylas and our own analysis of the interrelations between haciendas and peasant groups in the Mantaro region. We suspect that the same general pattern prevails throughout much of highland Peru. Large highland landholdings had little economic dynamic throughout the colonial and contemporary periods, and capital accumulation, outside of the mining enclave and a few large livestock haciendas, was mainly based on the internal differentiation and exploitation of the peasant economy.

Several studies in the 1950s and 1960s attempted to assess the factors that led some communities to adapt to change more effectively than others, using such indicators of modernization as the number of services available, the number of community projects, and the types and number of village associations. Some of these studies were carried out in the Mantaro area; thus, Maynard documented the high level of community service development in the area, attributing this development to the organizational capacity of the villagers and the stimulus provided by external linkages, such as regional associations, trade, and good communications. [48] More detailed studies of two of the Mantaro area communities—Mito in the valley and Chaquicocha on the plateau—explored the factors influencing "rates of progress." [49] These studies questioned the utility of a simple model of progress based on the presence of community services. Castillo contrasted Chaquicocha, which had a "progressive" spirit, despite its lack of service development, with Mito, which was high in service development but had declined severely in population and communal energy. These two studies indicate that community progressiveness represents a particular stage in the economic evolution of peasant villages. Thus Mito, described as the orphan of its illustrious children, had in the 1920s and 1930s an energetic town organization that built schools and obtained subsidies for a bridge, a road, and an electrical plant. Its "success" meant, however, that families seized the opportunities for education and improved income and, ultimately, left the village for larger centers. At the time of the study, Chaquicocha, a poorer and more remote community, was at the stage when villagers' energies were still directed toward building up local resources.

However, more in line with Mariátegui's and Castro Pozo's views, other studies reported that increasing integration into the national economy had not led to the social fragmentation of the community. In Pucará, at the southern end of the Mantaro Valley, communal organization seemed to be revitalized as the village became more closely connected to Huancayo and other urban centers through increasing trade and better road communications.[50] Migrants played a leading role in the introduction of new forms of agricultural technology and of new cropping patterns; also community resources were invested in the establishment of such cooperative enterprises as a bus company and a sheep cooperative.[51] A similar process was reported by Fuenzalida in his study of Huayopampa in the Chancay Valley, which shows how community organization and control of community resources were used to develop flourishing enterprises, marketing produce directly to the major urban centers.[52] With its increasing prosperity and closer external linkages, the number of communal enterprises in Huayopampa increased.

One recent attempt to try to explain such variations in village development and political organization on a regional basis is that of Lamond Tullis, who, like Alberti and others, used Frank Young's notions of "information-processing capacity" (usually indexed by levels of education, organizational complexity, and degree of solidarity) to assess the nature of the intervillage system in the Mantaro area.[53] Tullis characterizes the intervillage system he studied in the Mantaro Valley area (the Chupaca system) as having a relatively high centrality, that is, having relatively good access to government and other resources. However, within this system some villages will occupy a more central position than others, being the focuses of the main networks of intervillage contacts, trade, et cetera: these more central villages have a greater range of service and educational and associational activity. They also are more able to organize and defend their interests against other competing groups. Tullis contrasts the intervillage system of the Mantaro Valley with that of the adjoining Yanamarca Valley, where haciendas controlled most of the arable land and resources.[54] Most of the Yanamarca villages had been prevented from developing their own services, such as schools, and had little experience of effective community organization. Tullis claims that the "subordination" of this intervillage system necessarily led to peasant protest movements that were more radical and violent than those that occurred in the Mantaro Valley. This took place when through migration and increasing external contacts villagers became "aware" of their exploitation.

Tullis's findings on the high level of political activity in the Mantaro communities were, in part, confirmed by Handelman, whose study of peasant political mobilization included Mantaro villages.[55] Handelman argued that the more integrated the community was into the wider economy, the less radical the political objectives of its leaders. He also showed that village leaders in the departments of Junín and Pasco expressed a higher degree of confidence in the ability of their communities to influence central government policies than those leaders from Cuzco: only one third of those interviewed in the central highlands region said they were without influence, as against a half of those from the southern region.[56]

We question the preoccupation shown in the above studies with measuring the relative progressiveness of individual communities and with analyzing social change primarily in terms of the impact of modern communications and external work opportunities on supposedly isolated village populations. Such studies have tended to treat villages as relatively undifferentiated units placed within a hierarchical system of larger and smaller settlements. The latter approach, we believe, pays insufficient attention to the long-term economic processes and interrelationships among villages, towns, and social groups within a regional and national context.

The stress on "modernization" obscures the historical importance of peasant political activity. Stressing the land invasions and peasant syndicates that occurred in the central and southern highlands in the 1950s and 1960s, both Tullis and Handelman attribute this upsurge of political activity to the breakdown of the "traditional" system of domination in the highlands that followed the rapid extension of modern communications in the 1940s and 1950s. We have already indicated why we find it difficult to accept this concept of a "traditional" system of domination: as Spalding and some of the chapters of this volume show, the attempts by haciendas and allied interest groups to extend their control over land and labor resources is a feature of the early twentieth century, when capitalist development was intensified in the highlands as a result of the building of railroads and closer integration into the world market.[57] Moreover, there is in fact a long history of relatively successful political movements involving even the remotest of peasant villages prior to the twentieth century.

The importance of giving adequate historical depth to the assessment of contemporary patterns of village organization and politics is shown by the recent attempt of Alberti and Sánchez to develop a comprehensive approach to the Mantaro area.[58] They base their study of the region's development on case studies of the changes occurring in selected villages from the end of the last century. They show how power resources in the area have changed over time as a consequence of broader economic changes, such as the development of mining and the increasing concentration of population in the major urban centers. For example, the political fragmentation of valley districts, which, as Samaniego's paper also shows, is closely connected with these changes, reduced the power of village elites, destroyed the hierarchical pattern of political control in the valley, and hastened the out-migration of these elite families. Occupational groups emerge linked to new forms of economic activity, such as trucking, professional and administrative occupations, and new types of merchandizing. The dependency of these new groups on local resources and local support to secure their positions on a regional and indeed national basis becomes, in Alberti's and Sánchez's analysis, a more significant determinant of political change than the apparent level of integration of a village as a unit within a village system. This perspective leads Alberti and Sánchez to examine the unintended consequences of the state's attempts to reorganize the peasant community.[59]

Historical Background

The history of the Mantaro region is principally the history of a battle for control over land resources and labor in an area of relatively rich soils within an agricultural economy. This struggle has been fought out between richer and poorer *comuneros*, between neighboring *comunidades*, between *comunidades* and their satellites,[60] and between *comunidades* and haciendas. These latter struggles occurred mainly in the *puna* areas peripheral to the valley, since the hacienda system failed to establish itself in the valley itself. There were, however, more haciendas in the valley than has often been suspected; before agrarian reform there were a number of small haciendas in the vicinity of Jauja, Huancayo, and Apata, and in the adjoining Yanamarca Valley haciendas predominated.

We know from the early Spanish chronicles that the Mantaro Valley region had been the center of the Huanca (sometimes spelt Wanca)

Kingdom before being absorbed into the Inca Empire by Inca Cápac Yupanqui, brother of Pachacútec, the tenth Inca.[61] During the Spanish conquest, Pizarro passed through the Mantaro Valley on his way to Cuzco, and the Huanca *curacas* (local leaders) signed an alliance with him to assist with men and supplies in the defeat of their Inca overlords.[62] In return for their help the Huanca *curacas* were given favorable treatment under colonial rule, at least in the early days. They maintained their lands and even recovered land taken from their ancestors by the Incas. After the Spaniards had decided to abandon Jauja as the national capital, the *curacas* took control of the rural population on behalf of their Spanish masters. There is certain evidence to show that *curacas* who were prepared to cooperate with the *encomenderos* (Spanish overlords) benefited considerably from a freedom to exploit the local population that they had not enjoyed under the stricter hierarchical supervision and control of the Inca empire. Yet it has been argued convincingly that the greater autonomy of the *curacas* and the tendency for them to overexploit their people, while ignoring traditional systems of reciprocity, led to a steady decline in their power and authority.[63] Other reasons were demands by the Crown for *mita* (forced labor) service in mines, road construction, and the building of churches and towns. These demands, epidemics, and the disruptions brought by early colonial rule led to a drop in agricultural productivity and to a severe reduction in the numbers of the indigenous population.

Under these circumstances, it became increasingly difficult for the *curacas* to maintain the system whereby *ayllus* (localized corporate groupings based partly on descent) controlled the ecological zones (*puna*, valley, and jungle) necessary for a well-integrated production and distribution system. Murra describes this system as the vertical control of ecological levels.[64] Climates and soil types in the Andes change significantly with altitude and with variations in topography, making it possible to produce, within a small area, the variety of agricultural and livestock produce necessary for subsistence throughout the year. Murra claims that the Andean peoples conceive of their world in "vertical" terms: "Throughout the Andes, the village and ethnic communities had always attempted to control as many of these microclimates as possible . . . Control of far away ecological floors could be done through mutual concessions, through conquest and subordination or through colonists sent from the center."[65] The loss of control over complementary ecological zones has been shown to be a major factor in the "peasantization" of the rural sector after the conquest. Fonseca argues that the breakdown in the system of vertical control led to increasing specialization, as highland villages dedicated themselves to livestock production and valley and lowland populations to different types of arable farming.[66] This process entailed an increase in marketing and exchange, creating opportunities for traders and intermediaries, and the rural sector became increasingly dominated by town-based landed and mercantile elites.

Another contributory factor to the reorganization of the rural economy and its increasing integration into a national system was the colonial policy of resettling the scattered *ayllu*-based settlements into nucleated villages. These settlements or *reducciones* were organized during the last thirty years of the sixteenth century and the early part of the seventeenth through the ordinances of the Viceroy Toledo. The two main objectives of this resettlement policy were the effective control of the labor and resources of local populations and their conversion to Catholicism through the setting up of parishes and religious brotherhoods. In these settlements, the indigenous population was given land that they were to hold collectively as a *común de indios* (subsequently, *comunidad indígena*)—the minimum unit for the collection of taxes and a reserve of manpower. It ranged from about eighty to one thousand families. Individual families could receive land in usufruct but were not allowed to dispose of it without official permission.[67] Pasture land was for communal use, while arable land was usually divided annually according to Spanish or pre-Spanish custom. In addition to the community land, land was allocated to cover the expenses of the town council (*municipio*), to provide for a community grain store, and to support the *cofradías*. The latter were religious confraternities, each one dedicated to the worship of particular saints. Membership carried with it the responsibility of working the lands belonging to the *cofradía*, the proceeds of which financed the annual fiesta, and the obligation of passing through the hierarchy of offices in the organization (*alférez*, *capitán*, and *mayordomo*).[68]

As various authors have shown, this pattern of organization developed in the early colonial period in the Mantaro area and was the basis for the contemporary forms of community organization and cooperation that are the subject of this volume.[69] Early records for the central highlands mention the founding of the towns of Jauja, San Jerónimo, and Chongos in 1565, Sicaya and Huancayo in the 1570s, and Chupaca in 1571. Most of the present-day district capitals were founded in early colonial times, a number of them on sites occupied by Huanca settlements or religious centers: Sanos, Sicaya, Sapallanga, and Pucará.[70]

Due to inadequate documentation it is difficult to reconstruct the colonial pattern of community organization and land tenure in the Mantaro area. It appears that the *curacas* exercised political and administrative control within the towns and continued to be the principal individual landowners. They shared power with the Spanish settlers, some of whom married into their families. In the case of the Mantaro Valley two parallel councils emerged in the towns: the *varayoq* (Indian authority), which represented the indigenous inhabitants and administered the lands of the *comunidad indígena*, and the district council, which was composed of *vecinos* ("neighbors"—the Spanish colonial settlers). There was always tension between these two groups. It appears that after independence from Spain the *varayoq* found themselves in the position of defending the community lands from the aggressiveness and ambition of the *vecinos* supported by the official authority.

Arguedas puts great emphasis on the relative absence of haciendas in the Mantaro Valley, arguing that this was due to the alliance between Spanish conquerors and local chieftains and to the movement of Spanish settlers to other regions of Peru.[71] The relative absence of haciendas, according to Arguedas, is the principal factor accounting for the economic progressiveness of the valley communities. It is likely, however, that Arguedas exaggerates the uniqueness of the Mantaro Valley; as Samaniego shows in his study of the microregion of Chupaca in the southern part of the valley, important haciendas did develop in the colonial period on the basis of the holdings of the native *curacas* who intermarried with Spanish families.[72] On the *puna* these haciendas became the basis for what was to become one of Peru's largest hacienda complexes, Sociedad Ganadera del Centro. In contrast, the large holdings of important families in the valley fragmented over time into relatively small holdings. The point that Samaniego makes is that climatic, soil, and market conditions made large-scale arable farming a risky venture, whereas extensive livestock production on higher ground offered better possibilities for profit for most of the colonial and nineteenth century periods. Similar processes probably occurred in other areas of the highlands, but they have been insufficiently documented because of the tendency, in the discussion of land tenure, not to differentiate clearly enough between pastoral and arable holdings.[73]

Within the villages, while all land nominally belonged to the Crown, it was allocated to the *ayllus*, the church, the *cofradías*, and Spanish settlers. In the case of the village of Muquiyauyo, situated in the northern part of the Mantaro Valley, Adams talks of a possible division of land among heads of family and institutions from 1591 to 1604, followed by a second partition from 1642 to 1666.[74] By 1742, 33 percent of the total land area available was in the hands of individual Spaniards, criollos (people of Spanish origin born in Peru), and mestizos (those of mixed Spanish and indigenous origin); 65 percent was distributed among individual indigenous households through the *comunidad indigena*; and 1.5 percent was in the hands of the *cofradias*. The fact that the *comunidad* was nominal owner of much of the village land did not mean that it had effective control over the utilization of this land. Adams maintains that *comunidad* lands passed into individual ownership or more or less permanent individual usufruct between 1794 and the end of colonial rule. In 1904 the remaining 109.5 hectares of *comunidad* land were divided up among its members. Samaniego concludes from a study of the earliest village documents of Chupaca, at the southern end of the valley, that the *ayllus* controlled land only until the early seventeenth century, after which the arable land began to pass into private family ownership, until by the end of the eighteenth century only pastures and small plots of arable land remained under communal control.

Samaniego's study is interesting in that it describes a process of increasing internal differentiation within villages and widening inequalities between them at a time when, in other parts of the country, arable land was still controlled by the *común de indios* or the *comunidad*. Fuenzalida, for example, describes the *reducciones* in the upper part of the Chancay Valley as being reasonably homogeneous during the colonial period, and, while most of the communal arable land was allocated to male heads of households, the *ayllus* maintained control over its distribution.[75] In the Chancay Valley the transference of *comunidad* lands into private hands was to take place mainly during the nineteenth century.

Likewise, it was in the nineteenth century that communally controlled land in other areas of Peru passed increasingly into individual hands. Many writers attribute this to the impact of the liberalizing decrees of the early independence period. Piel writes, for example: "The liberal decrees of San Martín and Bolívar abolished the native communities' collective possession of land. To this lawful aggression, which was applied freely, or not, according to local circumstances, there was added later the offensive of a market economy which gradually extended into the most isolated regions of Peru."[76] It would seem that these processes occurred earlier in the Mantaro Valley than in most other regions of Peru.

The process of increasing economic differentiation in the Mantaro Valley was based on the market opportunities for livestock and agricultural products created by the nearby mines of Huancavelica and Cerro de Pasco.[77] These mining centers were important in colonial times and required fodder for the animals and foodstuffs for the working population. The proximity of Lima and the numerous mule trains and army contingents that passed through the valley to the jungle and to the southern highlands provided an additional stimulus to such production. The farmers who generally took advantage of this increased demand were the larger village-based farmers who had access to local labor and to communal pastures. They were, also, frequently the political authorities of the village. Thus, by the end of the nineteenth century the Mantaro villages were highly differentiated socially and economically, with a dominant mestizo elite. Children from these elite village families were being sent as early as the 1860s to be educated in the secondary schools and colleges located in the provincial capitals of Jauja and Huancayo.[78] These village elites were important since numerically they had, by 1901, greater voting power in national elections than did the elites of the provincial capitals. In the wars against Chile and in the subsequent civil wars, prominent families from the villages helped mobilize contingents of soldiers and took a major part in organizing campaigns. The large land owners of the area resided in Huancayo or Jauja, but there is little evidence that they exercised much political or economic control over the villages.[79] Their lands were mainly located in the high plateau and devoted to livestock requiring little labor. These families were also more likely to spend time in Lima and marry into Lima families. A fuller analysis of this process is taken up in the next volume.

At the turn of the present century, the haciendas on the high plateau surrounding the valley were being consolidated into large commercial enterprises. In the southern end of the valley, the Lima-based company Ganadera del Centro was formed in 1910 through the purchase of several family-owned haciendas; at the northern end of the valley, Cerro de Pasco Copper Corporation bought up land to form a large sheep-raising complex. Previous to Cerro de Pasco's hacienda, another commercial enterprise, Sociedad Ganadera Junín, was formed in 1906 out of a number of small, locally owned haciendas. As Samaniego shows in his paper in this volume, these commercial enterprises attempted to rationalize production through improving stock and fencing land. These activities brought the haciendas into conflict with peasant villages over traditional grazing rights.

Such conflicts accompanied and were, in part, produced by the contemporaneous expansion of small-holder farming. At the end of the nineteenth century in the Mantaro area, there was increasing production in response to the demand for foodstuffs for the expanding mining populations, for Lima, and for those employed in the construction of roads and the railroad. In addition, alfalfa and other fodder crops supplied the large mule trains necessitated by the increasing commercial and transport activity of the region. As Samaniego argues, the increasing demand for foodstuffs led to a more marked pattern of stratification at the village level, with richer peasants seeking to expand their production at the expense of fellow villagers and of those in other villages. This agricultural "boom" was not sustained. Population increased rapidly in the first decades of the century: the population of the department of Junín doubled between 1876 and 1940, from 209,758 to 428,855. Increasing population pressure on land meant subdivision and a reduction in the amount and period of fallow. Moreover, the market for foodstuffs fluctuated considerably as a consequence of economic depressions. By the 1950s there are signs that agricultural productivity was declining.[80] For example, the Ministry of Agriculture statistics show that the production of maize per hectare in Junín declined from 2,155 metric tons in 1948 to 0,922 tons in 1960. In contrast, in the department of Lima productivity increased from 1,236 metric tons per hectare in 1948 to 2,149 in 1960.[81]

From the 1960s onward, there seems to have been a partial recovery in agricultural production in the Mantaro area, due to the increasing use of chemical fertilizers and insecticides. Also, the Ministry of Agriculture initiated extension work and improved credit facilities; the impact of some of these schemes is reported in the papers by Long and Sánchez and by Winder in this volume. New cropping patterns developed in this period with an increase in vegetable production for the Lima market and more widespread dairy farming associated with alfalfa production and barley.

One major change in the political and economic organization of the Mantaro area was the emergence of Huancayo as the major urban center. Until the end of the nineteenth century Jauja, at the southern end of the valley, had been the most important center in the area. Its dominance was challenged by the creation of the province of Huancayo with that city as the capital and with the formation of a separate juridical authority. By 1931, when Huancayo became capital of the department of Junín in place of Cerro de Pasco, the predominance of the southern part of the valley was clear. The growth of Huancayo in the first thirty years of the century was considerably greater than that of Jauja, and by 1940 Huancayo had some 27,000 inhabitants in contrast to the 7,700 of Jauja.

The causes of Huancayo's growth and predominance are connected with the building of the railway and the improvement of communications to the southern highlands. Huancayo was the terminal point for the railway and a major communications node for the mining areas to the south; it also functioned as a marketing center for the prospering villages in the southern part of the valley. In contrast, Jauja was bypassed as a communication center and had less importance as a marketing center for agricultural produce. As Hutchinson points out when contrasting the growth of Jauja and Huancayo, Jauja's marketing region extended for only 40 kilometers to the north, whereas Huancayo served as the main outlet of produce for a region extending 280 kilometers to the south.[82] The villages in the province of Jauja were also less developed agriculturally, with a smaller extension of good arable land, than the southern portion of the valley.

Contemporary Social and Economic Processes

These changes in the Mantaro area must be analyzed in relation to migration and to the expansion, in the area, of income opportunities in mining, manufacturing, transport, and services. This analysis is the subject of a subsequent volume, but it is partly dealt with in Roberts's paper on the textile mill in Huancayo. We will summarize the main features of the region's economic development, focusing on migration. By the 1960s, Junín—and especially the Mantaro area—had become one of the major focuses of industrial development in Peru. In 1963, the total value of industrial production in Junín was second only to that of Lima-Callao.[83] Though this production was concentrated mainly in the mining sector and, consequently, had few linkages with the local economy, the value of wages and salaries in Junín was still one of the highest in Peru. Our studies show that much of these industrial earnings was directly or indirectly invested in agricultural production, transport, and commerce in the Mantaro area.[84] To these earnings must be added those obtained in labor migration to the cotton plantations of the coast and to Lima. These sources of small-scale capital accumulation help to explain both the changing pattern of investment in agriculture, such as the more extensive use of fertilizers, and the diversification of the local economy.

In the rural sector, the most fundamental recent change is from a system of stratification based on control of land to one based on access to nonagricultural work and, in particular, to urban wage employment. Whereas our data for the 1930s show a consistent correlation between size of landholding and other attributes (e.g., migration experience, educational level, and political office holding), the contemporary data for the different villages reveal that land is no longer so consistently correlated with these characteristics. Sources of differentiation at the village level, in the contemporary period, appear to be multiple, in that wage labor, trading, salary earning, and land are relatively independent means of building up a household's resources. The prevalence of *mini-*

fundia (small holdings) throughout the area and the relatively low returns for agricultural production mean that even the largest farmers of the villages earn less than some of the local teachers or retired, skilled mine workers.

One way in which village populations differentiate themselves is in the use of educational facilities. At the end of the nineteenth century it was the village families with most land that educated their children. This education enabled these children to capture the best wage labor opportunities and, in many cases, to follow a professional career elsewhere. Hence education contributed to maintaining the divisions of wealth and social status, but it also encouraged the out-migration of these very same families. For example, of the six families from Matahuasi that were educating their children in the secondary school at Jauja in the 1870s, only one appears to have remained in the village.

An important change in the nature of the education process began with the rapid expansion of public educational facilities in the valley and highland villages from about the 1930s onwards.[85] This made it possible for most villagers to become literate and for even the poorer families to send their children on to secondary education. In the 1961 census, 61 percent of the population aged seventeen and over in the Mantaro area (provinces of Huancayo, Jauja, and Concepción) were classed as literate; this percentage includes women and the populations of remote highland villages for whom the level of literacy is lower than for the rest of the population. One of the important consequences of generalizing literacy levels was that villagers were able to take full advantage of the types of wage-labor opportunities in the mines, textile mills, and plantations that multiplied in the same period. The savings from such wage-earning activities enabled many poorer families to improve their relative positions in the villages and increasingly blurred the sharpness of the pattern of socioeconomic differentiation.

How education did contribute indirectly to local patterns of differentiation was through increasing the number of villagers who aspired to and who obtained white-collar jobs (while often remaining based in the villages). In the larger villages, such as Sicaya and Matahuasi, where this type of out-migration has occurred, there has been a need to recruit farm workers from the neighboring and poorer provinces. These workers have become permanent residents in the villages and work the farms of absentee or resident landowners, many of whom are white-collar workers or professionals. Since, in Sicaya, the immigrants are illiterate and speak Quechua, this has led to a sharp division between Sicaya-born members of the village and these new immigrants. This division is expressed in the use of ethnic stereotypes and in a degree of internal political division in the village.[86]

The high educational levels of this area have often been commented on. They are related to this same process of economic differentiation and wage labor. The villages in the valley were very quick to provide land, building materials, and labor for schools, and much of the initiative for school building came from migrants in labor centers. Moreover, it is through education that villagers have been most successful in tapping the resources of the state. For example, in the village of Muquiyauyo, of the fifty or so schoolteachers in the local colleges and schools who are paid by the state, some twenty-four were born in Muquiyauyo. The state represents the single most important employer in the Mantaro area and the only economic sector that is both expanding and paying good wages. Educational investments, then, are one means whereby local people have, to a certain extent, reversed the outflow of capital from periphery to center.

It is through the analysis of the migration patterns that have linked the villages, cities, and metropolis that we attain a crucial understanding of how the current social and economic divisions of Peru are reproduced. One characteristic of migrant patterns in the area is that they do not reflect a vertically integrated economic and urban system. There is, for example, no evidence that, either at the present or in the past, people from villages have migrated by stages to Lima. There is some stage migration whereby, either in one generation or over several generations, people have moved from the smaller and more remote villages of the Mantaro area and its neighboring departments, through Huancayo, and on to Lima.[87] More characteristic, however, is the pattern of circulatory labor migration that from the 1930s to the 1950s linked villages to the mines, to the coastal plantations, and to the labor market of Lima and Huancayo. All the villages in the area were involved in an extensive circulatory labor migration, and in the larger and more central villages about 80 percent of the male heads of household had migration experience. This was of two types—seasonal migration to the plantations and longer-term (averaging three to four years) migration to the mines or to the textile industry of Huancayo.

In more recent decades, migration has more often been directed to the urban centers, especially Lima. Part of this migration consists of migrants who work in the mines or other labor centers and who then move on to Lima itself. Hence, urban migration is mainly a form of direct migration from either village or town to Lima. It is not clear, however, to what extent migration to Lima is for permanent residence. Our survey evidence indicates a high level of return migration from Lima, and we encountered these return migrants in the villages, in Jauja, and in Huancayo. Furthermore, the patterns that we can identify give reason to suppose that this return migration is likely to continue and is based on migrants' changing perceptions of their relative economic opportunities with changes in their life career. There is, for example, a pattern whereby white-collar workers and professionals originate in valley villages, get their education in Huancayo, move to Lima or other coastal cities for their early career, and eventually return (often with pensions) to live and work in Huancayo or Jauja, within easy traveling distance of their native village. As the infrastructure of the rural villages has improved and transport services have intensified, so too have some migrants (including professionals) returned to live in the village, explicitly explaining their decision in terms of the lower cost of living. Since Huancayo is an important government and administrative center, many of these professional and white-collar migrants find work in the city and commute daily from their home villages.

It is important to remember that Lima's economy is only partly based on large-scale industries and associated services, for almost half the economically active population of Lima is involved in a wide variety of very small-scale commercial, industrial, and service enterprises.[88] These enterprises are highly sensitive to economic fluctuations. Although they can offer a reasonable income for migrants, employment tends to be rather insecure because manpower needs vary considerably. There are many cases of migrants from the valley area who migrated to Lima, worked there for a number of years, and then returned. This typically occurs at a moment of job scarcity, or at a stage in the family cycle when the migrant has many dependents to feed, or when he has amassed sufficient capital or commercial contacts to enable him to establish a business in the Mantaro area.

The main advantage of the Mantaro area for migrants and residents alike is that its population and geographical concentration permit the combination of differently located business pursuits together with some farming. This has had the effect of reducing the subsistence cost of labor, cheapening it to a point where it can effectively compete with large-scale factory production.

This process has a further spatial dimension, since, as we have indicated, migrants come into the Mantaro area from the poorer high-altitude zones (mainly from Huancavelica) and provide an additional pool of cheap labor. Since these migrants retain claims on land and produce from their areas of origin, it is a migration that represents an example of the progressive exploitation of provincial areas. Indeed, the current retention of population in the Mantaro area is partly based on this in-migration, while, in contrast, Huancavelica has, over the past decade, suffered a net loss.

Migration from these poorer areas is historically differentiated according to size of community and occupations of migrants. The earliest migrations that we have recorded are of professionals and white-collar workers who came to settle in Huancayo, whereas later migrations consist mainly of laborers (who work in the agricultural villages of the valley) and craftsmen and traders (who settle in Huancayo). There is some evidence too that, like the valley migrants to Huancayo and to Lima, particular migrant groups have specialized in branches of activity that link them with their home areas. For example, some of the major potato traders in Huancayo are migrants from Huancavelica who originate from potato-producing villages. After leaving their home communities many of them worked for a period in the mines, where they not only amassed capital but also made the contacts that now allow them to supply the mines in bulk.

The analytical value of this description of migration patterns depends on its being placed within a discussion of the regional and national economy. We characterize the national economy as having a large informal sector in which small-scale activity predominates and in which very few stable career opportunities exist even for professionals, who are often on short-term contracts.[89] Also, there are very few linkages between firms or between sectors of the economy that would enable people to follow reasonably consistent career patterns. Peruvian capitalism, it seems, has little capacity either to organize extensively or to effect major transformations in the nation's economy. The analysis of processes, such as migration, through which small-scale activity continues to flourish both in Lima and in the provinces enables us to understand why this economic "incapacity" at the national level does not produce stagnation at the local level. It is individual life careers and the build-up of a series of short-term decisions and socioeconomic strategies that give shape to the overall pattern of economic opportunities. This is particularly clear in the Mantaro area, where the economic organization can be described in terms of the interlocking of various economic and social careers. There is clearly some degree of economic integration in the area, and spatial location is often significant for the range of economic activities practiced. Yet, nevertheless, it is fundamentally because people are able to combine social and economic resources in novel and changing ways during the course of a life career that the area retains an important degree of internal vitality, despite its being economically dependent on Lima, the metropolitan capital.

The study of migration histories illuminates the complex ways in which this vitality is achieved from the point of view of individual households. It also warns us that there is, at present, no economic and locational basis for the formation of coherent class groupings. We have been able to document this proposition in studies of political movements and political activities in the area—especially with reference to the APRA political party and with respect to peasant movements.[90] This relative absence of a distinct pattern of class organization in the Mantaro area is also important for understanding the responses to recent government attempts at planned change.

The Organization of the Volume

The chapters fall into three major groupings that, basically, result from the different historical periods to which the studies relate. We begin with two studies (Samaniego and Laite) that document certain crucial features of the agrarian structure of the Mantaro area at the end of the nineteenth and the beginning of the twentieth century. Samaniego describes the relationship between highland and valley villages and examines the impact of an increase in marketing opportunities on social and economic differentiation within these villages. The struggle to expand production within villages, between villages, and between villages and haciendas is shown to be central to the understanding of the political movements of the day, including the *indigenismo* movement. Laite's study also emphasizes the importance of the internal differentiation of the village communities and the uses made of community ideology and structure by local people seeking to expand their economic opportunities. In this latter chapter, we are also told about the initial impact of what was to become the major economic enterprise of the central highlands: the refining plant of the Cerro de Pasco Corporation. Interestingly, even the aims and strategies of this powerful, foreign-owned corporation were significantly affected by the changes taking place within the villages and small towns of the area. The chapters by Samaniego and Laite demonstrate that migration and small-scale commercial farming have long historical antecedents in the Mantaro area. Moreover, the level of political activity and sophistication described show how misleading it is to characterize highland Peru as "traditional" or politically backward prior to the coming of the railway, modern roads, and large-scale capitalist enterprise.

The next four studies explore the changes taking place in the Mantaro region in the period following the full development of the mining economy in the highlands and of the plantations on the coast. In this period, large numbers of villagers from the Mantaro area migrated for work outside. Thus wage earning helped to intensify the commercialization of the village economy and Huancayo developed as a distribution center for imported manufactures. Some of the profits of this expanding trade provided the basis for the development of the textile industry as described by Roberts. The other three chapters look at different cooperative "responses" to these processes. Smith and Cano examine the genesis of a successful land invasion campaign in the highland village of Huasicancha; Solano describes how a group of villagers in the valley village of Pucará first form an agricultural cooperative and subsequently purchase a hacienda for their private use; and Grondin provides an analysis of the formation, subsequent history, and final failure of an electricity cooperative in the valley village of Muquiyauyo. These three chapters show how various cooperative ventures are similarly affected by the increasing integration of the area into the wage-labor economy and by increasing government intervention in the local economy. The arena for local-level political and economic action includes, in all these studies, the provincial and national capitals and such other important work centers as the mines. Migrant associations and returned migrants play an important part in village decision-making. It is also clear that the village economy and associated social relationships remain focuses of interest even for those migrants who secured relatively permanent work opportunities outside the village. The history of the textile factory in Huancayo and of its labor turnover shows that even in this urban setting the village economy continued to exert a powerful influence.

The last three chapters in the volume concentrate on the attempts of the military government of General Velasco (1968–1975) to sponsor agrarian reform. All three, however, give considerable attention to the antecedents of the reform situation. Thus, Winder provides a short account of the history of the *comunidad* in Peru before examining the implementation of the Peasant Community Statute. Likewise, Samaniego and Roberts discuss the characteristics of the highland pastoral economy in order to identify the difficulties of restructuring the pastoral haciendas into cooperatives owned by local peasant communities. The chapter by Long and Sánchez provides detailed data on the operation of one milk-marketing cooperative that is supported by both the Peruvian government and a foreign technical mission. Here again, the problems this cooperative faces, despite its impressive backing, are traced to the long-standing processes of diversification and economic differentiation characteristic of the Mantaro area.

The chapters are intended to complement each other in the data they provide on the Mantaro region. The villages described are major sources of migration to Huancayo, the mining sector, and Lima. These villages have also been interrelated historically through political and marketing relationships, such as those between the highland villages of Huasicancha, Cacchi, and Yanacancha (discussed by Smith and Cano and by Samaniego and Roberts) and the valley villages of Chupaca and Sicaya (discussed by Samaniego and Winder). Moreover, the villages are all geographically close to each other and the inhabitants of the different villages know about each other, visit, and intermarry. These interrelationships are often competitive, as, for example, when a village like Sicaya consciously strives to provide a "better" fiesta than those of neighboring villages or when Pucará prides itself on being more "progressive" than Muquiyauyo. The diversity of cooperative ideology and practice found in this relatively compact region provides an interesting opportunity to assess the possibility of locally based cooperative organization in the face of increasing integration into the national Peruvian economy and polity.

NOTES

1. The most radical agrarian reform in Peru is that initiated in 1969 by the military government that came to power in 1968. It includes the expropriation and reorganization of the coastal estates and the highland haciendas, and a reform of peasant communities. See Ramón Zaldívar, "Agrarian Reform and Military Reformism in Peru," in *Agrarian Reform and Agrarian Reformism,* edited by D. Lehmann; José M. Mejía and Rosa Díaz S., *Sindicalismo y reforma agraria en el valle de Chancay*; César Fonseca, "Comunidad, hacienda y el modelo Sais," *América Indígena* 35, no. 2 (April–June 1975); Christopher Scott, "Agrarian Reform, Accumulation and the Role of the State: The Case of Peru," in *Dépendance et structure de classes en Amérique Latine,* CETIM; Eric Hobsbawm, "Peru: The Peculiar Revolution," *New York Review of Books,* December 16, 1971, pp. 29–36. Abraham F. Lowenthal, ed., *The Peruvian Experiment,* provides an overall assessment of the government's agrarian and other reforms.

2. Harry Tschopik, *Highland Communities of Central Peru*; Richard N. Adams, *A Community in the Andes: Problems and Progress in Muquiyauyo*; Gabriel Escobar, *Sicaya*; William F. Whyte and Lawrence K. Williams, *Toward an Integrated Theory of Development*; and G. Alberti and R. Sánchez, *Poder y conflicto social en el valle del Mantaro.*

3. David Winder, "The Effect of the 1970 Reform on the Peasant Communities and on the Community Development Process in an Area of Peru," M. Ed. thesis, University of Manchester, 1974. Winder quotes from a report of the Peruvian Indigenous Institute.

4. Other sources indicate that in 1960 there were only thirty-nine official *comunidades.* Dew attributes this low number to the legal and political difficulties of obtaining recognition, (Edward Dew, *Politics in the Altiplano: The*

Dynamics of Change in Rural Peru, p. 30). See Harry F. Dobyns, *Comunidades campesinas del Perú*.

5. *Censo Nacional*, 1940.

6. D. Norberto Padilla, *El Peruano*, July-October, 1974, cited in Ricardo Tello Devotto, *Historia de la provincia de Huancayo*, pp. 50–53.

7. Grant Hilliker, *The Politics of Reform in Peru: The Aprista and Other Mass Parties of Latin America*, pp. 77, 54; François Bourricaud, *Power and Society in Contemporary Peru*, pp. 237–254; and Carlos Astiz, *Pressure Groups and Power Elites in Peruvian Politics*.

8. Howard Handelman, *Struggle in the Andes: Peasant Political Mobilization in Peru*, pp. 140–147; F. Lamond Tullis, *Lord and Peasant in Peru: A Paradigm of Political and Social Change*, pp. 64–65.

9. Rodrigo Montoya et al., *La Sais Cahuide y sus contradicciones*.

10. We use the term *estate* to refer to the now expropriated haciendas. In the central highlands, these estates have been organized into cooperatives (*sociedades agrarias de interés social*).

11. For a technical assessment of the zone's agricultural potential, see Latin Project, *Training the Río Mantaro*.

12. *Población del Perú: Resultados Provisionales del Censo de 1972*, pp. 30–31.

13. Comité Interamericano de Desarrollo Agrícola (CIDA), *Tenencia de la tierra y desarrollo socio-económico del sector agrícola, Perú*, p. 106.

14. Ibid., p. 35.

15. Ibid., p. 47.

16. Montoya et al., *La Sais Cahuide*, p. 24.

17. CIDA, *Tenencia de la tierra*, p. 298.

18. *Boletín de Estadística Peruana*, 5, no. 6, 1962.

19. CIDA, *Tenencia de la tierra*, p. 299. Undoubtedly, a proportion of the animals counted on farms of less than five hectares must have been grazing either on communal pastures or illicitly on haciendas. See Juan Martínez-Alier, *Los huacchilleros del Perú*, for a discussion of this latter practice.

20. Montoya et al., *La Sais Cahuide*.

21. D. E. Horton, *Land Reform and Reform Enterprises in Peru*, p. X13.

22. Richard Schaedel, *Plan regional para el desarrollo del sur del Perú*, vol. 5, pp. 31–32.

23. Martínez-Alier, *Los huacchilleros*.

24. See, for example, Handleman's discussion in *Struggle in the Andes*, pp. 48–49.

25. See, for example, John Murra's interesting collection of papers, *Formaciones económicas y políticas del mundo andino*; also, Billie Jean Isbell extends this perspective to showing how these patterns are reproduced by migrants in the urban milieu ("The Influence of Migrants upon Traditional Social and Political Concepts: A Peruvian Case Study," in *Latin American Urban Research*, vol. 4, edited by W. A. Cornelius and F. M. Trueblood, pp. 237–262).

26. José Carlos Mariátegui, *Seven Interpretive Essays on Peruvian Reality*.

27. Hildebrando Castro Pozo, *Nuestra comunidad indígena*.

28. Mariátegui, *Seven Interpretive Essays*, p. 59.

29. Ibid., pp. 58–61.

30. Escobar, *Sicaya*, pp. 13–17.

31. Tschopik, *Highland Communities of Central Peru*, p. 55.

32. Paul L. Doughty, *Huaylas: An Andean District in Search of Progress*; and idem, "Behind the Back of the City: 'Provincial' Life in Lima, Peru," in *Peasants in Cities: Readings in the Anthropology of Urbanization*, edited by William Mangin, pp. 30–46; William Mangin, "The Role of Regional Associations in the Adaptation of Rural Migrants to Cities in Peru," in *Sociologus* 9 (1959): 23–36; Norman Long, "The Role of Regional Associations in Peru," in *The Process of Urbanization*, edited by M. Drake et al., pp. 173–191; Bryan R. Roberts, "The Interrelationships of City and Provinces in Peru and Guatemala," in *Latin American Urban Research*, vol. 4, edited by W. A. Cornelius and F. M. Trueblood, pp. 207–236.

33. Adams, *Community in the Andes*.

34. José María Arguedas, "Evolución de las comunidades indígenas," *Revista del Museo Nacional* 26 (1957): 78–151.

35. William Baxter Hutchinson, "Sociocultural Change in the Mantaro Valley Region of Peru: Acolla, a Case Study," Ph.D. dissertation, Indiana University.

36. Schaedel, *Plan regional*.

37. Dew, *Politics in the Altiplano*.

38. Schaedel, *Plan regional*, pp. 7–24.

39. Karen Spalding, "Class Structures in the Southern Peruvian Highlands, 1750–1920," and "Hacienda-Village Relationships in Andean Society to 1830," in *Economia y sociedad en el Perú moderno*, vol. 2, edited by Heraclio Bonilla.

40. Jean Piel, "The Place of the Peasantry in the National Life of Peru in the Nineteenth Century," *Past and Present*, no. 46 (February 1970), pp. 108–133.

41. Harry F. Dobyns, Paul L. Doughty, and Harold D. Lasswell, eds., *Peasants, Power and Applied Social Change: Vicos as a Model*.

42. Ibid., p. 61.

43. William W. Stein, *Countrymen and Townsmen in the Callejón de Huaylas, Peru: Two Views of Andean Social Structure*.

44. Ibid., pp. 24–25.

45. César Fonseca, "La economía 'vertical' y la economía de mercado en las comunidades alteñas del Perú," in Iñigo Ortiz de Zúñiga, *Visita de la provincia de León de Huánuco*, vol. 2, p. 335.

46. Fernando Fuenzalida, "Poder, raza y etnia en el Perú contemporáneo," in Fernando Fuenzalida et al., *El indio y el poder en el Perú*, pp. 15–87; Doughty, *Huaylas*, pp. 66–69.

47. As the reader may have noted, there is considerable ambiguity in the literature about the best way to categorize the types of settlement found in highland Peru. The terms *town* and *village* are frequently used interchangeably to describe the nucleated center of a municipal district, the basic unit of local administration in Peru, where one usually finds a church, a central plaza, and the offices of the district authorities. The district center is often the place of residence of the bigger farmers and traders of the district, while the other inhabitants live in scattered farmsteads or in small hamlets. Although in the early colonial period there were important status and occupational distinctions between the Spanish residents of the district centers and the Indian inhabitants, these gradually became blurred. Those types of settlement that in the Callejón de Huaylas and in the Mantaro Valley may be labelled "towns"

are also peasant "villages" in the sense that nowadays the majority of their inhabitants are small-holder farmers, some of whom supplement their incomes by nonagricultural activities. Even the "town elite" will own and often work farm plots of up to about twenty hectares, using both household and hired labor, and, in this sense, they constitute a rich peasant stratum.

48. Eileen A. Maynard, "The Patterns of Community Service Development in Selected Communities of the Mantaro Valley, Peru," *Socio-Economic Development of Andean Communities*, Report no. 3.

49. Hernán Castillo, "Mito: The Orphan of Its Illustrious Children," *Socio-Economic Development of Andean Communities*, Report no. 4, and "Chaqui-cocha: Community in Progress," *Socio-Economic Development of Andean Communities*, Report no. 5.

50. Manuel Alers-Montalvo, *Pucará: Un estudio de cambio*. Also, see Solano in this volume.

51. Alberti and Sánchez, *Poder y conflicto social*, pp. 75–90.

52. Fernando Fuenzalida et al., *Estructuras tradicionales y economía de mercado: La comunidad de indígenas de Huayopampa*, pp. 155–187.

53. Frank W. Young, "A Proposal for Cooperative Cross-cultural Research on Intervillage Systems," *Human Organization* 25, no. 1 (Spring 1966): 46–50.

54. Tullis, *Lord and Peasant in Peru*.

55. Handelman, *Struggle in the Andes*, pp. 139–154.

56. Ibid., p. 220.

57. Spalding, "Class Structures."

58. Alberti and Sánchez, *Poder y conflicto social*.

59. Ibid., pp. 179–193.

60. A full account of these struggles since the colonial period is provided in Carlos Samaniego, "Location, Social Differentiation and Peasant Movements in the Central Sierra of Peru," Ph.D. dissertation, University of Manchester, 1974. A similar account is provided for the neighboring region of Huanca-velica by Henri Favre, "Le Peuplement et la colonisation agricole de la steppe dans le Pérou central," *Annales de Geographie* 84 (July–September 1975): 415–440.

61. S. Waldemar Espinoza, "Los Huancas, aliados de la conquista," *Anales Científicos* 1, no. 1, Universidad Nacional del Centro, Huancayo, 1972; Garcilaso de la Vega, *First Part of the "Royal Commentaries of the Incas."*

62. Samaniego, "Location, Social Differentiation and Peasant Movements," pp. 60–69.

63. John Murra, "An Aymara Kingdom in 1567," *Ethnohistory* 15, no. 2 (1968): 115–151.

64. John Murra, "El control vertical de un máximo de pisos ecológicos en la economía de las sociedades andinas," in John Murra, *Formaciones económicas y políticas del mundo andino*, pp. 59–115.

65. Murra, "An Aymara Kingdom," *Ethnohistory* 15, no. 2 (1968): 121.

66. Fonseca, "La economía 'vertical' y la economía de mercado." For "peas-antization," see Steven S. Webster, "Native Pastoralism in the South Andes," *Ethnology* no. 12 (1973), pp. 115–133.

67. See Winder, "The Effect of the 1970 Reform on the Peasant Communities," pp. 9–11; José María Arguedas, "Conclusiones de un estudio comparativo entre las comunidades del Perú y España," *Revista Visión del Perú* no. 1, (Lima) 1964.

68. Fernando Fuenzalida, "La matriz colonial de las comunidades de indígenas andinas," in *La hacienda, la comunidad y el campesino en el Perú.*
69. Escobar, *Sicaya*, pp. 160–169; Adams, *Community in the Andes*, p. 18; Samaniego, "Location, Social Differentiation and Peasant Movements," pp. 406–409, for an account of the early history of Chupaca.
70. Ricardo Tello Devotto, *Historia de la provincia de Huancayo*, p. 12.
71. Arguedas, "Evolución de la comunidades indígenas," *Revista del Museo Nacional* 26 (1957): 98.
72. Samaniego, "Location, Social Differentiation and Peasant Movements," pp. 63–67, 89–91.
73. Our point is that in most areas of highland Peru where arable farming predominates, land is likely to be held in relatively small holdings. Regional statistics on landholding obscure this pattern by aggregating pastoral and arable holdings.
74. Adams, *Community in the Andes*, pp. 18–21.
75. Fuenzalida et al., *Estructuras tradicionales*, pp. 52–56.
76. Jean Piel, "Notas históricas sobre la evolución y la permanencia de las estructuras de dominación interna y externa en la sociedad peruana," *Revista del Museo Nacional* (Lima) 35 (1967–1968): 191.
77. John Fisher, "Silver Mining and Silver Miners in the Viceroyalty of Peru, 1776–1824: A Prolegomenon," in *Social and Economic Change in Modern Peru*, edited by Rory Miller, Clifford T. Smith, and John Fisher, pp. 13–26.
78. Data on the education of children from village families were obtained from the archives of the *colegios* of Jauja and Huancayo.
79. This is less true for Jauja. See Alberti and Sánchez, *Poder y conflicto social*, pp. 33–41. However, we examined carefully the proceedings of the Huancayo Provincial Council and could find no indication of any persistent policy of intervention in and control of the district councils.
80. *Boletín de Estadística Peruana* 5, no. 6, 1962, p. 405, table 12; David Slater, "Underdevelopment and Spatial Inequality: Approaches to the Problems of Regional Planning in the Third World," *Progress in Planning*, vol. 4, pt. 2, pp. 121–122, for the position of Junín at the beginning of the 1950s.
81. *Boletín de Estadística Peruana* 5, no. 6, p. 406, table 12.
82. Hutchinson, "Sociocultural Change in the Mantaro Valley," p. 10.
83. Instituto Nacional de Promoción Industrial, *Estadística Industrial, 1963*, p. 21.
84. The question of capital accumulation and investment in the village economy by migrants is taken up in the subsequent volume.
85. See Slater, "Underdevelopment and Spatial Inequality," pp. 114–134, for national trends.
86. Escobar, *Sicaya*, pp. 42–43, and Winder in this volume.
87. Bryan R. Roberts, "Migración urbana y cambio en la organización provincial en la sierra central del Perú," *Ethnica* (Barcelona) no. 6 (1973), pp. 237–258.
88. An analysis of this type of economic "dualism" is given by Richard Webb, "Government Policy and the Distribution of Income in Peru, 1963–1973," Discussion Paper no. 39, Research Program in Economic Development, Princeton University.
89. Bryan R. Roberts, "Center and Periphery in the Development Process: The Case of Peru," in *Latin American Urban Research*, edited by W. A. Cor-

nelius and F. M. Trueblood, vol. 5, pp. 77–106.

90. Gavin A. Smith, "The Social Bases of Peasant Political Activity: The Case of the Huasicanchinos of Central Peru," Ph.D. dissertation, University of Sussex, 1975; Samaniego, "Location, Social Differentiation and Peasant Movements."

2. Peasant Movements
at the Turn of the Century
and the Rise of the
Independent Farmer

CARLOS SAMANIEGO

This chapter[1] investigates a series of peasant movements that mark the transition from an agrarian, colonial structure dominated by feudal-like relations of production to one dominated by capitalist relations. These movements took place during the period 1870 to the mid-1930s in the zone of Chupaca, an important district capital, located at the southern end of the Mantaro Valley on the opposite side of the river from Huancayo. Parallel to this transformation, local and regional political authorities were gradually losing their relative autonomy with respect to central government. This weakening of local political power was perceived by the movements' leaders and was utilized in their strategies.

The movements that I describe have often escaped the notice of sociologists, anthropologists, and historians who have studied peasants, since they mostly occurred in a "silent" manner, using legal means and little physical violence. Many important changes were brought about in the rural zone by patient and obstinate use of legal means by the peasants. This is my objection to Quijano's division of the social struggle in Latin America into two main periods: a prepolitical period and the period of politicization.[2] This division is not adequate insofar as it implies the nonexistence of politics among the rural population before the twentieth century. Historically, peasants have always been involved in politics, although clearly the class of politics has not al-

45

ways been the same. In earlier periods the peasant was more involved in what we could call "traditional politics," whereas recently, since the beginning of the twentieth century, peasants in Chupaca and other zones of Peru have entered into modern politics through formally organized political parties and defined ideologies.[3]

The movements that occurred in the zone of Chupaca between the 1870s and the 1930s were reformist in nature. They were of two types and followed changes in the national capitalist economy as this gradually penetrated into the social, economic, cultural, and political life of the villages in the western zone of Chupaca. The first type of movement was an independence movement against the domination of the town of Chupaca. Its aim was to advance the economic interests of certain villages, especially those with greater resources of farming land and/or natural pastures. This movement toward independence occurred within two different political contexts, and the differences in these contexts determined the success or failure of the movement. The first political context was that of a period of crisis in the country as a whole, between 1874 and 1891, when the zone of Chupaca enjoyed relative economic and political autonomy. This was the period of the nitrate wars with Chile, of the subsequent Chilean invasion and occupation of much of Peru, and of the civil wars that followed the Chilean withdrawal.[4] The independence movement of this period occurred in the highland villages of the zone of Chupaca. A similar movement of lowland villages, headed by Ahuac, from 1903 to 1905, occurred within a political context in which the rural population began participating as wage labor in the production of the plantations, mines, and haciendas. This context meant that the peasantry had direct access to national-level organizations.

The second type of movement occurred during the 1920s and 1930s, when Chupaca was no longer dominant politically. This differed from the first type of movement in its greater utilization of formal political and economic organization, linked directly to national-level organizations. One movement was concerned with the process of legal recognition of the villages as *comunidades indígenas*.[5] In this movement, highland villages acquired exclusive collective ownership of pasture and took control of their communal labor force. The other movement was directed against the remaining landlords and against church lands.

In the zone of Chupaca, none of these peasant movements was the result of conflict between homogeneous villages or resulted from communities defending their collective resources of pasture, crop lands, irrigation water, or labor force. The movements were, in fact, a struggle between one set of farmers, landlords, and traders residing in the dominant valley towns and villages and another set who had emerged in villages dependent on these larger centers. With some exaggeration, one could say that the struggle was between an emerging petty bourgeoisie and an already established bourgeoisie, in Chupaca town, that was allied to the landlords and to speculating and profiteering tradesmen.

In the account that follows, I make frequent use of the term *independent farmer*. By this term, I mean a group of farmers who had sufficient land or animals to produce a surplus for the market and who used part of this surplus to reinvest in land or animals. Apart from the intensive use of their own household labor, this group made use of hired labor obtained for a cash wage or in return for a share of the crops. They contrast with the large farmers—the landowners—in the smaller size and direct exploitation of their property. Within their own social and economic context, this group has many similarities to the kulaks of Russia; their relationships to their laborers and to other farmers were based on complementarities of interest and, often, on kinship. The patterns of inheritance of the independent farmer group, based on a division of land among all the heirs, encouraged, as in Russia, a certain degree of social mobility within villages and from villages to urban centers.[6]

In using the term *independent farmer*, my purpose is to focus on changes in the mode of production in the Chupaca zone. I argue that "independent" farming is an identifiable, though subordinate, mode of production based on particular social relations of production and particular means of production.[7] Furthermore, as a mode of production, independent farming has a superstructure of political and cultural institutions. It is as part of this structure and of the processes of change associated with it that the social and political movements of the Chupaca zone are analyzed here.

The special position of the independent farmer was that he was a small-scale, commercial farmer who depended for extra labor neither on relations of a feudal type (that is, sharecropping, labor services), as did the landlord, nor exclusively on capitalist ones. Having greater direct control of his land, much of which was irrigated, the independent farmer of the lowlands responded, more effectively than the landlord who held large extensions of dry land, to changes in the demand for agricultural foodstuffs in Peru at the end of the nineteenth century.[8] However, the independent farmers needed to exploit their production resources directly and had to supplement their household labor by contracting laborers who, in exchange for a wage, would lose their right to the final product. The precondition for this labor market was the development of a money economy in the zone and an increase in the consumption of manufactured goods that could be acquired only with cash. This was a slow process, since it was not associated with the rise of a mass consumer market based on factory industrialization; hence, the independent farmers utilized the diverse traditional forms of labor combined with wage labor to expand their enterprise. The laborer still had ownership of his tools, with which he worked as a "peon" or agricultural laborer. In such a situation, technological improvement was slow with respect to the instruments of work, although other aspects of farming production could be improved through seed selection, crop rotation, and better techniques of produce conservation.

The Economic and Political Context

Toward the end of the nineteenth century, the political organization of the Mantaro Valley was based on a series of districts whose administrative centers were large villages based in the valley lowlands. The districts also included a number of small settlements (*anexos*). The jurisdiction of the district authorities included large areas of communal pasture, located mainly in the highlands. A number of small villages had developed on the highland pastures, and several of these had originated as the abodes of shepherds pasturing flocks that belonged to families living in the district capital or in other important valley villages.[9] These highland residents had, over time, secured a degree of economic independence through raising their own flocks and through crop cultivation. They remained dependent on the district capitals as market and political centers; this dependence also characterized families residing in the *anexos* located in the valley.

The district of Chupaca included in 1870 a substantial part of the southern end of the Mantaro Valley. Relationships between the town of Chupaca and villages (*anexos*) within the district were basically the same in 1870 as they had been during the Spanish Colony. Villages provided communal labor free and contributed such material resources as straw, adobe, and wood for the public works of the town of Chupaca. These relationships were enforced by local officials who were delegated representatives of the town of Chupaca. These officials were often forced to assist the Chupaca leaders in their private activities, acting as their commercial agents and sending personnel to work on their lands. On each visit of the Chupaca authorities, local officials expected "rich" households in the village to provide lodging and food and even to sell some of their livestock or produce to the visitors at reduced prices.[10]

The authorities of Chupaca were as heterogeneous as their economy. Although the landowners predominated, power moved among them, the traders, and the independent farmers. In the dependent villages, such as Ahuac, Huarisca, Iscos, and Yanacancha, the *agente municipal*, previously known as *alcalde auxiliar*, and the *teniente gobernador* were independent farmers and traders, as were their counterparts in the town of Chupaca.[11]

Apart from the population figures of the national census of 1876, there are no statistical data to describe the social and economic characteristics of either highland or valley villages in this period. To provide some basis for the subsequent discussion, I have compiled statistics on the crop and animal distribution for one highland and one valley village that belonged to the district of Chupaca; these villages figure importantly in the peasant movements of the southern end of the Mantaro Valley and provide most of the data for the analysis to follow. See tables 1 and 2. The statistics on crop and animal distribution were collected using local archives and local informants. The categories into which I group families are my own, based on my knowledge of crop and animal production in the zone, but they make use of informants' categorizations of the number of "rich" families or, in the case of Yanacancha, of the number of families without animals or pasturing the sheep of others. I also use case histories of individual families and of their land and animal ownership.

The Secession of the Highland Villages

The first social movement occurred in the 1870s in the Chupaca highlands and was led by the independent farmers. It was produced by the development of livestock raising on the communal pastures, where the former shepherds took control of livestock production and possession of the pastures. It resulted in the creation of a new district —San Juan—formed from the highland villages. On November 27, 1874, the *Congreso Nacional* legalized the creation of the district of San Juan, on the highlands of the western zone of Chupaca, formed by the villages of Acac, Jarpa, Quero, Yanacancha, and Potaca and the settlements of Sulcan, Cacchi, Chaquicocha, and Huarmita. The haciendas of Canipaco, Laive, Ingahuasi, Jatunhuasi, and Colpa were included in the new district. Six districts, Chupaca, Sicaya, Chongos, Colca, Mito, and Orcotuna, towns in the valley, thus lost the livestock villages that they had controlled from colonial times.

Social and economic differentiation in the highland villages had resulted in the fact that the majority of households had become largely independent of Chupaca livestock owners (table 1). These highland families needed to establish new commercial relationships to replace those with Chupaca, which, while placing them in a servile position, had also given them access to lowland crops through gifts and exchanges. The highlanders did not legally control the pastures and this

TABLE 1

OWNERSHIP OF SHEEP IN YANACANCHA CIRCA 1880

Social Category	Number	Average Number of Sheep	Own Sheep	Sheep of Chupaca Families	Total
Independent farmers	20	800	16,000	——	16,000
Subsistence households	31	300	9,300	——	9,300
Shepherds	30	300	4,500	4,500	9,000
Dependent families	20	——	——	——	——
Total	101		29,800	4,500	34,300

NOTE: Yanacancha village: an *anexo*, some thirty kilometers from the district capital located in pastoral highlands.

disadvantaged them in commercial relations. On the other hand, the Chupacans were the only animal traders of the zone and, in order to secure a monopoly of buying and selling of livestock, they had to have political control over the highland farmers and control of their pastures. The imposition of a rent on the pastures was, as well as a source of money, a means of holding down the highlanders.

The implications of the political dependence of the highlands on Chupaca had been emphasized seven months before the creation of the new district. As a result of fiscal crisis, the *concejo municipal* of the province of Huancayo ordered the *concejos municipales* of the districts to count the number of animals that grazed on the communal pastures and impose a tax.[12] The first municipality to ask for authorization to charge rent for the use of communal pastures was Chupaca, followed later by Sicaya, San Jerónimo, Chongos, and Colca. On August 11, 1874, the districts proposed a list of charges to the *concejo provincial*, based on the charges made by the haciendas in the zone. The charge for renting communal pastures was an innovation, since previously this rent had been paid only by livestock owners who were not from the district of Chupaca. Shortly afterward, the highland livestock farmers presented a formal complaint to the *alcalde* of the *concejo provincial* against this rent.[13]

By the end of July, 1875, the *concejo provincial* had approved the charging of rent by Chupaca, despite the creation of the new district. Almost immediately, on July 31, the authorities of Chupaca invaded the pastures of the village of Acac, to the north of Yanacancha. The following day the *alcalde auxiliar* of the village sent an official letter to the *concejo provincial* to inform them of the invasion. The authorities of Acac complained that, on the pretext of charging rent for the pastures, two authorities of the town of Chupaca, with the aid of twenty men, robbed the farmers of "the best steers, sheep, and donkeys . . . assaulting various people, as happened with the wife of Don Ciriaco Rojas, who was kicked and beaten when within a few days of giving birth and who is now in danger of her life. All this was committed by the horde of bandits . . . as this same *Aliaga and Laso* [authorities from Chupaca] *run the business of collecting the two classes of livestock and pack animals,* they have taken advantage of the situation *to force us to sell them our steers and sheep,* and obtain the strongest and most resistant donkeys for their business, simply at their caprice." [14]

The request of the Chupaca authorities to annul the law was based on two points: first, that the law was a maneuver of the hacendados and of some members of the national congress to divide the communities and take over their pastures. The second point was that highland inhabitants did not form towns or villages as appeared in the law but were simply "shepherds" of the *comuneros* whom the Chupacan authorities represented, so there were no persons qualified to hold the posts that each district demanded. [15]

Later, to justify their attempt to levy rent on pasture within the new district, the Chupacans stated that "no one can usurp what is ours, as these pastures were left by the ancient owners for the benefit of the town we legally represent; thus, the unaltering ancient ownership is ours. If the individuals of Achipampa (Yanacancha), Jarpa, and Acac have separated themselves . . . it was understood that this happened only on political grounds, not in order to appropriate another's estate." In contrast, the highland villages stressed the economic restrictions placed upon them by Chupaca. In one document it is stated that, once the population began to increase, the Chupaca authorities started to antagonize the people, usurping by force their labor power, livestock, and money for public works in the town of Chupaca and to the benefit of certain individuals. [16] The document mentions that the Chupaca authorities made a yearly trip to the highlands to collect a form of "gift" as their payment and that the value of livestock taken each year was from five thousand to six thousand soles.

Apart from the legal battle, there was also physical violence; on several occasions the authorities of Chupaca led armed incursions into the highlands, burning buildings and seizing animals. The highlanders organized their own defense, repelling the invaders until the army intervened to restore order. Under these circumstances, the highland villages acted cohesively despite marked internal differentiation. In the case of Yanacancha, the one hundred households organized themselves behind the independent farmers of the village.

The high degree of solidarity shown, especially in repelling invasions by the Chupaca authorities, was an expression of the network of social and economic relations among the different village groups. These groups were united through relations of labor service and kinship, and these relations organized the social and economic activity of both households and individuals. Those families without livestock were, for example, related by kinship to those for whom they worked and often resided in the same compound. Economic and political independence was an objective shared by all the households in a highland village, as it would expand the village economy; though, in practice, it was the better-off independent farmers who benefited directly from such an expansion, since they alone had access to the necessary resources, particularly labor.

Despite their cohesion and their use of legal strategies, the highland villages eventually lost their fight. On November 6, 1891, the president annulled the creation of the district of San Juan, and the highland villages returned to their old jurisdictions. The major factor in the victory of Chupaca and the other valley towns was their continuing political power within a national context in which the central government was weak. For example, the Chupaca authorities increased their political power in the region after the war with Chile because of their participation in the resistance led by General Cáceres. In the warfare of this period, the larger towns of the provinces, led by their landowners and traders, enjoyed a certain autonomy. Bartolomé Guerra, the principal landowner of Chupaca and one of the officials who invaded the highland village of Acac, was an important military figure of his day, helping to organize the resistance against Chile.

Independent Farmers and the Movements of Independence

By the turn of the century, the economic structure of the region was no longer consistent with the power structure. The increasing incorporation of the region into the national economy weakened the political power of the formerly dominant large landowners and traders resident in the district capitals, as a result of the direct and indirect alliances between independent farmers and nationally based economic and political interests. New economic opportunities gave the independent farmers a certain security in their struggle against their exploiters, the

Chupaca authorities. The rapid economic growth of plantations, mines, and cities at the turn of the century increasingly influenced the rural area, and, every year, new villages became more integrated into their economy through wage labor. In this way, the households began to liberate themselves from local exploitation based on tied labor and entered into capitalist relations of exploitation.

The growth of the national economy also created an increased interest in control of the rural population from the capital of the Republic. The organization of political parties and of groups for the protection of the "indigenous" population began to break down the political monopoly of power groups in the towns of the different zones of the valley.[17]

By the beginning of the twentieth century, Ahuac had become a prominent village. According to the census of 1876, Ahuac was the most heavily populated lowland village of the western zone of Chupaca. Ahuac was the center for supplying certain farming products to the neighboring villages. It had greater resources of land and water supply than other villages and was one of the most internally differentiated villages. About 19 percent of the households lived mainly from non-farming activities.[18] Many produced agricultural and nonagricultural products that were exchanged with other villages.

There were in Ahuac at least twenty-two independent farmer households (table 2); besides controlling the greatest proportion of irrigated lands, these households had, according to informants, an average of three years of schooling, and there were also four members who were studying at secondary school in Huancayo. All these households produced for the market and were the only ones to utilize wage labor for some of their farming and commercial activities. They were familiar with the mines through traveling there as mule owners or when taking their farming produce. Eight members of these households had worked on the construction of the railroad between Chicla and La Oroya; others had worked in the coal mines of the zone. Other members of these households were to be found in Lima. A general tendency of these households was to place many of their members in nonfarming activities. The heads of households encouraged their sons to study and took them on business trips or sent them to work in the mines, the coastal plantations, or Lima. Some joined the army or police force. Once they had become accustomed to the city, its institutions, and the possibilities of work, they often settled in Lima.

The other households, of which there were about 347, were heterogeneous. Many of them had some experience of the region as soldiers or mule drivers. Members of these households did not yet migrate for

TABLE 2

LAND OWNERSHIP IN AHUAC VILLAGE CIRCA 1880

Social Category	Number of Owners	Amount of Land Owned Within Ahuac* in Acres				
		Irrigated	Unirrigated	Average Irrigated	Average Unirrigated	Total
Independent farmers from Ahuac	22	257	117	11.7	5.3	374
Subsistence households	406	317	2,256	.8	5.6	2,573
Independent farmers from Chupaca	10	——	205	——	20.5	205
Landlords†	2	20	835	10	418	855
Saints and images of Chupaca‡	1	27	126	27	126	153
Saints and images of Ahuac	1	84	——	84	——	84
	442	705	3,539			4,244

NOTES: * Ahuac village: an *anexo* some five kilometers from the district capital located on the valley floor.
† These two owners are from the Guerra family, which, in turn, is descended from the colonial and precolonial landlords, the Apoalaya.
‡ These are lands granted to the church by landowners and richer peasants for the cult of the saints; their proceeds are intended to pay for the upkeep of the images and their festivals.

paid work in the region, in the mines, the plantations, or Lima. Not until the beginning of the 1910s did they begin to move to these areas as temporary wage laborers.

By the end of the 1890s and the beginning of the twentieth century, a strong opposition had developed in the western villages against the town of Chupaca. This had its origin in the intensive and continual use of the communal labor of the villages by the Chupaca authorities. After the end of the Chilean war, when General Cáceres was president, the Chupacans devoted themselves to rebuilding their town, which the Chileans had destroyed. Their greatest task was the rebuilding of the large church and municipal building. The villages worked continually for Chupaca from 1890 to 1902. Although communal labor took place only during the time of the year when there was no rain or farming activity, that is, part of June and all of July and August each year, these were the months in which households could realize extra activities complementary to their economy. Households producing for the market used these months to transport their produce to work and urban centers and to obtain new contracts for the following year. Subsistence households used the time to repair their tools, improve their houses or build new ones for young relatives, exchange products, or even look for seasonal wage labor in the region. Intensive livestock raising had begun on the lowlands and, during the dry months when good pasture was scarce, households led their cattle up to the highland pastures.

The situation was aggravated by an increase in population; each household engaged in subsistence farming needed to practice complementary activities in order to obtain the farming and livestock products that it could not produce. To develop their economy or even to remain as subsistence farmers, it was necessary for the villagers to be independent of Chupaca and not waste labor, time, or cash in activities designed to benefit Chupaca.

The struggle for separation began at the end of August, 1903. The authorities of Ahuac received an official letter from their counterparts in Chupaca ordering them to prepare ten thousand adobes, within a week, for the construction of a girls' school in the town of Chupaca. The Ahuacinos decided to send a committee of ten, headed by the authorities, to inform the Chupacans that the task was impossible, as the rains had already begun, and that the work should be left for the following year. If that were not possible, the Chupacans were asked to allow them to make fewer adobes and to have two weeks to make them.

Victor Fernández, the thirty-year-old leader of the Ahuac committee, was not from a household that held a large area of land. However, what he did possess was good, being near the springs and completely protected from the vagaries of climate. He had received four years of primary schooling. The other three leaders in the struggle had studied at secondary school and belonged to households with relatively large extensions of land.[19] In addition to these four men, all the independent farmers in Ahuac and the other villages west of Chupaca participated actively in the separatist movement; their names are listed in the project for the creation of the district of Ahuac that was laid before the Congreso Nacional, a project that was finally successful two years later.[20]

The first problem facing the leaders was that of finding a lawyer. They first approached Agusto Duarte Valladeres, son of the owners of Tucle Hacienda and the former owners of the Laive and Ingahuasi haciendas. As he was unable to help them, they asked the advice of a lawyer who was headmaster of the Colegio Santa Isabel in Huancayo, where one of them had studied. He was the father-in-law of the congressman Ernesto Ráez. The headmaster displayed such interest that he visited the western zone of Chupaca and was impressed by the solidarity of the people and the resources of Ahuac.

The leaders traveled to Lima to see Ráez, but he refused to help them, for the Chupacans had already spoken to all the congressional representatives from the province of Huancayo and had stirred up opposition to the project. The Ahuacinos were not discouraged and went to the office of a firm that specialized in economic evaluations and official transactions: M. J. Kando y Co., Comisiones y Consignaciones de Lima. This firm designed a project for the creation of a district, basing their plan on the possibility of the creation of a new department: El Mantaro, which would have four provinces: Concepción, Chupaca, Huancayo, and Tayacaja.[21] The new department was justified as a means of developing the rich mineral deposits, mainly coal, and crop and livestock farming. The project argued that the district of Ahuac was needed for the creation of a province of Chupaca to facilitate public administration over the large area of the existing district of Chupaca. It was also suggested that the separation of the towns was inevitable as a simple function of progress, and precedents in the United States were quoted as examples.

The Ahuacinos took the project to various congressional representatives and gained the support of the Constitutionalist party of General Cáceres. Finally, after a personal intervention by Cáceres, the district of Ahuac was created on November 14, 1905; the law was approved by the president of the Republic, José Pardo, who was later to become one of the largest shareholders in a textile factory in Huancayo. Though the Ahuacinos felt that the personal intervention of Cáceres was crucial for the creation of their district, their main ally was the changing situation of the central region of Peru. The idea of a new department was attractive to the Constitutionalists because the department would consist of towns and villages dependent on Huancayo, a rapidly growing town, which would be the departmental capital. In contrast to the city of Jauja, which had constantly opposed Constitutionalist policies, Huancayo represented a growth pole suited to developing the commercial and mining opportunities of the area. At the same time, the relative development of other villages in the zone and the existence of new economic opportunities in the form of wage labor broke the virtual economic monopoly and political autonomy of Chupaca.

The Second Type of Peasant Movement:
The Exploitation of Communal Institutions

In the Chupaca zone, the period from the turn of the century is one in which communal institutions and organizations appear to gain strength; the prominence of such institutions is due to the use of formal and legal organization to achieve local objectives and is directly related to the developmental strategies of the independent farmers. This use of formal organization is also partly based on the experience of wage laborers in cities, mines, and plantations.

The sequence in which the different localities were transformed by these movements was almost the reverse of the colonial sequence, in which Chupaca village served as a point of Spanish colonization and economic exploitation. Chupaca was the last locality to change in the early twentieth century, and its change was linked to the prior transformation of its dependent villages.

Interest in communal organization among the villages was a product of the conflicts between them and Chupaca over control of resources. The villages had to create their own identity, define their own resources and borders, and form a political unity vis-à-vis other villages. In the highlands, the organization of villages into officially recognized communities had as its aim the expansion of livestock farming and the defense of natural pastures against encroachment by other villages or the haciendas.

For the village population itself, the communities were never "Indian" or "indigenous." Only in their relations with the external world did the population present themselves as *indigenas*, thus coinciding with the image that urban populations and national organizations, both political and intellectual, held of the rural population. This self-labeling as *indigenas* was a legal strategy used by the villagers in order to take refuge in the colonial and republican laws that protected the lands and pastures of *indios* or *indigenas*. All colonial titles of communal ownership of lands and pastures specifically stated that the owners must be *indios*. The first liberal laws of the Republic reinforced the idea of the existence of pastures and farming lands belonging to *indigenas*.[22] Thus, formally, the village population became *indios* or *indigenas*, in order to have the support of the law. Villages in the Chupaca zone only formed themselves into *comunidades indigenas* after they had reached a point of marked social and economic differentiation: The *comunidad* represented an alliance among its various economic and social segments in opposition to external groups.

The livestock haciendas were also interested in the recognition of highland villages as *comunidades indigenas*. The ancient lowland villages had always been a strong obstacle to the haciendas because of their political and economic importance and because of their legal ownership of pastures and lands. The official recognition of highland villages as *comunidades* made the situation easier for the haciendas, as they found less difficulty in arriving at a compromise with villages whose boundaries had only recently been fixed and whose leaders had fewer political contacts than the lowland leaders.

With the development of an agro-mining capitalist economy, the *comunidad indígena* became a functionally convenient form of organizing the villages of the countryside. Because of its collective character, the *comunidad indígena* tended to slow down the process of social and economic differentiation that would eventually destroy the subsistence basis of a temporary wage labor force. At the same time, the *comunidad* encouraged the union of households for joint or communal action.

The division of the rural population into small units with limited resources meant that livestock and arable farming could satisfy only a part of the needs of the household. It was necessary for some members of the household to work in plantations or mines for a period each year to compensate for the deficit in their production. Likewise, plantations and mines were organized in such a way that they could absorb this rural labor force seasonally, cyclically, or permanently.

For the villages and for their labor power to be incorporated fully into the national economy, it was necessary for them to develop a money economy and to be brought into closer contact with the cities. This was achieved by the construction of highways and schools and by the introduction of the telephone. New roads were needed to stimulate crop, livestock, and mining production. Through the *Ley de Conscripción Vial* of 1920, all villages organized as *comunidades* were obliged to work on road construction. The division of the rural population into *comunidades indígenas* thus facilitated their manipulation, especially when their communal labor was required for undertaking public works, as specified by the *Ley de la Vagancia* of 1924.

Within this economic context, the *indígena* issue became a matter of interest and concern at the national level. Urban-based Peruvian intellectuals began a campaign in favor of the *indios* of Peru, organizing a series of pro-indigenist institutions to aid the villages in their struggle against the haciendas and the dominant towns.[23] At the same time, politicians began to speak of the integration of the indigenous population into the social, cultural, and economic life of the country. The result of these political movements was the full legal recognition of *comunidades indígenas* in 1920.[24]

At the village level, the resurgence of the *comunidad indígena* was due, in part, to the interests of the independent farmers. The development of the agro-mining economy did not create markets for agricultural foodstuffs in sufficiently large proportions to allow for the development of extensive food-crop agriculture. It thus only stimulated the development of a relatively small group of independent farmers who had sufficient irrigated land, had access to labor, and participated in the exchange economy. The independent farmers were continually seeking to control two fundamental resources: land and money in the form of capital. This control occurred within a framework of agricultural development that was limited by local resources and by competition between households.

Let us now outline briefly the various ways in which the independent farmers of Ahuac made use of the creation of the new district and its communal institutions. The activities of the district council both stimulated the development of a money economy and provided opportunities for commercial enterprise. The district council obtained one-third of its annual rents from the charge made for the use of communal pastures. It also received payment for the use of irrigation, for the renting of alfalfa plots on the church lands, and in taxes on the sale of certain products and on licenses to use new farming lands. This revenue, whose total apparently was never fully revealed, provided the authorities with a useful means of financing their own private business undertakings. Complaints about the misuse of council money are frequent in the minutes of the council and led, in 1920, to a lawsuit against a former alcalde for embezzlement of funds.

There was an annual auction of the right to collect taxes for the sale of liquor and coca, for the renting of council shops, and for licenses to open shops, sell eggs, bread, and fruit, and impose fines on trespassing livestock. According to the *Libros de Remate*, these rights were always won by people who occupied posts in the council.[25]

Competition over communal resources led to the appearance of two factions among the independent farmers. One faction consisted for the most part of those who had completed primary school or had some secondary school studies. These included former soldiers and men with experience of wage labor; most were young. The second faction could be described as "traditional" and held more land thon those of the first group. The young faction with less land sought individual benefits from the control of communal resources that would enable them to accumulate land and money. The more "traditional" faction sought to establish and develop their economic position by widening their field of activities.

The methods used by the two groups were also different. The young faction, by virtue of having worked for a wage externally, were in contact with the coastal trade unions and with such institutions as the Asociación Pro-Indígena, the Comité Pro-Derecho Indígena Tahuantinsuyo, and the Patronato de la Raza Indígena, which were interested in aiding the "indigenous" population. The "traditional" faction was more interested in local and zonal action, such as the cleaning of irrigation ditches and roads, road building, and so on.

The young faction had two basic desires: to increase their holdings of irrigated land and to increase their resources of money. In order to achieve these objectives they founded two associations; the first, the Sociedad Anónima Progresista Canalizadora de Huillaca (1913), aimed at improving irrigation and extending the amount of irrigated land; the second, the Centro Defensor de los Derechos Comunales de Ahuac, was founded in 1919 to expose the irregularities of the traditional faction, which was accused of having embezzled council funds. The Centro Defensor was initially formed by sixty *principales* of the village who, with the support of the provincial mayor of Huancayo, removed the mayor of Ahuac and elected new authorities. From that moment, the Centro Defensor took over direct administration of the church lands and the irrigation system of the village.[26] The Centro acted as a tenant of the council, for it paid the latter a fixed rent for the lands and water. Later, the Centro Defensor became a limited company with a capital of 1,960 *soles oro*, distributed among twelve members, one of whom held 47 percent of the shares while the rest were fairly evenly distributed among other members.

With this capital, the Centro Defensor worked the church lands, sharing the profits among its members. The members also worked the *cofradía* lands of Chupaca church when these came under the administration of the Sociedades Unidas de Chupaca. In the contracts undertaken by the Centro Defensor it was usual for part of the income to be used for some public work.[27]

The Centro Defensor achieved virtual control over the economic activities of the district council until 1928. The "traditional" faction allied with new groups that sprang up in the 1920s and formed the Sociedad Fraternal No. 1, which claimed some control of municipal revenue. Both the Centro and the Sociedad put forward their own candidates for the election of mayor in 1925; this led to open violence. In 1928, both organizations were banned by the government, although the Sociedad Fraternal No. 1 continued, informally, for several more years.[28] After this, the two factions disappeared, and, from this period on, households rarely participated in such locally based collective associations.

It is my view that the development of communal organization and other forms of local association is closely linked to the fact that the independent farmers perceived their major opportunities as being locally based. There is ample evidence in Ahuac that, in the first three decades of the century, the independent farmer group used their political control to open up new resources. As soon as the new district was created, the authorities of Ahuac issued licenses to convert communal pasture into privately cultivated arable land and about two-thirds of the lands in the zone intermediate to the valley and the highlands, about 1,700 acres, were so converted between 1900 and 1930. The beneficiaries were both the independent farmers of Ahuac and those of the *anexos* lying in the intermediate zone.

Another resource that was more intensively exploited was the land belonging to the church; this land was customarily farmed by the *priostes* and *capitanes* of the various fiestas and the product used to finance the celebrations. In 1908, the district council obtained the direct administration of these lands and, since they were irrigated, sowed them with alfalfa and sold the crop to the highest bidder; according to their account books, the purchasers were the richer dairy farmers of the village. The lands were worked by communal labor; a major part of the profits was used to finance public works, only a small proportion going toward the organizing of fiestas. Village informants claimed that this more limited support for the fiestas directly served the interests of the village authorities and their allies. The authorities brought pressure to bear on households to accept posts for the major village fiesta, but as these households no longer had the use of the church land, nor often the ready money necessary for the fiesta, they were forced to take out loans and mortgages on their land which they often found difficult to repay. One of the best known of the authorities, at the time of the creation of the district, obtained at least one-third of his irrigated land in this manner.

The extension of irrigation in the district was a further point of intense activity during this period. Through use of communal labor and district funds, an ambitious project for an aqueduct, including a tunnel, was commenced and eventually finished in the 1930s, irrigating 484 hectares in Ahuac.[29] This irrigation mainly benefited the independent farmer group, since they had the most and best-located land.

However, the system of *enganche* most clearly illustrates the significance of political authority for local enterprise. *Enganche* was a system whereby workers were contracted to give services for a fixed period in a certain place; they were given a certain amount of money in advance, in part payment of future earnings. They were thus indebted and under obligation for a specific period. The *enganchadores* were usually local authorities and acted as agents of the plantations and mines. During the first decades of the century, Chupaca had a monopoly of *enganche* for the mines and the cotton and coffee plantations. Between 1920 and the end of the 1930s, four individuals from Ahuac gained control of wage labor for the plantations of Cañete and Lima. These four Ahuacinos were able to break the Chupaca monopoly by developing direct contacts with the coastal haciendas. Their success also depended on the willingness of the local population to accept wage labor and on their ability as local authorities to bring internal political and economic pressure on those who did not want to work outside.

The Struggle for Ownership of the Communal Pastures

The final and successful struggle for independence by the highland villages was carried out through the formation of *comunidades indigenas*. In this way, villages dependent on lowland political and commercial centers formalized their collective ownership of the natural pastures they had held for several centuries. This movement of highland villages, aimed at securing ownership of the natural pastures, was general in the Mantaro region. In 1935, the former shepherds of Cacchi became independent of Sicaya on being recognized as a *comunidad indigena*. In a similar way, Muquiyauyo, a village in the lowlands, lost its highland pastures when it was forced to sell them to the shepherds who had established the community of Ipas.[30]

In Yanacancha, the highland village chosen for detailed discussion, an increase in population had led to the overgrazing of pastures. By 1910, the pastures of Yanacancha were reaching their full capacity.[31] Complaints by the Yanacanchans about the incursion of livestock from the haciendas and from neighboring villages increased in this period, indicating the interest of the Yanacanchans in keeping "foreign" animals off their pastures.[32] The *estancias* (hut, corral, and grazing area) of independent farmers had also, by this period, reached their maximum expansion.

The movement initiated in Yanacancha in the early 1920s to consolidate their boundaries was stimulated, sustained, and directed by the independent farmers. They were especially interested in consolidating their *estancias* under the umbrella of communal property.

They first took the step of allying themselves with the haciendas in order to gain political influence at the national level. The initiative came from men who were also the official local representatives of the Ahuac district authorities. The haciendas Laive and Ingahuasi were at a stage in their development in which the demarcation of boundaries with the villages surrounding them had become critical. This stage had begun when the first innovations were introduced in the haciendas Laive and Ingahuasi in the 1860s. Sheep were imported from England with a view to crossbreeding them with native stock in order to increase meat and wool production. There was also an attempt to improve the system of sheep management, but without altering the form of labor based on herding by *pastores huaccheros*, that is, shepherds who also tended their own private flocks.[33]

These innovations overextended the Laive and Ingahuasi haciendas and led them to financial ruin. They passed into the hands of a Lima family and in 1928 became part of a livestock company, Sociedad Ganadera del Centro, which included other large haciendas of the zone. This company gave priority to the demarcation and fencing of all boundaries, which, they hoped, would improve pasture lands and sheep breeding. In this respect, the hacienda and Yanacancha shared common interests.

Ahuac was so little concerned with the Yanacancha pastures that its authorities remained passive in the face of repeated incursions by livestock from the haciendas and from other villages. For example, in May, 1922, there had been a major incursion by the hacienda Laive and by the lowland village of Chongos Bajo. The Yanacanchans were therefore obliged to take matters into their own hands. They adopted a campaign of opposition to the Ahuac authorities; they refused to pay anything for the use of pastures or to buy licenses for new lands.[34]

At the individual level, relations between the haciendas and Yanacancha were good; Yanacanchans often worked on the haciendas on a temporary or permanent basis. Taking advantage of these relations, one of the Yanacanchan authorities, Pedro Cangalaya, began to negotiate with hacienda Laive. The basic agreement was that the hacienda would help Yanacancha with the procedures necessary to become officially recognized as a *comunidad indígena* and that, in return, once the *comunidad* came into existence, boundaries would be fixed without the intervention of Ahuac. The hacienda accepted the offer with alacrity, producing the first and one of the most rapid recognitions of *comunidades* in central Peru.[35] Yanacancha was also supported in its struggle by the Patronato de la Raza Indígena, the newspaper *El Sol* of Lima, and by Yanacanchans resident in Lima.

The leader of the movement, thirty-year-old Pedro Cangalaya, was one of the richest livestock farmers of Yanacancha and was noted for his opposition to the Ahuac authorities. He had only three or four years of primary schooling and had hardly moved outside the valley, but he succeeded in recruiting a well-known Yanacanchan, Víctor

Yauri, a teacher and part-time trader working in a private school in the neighboring village of Potaca. Yauri, twenty-eight years old, acted as the movement's "intellectual," for he was well acquainted with the political situation in the zone, the region, and the country as a whole. It was Yauri who traveled to Lima to conduct the negotiations.

When the *comunidad* had been recognized, the representatives of the hacienda brought pressure on the leaders to settle the disputed boundaries. When the boundary dispute was finally settled, the Sociedad Ganadera obtained a favorable definition of boundaries and the promise of help from Yanacancha's communal labor force for fencing. This boundary settlement gave rise to controversy within Yanacancha and to suspicion over the motives of the leaders. In the case of Yauri, it seems from existing letters that he was interested in a rapid settlement to enable him to return to his teaching and business affairs. Pedro, on the other hand, was more directly compromised. Because he was a large livestock owner, it was very much to his advantage to be on good terms with the hacienda; in fact, he ended up working as a labor recruiter for the Sociedad Ganadera in Yanacancha, contracting workers when the hacienda required them and even forcing down wages below the normal stipend.[36] Many years later, Pedro was accused by his fellows of having sold part of the community pastures to allow the hacienda to take possession. Irrespective of the truth of this allegation, this case demonstrates the various ways in which a hacienda is able to attain its objectives without resorting either to violence or to a crude show of political power; the social and economic differentiation of the villages provided many opportunities for internal intervention through bestowing favors on individuals.

The Ahuac authorities resisted the boundary agreement by trying, unsuccessfully, to take advantage of a split within Yanacancha; they encouraged the hamlet of Achipampa, which belonged to Yanacancha and also bordered on the hacienda, to seek recognition of its own *comunidad* status. The Ahuac authorities also led two invasions to destroy the fences between the hacienda and Yanacancha. These incursions ended when the Ahuac authorities and their supporters were imprisoned by the provincial authorities.

The complex intertwining of interests in the zone was nicely demonstrated when one of the Ahuac ringleaders was immediately released from custody through the intercession of one of Huancayo's largest landowners—the hacendado and businessman Javier Calmell del Solar. The Ahuac leader had acted as one of Calmell del Solar's political and business agents in the Chupaca zone. The independent farmers, too, usually had intersecting interests with big traders and landowners of Huancayo. Frequently they were economic and political agents for rich Huancayo families, especially for those who were provincial authorities or representatives in the national parliament. Through this relationship, the independent farmers had access to political power, which they used to maintain their position in their villages.

The Redistribution of Land in Chupaca

My final case is that of a movement that transformed the agrarian and political structure of the district capital of Chupaca. The power of the larger landholders, allied with traders and church authorities, had been centered on this town; consequently, Chupaca was affected by the development of the independent farmer group at a later stage than were the surrounding villages. Though there are many similarities between the changes in Chupaca and those in Ahuac and Yanacancha, the independent farmers were less dominant in the Chupaca movement and there were fewer internal resources on which they could base the development of their economy. In this period, the interests of the different social groups in the town focus increasingly on *external* economic and political opportunities, and their organization reflects this changing orientation.

The movement to change the agrarian structure in Chupaca evolved through the frustration of a group that could no longer extend its economic activities. The leaders of the movement were drawn from two groups, one composed of "semiproletarians" and the other of independent farmers; the former was more important, as it organized and directed the movement.[37]

The semiproletarians were all between twenty and thirty years old, with experience of wage labor and urban life. Some had taken part in the laborers' strike in Lima in 1918–1919.[38] Their level of schooling was relatively higher than the average. Their social and economic backgrounds were heterogeneous, but those whose parents were independent farmers predominated and there were even some from landlord families. Wage labor had brought them into contact with the indigenist organization of Lima, whose protection they now sought.

In actual fact, this group had little interest in either the "indigenous" population or in poor subsistence cultivators, but they utilized this latter population for their own ends. Their actions and their manner of conducting the movement show that their main goal was the organization of commercial enterprises, whether in farming, trade, or services. This entrepreneurial orientation of the movement's leaders can be seen in their attitudes towards the *cofradía* land and in the way in which they organized the subsistence cultivators. For example, they did not attempt to expropriate land from the church or landowners without paying for it, nor did they act illegally. They did not organize themselves within a *comunidad indígena* and, indeed, Chupaca never attained that status; instead, they formed commercial enterprises that retained that fundamental element of the community, namely, communal labor.

The organization of the movement followed the existing organization of the town into *barrios*. Each *barrio* was organized into a company (*sociedad*) that was commercial in character, under the leadership of the semiproletarian group. Within the company, each member was considered to be a shareholder and, at the same time, a *comunero*. Thus, each member shared in the company's successes and failures. This form of organization, which was also utilized by Ahuac and villages throughout the valley, was not of internal origin but was introduced by those who had been wage laborers in the cities and plantations.

The composition of each company varied according to *barrio*. The *barrios* in the town center mainly consisted of households with more experience of "city" life than those of the *barrios* in the "rural" parts. The most active members were those with little land but with long experience of wage labor. By 1921, the town was organized into eight companies: Sociedad Porvenir del Carmen Alto, Sociedad Fraternal Vista Alegre, Sociedad Fraternal Pro-Pincha, Sociedad Progreso Yauyos, Sociedad Avanti Callabayauri, Sociedad Porvenir Llacuas, and Sociedad de Molinopata.[39]

Then, on April 6, 1921, the companies were organized into a single institution, the Sociedades Unidas de Chupaca, in which each company kept its independence but was represented on a central committee. The number of members reached 560. The institution had two legal representatives, one of whom, Juan Wildeng, was a foreign immigrant and the other, a lawyer, Oscar Chávez of Huancayo, later represented the province several times in parliament.

But, as matters advanced, they became influenced by other political currents of the 1920s, such as those emanating from APRA and the socialist parties. Although socialist ideas were incompatible with their existing economic interests, the leaders utilized them to reinforce their activities. For example, the purchase of *cofradía* lands was justified on the grounds that the "Indian problem" was an economic one and that redistribution of land among the poorest was fundamental. Socialist ideas were also utilized to create uncertainty among the landowners so that they would accelerate the sale of their lands, as in fact happened with the Guerra family. In the end, it was the leaders and their allies who bought up the largest plots of land, which they used for commercial agriculture. They never felt themselves to be *indígenas* but, as informants attest, looked down on anyone who did not come from Chupaca and those whom they labeled as *indígenas*.

Opposition to the Sociedades Unidas was purely local in character, coming from the church, which was afraid of losing its lands without receiving any form of benefit from them, and from the landowners. To placate the church, the Sociedades Unidas followed the legalist line of renting and, later, purchasing the land. This organization threatened the economic and political power of the landlords and that of the established, large traders. This led the landowners, who occupied practically all the political and administrative posts in the district, to refuse to recognize it and to accuse the leaders of organizing a subversive movement against the government. They set in motion a campaign of intimidation against the members and had several of the organizers arrested.

Some days after the Sociedades Unidas had been formed, when the members were cleaning the streets and irrigation channels, the *alcalde* and the governor of the district, who were brothers, attempted to stop the work. They intimidated the laborers, ordering three policemen to shoot into the air near them. When the police ran out of ammunition, the authorities were captured by the company's members and taken to the local magistrate. The governor of the district claimed that the Sociedades Unidas were subversive and persuaded the subprefect of Huancayo province to send an army battalion, stationed in Huancayo, to arrest all the company's leaders. The members protested in the main square of Chupaca, occasioning a riot on April 17, 1921, which led to the death of five, the wounding of twelve, and the arrest of more than forty.

Two of the leaders escaped and traveled to Lima to complain. Finally, through the aid of the Comité Pro-Derecho Indígena Tahuantinsuyo, and the government's interest in attending to the problems of the *indígenas*, the Sociedades Unidas were recognized as a legal institution by the president of the Republic in December, 1921.[40]

Following this, the Sociedades Unidas took over the administration of all the *cofradía* lands. Any profits were to be used for the construction and repair of the town's public buildings, drawing on the communal labor of members. Under the rules of the Sociedades, these lands should have been distributed equally among their members. However, this was difficult to realize in practice. An analysis of the list of persons who bought *cofradía* lands, a total of 604, shows that 80 percent of the buyers of land in the Chupaca district were members resident in the center of Chupaca and the remaining 20 percent were resident in the *anexos* of the district.[41] My calculations indicate that 60 percent of the *cofradía* lands reached subsistence households. The other 40 percent went to persons engaged in commercial agriculture or trade.

Besides administering and selling the church lands, the Sociedades Unidas used the profits from the sales to finance many projects that benefited Chupaca. The most important was the construction of an irrigation system. They also built a hydroelectric plant, a market, and an electric grinding mill, and each *barrio* was given a piece of land on which to build a school and land to open up new roads. They financed the purchase of the Apahuay hacienda to provide income for the Escuela Normal de Varones, founded to form teachers to bring education to the *indígenas* under the indigenist policy of the times. The private companies of each *barrio* also financed several projects in their respective areas; for example, Chinyac bought a mill from the church of Chupaca.

Redistribution of the *cofradía* land was accompanied by that of the landlords' holdings. From the late 1920s, the major landowners—the Guerra family—began to accelerate the sales of their land; these sales, in part, responded to their fears that they would encounter difficulties with the *indios* over land titles or sharecropping practices. The actual heirs of the Guerra family estimate, however, that a further important factor was that members of their family had become professionals or city-based businessmen and no longer had a direct interest in the land. As in the case of the *cofradía* land, it appears that this land was sold in small plots. Some of these were sold to the actual sharecroppers of the land and others to households that had accumulated a certain amount of money from wage labor or from small trading activities. In one area of Chupaca on which I have data, the Guerra family sold forty separate plots of land between 1920 and 1939, averaging in size between one and two hectares.

The households that were able to benefit most from the land redistribution were those with capital—those households that had participated in wage labor and those that marketed some surplus. Yet, although some households did accumulate more land, the overall tendency was to reinforce the predominance of small holdings and to allow no more than about ten independent farmers to extend their farms. This redistribution began a leveling process in the Chupaca zone based on small holdings and acted against the development of large-scale commercial farming. The leaders of the Chupaca movement had, by the 1940s, become entrepreneurs, yet many of their economic interests were oriented outside the community. For example, they controlled the transport system and the local stores; they had acquired land in the tropical lowlands of Satipo and controlled trade in livestock and grain. Moreover, some of the more important achievements of the Chupaca movement, such as the construction of an effective local school system, further encouraged the focus on external opportunities.

Conclusion

In the preceding pages, I have described the various ways in which peasant groups in the Chupaca zone played an active part in regional politics at the end of the last century and at the beginning of the present one. This account is intended to counter the notion of the political conservatism of the peasantry or their subjection within a culture of domination imposed by large landowners and central government.

I have emphasized how competition for scarce resources encourages the development of individual interests that differentiate peasant groups. This differentiation, which was present in the colonial period, has been accentuated by the penetration of the capitalist economy. The heterogeneity of interests that emerged provides an understanding of the difficulties attending peasant movements as agents in the structural transformation of society.

The diverse agrarian structures of Third World countries make unlikely a peasant revolt on a national—or even a regional—scale. Two or more regions may simultaneously rise in rebellion when, for historical reasons, their respective agrarian structures become untenable at the same time. It is not only the lack of an external influence or an influence from above that impedes the development of a general peasant movement, as Hobsbawm suggests.[42] Such a movement is also impeded by the particular nature of the agrarian structures in the zones and regions of a dependent country whose internal contradictions do not crystalize at one and the same time. When agrarian structures are more fully developed, that is, the less heterogeneous they are, the possibility of simultaneous peasant movements through the country becomes greater, making more likely the growth of a movement at national level.

Notes

1. This chapter is an amended excerpt from Samaniego's Ph.D. thesis (Carlos Samaniego, "Location, Social Differentiation and Peasant Movements in the Central Sierra of Peru," Ph.D. thesis, University of Manchester).

2. Aníbal Quijano, "Contemporary Peasant Movements," in *Elites in Latin America*, edited by S. M. Lipset and A. Solari, p. 303.

3. Eric Hobsbawm, "Peasants and Politics," *Journal of Peasant Studies* 1, no. 1 (October 1973): 3–22.

4. These wars were partly the result of increasing foreign capitalist pene-

tration. See Ernesto Yepes, *Perú, 1820–1920: Un siglo de desarrollo capitalista*, pp. 103–123.

5. A detailed discussion of the origins and legal definition of the *comunidad indígena* is given by Winder in this volume.

6. Teodor Shanin, *The Awkward Class*.

7. A discussion of the relationship between dominant and subordinate modes of production is found in Maurice Godelier, *Rationality and Irrationality in Economics*, pp. 88–104. One attempt to discuss the variety of modes of production in Peru is Rodrigo Montoya, *A propósito del carácter predominantemente capitalista de la economía peruana actual*.

8. The historical evolution of these patterns of landholding in the valley is reported in my thesis (Samaniego, "Location, Social Differentiation and Peasant Movements," pp. 163–173).

9. Ibid., pp. 90–94.

10. This process is described for other Mantaro villages by G. Alberti and R. Sánchez, *Poder y conflicto social en el valle del Mantaro*, pp. 33–41.

11. The *agente municipal* is the local representative of the district council, carrying out their decisions at the village level. The *teniente gobernador* is the village representative of the district governor, with responsibility for police and judicial activities.

12. The Constitution of 1860 brought in the *concejos municipales* (municipal councils) at the level of district, province, and department; the departmental council had a certain authority over the provincial council and the latter had considerable supervisory powers with respect to the district councils. The original intent was to centralize government, but the Constitution limited their powers, especially those of the departmental *concejo*. See F. B. Pike, *The Modern History of Peru*.

13. Proceedings followed by the authorities of Mito, Orcotuna, Sicaya, and Chupaca on the abolition of the district of San Juan, and concerning the demarcation of limits of pastures and abuses, 1881.

14. Ibid. (my italics).

15. Ibid.

16. Ibid., pp. 10–13.

17. These pro-indigenous organizations are described by Winder in this volume. Also, see François Chevalier, "Official *Indigenismo* in Peru in 1920: Origins, Significance and Socio-Economic Scope," in *Race and Class in Latin America*, edited by Magnus Morner.

18. The Municipal Registration of Citizens for 1906, in the archives of the District of Ahuac, Ahuac, Peru.

19. A. S. Cerrón, *Breve historia de Ahuac*, p. 21.

20. Título de Creación del Distrito de Ahuac, in the archives of the district of Ahuac, Ahuac, Peru.

21. Ibid., p. 3.

22. E. Nieto, *Recopilación de leyes y decretos desde la independencia*, p. 873.

23. The principal pro-indigenist associations organized in Peru were: Asociación Pro-Indígena (1900s), Comité Pro-Derecho Indígena Tahuantinsuyo (1920), Patronato de la Raza Indígena (1922). For information on the organizations for the protection of the rural population, see W. Kapsoli and W. Reátegui, *El campesinado peruano: 1919–1930*.

24. Jesús Chavarría, "The Intellectuals and the Crisis of Modern Peruvian

Nationalism: 1870–1919," *Hispanic American Historical Review* 50, no. 2 (May 1970).

25. *Libro de Remates*, 1906–1931, in the archives of the district of Ahuac, Ahuac, Peru.

26. Cerrón, *Breve historia*, pp. 27–28.

27. Concerning the contract see Libro de Sesiones Extraordinarias, 1922–1931, in the archives of the District of Ahuac. On the distribution of shares among other members see the "Cuaderno de anotaciones privades" of the late Sr. Severo Cerrón A., which is in the possession of his elder son, who lives in Huancayo.

28. For a fuller exposition of these events see my thesis (Samaniego, "Location, Social Differentiation and Peasant Movements," pp. 212–225).

29. E. Teogonio Ordaya, *Chupaca: Estudio monográfico*, p. 132.

30. See Marcelo Grondin in this volume.

31. See table 1 on the development of sheep farming in Yanacancha in Roberts and Samaniego in this volume, where details on the later economic and social development of Yanacancha are given.

32. These complaints were frequent in the sessions of the district council of Ahuac.

33. Juan Martínez Alier, *Los huacchilleros del Perú.*

34. Libro de Sesiones, 1919–1932, in the archives of the district of Ahuac, Ahuac, Peru.

35. ADPC, Expediente 861.

36. On January 5, 1921: Letter sent to the administrator of the Laive hacienda in Correspondencia con comunidades, 1929–1933, 11–D–5, Centro de Documentación Agraria, Lima.

37. I use the term *semiproletarian* to describe a person or a household that, because of lack of control of significant financial capital or land and/or livestock, has to sell his or its labor systematically, on either a temporary or a permanent basis (Samaniego, "Location, Social Differentiation and Peasant Movements," pp. 245–247).

38. Yepes, *Perú: 1820–1920*, pp. 281–282.

39. Ordaya, *Chupaca*, p. 194.

40. Ricardo Tello Devotto, *Historia de la provincia de Huancayo*, p. 181.

41. Manifiesto de Caja y Razón detallada de los bienes adqueridos, Tesorería Central, Sociedades Unidas de Chupaca, in the archives of the district of Chupaca, 1930.

42. Hobsbawm, "Peasants and Politics," *The Journal of Peasant Studies* 1, no. 1 (October 1973): 3–22.

3. Processes of Industrial
and Social Change in Highland Peru

JULIAN LAITE

During the short space of thirty years—from 1893 to 1922—the small village of La Oroya, lying thirteen thousand feet above sea level in the Andes fifty miles northwest of the Mantaro Valley, was transformed into a bustling city; today it is the largest mining town in Peru and one of the most important railway centers. This transformation was brought about first by the arrival of the railway and second by the location in the town of the ore refinery of the Cerro de Pasco Copper Corporation.[1] The refinery currently employs some 6,000 people, mainly workers recruited from the rural hinterland. Today La Oroya contains 26,000 people and is surrounded by an area of desolation created by the poisonous fumes of the refinery. The situation is a complete contrast to that in which—only eighty years ago—several hundred villagers raised crops and livestock on the nearby pasture lands.

The major outcome of the changes occurring in La Oroya has been the creation of a modern industrial location, characterized by desolation and exploitation, in place of an agricultural milieu of village communities and haciendas. First impressions of the region today suggest that, similar to industrialization processes in the "developed" world, a depressed peasantry has been transformed into an industrial proletariat. Previous analyses of this situation have focused on this outcome and explained such a transformation through stressing the power differential that existed between the competing industrial and agricultural interest groups.[2] Here, as elsewhere in the Peruvian highlands, the "traditional" rural social structure was seen as having collapsed or ossified in the face of "modern" economic change.[3]

A closer inspection of this region, however, reveals a more complex relationship between economic and social changes and interesting differences between this and other industrialization processes. This account, then, inspects the variety of outcomes accomplished by, and emergent from, the interaction of actors participating in the social process.[4] Economic changes will be differentiated according to the nature of their technology, purposes, and impact; rural social structure will be seen as providing for the actors involved a range of cultural vehicles through which they were able to organize a response to the problems posed by economic change. In particular, the concept of *comunidad* will be treated as an organizational device available to actors to give a sense of order to the social processes in which they were involved, rather than as a description of a "traditional" social structure.

The industrial and social changes occurring in this region, then, were achieved through the bargaining and actions of parties whose interests and resources differed and also changed over time. During the nineteenth century the resources of the haciendas may have been greater than those of the *comunidades*: rights to communal land were not clearly established in law, and the hacienda owners had more influential political and legal connections. However, the bargaining position of *comunidades* lay in the perennial threat of peasants to defend their own land, and over the years both their legal rights and their political influence were to increase.[5] At the beginning of the twentieth century, the favorable situation created by the arrival of the railway was characterized by a relative harmony of interests and did not accentuate the resource differences of participant groups. It was not until the arrival of the Cerro de Pasco Corporation in the twentieth century that major differences emerged in interests and resource mobilization.

Undoubtedly, the resources of the corporation in terms of finance, knowledge, and political networks were larger than those of the other competing groups and considerably enhanced its bargaining position. Yet, just as the interests and resources of the haciendas and *comunidades* changed over time, so too did those of the corporation. The resources of the corporation were not infinite; at different times it faced debts, political threats, legal reverses, and changeable mining operations. Nor were its interests always clear-cut and opposed to those of other groups. Rather, agreements or conflicts among participants were continually reassessed in the light of changes in their interests and resources, leading to further compromises and conflicts. The existence of a simple, continuous power differential in favor of one party in this process is thus not enough to explain fully the variety of outcomes. Therefore, it is on the process of bargaining that this account focuses, but in order to understand some features of those negotiations it is necessary to look at the social and economic situation in the area prior to industrialization and, in particular, at the processes of migration.

The Situation at the End of the Nineteenth Century

During the nineteenth century the region around La Oroya was divided into five haciendas and three *comunidades*, including that of La Oroya itself. The haciendas ranged from fifteen hundred to six thousand hectares in size and were owned by families living in the region, by families from the nearby town of Tarma, and by a joint stock company in Lima. This company rented out a hacienda for $4,500 a year under the guarantee that the rentee would also provide an annual income from production. The remainder of the year's product accrued to the rentee.

The economic activities of the haciendas were, overwhelmingly, the raising of cattle and sheep. This meant that their labor forces were small, since one shepherd could control many animals and the hacienda families themselves provided a labor input. These haciendas also used the practice of *huaccha*, whereby shepherds from nearby villages would tend their own, as well as hacienda, sheep on hacienda land.[6] A full-time shepherd received some $2 (four *soles*) per one hundred head of sheep, while a cowherd was paid around $35 per annum. One of the shepherd's principal duties was to herd the animals from one grazing area to another, crossing the toll bridge at La Oroya, which was the focal point for the passage of animals and men in the region.

The *comunidades* of La Oroya, Huaynacancha, and Sacco ranged in size from 1,000 to 2,200 to 7,000 hectares respectively, with adult populations of 150 for La Oroya and between 200 and 300 for the other two. Again, the economic activities of the *comunidades* were predominantly the raising of cattle and sheep, but a socioeconomic breakdown of La Oroya and Sacco at the beginning of the twentieth century reveals that there was some economic differentiation both within and between them.[7] Of the *comuneros* of La Oroya 56 percent were described as solely agriculturalists, with 80 percent of these being shepherds. Mining and trading accounted for another 25 percent of the *comuneros*, while the remainder were employed in either the municipality or the newly arrived railway.

Among the agriculturalists there was also considerable differentiation. Of those who held usufructuary rights to the main area of arable land controlled by the *comunidad*, 63 percent had less than 0.5 hectare, while 37 percent had between 0.5 and 2.5 hectares. Differences in wealth among the pastoralists are indicated in the documents concerning the claims of the local population for compensation for the near total loss of their animals as a result of pollution from the refinery.[8] Ten percent of the pastoralists claimed that they had lost over one hundred sheep, 20 percent claimed that they had lost between twenty and one hundred sheep, and 70 percent claimed that they had lost less than twenty sheep.

In addition to these differences, there were some *comuneros* who controlled land in the village of La Oroya that was later to become valuable urban property. In Sacco, 51 percent of the *comuneros* were agriculturalists, nearly all of them shepherds, and 4 percent were engaged in trading. The main economic activity of the remaining 45 percent was work in the small silver mine that was operational in Sacco during the nineteenth century. This picture of the region was to change dramatically with the industrial changes about to occur; yet the industrial changes were but some of the many important processes that had been affecting the area for some time.

The effects of migration were already being felt in La Oroya and the surrounding region during the first half of the nineteenth century. Drawn by the mines of Cerro de Pasco and Yauli province and by the opportunities to raise sheep and cattle, the migrants came, settled, and bought land. Analysis of the parish records in Yauli, the nearest parish seat to La Oroya, shows that during the fifteen years preceding 1850 there was a marked pattern of both short- and long-distance migration.[9] Forty-four percent of the spouses married in the central parish church had migrated from the outlying districts of the parish; a further 13 percent were from outside the parish, 54 percent of these being from the Mantaro Valley and 13 percent from Tarma. As well as place of origin, occupation and length of residence in the parish are recorded, and it is clear that many migrants were medium-term residents in the parish.

For as far back as records could be traced there was a steady turnover of land in the region surrounding La Oroya; during the 1850s the world prices of meat and wool rose dramatically, stimulating property transactions over the predominantly pastoral haciendas. The documents show that the role of women, at least as legal figures, was crucial in these transactions; in 1861 the mother of the Santa María family from Tarma bought the first hacienda from a group of three widows and two spinsters. In 1869 her son expanded the family interests along the river bank, and in 1874 he bought the neighboring hacienda from its widowed owner. This sale was reversed in 1890 when a daughter of the widow bought back a share from the Santa Marías, while in 1895 a second daughter bought out her mother and sister. At the end of the nineteenth century the third hacienda in the region was also in the hands of a woman, one whose father had bought out the last remaining Spanish family in 1845.[10] The fourth hacienda was owned by a public company in Lima, and ownership of the fifth was under dispute. This last hacienda—Tallapuquio—had once been part of the communal land of Sacco but was worked in usufruct by a *comunera*; when she died her communal rights to this land passed to her two children. In 1870, however, two other *comuneros* from Sacco occupied the land, claiming that it was common land, and the case was taken to court. The children of the *comunera* won the case but lost the land, for it was promptly claimed by their lawyer in payment for his fees. In 1891 the lawyer died and the hacienda passed to his daughter.

The alienation of communal land was taking place not only in the *comunidad* of Sacco but also in that of La Oroya. During the nineteenth century, tolls on the bridge at La Oroya provided the Tarma municipality with 30 percent of its annual income,[11] and in 1842 a Tarmeño had come to La Oroya to take up the post of toll collector. He began buying land and houses in the village itself. The *comunidad* records reveal that his son began to buy communal land in 1884 and that this process of alienation had been going on in La Oroya since at least 1880. A similar process was affecting the communal land of Huaynacancha, the second *comunidad* in the region. In both *comunidades* the tendency toward the dispersal of communal land through inheritance and consequent subdivision of usufructuary rights was being reversed: the countervailing tendency was for rights to land to become concentrated in the hands of outsiders.

It is also necessary to differentiate among the various phases and types of industrial activity occurring in the region. It is clear from the extensive literature on mining in Peru that for centuries mining has involved linked production and refining techniques.[12] Mines also made large-scale use of labor and organized transportation and distribution to worldwide markets. The industrial changes that are the subject of this paper differ from previous industrial activities in the massive acceleration of technological change, in the increasing use of larger and more integrated machinery, in the adoption of more rational accounting techniques, and in the more widespread use of wage labor; however, these changes do not imply the introduction of novel techniques.

This acceleration of industrial change took place in La Oroya as part of two major developments—the expansion of the railway network and the expansion and rationalization of the mining sector. These two developments gave rise to differing social outcomes, and each development may now be analyzed in turn.

The Railway

In 1893 Thorndike and Meiggs finally completed the rail link between La Oroya and Lima.[13] They used a large hired labor force working to a cost-accounting rationale with materials shipped in from the United States; Meiggs intended to continue the railway to Cerro de Pasco, where he had already purchased the rich ore deposits. In a short space of time, La Oroya became a railhead and the convergence point for routes from the northern highlands, the southern highlands, and the jungle; further commercial possibilities seemed promised by the continuation of the railroad and by the expansion of the mining sector. The opportunity was seized by those who could readily mobilize resources and so take advantage of the fluidity of the land situation.

One method of mobilizing cash to exploit the new opportunities was to float a joint stock company. In 1892, while the government debated plans concerning the creation of a new town in La Oroya, the Santa María family formed itself into a limited company, La Compañía Mercantil de la Oroya, to control a strategic forty hectares of the family's hacienda land. The capital of $48,000 was divided into one thousand shares of $48 each; in the newspapers of Lima, the company advertised that its aims were to rent land, construct hotels, offices, and markets, and exploit commercial opportunities.

The shareholders of the company were the descendants of the woman who had first bought the land in 1861. One of the five directors was Thorndike himself, and it was he, together with the younger son of the family, who became the main force behind the Mercantil. Household servants who had been granted land by the family during the farming days sold back their plots; in turn the Mercantil started to sell and rent land for development. Land was sold first to the railway company in 1892 and subsequently to individuals for the building of houses and shops. Among these was the elder son of the Santa María family, who, in 1901, sold a part of his share in the Mercantil and then used the cash to set up a general store.

However, by the turn of the century the extension of the railroad had not materialized. A proposal by the Backus and Johnson Company to construct the line had been frustrated by the Peruvian Sociedad Nacional de Minería, which did not want foreign interests to control this vital link in the chain of production and distribution.[14] The line was again offered for tender; since Thorndike was the only one to bid, it passed into his control and he began to make preliminary studies. This meant that coal continued to be taken by llama to the Cerro de

Pasco furnaces at the almost prohibitive cost of twenty dollars per ton. The increasing scarcity of high-grade ores in Cerro and the fall in the price of copper in 1901 and again in 1902 forced many small-scale mines to close. Thus, although La Oroya was a bustling railhead upon which was focused much agricultural commerce, the precariousness of its prosperity meant that government and private plans for the new town were not fully implemented.

Then, in 1902, a syndicate of American financiers and engineers undertook to exploit the Cerro de Pasco mine; this was the first ripple of the second wave of industrial change that was to affect La Oroya twenty years later. The syndicate, entitled the Cerro de Pasco Investment Company, formed the Cerro de Pasco Mining Company and the Cerro de Pasco Railway Company. The latter immediately began to construct the line to Cerro, the rights to which it had acquired from Thorndike. Once more, railway workers came to La Oroya, raising the level of commercial activity. Although the railway construction was terminated in 1904, the Cerro mining region had been opened up and production was expanding. The position of La Oroya as an urban center was consolidated; the expansion of the railway network was accompanied by the formation of a joint stock company to the south of La Oroya, where the Sociedad Ganadera de Junín was formed during the years 1904–1906, amalgamating six large haciendas.

Negotiations involving communal land were also influenced by the coming of the railroad. For the period 1900 to 1920, seventy-seven transactions involving the communal land of La Oroya were documented. Through these negotiations the land holdings of forty-three *comuneros* became concentrated in the hands of fourteen individuals, of whom eleven were migrants—seven from Tarma, two from the southern highlands, one from the Mantaro Valley, and one from Bolivia. The occupations of this migrant group ranged from shopkeeper, hotel owner, cobbler, and landlord to employee of the railway company. The integration of this group into the new commercial activity of La Oroya meant that they were able to mobilize resources and transform the distribution of landholdings of the *comunidad*. In contrast, the resident *comuneros* were mainly agricultural workers and temporary miners who had neither the resources nor the inclination to combat this transformation. Indeed, they seemed quite willing to exchange their land for cash that they themselves could then invest in the economic opportunities opening up.

The initial response to these industrial changes from the actors in the situation was to reinforce processes that had been going on during the nineteenth century. For both *comunidades* and haciendas the rate of land transactions increased and more land passed into the hands of migrants and outsiders. However, differences emerged in the way particular actors mobilized resources, based on their interests and economic potential. While the hacienda families were acting in concert, splits were appearing in the ranks of the *comunidad* members. The reinforcement of these processes was an emergent consequence of the industrial changes initiated by the railway and intimately affected the rather different social developments occurring with the second type of industrial change.

The Refinery

In the period in which the effects of the railway were being felt on landholding in La Oroya, changes were also occurring due to the expansion of the Cerro de Pasco Mining Corporation. The relative location of coal and ore deposits is a perennial problem for mining companies, often involving the costly transportation of materials. In 1908, the railroad from the smelter at Cerro to the nearby coal deposits was completed, and coal freight costs came down from twenty dollars to four dollars per ton.[15] The dispersal of the corporation's locations through the purchase of mines at Morococha and Casapalca again raised the problem of transport costs. The new purchases had their own small ore concentrators, but these could not cope with the massive increase in output, estimated to have jumped, for Casapalca, from 1,000 tons in 1889 to 160,000 tons in 1916.[16]

In order to increase output and at the same time minimize unit costs, it was clear to the corporation, a centralized refining process needed to be installed.[17] Such an installation required land for plant and workers' accommodation, the proximity of an available labor force, access to water for in-process use, and an outlet for the processed waste that would emerge as smoke and refuse. These latter considerations made location on the coastal side of the Andes fraught with difficulty, for Casapalca straddles the river Rimac, which flows directly to Lima. The former considerations, however, favored La Oroya as the possible new site; the fluidity of the land situation there offered an opportunity for the corporation to procure land.

At that time, mining companies could, in law, lay claim to tracts of land that they wished to annex for mining purposes. The legal limits of such claims, set out in the mining code, referred to the nature of the land claimed—private, communal, inhabited, urban, et cetera—and to the purposes for which the land was wanted—drilling, installation, transport, and so on. The land needed immediately in La Oroya was that of the Compañía Mercantil; in March 1918 the corporation laid claim to that land, stating that it wished to build the refinery on it.

By 1918 the status of the land owned and controlled by the Santa Marías and by the Mercantil was very involved indeed. In 1905 the government had planned to annex all the land of the Mercantil. Instead it annexed only half in order to build offices and shops; twenty hectares were left to the Mercantil so that it too could implement investment plans. Between 1905 and 1918 the Mercantil did erect some shops, which it rented out to petty traders; the promise of major investment was never fulfilled, and the main activity was the buying and selling of small plots by the railway, the municipality, and assorted individuals.

As soon as the corporation's claim was laid, Thorndike offered to sell all the Mercantil to the corporation for $115,000, arguing that the Mercantil's land around the railway station would also be useful to the corporation. The corporation calculated that extending the claim to land while offering to buy out the Mercantil would be their best move.[18] The Santa Marías would be likely to compromise, since if the corporation did not purchase the land it would be valued at the low agricultural rate. Because the Mercantil had not fulfilled its promise to the government, there was also a lawsuit pending in favor of the government that made the property virtually state land.[19] In April the corporation extended its claim amid a protest from the Santa Marías that corporation claims were confusing the land situation. In 1919, a director of the corporation became the president of the Mercantil, buying up 2,880 of the then 3,000 shares.

The corporation had already bought the hacienda Tallapuquio in 1912 in order to construct a hydroelectric plant there. Once the location of the refinery was fixed, it set about acquiring other hacienda land through claiming and then buying needed tracts. In 1920, the 6,000 hectare hacienda of the Santa Marías was bought for $19,000, and in the same year the younger Santa María brother finally sold the remaining 2,800 hectares of the family hacienda for $7,200. Although there were now ongoing disputes with the *comunidades* of the region over corporation mining claims, the major land problems posed for the corporation by the building of the refinery had been solved, and in 1919 construction work commenced.

However, while the corporation had achieved favorable solutions to its problems of location and production, in the market situation the corporation's position was becoming extremely unfavorable. When the decision was made in 1917 to construct the new refinery in La Oroya, metal values were high—copper stood at thirty-three American cents per pound. The corporation was paying dividends, and it was calculated that the six-million-dollar estimate for the construction was a worth-while investment. So, in 1919, capital equipment and skilled labor on two-year contracts were shipped in from the industrialized nations and unskilled labor was recruited from the surrounding regions.

The corporation solved its labor problems through the method of *enganche* or subcontracting.[20] In this method, the mining company contracted with the *enganchador* to provide work for a certain period of time for a certain number of men supplied by the *enganchador*. In his turn, the *enganchador* contracted these men through the method of paying them all or part of their fee in advance and then requiring them to work off the required number of debited working days in the mines. Under *enganche* there was no legal relation binding the company and the worker, only a mechanism linking work and payments. It was in this vacuum that the *enganchadores* flourished, supplying labor both to the mines and to the haciendas of the coast and jungle.

This mechanism was seen to be so pernicious in its operation that a law had been passed in 1910 limiting its scope. Immediately, the large mining companies blamed the growing mining recession on the subsequent shortage of labor; later in the same year the Peruvian Senate and Executive split over the implementation of the law. So, by 1920, the system still flourished among mining companies as the only way to guarantee a stable labor force to carry through operations, for independent workers tended to drift away at planting and harvesting times. This problem of labor stability became suddenly acute for the Cerro de Pasco Corporation, whose financial position during 1920 began to deteriorate rapidly.

The original estimate of six million dollars for the construction of the refinery had risen to fifteen million dollars, so the corporation borrowed eight million dollars by floating stock. The plans for the refinery, the ordering of materials, and the cost estimates had all been initiated before the United States entered the First World War. The dramatic rise in the cost was mostly due to the increased values of materials subsequent to United States entry. However, from their "high" just after the war, copper prices then slumped in 1920 to fifteen American cents per pound, and this became a crisis year for the corporation. As well as reducing freight costs, the new refinery promised to cut fuel costs through heat conservation by at least 50 percent.[21] All the time that the new plant was not in operation the older installations kept unit costs high and restricted large-scale exploitation of the rich ore bodies at Cerro and Casapalca. There was thus great urgency to start the new refining operations to pay off the corporation's debt; this, coupled with their attitude toward labor stability, persuaded the management that *enganchadores* should be employed on a large scale to provide a steady stream of labor. In only two and a half years the refinery was completed, and operations commenced in November, 1922.

Negotiations orientated to the arrival of the railway had reinforced and accelerated existing processes of change, whereas the arrival of the corporation and the building of the refinery initiated new developments. Ownership of the haciendas was concentrated into the hands of one organization, which, although it continued farming cattle and sheep, was using some of the land for purely industrial purposes. The fresh influx of migrants had again increased commercial opportunities in La Oroya, but the bargaining between the *comunidades* and corporation was balanced between a suspicion of mining claims and an interest in further commercial expansion. Above all, the readiness to compromise, the complementarity of interests, and the accordance with the legal process that characterized the land negotiations of both the railway and of the corporation's initial settlement were in sharp contrast to the public outcry and bitter disputes and bargaining that followed upon the operation of the refinery.

Technological Changes

In 1915 the interests held by the Cerro de Pasco Investment Company had been amalgamated into the Cerro de Pasco Copper Corporation, whose chief concern was the extraction and processing of copper. Even though lead was present in the ores extracted from this region, this was disregarded altogether; the new La Oroya smelter provided only for the recovery of blister copper and some gold and silver from ores carrying 10 percent to 12 percent of copper. By comparison, in Bolivia ores of only 1 percent copper were considered worth processing. The main smelting operation was to be the blast furnace. Only relatively short flues were provided to recover metals from the smoke; these were designed for returning the solid particles of ore carried mechanically in the gas streams. Financial expediency meant that there was no provision for processing wastes consisting of volatilized metals: "The new Oroya plant was therefore practically without what now would be classified in any form as smoke control . . . The Oroya plant gradually took over all smelting operations of La Fundición and Casapalca, and, *due to the urgency of cancelling the debts,* the mines and the smelter were being driven to the utmost."[22]

Consequently, 100 to 125 tons a day of lead, bismuth, sulphur dioxide, and arsenic were immediately deposited on the surrounding countryside. In 1919 the corporation had foreseen this happening and, in order to observe the effects of the smoke, the general manager of the time installed cattle, horses, and sheep on the recently purchased haciendas surrounding La Oroya.

The effect on the crops of the *comunidades* and haciendas around La Oroya was cataclysmic. A fresh seven-year agricultural rotation cycle was just starting for the *comuneros* of La Oroya, and they had planted the hill opposite the smelter with barley. Almost overnight the sulphur dioxide destroyed the barley; the *comuneros* later claimed that seventeen hectares of land directly opposite the smelter had been rendered useless. The high walls of the Mantaro River valley acted as a flue conserving the concentration of sulphur dioxide for long distances. The heavy quantities of solids present in the smoke tended to drag it down to ground level. The barley on the communal land of Huaynacancha was destroyed, as was that at Pachacayo, twenty-five miles from La Oroya.

Stock, too, was affected; many died through diarrhea and lack of edible vegetation, while others died of direct poisoning. The large haciendas began to recognize the damage; the Sociedad Ganadera de Junín claimed that the death rate in cattle had risen from 3 percent to 18 percent per annum. Owners of stock in the Mantaro Valley, fifty miles away, found flakelike particles adhering to the inner lining of animal stomachs as a result of the corporation's dumping all its slag into the Mantaro River. In the two years from 1922 to 1924, the *comunidad* and some individuals of La Oroya claimed that 278 cattle, 3,874 sheep, and nearly 200 mules and horses had perished due to smoke poisoning. And the smoke took its toll of humans too. Residents in La Oroya claimed that the ash fell like rain, causing skin irritation and hair loss. One letter to the corporation ran: "We all had a very clear idea of what was meant by the establishment of Industries in the Country, but we never believed that the smoke would bring illness to our families and ruin our interests." [23]

The Bargaining Process

The immediate demands of the affected parties were unanimous— the smoke must be controlled and indemnification must be paid. As in the cases of the arrival of the railway and the location of the refinery, these parties entered the negotiating arena with differing interests and resources. Also, the outcomes of the negotiations depended not only on the interests and resources of the participants but also on features of the bargaining situations themselves.[24] The outcomes of the arguments and deals that followed the opening of the refinery were affected by such factors as the overtness of the bargaining, the role of third parties, and the range and relationship between one negotiating topic and another. In the short run, the strategies of the *comunidades* and haciendas diverged, as Huaynacancha threatened to blow up the refinery, whereas the Sociedad Ganadera de Junín tried to bring political pressure to bear.

The law relating to land transactions stated that, while private land could be bought and sold, communal land could not. Compensation for communal land expropriated through mining claims had to be through an agreed donation of land situated elsewhere. Also, inflexibility in the public negotiations over land was reinforced by the legal protection of communal land by President Leguía against the encroachment of private landholders and by the growing activities of the *indigenismo* group.[25] In this context the very public dealings between the corporation and the *comunidades* had to be of a different order from the covert, individual transactions over communal land in the late nineteenth century.

The corporation's managers and lawyers considered that they could either embark on a process of continual indemnification for loss of crops or livestock, or compensate the affected parties once and for all, depending on the extent of damage and the legal negotiations. Pressure on the government from the wealthy and influential families in the region produced the establishment of a smoke commission in 1923—it was to be the first of five. During the two years the commission took to complete its investigations, more and more claims for damage were lodged against the corporation. In 1925 the corporation decided to reduce the smoke and to negotiate over particular claims upon the following reasoning:

> New smoke claims are being presented from various points. . . .
> First, these points are scattered in all directions and, second, there are numerous other properties contingent to them, for which claims have not yet been made. . . . To recognise all of these new claims is to invite a probable continuance of other claims from contiguous properties . . . the settlement of which will involve enormous sums of money. . . . something must be done . . . to put an end to these claims.

Two methods were suggested, namely:

> To fight the cases by law, and thus prove the limit of damage. To install in the plant the necessary machinery to stop, or at least decrease, the damage, and localise it to known and recognised limits.

> Owing to the very strong sentiment now existing in this country against the Corporation, due to the Tacna and Arica affair, to the well-known general feeling of opposition to corporation interests, to

other natural causes, and especially to the campaign conducted against the Corporation by the *Ganadera Junín* regarding smoke damage, it is very doubtful if the Corporation could win a smoke suit under any conditions. The tendency to legislate against the Corporation, the recent frankly unjust decisions by the Labour Commission against it, and the public demonstrations at the time of the Tacna-Arica decision, showing disfavour to foreigners (which were not confined to the lower classes), prove quite conclusively that the Corporation would attain justice in any suit only with the greatest difficulty, if at all, and it would practically be impossible to win a smoke suit.

But the Government has indicated to the Corporation a way out of the difficulty, namely, by following the directions of its engineers . . . a declaration by the Corporation . . . that it would comply with their recommendations within a reasonable time would make easy all of the settlements now under negotiation. The recommendations of the Government engineers . . . do not constitute the best or most economical method of handling the cases. But it is necessary to have the Government's approval of the methods ultimately installed . . .[26]

Clearly, the way in which one bargaining situation was seen to relate to another affected both the ordering of topics and the degree of commitment to principles. Faced with claims from a large number of sources, the corporation could not afford to lose such a claim as that of Sociedad Ganadera de Junín and so present an opportunity for that one to be cited as the governing case or principle upon which the others would be decided. On the other hand, fighting each case to win meant a heavy drain on corporation time and money, often about particular instances of little importance in themselves.

At the same time, the corporation was experiencing a decline in the metal content of its ores. The ore from Morococha that had yielded 12.84 percent copper in 1911 was, by 1922, yielding only 7.38 percent; the content of the Cerro de Pasco ores had dropped from 12 percent in 1906 to 5.1 percent in 1922.[27] The lower-grade ores were too poor to pay for transportation, so a concentrator was built in Morococha. Traces of lead and zinc began to appear in the concentration process; with the discovery of enormous quantities of zinc in the pyrite ore bodies of Cerro de Pasco, the corporation reconsidered its position as solely a producer of copper. Thus, under pressure from two sources— public opinion and falling ore copper content—the corporation installed smoke filtering processes. The filtered particles were fifty percent lead in content and one ton a day of bismuth was recovered, with a value of one and a half million dollars per year.

However, the damage had been done to the haciendas and *comunidades*, and claims against the corporation were still outstanding. The corporation was itself split over which strategy to adopt with regard to the extent of fume recovery; however, it was unanimous over the strategy of removing future claims on the corporation by buying the lands, crops, and livestock of the haciendas. The corporation knew from the experiments carried out with its own stock that seemingly inebriate animals could recover given proper care and attention. Given the fact that smoke output was being reduced, the costly investment in the purchase of the haciendas would have some financial payoff.

American-trained experts were hired to continue the experiments with livestock; a new corporation farms department was created, under the control of a chief accountant from a recently closed mine who was himself a large land and stock owner. The buying of the haciendas began, and those with the prominent outstanding law suits were the first purchased. The Sociedad Ganadera de Junín, with fourteen thousand head of cattle, sixteen thousand sheep, and one thousand horses, and extending over 115,358 hectares, was purchased in 1924 for $1,368,000. Next came Quiulla, then Punabamba, Paria, and Paucar; by 1930 the corporation had purchased 228,490 hectares with a total payment of $1,851,800 to their owners for smoke damage over the years.

The Concept of *Comunidad*

Negotiations between the *comunidades* and the corporation, however, were of a very different character. For the different groups engaged in the negotiations over communal land, the concept of *comunidad* became a crucial bargaining device. In focusing on the concept as a means through which competing groups could establish and order their particular interests, this account echoes the material found elsewhere in this volume that emphasizes the pragmatic nature of the concept of community in highland Peru. The concept of *comunidad* is used to order both interactions among its members and interactions between those members and external interests.

Individual *comuneros* saw the situation as one in which a better deal, and perhaps one in cash, could be made through an individual transaction with the corporation. This strategy was preferred to that of being part of an overall communal transaction; thus, the definition of land as private or communal became a crucial issue. In 1918, the corporation had gone ahead with its annexation of the land belonging to the Mercantil, but the same mining claim had included land belonging to the *comunidad* of Huaynacancha. Although the state ratified possession of the private land, it left the position regarding the communal land unclear; in 1920, the *comunidad* was successful in calling for a government inquiry.

The *comunidad* argued that in Peruvian law the government had to show "sufficient need" for developments before it could evict people and that the same conditions applied to the corporation. Three hundred people lived on the expropriated land; since alternative sites for a refinery could be found they should not be evicted. This land, maintained the *comunidad* lawyer, was actually divided among individuals who paid individual taxes and so could not be considered as communal land at all. The corporation replied that its need was a real one, due to the dispersion of its mines. In contrast to the position of the *comunidad* lawyer, the corporation claimed that the land was communal, arguing that in 1795 a viceroy had given this land to Huaynacancha as a fief to the ancestors of the actual possessors.

The *comunidad* replied that they were certainly not a "community," but that the "neighbors of Huaynacancha" had bought from the king of Spain the land that they now occupied through inheritance. In fact, continued the *comunidad*, the land had been usurped by the Santa María family; the government had permitted this transfer for a specific purpose that had not been accomplished, and the family had no right to cede that land to a private corporation. Further, claimed the *comunidad*, the corporation was aware of the flaws in the Santa María land titles and had claimed the land in order to obscure the issues. Finally, Huaynacancha argued that the mining code referring to *comunidades* had been relevant only when *comunidades* existed; the code could not be applied in the Yauli region, where *comunidades* were generally defunct. In December, agreement was reached that cash compensation could be paid for this small portion of "communal" land. The corporation increased its previous valuation and paid up.

It was also in 1918 that the corporation had begun to obtain the land of the *comunidad* of La Oroya by the purchase of thirty-six hectares. In compensation for this and a later purchase in 1920, the *comunidad* received cash and grazing rights on a nearby corporation hacienda. The second purchase projected by the corporation included land where *comuneros* were living; the fact that the land was peacefully occupied posed a problem for the corporation. By 1923 this problem, still unresolved, became incorporated into the larger problem of smoke indemnification. Faced with the ruined harvest of 1922 and recurrent corporation encroachment on *comunidad* land, all parties agreed that indemnification for smoke damage alone would not be enough; compensation would also have to be made for the land itself. So the *comunidad* land was measured and priced.

The immediate response to valuation from the La Oroya inhabitants was from a group protesting their independence from the *comunidad*. The extent to which land alienation had been going on over the previous forty years was suddenly revealed as the fourteen private holders of former communal land presented their claims for individual settlement. Over twenty hectares of cultivable land had passed into the hands of this group. Their claims were supported by the *comunidad*, and they gained private cash awards. It was necessary to indemnify the remaining *comuneros* with land. A hacienda near Tarma was bought by the corporation and ceded to the *comunidad* in 1924, along with compensation for damage to crops and livestock calculated over a projected twenty-year period, 1924–1944. The idea was that those *comuneros* who had lost land through smoke damage should resettle on the former hacienda land. Again, a split appeared in the *comunidad* ranks but, this time, over the decision to move.

Only *comunidad* land that had been rendered completely useless was being exchanged for hacienda land. This exchange produced an overall division in the *comunidad* between those who had rights pertaining to the affected land and those who did not. The latter group received only indemnification for crops and stock lost; the former group had the choice of moving near Tarma or accepting cash indemnification for the land lost. Roughly half of the latter group chose land and half chose cash. It was predominantly the older, larger landholder who preferred to take up the land option. The *comuneros* who stayed were younger and either worked for the corporation or the railroad or were equipped with skills in house building and carpentry.

The members of the committee representing the *comunidad* chose to go, distributing the cash indemnification to those who stayed. This division between the separate parts of the *comunidad* was not a complete one. The agricultural activities of the *comunidad* were mainly pastoral. Some families preferred to remain in La Oroya and use the land in Tarma only for grazing cattle and sheep; in other cases the household moved to Tarma and left behind sons to work in the refinery and on the railroad. A further dimension to *comunidad* membership was added by the claims of the former hacienda workers already resident on the Tarma land. The application by these workers to become members of the La Oroya *comunidad* was at first refused, but seven years later a court order gave them full communal rights.

As the years passed, further smoke damage in La Oroya led the residents there to see the old cash settlement as a mistake. But this settlement had been a twenty-year agreement; in this situation, the government of Leguía, which was heavily dependent on foreign capital, offered little support for a fresh inquiry. Then in 1943 the first twenty-year period ended and a new smoke commission was established. A new compensation rate was fixed, which the corporation agreed to pay on a yearly basis. The yearly compensation was designed to prevent the rapid dispersal of the cash, avoid the buildup of grievances that occurred under the previous settlement, and keep temptation out of the hands of the *comunidad* leaders. The head of the farms division of the corporation, however, supported another land settlement to the *comuneros*: "Proof of the wisdom of such a plan is the Hacienda 'Cari' which was given to half of Oroya (community) twenty years ago and on which now the whole community has crowded so that no one family has sufficient ground." [28] Since the smoke commission agreed to this, the corporation began to seek another hacienda to buy. By 1947 it had not found one, and the *comunidad* began public pressure to achieve a solution.

Bustamante had been elected president in 1945, supported by APRA, and under his government the APRA party was able to extend its organization. The federation of *comunidades* of the province of Yauli was established under the guidance of the *personero (comunidad* leader) of La Oroya, a well-known *aprista*. The federation pressed for increased indemnification for damage to crops and livestock, encouraging La Oroya and Huaynacancha to push in concert for a land settlement. In the same year, the corporation decided to clean its chimneys, which meant shutting off filtering processes and increasing smoke output. The La Oroya *comunidad* leader persuaded the *aprista* deputy of Yauli, Pedro Muñiz, to raise the problem in the House of Deputies. The federation demanded that the refinery should close altogether. Under this pressure the corporation decided to finish with the claims once and for all by compensating the *comunidad* with land. Another hacienda in the Tarma district was bought by the corporation for twenty thousand dollars; in late 1947 the exchange of land went through.

But neither for La Oroya nor for Huaynacancha was the wheeling and dealing complete. In 1945 the problem of compensation for the thirty-six hectares of La Oroya land bought by the corporation in 1918 was again revived. The same *personero* of La Oroya demanded the return of the land, which by then was settled with corporation houses. He suggested that exchange of this land for corporation land in the city center would be acceptable. On this basis agreement was reached.

By this time, the use of land for agricultural purposes had become a minor consideration compared to its use as a "chip" in the urban dwelling and consumption situation. The continued location of the *comunidad* office in La Oroya served both as a demonstration that the institution was functioning and as a base from which *comuneros'* urban affairs and negotiations with the corporation could be carried on. In the case of Huaynacancha, the corporation and the *comunidad* finally settled in 1966 on a land grant by the corporation of 3,300 hectares of old hacienda land near La Oroya to compensate the *comunidad* for smoke damages assessed in 1946 by the Ministry of Agriculture.

The role of third parties, or bargaining agents, clearly affected the outcome of the negotiations involving these *comunidades*. In this instance, the third parties most frequently appealed to were the legal code and the government; the responses from these two sources were both negotiated and emergent phenomena, changing with the passage of time. Documents referring to the *comunidades* show that even within the legal code the correctness of definition and the stringency of application were both matters for bargaining.

Whereas appeal to third parties had led to a division in the *comunidad* of La Oroya, in the case of the *comunidad* of Sacco the effect of this appeal was a unifying one. As was noted above, the corporation had purchased in 1912 the hacienda Tallapuquio, and during the 1930s it rented this land out to an intermediary who, in turn, sublet it to stock herders. The intermediary and the *comunidad* of Sacco were in permanent conflict over the property and over grazing rights to it; the conflict came to a head in 1934. The *comunidad* threatened legal action over the land titles held by the corporation, but the removal of the intermediary and the low probability of winning the court case placated them. In 1954, the *comunidad* recruited the senator of San Martín as their lawyer and by 1958 had successfully reintegrated the Tallapuquio land with the *comunidad*.

In 1962, however, the corporation's appeal was successful and the land returned to its hands. The projected cost for Tallapuquio of future appeals and the difficulties for the corporation in removing the settlers on the land brought both sides to the negotiating table. A solution was hammered out in which the *comunidad* ceded its rights to part of the land in return for the benefits of building materials and water for the village schools. In its turn, the corporation ceded rights to land that did not encroach on corporation installations, obtaining promises from the *comunidad* of an end to smoke and land litigation. In effect, the *comunidad* regained most of its land and was prepared to cede parts of it in return for improvement in living standards. The corporation occupied the strategic land around canals and installations and was promised freedom from continual legal negotiations.

Of course, the legal arena was not the only one used by interested parties to further their aims, although it does seem to have been the most important for the bargaining in the La Oroya region. Smith and Cano (in this volume) and Kapsoli have shown how *comunidades* can extend the arena of negotiation through land invasions.[29] The corporation, too, had its own techniques, as is indicated in this letter of one of its managers: "It is not very comforting to face and argue with 50 to 200 half-drunken members of an opposing *Comunidad*, while standing on the land they claim as theirs. I ceded a small strip under these circumstances once, and I regret it to this day, but I learned to withhold my strongest objections until they are much fewer in numbers and usually in my office or some other safe place."[30]

Outcomes

At first glance, the outcome of these changes and negotiations has been a uniform picture of industrial desolation and exploitation, but for the various parties involved there also emerged other, differing outcomes.

In the case of the *comunidades*, the occupations, interests, life styles, and even location of *comuneros* had changed radically since the 1890s; each change that occurred provided the basis for further change. Within the *comunidades*, negotiations oriented to the arrival of the railway revealed divisions that, with the arrival and building of the refinery, became major splits. Between the *comunidades* the long-standing disputes over lands and boundaries—exacerbated by the arrival of the railway and the refinery—were put aside in 1947 with the formation of the federation. The occupational diversification of *comuneros* had enabled some of them to capitalize on the expansion of the railway, reinforcing previous tendencies toward the alienation of communal land; this diversification increased with the construction of the refinery and became one means by which the land situation was radically altered.

While continuing to bargain with the corporation, *comuneros* could support themselves by either working in the smelter or carrying on entrepreneurial activity in La Oroya. Cash provided in compensation for land or crops lost was invested in the construction of houses and shops in the urban center. The houses were rented out to the incoming industrial workers, while the shops and restaurants catered to their consumption needs. At the same time, the property owner would himself work in the refinery or leave the management of the property in the hands of his family. Fortunes were to be made through renting in this way. Examples of such fortunes are those of the APRA *comunidad* leader and his brother; their nephew is the present-day leader of the *comunidad* and a large landlord in the town. Today, the renting of houses is still big business, enough to lead the workers of the refinery to the brink of a strike over their demands for rent subsidies from the corporation. The "front" occupation of many petty traders is secondary to their management of their own or others' property interests. The dependence of such interests on the prosperity of the corporation was, however, a perennial negotiating dilemma: "We have written to the company three times on this matter, and while . . . we wish to maintain good relations with a mining company in which the majority of our *comuneros* work, since you are not using the land we would like it returned to us." [31]

For the hacienda owners the industrial changes meant first amalgamation and then withdrawal. In contrast to the initial divisions that characterized the *comunidades*, the unity of purpose and of control among the hacienda owners was a useful resource. In the negotiations carried out by the Mercantil at the time of the arrival of the railway, unity was achieved through the manipulation of kin links. Apart from the small group of Lima directors, only members of the Santa María family were allowed to be shareholders; the majority of the negotiations were carried on by the younger brother. Through their somewhat dubious purchases of land in the nineteenth century and through the negotiating activities of the younger brother, the Santa María family were able to turn their control of strategic hacienda land to very profitable advantage. In this they contrasted with the other hacienda owners of the region, who perceived the situation as one in which agricultural opportunities had closed while commercial opportunities had opened. This latter group sold out and invested cash in La Oroya and elsewhere. Such a strategy was shortsighted, however; over a large area the extent of the damage caused by the refinery was less severe than threatened, and the corporation was able to turn the purchase of the haciendas into a profitable investment, creating its own livestock company.

Such a profitable return was not envisaged at the time of purchase and the corporation was divided by perceptions of where its interests lay. There is little doubt that the corporation knew what the effects of pollution would be, since similar problems had occurred around the old smelter of Cerro, and control animals had been introduced in La Oroya to observe the extent of damage; however, the final decisions to filter the smoke and purchase the adjoining land were not at all unanimous, for the then general manager ". . . always felt that the claims for damage from smoke were mostly visionary. . . . 'Smoke-farming' he called it, and he was opposed to an all-out plan of fume recovery. When the new plant was in operation . . . he came to the writer's office in a rage and told him that had he known he would never have authorised it." [32]

Once the corporation decided, however, its potential for rapidly mobilizing legal, technical, and political aid placed it in a strong bargaining position, evidenced by the rapid creation of its farming division.

Despite the differences in interests and resources, both *comuneros* and the hacienda owners had rights to land that provided them with a basis and a focus for negotiation that, in turn, differentiated them from certain hacienda workers. Workers on the haciendas ranged from *comuneros* of villages encircled by hacienda land, through seasonal laborers, to landless wage laborers. Many of the last migrated to look for work in La Oroya in the period between the onset of the smoke damage and the increase of production by the new farms division. Thus, one outcome of the pollution and the purchase of the surrounding land was to provide the corporation with an available labor force and a supply of timber and stock to house and feed its workers. This is the outcome that has led Malpica and the Centro de Investigación de Desarrollo Agrícola to deduce that the corporation had planned this result from the start.[33] Such a deduction, however, relies on the mechanism of an omnipotent corporation working to a profit-and-loss rationale, while ignoring the activities of other participants in the processes of change; it does not account for the range of outcomes that emerged. Nor does it explain one striking difference between this refinery labor force and those in industrialized societies. Unlike the stable industrial proletariats laboring in the refineries of Europe and the United States, over 80 percent of the contemporary La Oroya workers are migrants. Although the corporation has attempted to stabilize its labor force, the social and economic institutions of the Peruvian highlands have supported a circulatory migration response to the problems and opportunities posed by industrial change.

Conclusion

In order to understand fully the processes of industrial and social change occurring in this region, it has been necessary to differentiate between types of industrial activity and the social interaction associated with them. Previous analyses of industrial and social change in highland Peru have tended to focus upon outcomes rather than the processes by which they are achieved. This focus has led to the difficulty that an overdeterministic view of industrial change is presented, one that does not distinguish between one type of industrial change and another. Likewise, such a focus has tended to subsume the range of social processes of contemporary Peru under the categories of "traditional" and "modern." In the La Oroya situation, the different industrial changes could not simply be classified as a "modernizing" process, nor could the forms of highland socioeconomic organization be characterized by "traditional" values, homogeneity, or static landholding. Rather, fluid land situations within a variety of cultural institutions enabled different groups to pursue a range of interests, producing a spectrum of changes that, in turn, fed into further dynamic social interaction.

Accounts of industrialization in Latin America have been constructed in the social sciences by authors working within different disciplines and from markedly divergent viewpoints. There has, however, been one similarity among these different approaches: the search for general conclusions from analyses of particular situations. Industrial change is often described only quantitatively, and the social changes associated with it are seen as determined by it.[34] Those attempts that distinguish between types of industrialization have been at only the most general level.[35] In this search for generalization, accounts of industrialization and social change become too deterministic and too simplistic. In contrast, this paper has sought to understand the relationship between industrial and social change in a particular situation in terms of the particular factors operating in that context. The aim has been to highlight the interesting differences, as well as similarities, between this and other situations. Such a method of attending to the differences between processes and outcomes allows for contrasts to be drawn between this and other situations in which industrial change has occurred. On the one hand, the outcome of circulatory migration to handle the problems of industrial change in Peru is in marked contrast to the creation of an urban-bound proletariat in the industrialized nations. On the other hand, the mobilization of such cultural vehicles as the *comunidad* to support the migratory solution is quite different from the social and economic institutions available to the peoples of Africa south of the Sahara, even though the problems posed by imperialism, and their present solutions, are similar. These contrasts would indicate that the consideration of industrialization as a homogeneous process with "convergent" outcomes is, at the least, premature.[36]

NOTES

1. An American-owned corporation, referred to in the account as "the corporation," and in the footnotes as C. de P.C.C.

2. CIDA (Centro de Investigación de Desarrollo Agrícola), *Perú: Tenencia*

de la tierra y desarrollo socio-económico del sector agrícola, 1966; Carlos Malpica, *Los dueños del Perú.*

3. J. Cotler, chapters in José Matos Mar et al., *Dominación y cambios en el Perú rural;* José Matos Mar, "Migration and Urbanization—The 'Barriadas' of Lima: An Example of Integration into Urban Life," in *Urbanization in Latin America,* edited by Philip Hauser; Allan R. Holmberg, "Changing Community Attitudes and Values in Peru," in R. Adams and R. Gillin, eds., *Social Change in Latin America Today;* Harry F. Dobyns, Paul L. Doughty, and Harold D. Lasswell, eds., *Peasants, Power and Applied Social Change, Vicos as a Model.*

4. H. Blumer, "Early Industrialization and the Laboring Class," *Sociological Quarterly* 1, no. 1 (January 1960).

5. See Smith and Cano in this volume.

6. Juan Martínez-Alier, *Los huacchilleros del Perú.*

7. C. de P.C.C., internal correspondence, 1918.

8. C. de P.C.C., internal correspondence, 1924.

9. Marriages were conducted both in Yauli and in the outlying villages, so that the records reflect place of residence as well as place of marriage.

10. A direct descendant of a Spaniard, granted land by the king of Spain.

11. I am grateful to Fiona Wilson of the University of Liverpool for this information.

12. Denis Sulmont, *Mining Bibliography.*

13. Watt Stewart, *Henry Meiggs, Yankee Pizarro.*

14. W. S. Bollinger, "The Rise of the United States Influence in the Peruvian Economy, 1869–1921," M. A. thesis, University of California, 1972.

15. Ibid.

16. P. D. Lisson, *El Comercio,* Lima, November 30, 1919.

17. A. Jachanowitz, "La instalación metalúrgica de La Oroya," *Boletín Oficial de Minas y Petroleo,* no. 3, Lima.

18. C. de P.C.C., internal correspondence, March 22, 1918.

19. Ibid., April 22, 1918.

20. There exists a growing bibliography of works on *enganche:* see M. A. Denegri, *La crisis del enganche;* F. Mostajo, *Algunas ideas sobre la cuestión obrera (contrato de enganche);* A. Noriega, "El enganche en la minería en el Perú," *Boletín de Minas,* nos. 4–6; and A. Noriega, "La crisis del enganche," *El Comercio,* May 17, 1911.

21. Jachanowitz, "Instalación metalúrgica."

22. B. T. Colley, "Memoirs." He was once a high ranking employee of C. de P.C.C. and for many years head of the farms division.

23. C. de P.C.C., external correspondence, January 18, 1927.

24. Thomas Schelling, *The Strategy of Conflict.*

25. David Winder in this volume.

26. C. de P.C.C., internal correspondence, July 10, 1925. In 1925 President Coolidge of the U.S.A. attempted to solve the dispute between Chile and Peru over the regions of Tacna and Arica by ordering that the resident populations there should decide their nationality by plebiscite. The Peruvians were incensed at this foreign interference in a domestic affair and there were many demonstrations.

27. See A. De Wind, "From Peasants to Miners"; C. de P.C.C., internal correspondence, August 20, 1947.

28. W. Kapsoli, *Los movimientos campesinos en Cerro de Pasco: 1880–1963*.

29. Ibid.

30. C. de P.C.C., internal correspondence, June, 1952.

31. Ibid., external correspondence, 1934, Sacco to corporation.

32. Colley, "Memoirs."

33. See Malpica, *Los dueños del Perú*; CIDA, *Perú: tenencia de la tierra*.

34. Fernando Henrique Cardoso and J. L. Reyna, "Industrialization, Occupational Structure and Social Stratification in Latin America," in *Constructive Change in Latin America*, edited by C. Blasier; André Gundar Frank, *Latin America: Underdevelopment or Revolution*.

35. Anibal Quijano, "Tendencies in Peruvian Development and Class Structure," in *Latin America: Reform or Revolution?* edited by J. Petras and M. Zeitlin; G. A. O. Soares, "The New Industrialization and the Brazilian Political System," in Petras and Zeitlin, *Latin America*.

36. R. E. Scott, *Latin American Modernization Problems*.

4. Peasant Cooperation and Dependency: The Case of the Electricity Enterprise of Muquiyauyo

MARCELO GRONDIN

Introduction

In 1912, only thirty years after Edison turned on the electric light for the first time in New York, Muquiyauyo, a small village in the central highlands of Peru, conceived of the idea of constructing a hydroelectric plant in the Andes.[1] By 1921, when many cities and towns of Western Europe and North America still depended on gas lamps for lighting, the project was completed and the village began to sell electricity to the nearby provincial capital of Jauja. The building of the electricity plant affected the social organization and development of Muquiyauyo, and it is cited by several writers as one indicator of the "progressiveness" of the community.[2]

In comparison with the other valley villages discussed in this volume, Muquiyauyo is characterized by a more extreme form of minifundist agriculture, and by the turn of the century it was already experiencing acute problems due to pressure of population on land. Population statistics for 1900 suggest that, with a resident population of 1,650, the average size of private arable holdings was about 1.5 hectares per household. Productivity had been improved in 1846 with the building of an irrigation system that served some 50 percent of holdings and that allowed for the intensive cultivation of alfalfa, a valuable fodder crop used for pack animals; yet, nevertheless, population was clearly beginning to outstrip resources, as was indicated by the decision taken in 1904 to make more land available to individual households by dividing up the remaining communal land. Four years later the problem was exacerbated by the opening of the railway to Huancayo. The railway had a major impact on alfalfa production, since it reduced dependence on pack animals for transport and thus resulted in many muleteers' going out of business.[3]

Land shortage in Muquiyauyo had a further consequence: it led to a narrowing of the gap between so-called Indians and mestizos[4] and inhibited the development of an "independent farmer" class that had assumed a position of economic and political influence in other parts of the Mantaro region.[5] Indeed, socioeconomic differentiation in Muquiyauyo, it seems, was less a function of control over agricultural resources and more related to the capacity of particular families to make judicious use of outside nonagricultural opportunities. In addition to the part played by Muquiyauyinos in the running of the mule trade, many had spent time outside the valley working in the mines established during the colonial period. This and other nonagricultural forms of work served as a necessary supplement to household income for many families. One Muquiyauyino achieved distinction as a mine owner in 1888 by purchasing two mines. One of these mines (San Francisco de Morococha) was later sold to the Cerro de Pasco Corporation when it began operations.[6]

The involvement of Muquiyauyinos in nonagricultural occupations intensified after the completion of the railroad to Huancayo in 1908. This was primarily due to the expansion of employment opportunities in the coastal sugar and cotton plantations and in the mining sector. The latter was particularly attractive to Muquiyauyinos, as the newly opened Cerro de Pasco mines were within easy traveling distance by rail, and many Muquiyauyino families had already had some mine experience. Data for the 1910–1930 period indicate that about 67 percent of householders worked at the mines and a further 14 percent found employment in Lima after short spells in one of the mine towns.[7] From about 1930 onward Muquiyauyo, like other villages, was affected by the vagaries of mining production: during the economic recession of the 1930s large numbers of men were laid off and had to return to their villages; later, mining was revitalized during the war period, but it again suffered major fluctuations in demand in the years that followed. Yet, despite these changing conditions of employment, Muquiyauyo continued to be closely integrated into the mining sector. Indeed, as the following analysis shows, the participation of miners in both the planning and the implementation of the electricity scheme was critical to its success, although, at the same time, it also contributed to internal conflicts over its aims and use.

Previous observers have been impressed by the achievements of Muquiyauyo: it built and developed a complex system of irrigation, established a hydroelectricity plant that provided lighting for Jauja, the provincial capital, and for Muquiyauyo itself, and undertook numerous other infrastructural developments (e.g., schools, a piped water scheme, a cemetery, a new central plaza, a flood protection wall along the banks of the Mantaro River). Most of these projects were carried out utilizing unpaid labor and financial contributions from the village. In contrast to other highland communities, Muquiyauyo thus appeared to show a high degree of social solidarity and self-help. Underlining this interpretation is the fact that the original ethnic division in the pueblo was gradually eroded, with increased homogenization of the population as a result. At the same time, Muquiyauyinos were drawn into a new set of urban relationships, which enabled many of them to learn new technological skills and acquire more "progressive" attitudes and interests.

The present chapter attempts to demonstrate the inadequacy of such an interpretation. It argues that, far from exhibiting solidarity and being a means of democratic participation, community organization became an instrument used by certain individuals and interest groups (both inside and outside the village) to gain access to community funds and to community unpaid labor. The argument concentrates on a detailed exposition of the electricity project.

The capital generated through the sale of electricity was not used to invest in production to improve the economic situation of the majority of villagers; rather, it served to provide services to be used by the better-off residents. It is not my intention to suggest that this outcome was systematically planned and executed by the more dominant members of the village; it arose from the types of decisions taken by the community and as a result of the interplay of various internal and external processes. The chapter is divided into three main parts corresponding to the three important stages in the history of the enterprise.

Historical Antecedents

Before 1906 Muquiyauyo was composed of four different political entities: *la comunidad indígena* (the indigenous community), *el común* (a type of communal organization involving both Indians and mestizos), *los cuarteles* (the village sections), and *el concejo municipal* (the district council).

Under colonial rule, the village was divided into two broad socio-cultural groupings: the Indians (los indios) and the non-Indians (los mestizos). The former possessed communal land granted to them by the Spanish crown and controlled their own political institution (la comunidad indigena). The mestizos were administratively dependent on the Huaripampa district council, although there was also a small group of higher-status individuals (los notables) resident in the village who exerted considerable influence in political matters. Then, in 1886, after some ten years of legal procedure, Muquiyauyo achieved independent status as a district, thereby gaining control of various local government functions. Prior to this, the village had been organized into four sections (los cuarteles) so as to assist with the mobilization of labor for public works. Each cuartel was made up of all Indians and mestizos living in the particular section of the village and was headed by a municipal agent (agente municipal) who acted as go-between with the district council. With the formation of the new district, these municipal agents came under the control of the Muquiyauyo district council rather than Huaripampa.

As table 1 shows, the Indian population had gradually, during the eighteenth and early nineteenth centuries, lost control of a substantial part of its communal land. This led eventually, in 1904, to the par-

TABLE 1

A COMPARISON OF THE DISTRIBUTION OF
LAND IN MUQUIYAUYO IN 1742 AND 1819

	1742		1819	
Type of Land	Extension in hectares	Percentage of total	Extension in hectares	Percentage of total
Land held by *indios* and la comunidad indigena	329.3	47.1	109.1	15.6
Church and *cofradia* land	10.7	1.5	36.4	5.2
Land on *Isla* (an island in the Mantaro River) probably under communal control	125.0	17.9	125.0	17.9
Land held privately by Spanish, mestizos, and caciques	235.0	33.5	429.5	61.3
Totals	700.0	100.0	700.0	100.0

SOURCE: Richard N. Adams, *A Community in the Andes*, pp. 20–21.

titioning of the remaining communal land among the 239 heads of Indian households[8] and to the disappearance of the indigenous community as a specifically Indian institution.

A fourth institution of importance was *el común*, which, it appears, was formed during the period when Muquiyauyo was still a satellite of Huaripampa. It was organized to facilitate the integration of Indians and mestizos in order to carry out specific community projects, such as the construction of the irrigation system[9] or the building of the new cemetery. In 1879, when Muquiyauyo purchased 1,020 hectares of high-altitude pasture land to the west of the village, the new property was registered in the name of *el común*.[10] However, the legal status of this institution remained somewhat indeterminate, and major difficulties arose later with the district council of Muquiyauyo when the latter used labor from the *cuarteles* to cultivate *cofradía* land that had in fact been rented from the church by *el común*, not by the district council.[11]

These problems continued until 1906, when it was proposed to create a new community organization, completely independent of the district council, consisting of the four *cuarteles*.[12] Each *cuartel* was to elect three members each to the *junta directiva* (executive body), and there was to be, in addition, a general assembly to decide on major policy. The idea was received with enthusiasm and the new organization was quickly inaugurated. Unlike the earlier *comunidad indígena* but similar to *el común*, the new community (also designated *la comunidad*) was composed of both Indians and mestizos, equally represented on the governing body.

The new community organization had access to important capital resources and free labor. It possessed communal land and controlled the irrigation channels. This gave economic power and provided sanctions, since the use of these facilities was made conditional on members' participating in various communal work tasks. This led over time to the displacement of the district council as the most important center for decisions in the village.

The Electricity Project: Establishment Phase, 1912–1929

The turn of the century was a period of much activity for Muquiyauyo. Once the district had been formed, the attention of leaders focused on the improvement of public services, such as the repair of the bridge over the river, the building of schools, and the installation of public lighting. Yet two major problems remained: the first concerned the necessity of increasing village income in order to finance these public services; the second, the general improvement of living standards. The combined effects of *minifundia* and population growth had meant that the traditional system of agriculture was no longer able to provide the population with sufficient food for subsistence, let alone offer a way to economic betterment. In order to supplement their household budgets, many Muquiyauyinos, including women and children, had to leave for work in mining centers or coastal plantations. A majority of the population, therefore, relied economically on three sources of income: the cultivation of their private plots, a share in communal land, and earnings from wage employment or from trade and crafts.

The district leaders (most of whom were professionals), bigger farmers (possessing from three to ten hectares of land), or craftsmen and businessmen were less worried about the problem of family income and more interested in obtaining rent to finance new public services and renovate existing ones.[13]

This situation gave rise to two projects, one agricultural and the other industrial. Support for the former was led by the larger farmers, who were interested in mechanizing agriculture. With this goal in mind they proposed in 1912 the reconstruction of the hydraulic mill that had existed since colonial times but had lain unused for many years. They aimed to reopen the irrigation channels and to install a modern grinding mill,[14] making it possible for residents to have their corn ground in Muquiyauyo, instead of having to transport it to nearby towns.

Such an enterprise, however, could not produce much income for the community, since the current price for the grinding of one arroba (twenty-five pounds) of corn was only two cents, and cereal production was stationary and unlikely, given the land shortage, to expand much. Moreover, the existence of other mills in the neighboring towns limited the possibility of obtaining customers from outside Muquiyauyo. The improvement of agriculture through more extensive irrigation also encountered major difficulties. Irrigated land already amounted to approximately 50 percent of arable valley land and, due to the topography, it was not possible to expand more than 10 percent on the existing network of channels.

These difficulties prompted another group of people to look for an alternative solution. In 1912, an "industrial" group proposed an electricity scheme that had three basic aims: first, the replacing of the lighting supplied by an existing petrol generator; second, the renting of electricity to neighboring towns; and third, the improvement of household incomes with the creation of local industry and work. The proposal was first made by a schoolteacher who, at the time, occupied the position of mayor (*alcalde*).[15] He was supported by a group of miners and former miners, as well as by professionals who, like himself, had spent periods working in the mining centers.[16] Although the miners were not living in Muquiyauyo at the time, they were given the same rights and were expected to meet the same obligations as residents. Most miners worked at the mines for three or more years but kept up regular contact with their village, where their wives and kin cultivated small plots for them. Also, many of them returned for the planting and harvesting seasons.[17]

The miners and former miners had learned about the use of electricity in the mining centers. The petrol generator had been installed in the town in 1906, but it was very inefficient and many people were anxious to change it for a hydroelectric system.[18] The use of public and private electricity, however, was as much a question of prestige as of economic necessity. For most people the workday finished around six o'clock in the evening, and they went to bed fairly early so that they might make an early start on the farm. Thus the use of electricity did not improve the rhythm of productive life, nor did it bring much immediate economic advantage. However, it was thought that electricity would promote industrialization and give employment to the people of Muquiyauyo, without which many would have to migrate. In addition, the provincial capital of Jauja, only a few kilometers away, offered an extensive market for the sale of electricity that, it was hoped, would provide enough rent for the financing of various public works programs.

The final decision to go ahead with the electricity scheme was not the result of spontaneous enthusiasm. It was the outcome of six years of analysis and reflection during which the two groups presented their various arguments. In 1912 the project for the grinding mill received the approval of a communal assembly, and a commission was named to undertake a feasibility study. At the same time, the community approved, in principle, the electricity plant and hoped that it could be realized when the necessary funds were available. A few months later they received a tender from a businessman in Huancayo to build the hydroelectric plant. The community agreed to review the offer but later rejected it; in the meantime the commission for the mill advanced its work.[19]

At last, following a heated debate, the electricity project was finally and unanimously approved in 1918.[20] The assembly nominated a commission responsible for its organization, and the *comuneros* (community members) present promised to collaborate by raising money and giving labor.

The minutes of this assembly provide insight into the basic objectives of the project. The orientation, it seems, had shifted from the industrial toward the mercantile. Besides providing light for the village, the principal aim of the project, as stated in the minutes, was to sell electricity to Jauja in order to raise revenue. It was only subsequent to the assembly that the creation of industries was included as a major goal. With Jauja nearby as a ready purchaser, the mercantile strategy was less complicated than that of setting up industry, since the latter implied the purchase of production tools and the obtaining of raw products and their processing and marketing. Muquiyauyo was short of capital even for the installation of the turbines and for the distribution system.

Nevertheless, the marketing of a strategic product that was also a public service could create serious difficulties in the near future, and village leaders were well aware of this. They recalled the competition with Huaripampa over the building of a toll bridge across the Mantaro River. A new bridge constructed by Huaripampa in 1899 offered a shorter and more economic route than the bridge Muquiyauyo had built in 1857. This competition had destroyed the monopoly Muquiyauyo exercised over transport and trade.[21] For this reason, the leaders explored the possibility of obtaining monopoly rights over the supply of electricity. The electricity project created a good deal of expectation among *comuneros*, who believed that its construction would herald the beginning of a new era of economic improvement.

The building of a hydroelectric plant demanded a considerable input of material and economic resources. Muquiyauyo was reasonably endowed. It had a large acreage of pasture land, called Ipas, which was rented to the people of Paccha and Llocllapampa. It had some 25 hectares of land on an island in the river and a further 250 hectares of arable land that was distributed among members of the *comunidad* on payment of a small rent. From 1888 on, the community (*el común*, later called *la comunidad*) had rented *cofradia* land from the church. Any profits deriving from the sale of products went to the community, with a small sum or proportion going to the individual members of the *cuarteles*. The principal source of capital and capital accumulation in Muquiyauyo, however, consisted of a banking system run by the community. Money belonging to the community was loaned equally to all members at a monthly interest rate of 2 percent. This ensured a regular revenue.[22]

Perhaps the major advantage of Muquiyauyo was, as today, its irrigation channels. The inlet pipe situated in the Mantaro River carried a huge volume of water to the viaduct, sited on the higher ground belonging to the village.

The hydroelectric project required a large amount of labor to build the installations and distribution system. This was obtained through the use of collective work parties. The existing system of *cuarteles* served as a framework for organizing labor, and the relatively low level of socioeconomic differentiation meant that members had common interests. Most individuals depended to some extent on agriculture, and all were interested in making use of communal resources. It was relatively easy, therefore, to exert pressure on individuals to participate in work parties and to fulfill their community obligations, since non-participation could be penalized by refusal of permission to use communal land or by an increase in the tariff for irrigation water.

After final government approval for the project was secured and after the contract with Jauja, in October 1919, for the supply of electricity was signed, the work began. It was supervised by an engineer from the nearby town of Concepción, assisted by a technician from Muquiyauyo itself. During its construction a total of 391 members, including the sons of miners, worked for some 270 days each between May 1920 and August 1921. But shortage of capital forced the community to borrow some 16,000 *soles* from an Italian immigrant in the village of Huamali, repayable at a rate of 2 percent interest per month. The first current flowed to Jauja on 28 July 1921, some two years after the work was started.[23] Numerous reports in the newspapers of the time suggest that the project had a major impact on the region and in the country at large. It also became the focus of political struggle between competing groups, both within and outside the village.

The Nature of the Social Contract

The first difficulty met by Muquiyauyo was that of obtaining the legal authority to sell electricity to Jauja and other towns, once the plant had been constructed. This was the first time that a community (*comunidad*) had launched itself into commerce on a grand scale and there was no legislation to cover such a contingency. In order to solve this problem, the community had formed a limited liability company (*sociedad anónima*) composed of five associations of shareholders: the community (*comunidad*) together with the four *cuarteles*. Thus the enterprise (known as La Empresa Eléctrica FEBO) was the property of the community but was to be administered by the *sociedad anónima*.

On the third of June 1918, a contract[24] was signed inaugurating the electric company. The contract specified that the community, as major shareholder, would contribute fifty-seven shares of 1,000 *soles* each, and each *cuartel* seven of 1,000 *soles* each. This totaled 85,000 *soles* (or $42,500), of which the community provided 15,000 *soles* and the *cuarteles* 10,000 *soles* in cash. The rest was made up of the contributions of labor, materials, and other items necessary for the construction. Each *cuartel* or association of shareholders was accorded a special name—Sociedad Obreros, Sociedad Industrial, Sociedad Asociación Obrera, and Sociedad Unión Progresista—and given proportional representation on the general assembly of shareholders. This meant that the community had effective control over the enterprise and a major say in the nomination of the board of directors (*el directorio*). Figure 1 presents a schematic view of the organizational structure of the enterprise as it existed up until 1972. The diagram shows how community organization paralleled that of the *sociedad anónima*. The arrow indicates that the general assemblies of *comuneros* were frequently converted into meetings of shareholders. During the earlier period, eleven individuals were selected for positions on the board of directors, though later there appears to have been some fluctuation in the size of this group. All official posts were salaried.

The *sociedad anónima* was founded with a basic contradiction that was to be a source of conflict for the next fifty years. The enterprise was at one and the same time both a limited company, made up of the community and the *cuarteles*, and an enterprise of the communal type.

The social contract failed to define precisely enough either the property rights of the five member institutions or the position of individuals within this structure. It was unclear as to the differences between those who had contributed labor and other resources toward the construction of the plant and those who joined later. Also, the committee controlling the community, it seems, could dispense the capital and profits of the business without consulting individual members of the community but was expected to consult the *cuarteles*. These ambiguities meant that, while the board of directors of the electric company was theoretically responsible to the general assembly of shareholders, in the everyday operation of the business it acted rather independently and in many ways like the directorate of a capitalist enterprise.

Little by little, then, the conflict between these two tendencies (the communal and free-enterprise elements) and between competing factions within the community was accentuated. Hence, in 1922, when the first board of directors attempted to remain in office, they were accused of maladministration and replaced by a new group.[25] These original founders were predominantly professionals and former miners. The new group was of similar composition, although it contained a larger number of more recently returned miners who demanded a major part in the running of the enterprise. However, administrative troubles

FIGURE 1

ORGANIZATION AND ADMINISTRATION OF THE ELECTRICITY ENTERPRISE FEBO, 1918-1972

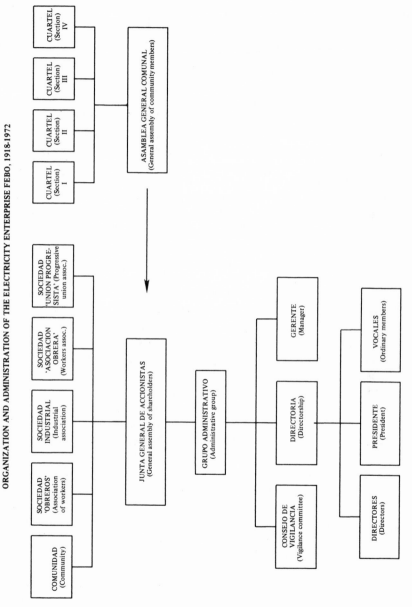

persisted, and the community found itself increasingly unable to meet its expenses. This led, in the following year, to the decision to rent out the plant to a man who had a medical practice in Jauja and who, at the time, was *alcalde* of Muquiyauyo and a close associate of the original group of founders. On taking control of the business, he immediately offered employment to several of his friends, and in this way the founders were able to regain influence in the running of the plant, although this time their power was indirect.[26]

The Electricity Enterprise and Communal Organization

The creation of the electricity enterprise had a profound influence on the political structure of the village. As the major shareholder, the community acted as the central focus of cohesion for the *cuarteles* and for the population in general, and, at the same time, became a major center of decision-making. The position of the *cuarteles* within the village was strengthened by their participation in the enterprise as shareholders. From now onward, the *cuarteles* became more than just territorial divisions designed to rationalize labor: they were institutions with important economic power and subcenters of decision-making within the political organization of the community. Indeed, the hierarchical organization of the member institutions of the enterprise into large and smaller shareholders gave shape to the future federated structure of the community and represented the two dominant tendencies in the political system: the trend toward centralism (i.e., the concentration of local government in the hands of the community) and federalism, which expressed the desire of the individual *cuarteles* to achieve their own autonomy or independence.

The district council, which was not accorded shareholder status in the new enterprise, was without economic resources. The conflicts between the leaders of the district council and the leaders of the community over the control of productive wealth in the village had, it seems, been solved in favor of the latter. In 1886 the district council had controlled the *cuarteles*, but thirty years later the community had reasserted itself and was rapidly replacing it as a center of power and decisions.

The electricity scheme was planned as an investment that would, it was hoped, stimulate development in the village, but in fact it had a negative impact on the village economy during the early years. The payment of individual contributions for the construction of the plant drained the savings of families, both those living in the village and those away at the mines. The enormous amount of time and effort put into the construction of the project in 1921 by *comuneros* also had an unfortunate effect on village production because it diverted labor from agriculture. On the other hand, the capital reserves of the community and the *cuarteles* were negligible. Indeed, the community had acquired a debt of about sixteen thousand *soles* due to the purchase of machinery and, in order to clear this, had to sublet to individuals and *cuarteles* the *cofradía* land it had rented from the church.

Phase Two: 1930–1955

In 1929, after six years of renting out, the community decided to resume control of the electricity enterprise. The main reason for this was economic. More revenue was urgently needed to finance various public work projects, and the electricity business had, by then, shown itself to be fairly profitable. The letting of the plant had made it possible for the community to pay off its 16,000 *soles* debt. Also, by all accounts, the lessee was making a substantial monthly profit, and the *comuneros* wished to reap the benefits as well. In 1929, when the renewal of the contract was refused, the lessee demanded an extension of at least another two years or the payment of compensation to the value of 15,000 *soles* for the improvements he had made.[27] Taking advantage of his official position as *alcalde* of Muquiyauyo and his good connections with the subprefect and others in Jauja, he threatened the community with a lawsuit that, in all probability, he would win. The community finally reached a settlement, agreeing to pay him 12,500 *soles* in compensation for recovery of the enterprise.

The village removed the former lessee from his position as *alcalde* and expelled him from his *cuartel*.[28] It was also decided to establish a new post, president of the *comunidad*, and to make the community organization completely independent of the district council. Up to this time, the district council was the titular head of both the municipality and the community. Later, in 1932, the community obtained full legal recognition under the new statute for *comunidades indígenas*[29] and became officially registered as La Comunidad Indígena de Industriales Regantes de Muquiyauyo. The new name once again expressed the community's emphasis on industry as well as on agriculture.

At this time, the contract for the supply of electricity to Jauja was near termination, raising the question of how best to utilize the plant. Should the community continue to sell electricity to Jauja or attempt, instead, to use it to develop industries in Muquiyauyo itself? The relatively low capacity of the plant made it impossible to do both at the same time.

In 1930 the Cerro de Pasco Mining Corporation was forced to lay off large numbers of workers as a result of the world economic slump:

from a total of 13,066 workers employed in 1929, the work force was reduced to 5,686 in 1930 and to 4,330 in 1933. As a consequence, a large number of Muquiyauyinos returned to their home village, as there was no way of supporting their families in the mine towns. This massive return migration coincided with a renewed interest in industrialization. One leader declared in 1930: "Let us forget [our divisions] and unite to develop industry that will bring true benefits to our renowned village for already agriculture cannot cover satisfactorily our basic necessities." [30]

In February 1931, the communal assembly nominated an industrial commission made up of persons experienced in industrial matters; the purpose of the commission was to analyze which sorts of industry would be most appropriate to establish in Muquiyauyo and to prepare an estimated budget.[31] This initiative received little support from the leaders of the community and, in August 1932, the general assembly of FEBO decided, on the basis of fourteen votes for and three against, to continue to sell electricity to Jauja instead of encouraging the establishment of industries.[32] In later meetings, up to 1955, some members occasionally repeated this plea for industry but with no success.[33]

The main reason for the failure to develop industry was, paradoxically, the predominance of nonagriculturalists in the community and electricity plant. Nonagriculturalists tended to occupy the more important posts of president, secretary, and manager. Table 2 provides evidence of this and indicates that over the first forty-year period the trend became more marked. The farmers who did hold office tended to be the larger landowners of the district, whose interests were generally opposed to those of the mass of small holders. Like their associates, the professionals, businessmen, and craftsmen, this group of farmers was more concerned with the creation of better public services than with the development of a sounder economy for the village as a whole.

TABLE 2

PRINCIPAL LEADERS OF THE *COMUNIDAD* AND OF THE ELECTRICITY ENTERPRISE

Occupational Category	Periods		
	1918–1922	1930–1932	1956–1959
Farmers	50%	46%	37%
Others	50%	54%	63%
Totals	100% (n=30)	100% (n=28)	100% (n=44)

The list of public works completed during this period, and in part financed by the electricity plant, attests to this orientation:

Public Works Completed between 1929 and 1955
1929–1930: The purchase of two electric grinding mills
1931–1933: The reconstruction of the bridge over the Mantaro River
1934: The building of a girls' school
1936–1937: The construction of the central plaza
1938: The purchase of church land
1938: The building of a boys' school
1937–1955: Various schemes concerning piped water
1942–1944: The installation of the office of FEBO in Jauja
1943: The building of a secondary school for girls
1949–1950: The construction of the new cemetery
1950: The establishment of a training school for sewing and design
1953: The reconstruction of the flood walls along the banks of the Mantaro River

FEBO's assistance in such work was not always in the form of individual contributions or levies on members. In the most important instances, large loans, repayable over a set period of time, were provided to the community.[34] In 1933, the general assembly decided to set aside some 25 percent of its profits for educational schemes and to invest the rest in the expansion of the enterprise itself.[35] Yet, by 1957, though it had collaborated in the financing of several expensive projects, its capital reserve still amounted to some 1,636,821 *soles*; none of its capital had been directed toward the creation of industry. The development of industry required long-range investment with little prospect of immediate return, and therefore it seemed less attractive than the expansion of the existing service and the provision of short-term loans. A change in policy would have demanded a basic change in the ideology and objectives of the leaders.

From 1933 onward, the improved economic situation in the mines had led to the reemployment of many former workers. This saw the gradual drift of many Muquiyauyinos once again to the mines for work, although, as the years passed, the migration flow shifted toward Lima, the national capital. The reabsorption of Muquiyauyinos into the urban labor markets reduced the pressure to establish industry in the home village.

This struggle, however, was replaced by an opposition of interest within the mercantile group: one sector favored the strengthening of communal organization and the other wished to develop the enterprise into a fully fledged limited company (*sociedad anónima*).[36] Those who promoted the former view sought to utilize FEBO funds to improve the infrastructure of the village and stressed that the electricity enterprise was primarily communal property and should therefore be administered directly by the community and *cuarteles*. The other group attempted to capitalize the business and extend its commercial influence. But, in spite of this internal antagonism, Muquiyauyo was able to present a united front in the face of external threats.

The main threat to Muquiyauyo came from Jauja. During the previous fifty years Jauja had gradually lost its economic and political dominance in the Mantaro Valley while Huancayo rose to prominence as the main administrative and commercial center for the central region. This coincided with Muquiyauyo's attainment of district status and with the launching of the electricity plant. The provincial elite of Jauja showed little apparent concern about the activities and profits of individual entrepreneurs—for example, they did not object to the selling of electricity by the tenant-manager of the plant. However, when Muquiyauyo reclaimed control of the administration of the business and began to use its capital to increase its own economic power, Jauja responded by trying to obstruct development in every conceivable way. Jauja took advantage of its politico-administrative and juridical powers as the provincial headquarters, imposing fines on Muquiyauyo for supposed defaults in the electricity service. During this period of litigation several Muquiyauyino leaders were arrested and accused of being Communist agitators.

The Jauja authorities also aided in the formation of a competing electricity company. In 1931 a group of Jauja businessmen, led by the Landa family, met to form the Empresa Eléctrica Siclachaca, S. A., which built a hydroelectric plant some five kilometers from Muquiyauyo. By 1934, this company was supplying many private residents of Jauja with lighting, and by 1936, with support from central government, it took away from Muquiyauyo the contract for public lighting.

Muquiyauyo attempted repeatedly to pressure government to rescind this decision, but it was not until 1957 that it was able to secure a new concession for the sale of electricity in the Mantaro Valley. During the interim period, it fought a hard and long-drawn-out campaign. A major obstacle to its success, it seems, was that the system of communal enterprise did not fit easily into the prevailing capitalist structure of the country; in fact the new statute for indigenous communities afforded community institutions special privileges with respect to taxation that worked to the disadvantage of private competitors. The granting of an important concession to Muquiyauyo, then, would have meant supporting the community against the group of mercantile capitalists in Jauja who were themselves closely linked to professional and business circles in Lima[37]; this was a practical impossibility.

On the other hand, the prestige and influence of Muquiyauyo in the region continued to grow. Several peasant communities, inspired by its example, sought advice on how to set up comparable communal institutions; political parties also visited Muquiyauyino leaders to discuss mobilization and tactics. The nearby districts of Huamali, Concepción, and San Jerónimo offered to purchase or take charge of the administration of its electricity installations. The formal registration of Muquiyauyo both as an indigenous community and as a business company opened the way for other communities with electricity centers or other types of enterprise to demand similar treatment.

Finally, however, through the intervention in 1957 of a senior government official, described as "a friend of Muquiyauyo," a concession was granted. But one of the conditions of this agreement[38] was that FEBO would be expected to meet the same legal obligations and pay the same level of taxes as any private commercial business. This was the first step toward a radical restructuring of its organization.

The Final Phase, 1956–1972: An Attempt at Autonomous Development

This last period in the history of the electric plant marks the expansion of the service to cover a large part of the Mantaro Valley. The concession of 1957 gave Muquiyauyo exclusive rights to supply electricity to an area of some 212,043 square kilometers for the period of fifty years. In its fight to secure this right, Muquiyauyo not only wished to eliminate the competition of the Landa Company and regain its customers in Jauja, but it also sought to extend its network of distribution so as to obtain a monopoly over electricity throughout the northern zone of the valley. It was only partially successful in achieving this, since the government allowed the Landa Company to continue operation until 1965.[39]

The Muquiyauyo miracle lasted for several more years. In 1957 Muquiyauyo purchased a second hydraulic turbine of 334 KWA and installed a new powerhouse and larger water channels. This work deployed communal labor and used capital from the enterprise. The total cost of the installation of the new machinery, including both materials and labor, was $60,159. Later, in 1964, an electric generator of 240 KWA, valued at $21,400, was installed in Jauja, and this was amplified, in 1971, by another more powerful one costing some $51,000. All this machinery was financed through short-term loans from government, but this left FEBO with a regular annual deficit, which meant that it had to retain its dividends for debt repayments. Whereas from 1957 to 1963 it was able to contribute toward various public work projects, including the building of two new schools, from 1963 onward it contributed virtually nothing. The new concession necessitated an expansion of operations to meet the increased demand and to conform with the contract provision that required a 10 percent extension of the electricity lines each year.

Throughout these years, the number of non-*comuneros* and passive *comuneros* in Muquiyauyo had increased. There was also greater social differentiation in the village, due to the widening of employment and income opportunities. This led to a lack of interest in communal work on the part of many residents. It was not worth their while giving up other work in order to take part in *faenas,* and the advantages of community membership were few. For these reasons, many residents refused to work on the construction of the second electricity plant. To encourage community participation, a system of work cards was introduced to record the amount of work done by individuals and their contribution to the building of the first plant.[40] Thus, at the same time that the community was showing signs of disintegration, there developed an emphasis on individual as against collective shareholding. This saw the reemergence of the struggle between those who stressed the communal nature of the enterprise and those who favored the idea of the *sociedad anónima.* In 1956, under the influence of the latter group, the members voted for the elimination of the community as a shareholder, recommending that the shares should be distributed among the remaining four *cuarteles* because, as one member put it, "the community had contributed nothing."[41] This decision was reaffirmed in 1962, but it was never in fact put into effect because of fears that the community institution would thereby be dissolved.[42]

In 1965 the communal group gained the approval of the general membership to change the name and character of the enterprise. From being known as The Electricity Enterprise FEBO, Sociedad Anónima, it was renamed The Communal Electricity Enterprise, and the *cuarteles* transferred their shares to the community. The administration of the business was to become the responsibility of the community.

However, a new state law for commercial enterprises promulgated in 1966 did not recognize collective associations, so the communal enterprise was once again forced to change its name and revert to the previous pattern of organization. In 1968 the government intervened to revise the original 1918 social contract. The text of the new constitution was ambiguous, for it both recognized the property of the enterprise as being communal and at the same time gave to the general assembly of shareholders the right to dissolve the organization.[43] The new contract was also unclear concerning shareholders: on the one hand, it stated that the only authorities that could hold shares were the five original shareholders (i.e., the four *cuarteles* and the community), but, on the other hand, it distinguished between preferential and ordinary shares, which were to be distributed proportionally according to the individuals' participation in the construction of the two plants, and deferred shares, which took no account of work done. A distribution of small dividends also took place, and, although it was of little economic significance, it did symbolically reaffirm the conviction of some members that the enterprise was essentially a limited company of the capitalist type.[44]

From this time onward, the division between those emphasizing the communal nature of the enterprise and those treating it as a *sociedad anónima* became much sharper. New *comuneros* were not offered shares in the enterprise, and former *comuneros*, who retired either voluntarily or by compulsion, claimed shares in payment for the work they or their fathers had contributed to the construction of the two plants. It also seems that there were persons listed as shareholders in the *cuarteles* who in fact took no part in communal activities. The latter were regarded as passive *comuneros*. All this, then, posed the fundamental problem of whose enterprise it was. Did it belong to those who had worked to build it or merely to those who were registered as *comuneros*?[45]

In 1968, an association of founders (Asociación de Fundadores de la Empresa) was organized to assist the directors of the *sociedad anónima* to defend the privileges of the founder members and to watch over the development of the enterprise.[46] Then, in 1971, under the influence and with the help of the political authorities of Jauja, the directors proceeded to introduce yet another organizational reform. This was aimed at eliminating the community and *cuarteles* as shareholders and at handing over the control of the business to those individuals who had collaborated in the construction and financing of the project. The leaders of the community, supported by groups of migrant Muquiyauyinos in the mines and Lima, reacted fiercely to this new initiative.[47] In a communal assembly *comuneros* refused to accept the proposal and reiterated that the enterprise was essentially a communal institution.[48] This declaration received the backing of a resolution passed by the Dirección de Comunidades Campesinas (the government agency concerned with peasant or indigenous communities).

In addition to this internal struggle, Muquiyauyo faced several other problems. The expansion of the enterprise demanded a relatively high level of technical and administrative expertise among both the leadership of the enterprise and the community. Many of the occupants of these key posts, however, were ill-prepared for the tasks facing them. Eventually, the leadership of the community lost control of the board of directors and the bureaucracy of the electricity plant and, despite their victory concerning communal versus private ownership, seldom assumed a major role in its operation. On the other hand, the electricity enterprise itself apparently suffered from maladministration and irregularities in financial matters. Periodically members of the general assembly called for some reform or other: for example, in 1961 a technical reorganization of the management of the business was suggested with a view to appointing persons with proven skills in the running of such enterprises. However, nothing appears to have been done to implement this policy.

The situation was aggravated by numerous irregularities in financial management. Despite the commonly-held view in Muquiyauyo that fraud and embezzlement of funds is a relatively recent development in the business, the minutes of the community and of the enterprise reveal that these problems first arose shortly after the founding of the enterprise. The only noticeable difference is that during the first twenty years there was a closer surveillance by the community. Throughout its history the enterprise has been both a source of revenue for the financing of public projects and a means by which particular individuals supplemented their domestic budgets. The sums withdrawn from the enterprise, in the form of salaries and allowances paid to officers, were at times very large.[49] According to data taken from the minutes of the general assembly of shareholders, capital reserves, from about 1936, have diminished more or less year by year; in addition, since 1963 the business has, with the exception of one year (1965), had a fluctuating annual deficit. This reached major proportions in the late sixties and early seventies:

Annual Deficit: 1968–1971 (in *soles*)
1968: 461,442.65
1969: 344,220.46
1970: 111,776.80
1971: 506,678.60

On various occasions after 1953 the government threatened to intervene because of deficiencies in the accounting system, but it never once offered direct technical assistance. In 1972 an auditor working for AUDICOOP petitioned the Ministry of Energy and Mines to declare the enterprise in a state of emergency, needing urgent help.[50] The

population of Muquiyauyo, too, had a clear appreciation of the difficulties, for in 1972, in response to my questions about administrative
problems, some forty (51 percent) of seventy-eight persons interviewed
indicated that they felt that the enterprise was handicapped by bad
—and at times dishonest—administration.

The problem of leadership was exacerbated by migration to urban
centers. During the 1940s and 1950s some 300 to 500 Muquiyauyinos
worked in the mines: by 1972 this number was reduced to about 111
persons dispersed among twenty-eight different mining towns. The drop
in the number of mine migrants, however, coincided with an increased
flow to Lima, following the urban-industrial development that took
place after the Second World War. A high proportion of these urban
migrants originated from the central highland region, and, like other
valley villages, Muquiyauyo made its contribution to this process.
Survey data collected in 1972 indicated that some 65.8 percent of absentee children lived in Lima; the rest were distributed among Huancayo (13.6 percent), Juaja (6.9 percent), and the mines (13.7 percent).
And a similar pattern was discernible for siblings.[51]

The two prime motives for migration were education and work. Our
1972 survey identified forty-nine young people studying outside Muquiyauyo in various Peruvian cities: of these, thirty-three lived in Lima.
In addition, there were another thirty migrants working as domestic
servants in Lima, and a further thirty-five who had recently completed
their schooling and had decided to seek work in Lima or other cities.
It is difficult to obtain precise information on the occupational structure of groups of migrants, but the majority appeared to be tradesmen,
skilled workers, and businessmen. Also, several Muquiyauyinos who had
higher education became teachers. Teaching is one of the few professions where employment is available in or near Muquiyauyo. In
1972 there were some fifty teachers based in Muquiyauyo, of whom
thirty traveled out each day for work in other parts of the valley. The
remaining twenty were employed in the large number of schools and
educational centers located in the village itself. Although most of these
professionals do not participate actively in the community (i.e., they
are non-*comuneros* or passive *comuneros*), they benefit from the lighting
and other public facilities provided by the village and are able to
reduce their living expenses by cultivating gardens and residing in
rent-free housing.

One consequence of this long history of emigration is that, over the
years, Muquiyauyo has lost many of the younger and more dynamic
members of the village. On the other hand, the leaders in the village
have relied on the collaboration of various "sons of the village" (*paisa-*

nos) living in the mining towns and Lima. They contributed significantly to the establishment of the electricity plant, collected funds,
provided specialist advice and practical expertise, and also acted as
brokers with central government. The latter function was especially
important, since they were on the spot for lobbying government ministries and for representing the village and electricity enterprise in their
various negotiations. Several migrant associations were formed to provide an organizational framework for such activity. In the early years
it was the various social clubs based in Morococha and Huarón, where
a substantial body of Muquiyauyinos worked, that played the dominant
role; later it was the Lima associations.[52]

This involvement of migrant associations in the affairs of the village
led in the 1960s to their assuming major influence over village development policy. A consultative committee (*consejo consultivo*), made up
of intellectuals living in Lima and elsewhere, was set up in 1961 with
the aim of resolving the numerous internal and external problems of
the village.[53] Special attention was to be given to the difficulties facing
the community (*comunidad*) and the electricity enterprise, to the fund-
ing of a project for piped water, to irrigation and agricultural matters,
and finally to the defense of legal rights of various kinds. Later in
the same year delegates were nominated to represent the various *cuarteles* in the Centro Comunal, Muquiyauyo, the main migrant club in
Lima[54]; in 1956 it was agreed that all members of such clubs should be
accorded full rights as *comuneros* of the community.

While of considerable value to the village because of the migrants'
specialist knowledge and access to urban networks, this arrangement
also had certain negative consequences, since migrants and professionals
were not always best able to appreciate the needs and priorities of
the village population. There were also difficulties over the delays in
communication between the village and the city, which were often
critical when the community needed to act quickly over some issue.
All in all, then, the increasing involvement of nonresident professionals
and others merely added to the social fragmentation of the village,
making it increasingly difficult for them to unite in the face of external
pressure.

The Final Phase, 1972–1973: The Defeat

Internal divisions and administrative inefficiency were at their height
just at the point when Muquiyauyo desperately needed a united front
in the face of outside forces. In spite of the new machinery that had
been purchased, the electricity enterprise was still not producing sufficient current. It could not deal adequately with the Jauja demand,

let alone that of other villages in the vicinity. By 1972, Muquiyauyo had not yet expanded its distribution network beyond Huaripampa, Tambo, and Sauza. Finally, in July 1972, taking advantage of the continuous complaints made by Jauja and other towns and of the fact that AUDICOOP had called attention to the seriousness of the financial situation, the Ministry of Energy and Mines announced that the original concession would be terminated.[55]

It is significant that, on this occasion, the community and its various organizations quietly acquiesced to this decision. Also, when the functionaries of SEN (Servicios Eléctricos Nacionales) visited the village in November 1972 to discuss the proposed takeover of the electricity enterprise (FEBO), a mere one hundred persons, not all of whom were *comuneros*, were present.[56] The questions raised at this meeting were limited to a request that the central hydroelectric installations in Muquiyauyo, the canal, and the distribution system in Huaripampa, Sauza, and Muquiyauyo be left in the hands of the community until the situation was more clearly defined legally. The meeting agreed that the Ministry of Energy and Mines should assume control over the electricity services in Jauja through SEN.

Two weeks later SEN intervened by taking over the installations in Jauja and assuming control of the enterprise's bank account, which is estimated to have been valued at about 300,000 *soles*.[57] The action provoked the community into one final effort to recoup some of its losses. It was decided to implement a partial boycott of the supply of electricity from Muquiyauyo to Jauja.

Because of the split within Muquiyauyo between the *sociedad anónima*, which had been reorganized by the association of founders, and the community, the government had to conduct its negotiations both with the directors of the *sociedad* and with community leaders. This allowed for considerable manipulation. Thus the initial discussions of SEN were conducted with the community and its leaders, thereby implicitly recognizing the community as the formal legal body controlling the electricity plant. But later, in a letter of May 1973, ELECTROPERU, the national electricity agency, addressed itself to the directorate of the *sociedad anónima* as the responsible body.

By the end of 1973 nothing had been settled. Government tactics were to procrastinate in the final settlement. This had the effect of undermining what village solidarity remained and reinforcing the opposition between communal and entrepreneurial interests. During this period, participation in communal work was at a low ebb: in fact only 35 percent of heads of household could be regarded as active *comuneros*. Not only had Muquiyauyo's human capital diminished, but also its financial assets were frozen. The majority of residents and migrants waited eagerly for compensation for the Jauja installations, estimated to be about 5,500,000 *soles*, and most argued that it should be divided among the individual members. There was now little confidence that community leaders would invest the capital wisely. When I left the field at the end of 1973 the matter of compensation was still not resolved, nor was the question of the relationship between the local plant and ELECTROPERU, although the dissolution of the enterprise as a community project was clearly within sight.

Conclusion

The history of the electricity enterprise is in microcosm the history of the community of Muquiyauyo. The analysis of the enterprise has enabled me to examine the significance of communal organization as an instrument of development. I have emphasized that communal organization in Muquiyauyo served to benefit certain socioeconomic groups, such as the better educated and those with more land and capital resources, at the expense of the mass of the peasant population. This exploitation occurred, in part, through using the labor power of villagers to build projects that gave financial benefit to the few. For example, only a relatively small number of members were, by virtue of their education and experience, able to assume control of the electricity enterprise; these became officers of the executive, receiving expenses for committee work and, at times, having the opportunity to embezzle sufficient funds to establish private businesses. This same group also monopolized the paid posts as administrative and technical staff. More important, inequalities resulted from the implementation of projects that, by their very nature, would benefit only those of elite status in the village. With very few exceptions, the projects undertaken in Muquiyauyo contributed to the amenities of the village, making it a more convenient and agreeable place of residence for professional and commercial people. The proliferation of the educational services, including a university, provided sources of employment for members of the better-off families in the village; in turn these educational services ensured that their children would be educated to a level that gave access to better-paid jobs in the region or farther afield. Such services have inevitably been used differentially by people in Muquiyauyo, since they incur financial costs and investments of time that are difficult for poorer families to meet. For such families, the development of Muquiyauyo's productive base would have been a more significant contribution to their economic and social security.

The role of communal organization in exploitation at the village level is intimately linked to the development of a national capitalist economy. Muquiyauyo provided infrastructural services required for national integration and, in effect, helped to subsidize the development of private and state enterprise. The electricity provided to Jauja not only gave public lighting but also provided current for the operation of various small industries. Also, the public works undertaken in Muquiyauyo were of the type that, in other circumstances, would be financed by central government through taxing the more prosperous sectors of the population. Yet a poor Andean village was to finance not only the building of roads, irrigation schemes, and schools but also the construction of a national university.[58] The willingness of the community to undertake these functions is explained by the characteristics of its leaders: they were people whose own careers and those of their children had become increasingly oriented to the opportunities created by national economic integration and the consequent growth of the bureaucracy. The relative success that these leaders had in persuading other groups to support their projects requires a detailed analysis of social and economic relationships within the village and of the ways in which these were modified over time. These aspects are explored elsewhere.[59]

Muquiyauyo's contribution to national development was acceptable so long as it did not threaten existing political and economic hierarchies. As soon as Muquiyauyo's communal organization sought to develop a monopoly over an important resource like electricity there was a concerted attempt by provincial and national government to limit its influence. The network of distribution for electricity never developed beyond the neighboring towns and villages, despite the fact that Muquiyauyo was granted a concession to supply a large part of the valley region. Jauja took advantage of Muquiyauyo's enterprise, but it used its political position and influence in Lima to extract the service at minimum cost. Through the imposition of fines for "inadequate" supply, Jauja managed to receive electricity free over a number of years.

The political implications and example of Muquiyauyo's communal enterprise were not tolerated by the existing national and regional elite. Indeed, Muquiyauyo became a target for accusations of Communist subversion, and in several periods Muquiyauyinos were jailed for political agitation.[60] This illustrates the basic contradiction in the use of the *comunidad* in national development: it enables development to be carried out "on the cheap," but if allowed to become too successful it can present an alternative political and economic model. This explains the ambivalence of successive Peruvian governments toward the "progressive" community of Muquiyauyo.

One other interesting lesson to be learned from the Muquiyauyo experience is the limit imposed on communal enterprise by a wage labor economy. Except for certain short periods, there was no surplus of labor in Muquiyauyo; hence there was no consistent local pressure to invest in the development of agricultural and industrial production. Although Muquiyauyo experienced extreme land fragmentation, this did not lead only to permanent migration but also to the retaining of small plots as a complement to external employment. In practice, this entailed women and older people being left to cultivate and tend the livestock, while men were absent for much of the year. At the local level the problem was to obtain enough labor for sowing and harvesting, rather than the creation of new local work opportunities.

The process of Muquiyauyo is one in which communal enterprise is constantly subject to the intrusion of individual interests that result from, and are reinforced by, Muquiyauyo's increasing incorporation into the capitalist economy. The types of occupational groups that played a leading part in the history of the electricity enterprise at different periods—miners, teachers, commercial farmers, traders—attest to this incorporation.

This incorporation took place through the growth of opportunities for trade and for work in the urban labor market; also, the community became increasingly subject to legislation protecting private enterprise. This is a good example of why it is that cooperative organization cannot work effectively when the overall institutional framework of laws and economic practice is based upon a free-enterprise rationality.

Despite these reservations, communal organization in Muquiyauyo did restrict the more destructive and blatant tendencies of individual enterprise. Its history is dialectical, reflecting the ways in which communal forces reasserted themselves in face of the attempts of particular interest groups to take control, but in which communal organization also becomes an instrument of individual or sectional interests.

NOTES

1. The material for this chapter was collected during two periods of field research, in August–December 1972 and April–September 1973. The main findings of the research are contained in Marcelo Grondin, "Un caso de explotación calculada: La comunidad campesina de Muquiyauyo, Peru," Ph.D. thesis, Universidad Iberoamericana, Mexico City, 1975.

2. See Hildebrando Castro Pozo, *Nuestra comunidad indígena*, pp. 63–68; Harry Tschopik, *Highland Communities of Central Peru*, pp. 46–48; Richard

N. Adams, *A Community in the Andes: Problems and Progress in Muquiyauyo*, pp. 1–2, 49.

3. Grondin, "Un caso de explotación," pp. 42–46, 176–180.

4. It is estimated that in 1900 there were some twenty households possessing between 3.3 and 8.3 hectares of private land. The ownership of these larger holdings was not confined, however, to members of the mestizo category, since several *indios* or *indigenas* were among the group. For a discussion of changes in the ethnic system of Muquiyauyo, see Adams, *Community in the Andes*, pp. 82–92.

5. See Carlos Samaniego in this volume.

6. Adams, *Community in the Andes*, p. 94.

7. Grondin, "Un caso de explotación," p. 193.

8. Adams describes this as "the most important act in the recent history of the town, since it symbolized the official extinction of the difference between Indians and *mestizos*" (*Community in the Andes*, p. 40).

9. Decreto del sub-prefecto, Jauja province, 16 July 1846.

10. Testimonio de venta, Don Lucán Hinostroza and wife in favor of *el común* of Muquiyauyo, Jauja, 31 March 1879.

11. Libro de cuentas, La Comunidad, 9 February 1903: 32.

12. Libro de acuerdos, La Comunidad, 3 February 1906: 3–5.

13. Actas del Consejo, Muquiyauyo district, 24 April 1909: 192.

14. Libro de acuerdos, La Comunidad, 28 June 1913: 111.

15. Actas del Consejo, Muquiyauyo district, 5 June 1912: 265.

16. Mariano Cárdenas Terreros, "Iniciadores y fundadores de la Empresa Hidroeléctrica FEBO de Muquiyauyo," ms., p. 2.

17. Grondin, "Un caso de explotación," p. 197.

18. Actas del Consejo, Muquiyauyo district, 30 June 1906: 80.

19. Actas de la Comunidad, 16 February 1913: 104.

20. Ibid., 24 February 1918: 135.

21. Adams (*Community in the Andes*, p. 183) explains that until 1895 the primary source of income for the district was the collection of tolls for using the Muquiyauyo bridge. As a result of opposition from Muquiyauyo, the construction of the Huaripampa bridge was delayed for about four years. Also later, in 1908, when excessive flooding damaged it, Muquiyauyo was able to raise the toll price for its own bridge once again, for a period of nine months, until the Huaripampa bridge was repaired.

22. Actas del Consejo, Muquiyauyo district, 11 February 1904: 39.

23. In order not to break the contract and have to pay a fine for failing to supply electricity to Jauja within the specified period, Muquiyauyo had to provide light by 28 July 1921, in time for the centenary celebrations of Peruvian independence.

24. Contrato de La Compañía Empresa Hidroeléctrica FEBO de Muquiyauyo, Jauja, 6 June 1918: 11.

25. Actas del Directorio de la Empresa, 12 July 1920; 16 June 1922: 58.

26. Actas de la Comunidad, 9 September 1923: 209.

27. Ibid., 3 December 1929: 43.

28. He subsequently left the village and took up residence in Jauja as the director of the medical center of Jauja.

29. For details see Winder in this volume.

30. Actas de la Comunidad, 12 October 1930.

31. Ibid., 23 February 1931: 257.

32. Actas de la Junta General de Accionistas, 12 August 1932: 137–138.

33. In 1951, a former leader of the community planned to set up a textile factory in Muquiyauyo, with the community acting as a minor shareholder and the entrepreneur's family being the major shareholder. However, although the machinery arrived in Muquiyauyo, it was never put into operation because the company was dissolved shortly afterward. In 1973, the machines were still lying idle.

34. For example, the electricity enterprise loaned capital to the community for the purchase of land from the church that cost fifteen thousand *soles*. See Actas de la Junta General de Accionistas, 3 August 1938: 153, and Actas de Sesiones del Directorio, 3 September 1938: 198.

35. Actas de la Comunidad, 11 March 1933: 108; also Actas de la Junta General de Accionistas, 4 April 1934: 106.

36. Actas de la Junta General de Accionistas, 21 October 1932: 198–200.

37. G. Alberti and R. Sánchez, *Poder y conflicto social en el valle del Mantaro*, pp. 33–47.

38. Contrato de Adaptación de Concesión de Servicio Público de Electricidad, 26 December 1957. For details see Grondin, "Un caso de explotación," Anexo 9, pp. 542–551.

39. In spite of its objections to the government ruling, the company was forced to close down. See the resolution of the Ministerio de Fomento, no. 342, 1965.

40. Actas de la Junta General de Accionistas, 30 September 1956: 232.

41. Ibid., 233.

42. Actas de la Comunidad, 11 February 1962: 174. The voting was 80 percent for, 20 percent against.

43. Inscripción de Modificación de Estatutos y Aumento de Capital Social de la Empresa Hidroeléctrica FEBO de Muquiyauyo, S. A., 23 March 1968. For details see Grondin, "Un caso de explotación," pp. 552–562.

44. Some twenty thousand *soles* each were distributed to the five component institutions. This gave approximately two hundred to three hundred *soles* per individual.

45. Actas de la Sociedad Obreros, 15 April 1967: 5.

46. Asamblea de Constitución de la Asociación de Fundadores de la Empresa Hidroeléctrica FEBO de Muquiyauyo, S. A. See Grondin, "Un caso de explotación," p. 563.

47. Actas de la Comunidad, 20 February 1972: 75.

48. Ibid., 23 February 1972: 3–7.

49. Grondin, "Un caso de explotación," p. 468.

50. Informe de Trabajo Especial, no. 142/72, 9 June 1972.

51. Grondin, "Un caso de explotación," pp. 352–353.

52. For details see Adams, *Community in the Andes*, pp. 95–97; Norman Long, "The Role of Regional Associations in Peru," in *The Process of Urbanization*, edited by M. Drake et al., pp. 182–184; Grondin, "Un caso de explotación," pp. 397–400.

53. Actas de la Comunidad, 26 February 1961: 134.

54. Ibid., 8 April 1961: 147.

55. Resolución no. 1130, Ministerio de Energía y Minas, 8 July 1972.

56. Actas de la Comunidad, 5 November 1972: 61–62.

57. Acta de recepción por SEN de los bienes de la Comunidad Campesina de Muquiyauyo, Jauja, 17 November 1972.

58. Muquiyauyo built and partially funded the local branch of the Universidad Nacional de Educación "La Cantuta"; this branch specializes in physical education, and some 8 percent of its students are from Muquiyauyo. These local students are paid for entirely by the community. See Grondin, "Un caso de explotación," pp. 409–411.

59. In my thesis I label this process that of "calculated exploitation" (see ibid., pp. 156–172).

60. Adams, *Community in the Andes*, pp. 98–99.

5. The Bases of
Industrial Cooperation in Huancayo

BRYAN R. ROBERTS

From the early 1930s to the late 1960s, Huancayo was the location
of a substantial textile industry, employing, at its height, some 3,500
workers. This industry was made up of four large factories and perhaps
a dozen medium-sized ones; all were established by private capital,
and the four large factories were subsidiaries of large family enterprises
with factories in Lima and other parts of Peru.[1] This is an account of
the largest of the textile factories—Manufacturas del Centro—which,
at one time, employed over a thousand workers. The history of the
factory illustrates two social and economic processes that are often
thought to be crucial to economic development: the formation of an
industrial labor force recruited from a predominantly agricultural
region, and the development of industrial entrepreneurship on the basis
of commercial activities.[2] The outcome of these processes was somewhat
different from that envisaged by models of urban-industrial growth that
emphasize linear development: in Huancayo these processes ended in
the deindustrialization of the city. Although the decline of the industry was relatively sudden, and although there were no alternative
sources of industrial employment or investment, this deindustrialization
was achieved with the apparent compliance of most of the workers,
industrialists, and local authorities. Indeed, it was a former mayor of
Huancayo and prominent local businessman who, as minister of labor
in the Peruvian government, was to preside over the closure of the
factories without seriously considering government intervention.[3]

I aim to explore this failure of "industrial nerve" by examining the
origins and characteristics of both the workers and the industrial entrepreneurs and by placing their life careers within a broader regional

129

and national perspective. These factory workers and industrialists are occupational groups with few contemporary representatives in the region; their histories provide one means of assessing the difference that an urban-industrial milieu makes to the life careers and regional commitments of the inhabitants of the Mantaro area. They are useful points of comparison with the small farmers, middlemen, craftsmen, and government employees who now dominate the valley's occupational structure.[4] Since most of these factory workers also originate from, and are still linked to, an individualistic village system of land tenure, land exploitation, and local commercial activity, their behavior helps us to assess the extent to which factory work and interaction "overcome" such background experiences and promote cooperative action. Textile work was also highly paid in comparison with other occupations in the region, and the workers' struggle to form a cooperative provides a case study of the political characteristics of workers whose work situation encourages class solidarity but who represent an elite of workers.[5]

In 1968, after the bankruptcy of the private firm, the factory and its remaining two hundred workers were formed into an industrial cooperative. This cooperative solution proved successful and, by 1973, the factory, now owned and run by its workers, had made substantial profits and begun the modernization of its machinery. Though the labor force is substantially less than in the heyday of the mill, these workers have managed to make a success of a complex industrial and financial operation where private enterprise failed to do so. The success of the enterprise is the more remarkable since the cooperative is formed only from the manual workers of the old factory and does not include the technicians or office workers. Moreover, an industrial cooperative of this size has no precedent in either Peru or Latin America as a whole.

Many of the problems that have faced the cooperative stem from a lack of experience with industrial forms of cooperative organization. Other difficulties arise from limitations that are more general to this form of social and economic organization, such as the tension between individualism and altruism that can become expressed in the exploitation of those within the organization and, to an extent, in the exploitation of the society outside it.[6] It is a tension that stems from members of the Huancayo cooperative being the individual owners and beneficiaries of its capital, while espousing important principles of equity, such as the principle of one man, one vote, and such social aspirations as the continuing education of all members in technical skills and cooperative principles. The tension is aggravated because cooperative organization can become a mediating element in the relationship between the state and its individual citizens. In Peru the state recently has greatly expanded its presence at both national and local levels without possessing the resources for extending bureaucracy to implement fully its control. Cooperative organization thus acquires the added tension of both implementing state control and being the means whereby individual citizens obtain privileged access to government resources.

I argue that Huancayo workers and industrialists had only a limited commitment to industry and industrial work and that their behavior reflects their involvement in social and economic situations apart from those of the industrial enterprise. Yet, in countries like Peru, where the tertiary sector of the urban economy is expanding fastest, industrialization may not be a historically inevitable part of the development process. Also, the power of industry to transform local structures is a reduced one when, as in Peru, it is concentrated in the national metropolis and in capital-intensive production.[7] For both Huancayo workers and industrialists, industry was but one among several possible ways of making a living, rather than a way of life that would increasingly dominate their future and that of the region.

The Huancayo region is economically dependent on Lima and, indirectly, on foreign capital. This dependency is not only a question of the increasing dominance of Lima through its technologically advanced industry and through control of capital and markets. The absence of any self-sustaining regional development in the Mantaro area is mainly due to structures of class relationships that have prevented any large-scale economic initiative developing at the local level.[8] The Huancayo industrialists and businessmen did not develop any major social or economic commitment to the region, to their employees, or to their clients; these latter groups were themselves so differentiated that there was not a sufficient solidarity of interests to identify, and to fight for, a possible basis of regional economic autonomy. This account of a textile factory aims to show that dependency is not only a process imposed from the center—but is also one that is contributed to and, often, sustained by the activities of local people. In this situation it is not surprising that a region's evident relative disadvantage and underdevelopment is not more questioned at the local level.

The Formation of an Industrial Labor Force

In this section, I want to consider certain social and employment characteristics of the workers who entered the factory between 1936 and 1968. The record cards of this entire labor force were available for analysis and provide complementary data to Chaplin's study of the

Lima textile industry.[9] My aim is to assess whether employment in the
factory was, in effect, monopolized by particular social groups from
within the region. Where jobs and access to jobs become controlled by
people from particular villages and particular social backgrounds, the
capacity of management to control and define the nature of its labor
force is limited. Likewise, the impact of the urban and factory milieu
on workers' commitments and orientations is likely to be less when
workers continue to have important social and economic links with
their villages of origin.

From its inception, the factory recruited a predominantly male, and
local, labor force; over the period 1936 to 1968, 60 percent of the 2,457
workers who were ever employed by Manufacturas del Centro were
born either in Huancayo or in the villages and small towns within
fifteen kilometers of the city (table 1). These recruitment patterns
contrast with the trends in the migrant composition of Huancayo's
labor force. Though it is difficult to be sure about the situation in
earlier periods, it is probable that in 1940 about half the adults in the
city were born in Huancayo or in the nearby villages; the life history
data from our 1971 Huancayo survey and data from the village surveys
suggest that from the 1940s onward migrants to Huancayo came predominantly from the more distant villages. By 1972, 60 percent of the
city's adult male population were born in places located more than
fifteen kilometers from Huancayo.[10]

Despite the increasing numbers of migrants "available" for recruitment, the relative predominance of local recruitment to the factory
increased over time. This predominance of a locally recruited textile
labor force contrasts with Chaplin's data on the Lima textile labor
force. In Lima, over half the textile workers were migrants, and the
relative proportions of migrants among textile workers increased as
migrants became a higher proportion of the economically active in
the city.[11]

In the Lima case, there is evidence that patterns of recruitment
were influenced by management policy; many managements expressed
preference for migrants, claiming that they represented a more ame-
nable labor force. The Lima textile migrants came predominantly from
coastal and non-Indian areas; almost all of them had previous nonagricultural work experience before their first textile job. Though
kinship and friendship ties were important in recruitment to the Lima
factories, Chaplin argued that their significance should not be over-
stressed and that some managements discouraged such recruitment.[12]

It is unlikely that the recruitment of a local labor force in Huancayo
was the result of management policy. There is no evidence of any such

TABLE 1
BIRTHPLACE OF FACTORY WORK FORCE AND YEAR OF RECRUITMENT TO FACTORY

Year of Recruitment	Huancayo	Mantaro: Villages within 15 km.	Mantaro: Villages within 40 km.	Huancavelica	North Central Sierra	Southern Sierra	Northern Sierra	Lima	Coast	Foreign	
1945 and before	34	21	12	10	10	1	3	6	2	1	100% (274)
1946–1950	26	34	10	9	7	1	4	4	3	2	100% (943)
1951–1955	28	32	8	8	8	1	5	7	3	—	100% (992)
1956–1960	27	39	9	8	5	1	1	7	2	1	100% (229)
1961–1965	26	53	—	11	—	—	5	—	5	—	100% (19)
Total	28	32	9	9	7	1	4	6	3	1	(2,457) 100%

NOTE: The Mantaro villages within fifteen kilometers are those in the valley surrounding Huancayo, e.g., Sapallanga, Chupaca, Sicaya, San Jerónimo, Ahuac. Those Mantaro villages within forty kilometers are, in practice, those of the provinces of Concepción or Juaja, such as El Mantaro, Quilcas, etc.; these are also valley villages. The villages of Huancavelica are kept separate, although most of these are also within forty kilometers, since they have a separate cultural identity and, on the whole, are poorer than those of the valley.

policy in existing records; when recalling their own recruitment, workers, while stressing the importance of friendship or kinship links or the possession of letters of recommendation, make no mention of there being any explicit preference for those born locally. Indeed, although most of these workers were born locally, many of them had extensive migration experience prior to their factory job. It is also unlikely that management would see any advantage in showing preference for local recruits. The cultural distinctions needed to discriminate between local villagers and those from more distant parts were not part of the cultural stereotypes used by the managers, businessmen, and technicians who formed the industrial elite of Huancayo. Recruitment into the factory was mainly in the hands of two men: a Swiss technician who arrived in Huancayo in the early 1940s and a Lima-born member of an important family of the Peruvian oligarchy, who came to the city to manage the factory. The stereotypes with which these men operated with respect to their workers appear to have been relatively undifferentiated; the workers were regarded as almost entirely of migrant origin and of mainly *cholo* social background.

The relative success of local people in obtaining work in the textile industry is not surprising in the light of the dense population of the valley area and the advantages that proximity gives to those seeking work. Also, employment opportunities in the textile industry of Huancayo suited the patterns of local labor migration. From at least the turn of the century, male heads of household of the valley villages and their elder children left for seasonal and longer-term work in the mines, the coastal cotton plantations, construction, and the cities.[13] This wage labor had become an essential part of the economic fabric of village and small-town life, permitting households to continue farming on small plots and promoting the diversification of local economies in trade, crafts, and small-scale industrial activities.

In the 1940s, there was a decline in opportunities for wage labor in certain sectors of the regional economy; the cotton plantations were in decline and did not need the masses of seasonal workers that had been previously recruited from the Mantaro area. Though the mining labor force was still large, modernization was severely reducing the rate of growth of its labor force and the recruitment of new workers; also, the large-scale construction projects in railways and roads were coming to an end in this period. Perhaps a more significant factor, however, was that the textile industry provided work that was qualitatively suited to the employment needs of local families: it was close to the villages, permitting workers to help out in farming when necessary; it was not an especially arduous or unhealthy job when compared with construction labor or certain mining activities; and the wages paid were relatively good. The relatively high educational levels of the valley population meant that villagers were attractive recruits for the factory.

Wage labor had always been part of the economy of all village households, not just of the poorest. Villagers with more land, a more diversified household economy, and more education had, in general, been able to obtain the better-paid jobs in the urban and mining centers. The poorer families of the valley villages not only could not compete so effectively for jobs as families with more material and cultural resources, but they were often closely tied to subsistence farming and were unable to afford to have members absent for long periods of time. The wealthier village households had developed their economies on the basis of some members' being absent in wage labor or trading ventures and being replaced, where necessary, by hired laborers. These are general patterns, however, and kinship and other relationships were, increasingly, to give even poorer villagers access to good jobs.

Evidence of the social origins of these workers is given by data on their fathers' and on their own educational levels. These data were not available for the whole work force but only for those workers who "survived" until the closure of the factory in 1968. As we shall see, this sample does not differ significantly from the remainder of the work force in those social characteristics that are available for all (i.e., previous employment, age at recruitment, and place of origin).

Of the fathers of workers, 41 percent had completed primary school and a further 16 percent had some secondary education. Forty-seven percent of the fathers had worked most of their lives in jobs other than agriculture, while 53 percent had been small farmers. Half of the fathers had been born in the villages within fifteen kilometers of Huancayo and another 14 percent in Huancayo itself. Some fathers born in the more distant villages of the valley and in the neighboring department of Huancavelica had migrated to Huancayo in the first half of the century. Their city-born children make up almost half the workers born in Huancayo (table 1). The characteristics of workers' fathers and the educational levels of the workers themselves (table 2) are typical of the more prosperous householders in the larger valley villages.

The recruits to the textile industry in Huancayo appear to have come from the more economically diversified village households, and of all recruits only 19 percent claimed to have worked in agriculture previous to employment in the mill (table 3).

The proportion of recruits with experience of nonagricultural work is smaller than is the case in Chaplin's Lima textile sample, but it still amounts to over half a labor force recruited from a predominantly

TABLE 2

LEVEL OF EDUCATION OF FACTORY WORKERS IN 1972

	Percentage
Did not finish primary school	30
Completed primary school	33
Some secondary school	24
Completed secondary school	8
Higher education	5
	——
	100
	——

TABLE 3

PREVIOUS JOB BEFORE EMPLOYMENT IN
MANUFACTURAS AND YEAR OF ENTRY

	1945 or earlier Percent- age	1946– 1950 Per- cent- age	1951– 1955 Per- cent- age	1956– 1960 Per- cent- age	1961– 1965 Per- cent- age	No.
Agricultural	6	16	21	35	19	(171)
Unskilled laborer	15	24	29	19	24	(223)
Construction	—	8	2	6	4	(35)
Transport	1	5	2	5	3	(24)
Textile factory	20	13	12	7	13	(117)
Craftsman	1	6	4	5	4	(38)
Trade	1	1	2	2	2	(16)
Clerical work	—	3	2	2	2	(19)
Student	17	11	16	10	14	(127)
No work or no reply	39	13	10	9	15	(133)
	100	100	100	100	100	

agricultural area.[14] As the years went by, recruits to the factory were increasingly more likely to have had a previous job experience. The rise in the number of agriculturalists recruited over time is likely to reflect both the tendency of workers to sponsor kin or friends who had remained as farmers in the villages and the relative decline in the "availability" of nonagricultural workers as better opportunities developed in Lima and elsewhere.

Evidence of the way in which textile employment fitted into the pattern of job opportunities in the Huancayo area is provided by the age of these workers on first employment in the factory. These workers were first employed in the factory at a relatively late age if compared with Chaplin's Lima sample.[15] The age on employment for the Lima sample varied between eighteen and twenty-two, with the tendency for workers to be recruited at older ages as time went on. The migrants in Chaplin's sample were first recruited when between twenty and twenty-six years of age. The average age on employment in Huancayo, however, was twenty-five, and 17 percent of the workers were recruited when thirty-eight years of age or older. This relatively late age of first recruitment reflects the migration patterns common to the region; migrants of the social backgrounds from which these workers were recruited move around from job to job. This does not reflect any inherent instability in their job commitments but caters to the complex patterns of a household's development. Some job mobility is connected with education, as elder sons leave for the city to work and to obtain education. Three of the union leaders in the factory, for example, came first to Huancayo to get secondary education. They worked to pay their expenses and, in all three cases, claimed that they took the job in Manufacturas as an expedient to allow them to save to continue their studies. The necessity of providing for younger brothers or parents at home was cited in all three cases as the reason why they could not carry out their plan.

Within this context, the job plan of any one household member is necessarily dependent on those of others; the illness of a parent, the ambitions of younger brothers, or changes in marital and family status mean that migrants give up one job and return home or look for another that is more suited to their circumstances. In the sample of workers who survived until 1968, many of their prefactory job careers were influenced by factors of this kind. Some of them initially worked seasonally on the cotton harvests, but when these opportunities ceased and when their own family responsibilities grew, they sought longer-term work in the city. Others had worked in the mines for short periods but returned because their own illness or that of family members made it necessary for them to be nearer home.

The Huancayo textile labor force was relatively unstable when compared with textile workers in Lima. In comparison with Chaplin's Lima sample, turnover in the Huancayo mill is extremely high (table 4).

These differences cannot be accounted for by the relative age of the factories, since Manufacturas is, in fact, older than either La Plata or La Junta; Manufacturas is larger than these latter two but about the same size as Avenida Garibaldi. Part of the reason for Manufacturas's high turnover index is a managerial policy of taking on workers and laying them off with seasonal and cyclical fluctuations in demand for woolen products—a policy that was made easy during the restrictions

TABLE 4

TURNOVER INDICES FOR LIMA AND HUANCAYO
TEXTILE FACTORIES

Huancayo		Lima Sample					
		Avenida Garibaldi		La Plata		La Junta	
1941–1945	32.2	1889–1910	10.7	1942–1946	12.6	1941–1945	4.3
1946–1949	32.3	1911–1920	6.8	1947–1951	3.7	1946–1950	3.4
1950–1953	38.0	1921–1930	3.6	1952–1958	6.9	1951–1959	4.6
1954–1957	15.4	1931–1940	2.5				
1958–1961	12.9	1941–1950	5.1				
1962–1964	3.2	1951–1958	1.0				
1965–1968	13.0						

SOURCES: David Chaplin, *The Peruvian Industrial Labor Force*, p. 148, table 7,
and my own data on the Huancayo factory. The turnover index is
constructed by the following equation:

$$T_i = \frac{\text{Accessions} + \text{Separations}}{\frac{\text{Size of Plant}}{\text{at start of period}} + \frac{\text{Size of Plant}}{\text{at end of period}}} \times 100$$

on worker organization during Odria's authoritarian government (1948–
1956). This explanation is, however, not sufficient to explain the differences, because both the Avenida Garibaldi plant and the La Plata plant
were owned by the same family that owned Manufacturas del Centro.
Management policies of the three mills were coordinated and there was
some interfactory transfer of workers and technicians. While management was probably able to "get away" with more in the provincial
situation, which was less sensitive politically and where the tradition
of worker organization was weaker, the higher provincial labor turnover
is also based on the readiness of this provincial labor force to work for
only short periods.[16]

   To appreciate the possible career strategies of these workers, it is
necessary to place textile wages and the advantages of textile employment within a broader regional context. By using the comparative
wage rates for different jobs, at different times and in different locations,
compiled by Julian Laite, it becomes clear that a job in textiles was
neither consistently better paid than other jobs nor worse paid. For
example, in 1946 one of the sample entered the textile factory, as an
assistant to a weaver, at a wage of 12 U.S. cents a day, which in the
space of a few months, after union bargaining, was raised to 37.5 cents.
In the same year, a foundry worker at Oroya could earn between 61
cents and $2.40 depending on his seniority; transport workers in the

area were reporting wages of around $1.20 a day. The incomes of small traders, in this year, were being estimated at rates of up to $3 a day. All these rates were several times higher than those paid to agricultural labor. After a short time in the textile factory, the worker who had entered at 12 cents a day was put in charge of a loom and started earning a basic rate of 93 cents a day, at age eighteen, which soon increased to $1.50. In 1952, when the mines were paying between 77 cents and $2.60 a day, another entering textile worker began at 64 cents, which was increased in the same year to $1.53 a day at age twenty-two, when this man became a spinning machine operator. Although a weaver, working overtime, could earn almost $260 a month in 1968, assistants and semiskilled workers earned less than a third of this amount, less than they would be paid in the mines or could potentially gain in trade.

Many of the entering workers could not expect significant relative improvements in their situation. The number of well-paid jobs was limited: the weavers, for example, were 10 percent of the labor force. Workers in other sections were less well paid and only the skilled operators of some of the spinning machines approached the earnings of weavers. The opportunities for occupational mobility were limited; the number of workers in charge-hand positions was perhaps 5 percent of the labor force, and the technical supervisors were foreigners. Even among those workers who survived until 1968 and who had an average seniority of some thirteen years, only 14 percent had held a charge-hand position. These surviving workers included disproportionately more weavers and skilled operators than did the work force as a whole, which illustrates a further problem for entering workers—that the best jobs were filled by seniority. Among the weavers, there appears to have been little turnover. The average seniority of the sixty-nine weavers in 1965 was sixteen years, compared to the nine years of what was, by then, a stable work force.

Under these conditions, the existence of more favorable wage-labor opportunities elsewhere would attract workers away at certain conjunctures: the need for extra cash because of a change in family status, helping siblings in education, and so on. For some, textile employment offered the possibility of obtaining a little capital from severance pay and from other benefits to which they were entitled under the law. They could use this capital to set themselves up in business or to buy land or animals. In our 1972 city-wide sample of Huancayo, we interviewed fourteen adult males who had worked, at one time, in the textile industry and had left before its closure. Ten of them had set themselves up, independently, in commerce or small workshops after leaving the industry. Of these, five claimed that they improved their incomes after separation and three registered a decline in income. Some of the labor force were prepared to view their job in the textile factory as temporary wage labor—a source of cash that might lead to a permanent job but might also lead to other forms of wage labor. The owner of one of the smaller Huancayo textile factories reported in an interview that at the height of the textile boom in Huancayo, in the late 1950s, it was quite common for his workers to treat their work seasonally, combining it with farm production, independent craft activity, or commerce.[17] Such patterns of employment are not likely to have been common or to have been permitted in a large factory like Manufacturas, and there are few recorded cases in the factory archives of repeated entries and separations.

The extent to which textile employment fitted the general pattern of wage labor in the area is also seen in the characteristics of two overlapping groups of workers: those who stayed less than a year in the factory and those who were employed in the construction department of the factory. This latter group is one of the lowest paid groups and is a category that textile employers find useful because such workers are not protected, to the same extent as other workers, by the laws pertaining to length of service and protection against dismissal. In the case of both groups, their social characteristics might be expected to differ significantly from those of longer-serving workers in the production branches of the factory. However, both those who stay less than a year and the construction workers are quite similar to other workers. The range of previous employment is almost identical to that of all factory workers; their places of origin are similar and their age on recruitment is, on average, the same. This is not, then, a clearly stratified industrial labor force in which the best jobs are kept by experienced and well-qualified firstcomers, leaving the temporary, ill-paid work to a "reserve army" of recent migrants. The longer-serving workers retained an interest in agriculture, keeping their rights to land in the villages and, at times, farming the land on weekends or with family and kin labor. Of the present textile workers, 44 percent farm land, usually with the aid of their relatives in the village of their origin.

Present-day workers in Manufacturas report that the accommodations of the workers in the 1940s and 1950s were mainly rented, and many, if not most, of the workers made a practice of returning to their home villages on weekends. One of the union leaders commented that these residential patterns changed when the development of the transport system in the valley made it possible for people to live in their home villages and commute, early in the morning, to the factory. He attributed the lessening of social activity outside the factory to this change, and at present almost 20 percent of the textile cooperative's work force lives in the nearby villages.

For some of the workers, the villages served as much more than simple dormitories; at least three of the present cooperative leaders were active in village politics and administration during the 1940s and 1950s, holding office in the village while still working in the factory. Nor was the textile work force separated from other economic activities in the region. Their close kin, including wives, were involved in a variety of jobs in trade, the services, and small manufacturing, as well as agriculture; some of this work complemented the factory work, as in the case of those who traded in cloth or set up tailoring or dressmaking establishments. Workers recruited others through kinship and friendship ties. In the sample of workers who survived until 1968, 53 percent claimed that they obtained their job through the recommendation of a relative or friend, and over half had relatives, friends, and fellow villagers working in the factory before they themselves joined. Of those who originated in the villages near Huancayo, only 12 percent had no fellow villagers working in the factory before they themselves began to work there.

Throughout the factory's history there were many cases of brothers, fathers and sons, mothers and daughters, uncles and nephews working together. Groupings of fellow villagers were also an evident part of the factory's organization; the fiesta of a large village such as Sapallanga would deplete the factory's work force for a few days, and, on occasion, both management and union were asked to contribute material or financial help to a village fiesta or project. These relationships with the villages and towns of the region were extended to work centers where these textile workers had lived previously or where they had relatives or friends living. It was quite common for them to spend their holidays visiting kin on the coast or in Lima or to return to their villages; they frequently report taking a few days off from the factory to visit and help a sick relative. The facility with which these workers moved around is one factor that, as we shall see, contributed to management's inability to confine industrial conflicts to the factory environment.

This emphasis on the interrelationships of factory and region must be complemented by a consideration of the nature of the factory and its organization. In the factory there was considerable interaction and mutual aid within the different sections. Interaction was more limited between sections, partly because of rules restricting movement within the factory and the prevalence of shift work. In certain sections, such as that of the loom operators, mutual aid was important in handling the job; though each loom had its operator, it was possible for one operator to keep an eye on another loom and, occasionally, on two or three looms, while the other weavers took a break or went for a meal. These and other mutual services, together with the concentration of looms in one place, meant that weavers were among the most cohesive groups in the factory. They were also the best-paid workers and were active in union politics, especially in defense of their particular privileges and relative rates of pay. The factory also operated a seniority rule, so access to the looms depended more on length of service than on evaluations of performance or potential performance. This did create internal divisions among the work force, and some workers complained that insistence on this rule by both management and union barred good workers from the more lucrative operations and prevented higher rates of production. For most of this period workers were paid by piece work.

The factory was a fully integrated textile mill containing all the essential processes, from washing the raw wool and spinning to weaving and finishing. This organization entailed a relatively high degree of worker interdependence, as production in one section depended on the levels of production in other sections. Within most sections, the antiquated machinery also necessitated a great deal of worker interaction on such matters as loading and changing spools. At the same time, there was a relatively large span of control in the factory hierarchy; sections had a charge-hand and a technical supervisor, and these supervisors reported directly to management. The supervisors were foreign, usually Italians, and were recruited directly to their positions. This technical supervisory staff had little social contact with the workers and knew little of local cultural practices; present-day workers remember these technicians with much more hostility than they remember the management itself. The complaints made when recording their impressions of these years of private enterprise are mainly against the authoritarian practices of the supervisors and their readiness to fault the work force.

The overall picture is that of a relatively mobile textile labor force that was not committed to an urban-industrial life career. This situation reflects the absence of a clear separation of the urban and its occupational world from the rural and its economic activities. The industrialization exemplified by the textile industry of Huancayo was one economic venture among many in the region; there was no reason, then or later, for local people to attribute to it any especial place in the trends of the future. We need now to consider whether such perceptions had any echoes in the ways in which the owners of the factory viewed the process they had helped initiate.

The Development of an Industrial Capitalism

The first textile factory was established in Huancayo in 1928, but it was at the end of the 1930s that the industry began to develop rapidly. Its expansion, in Huancayo, was based on proximity to the sources of the raw material, wool, on the availability of a labor force in a densely populated region in which wage labor was well established, and on the growth of a local market for the finished product. The expansion of the mining labor force, in particular, created a demand for woolen clothing suited to the cold temperatures of the mine altitudes. Manufacturas was started by a Central European Jewish trader in woolen textiles whose business had become increasingly based on selling to the mine townships. The major obstacle to the expansion of his business was the difficulty of obtaining supplies. On the bankruptcy of one of his debtors—a small Huancayo producer of hats and other traditional garments—he took over the factory and began cloth production. This original factory became the basis of three of Huancayo's major textile factories. The original Manufacturas del Centro was transferred in 1950 to a new and larger site and the old site became Manufacturas de Seda, specializing in rayon goods. A third factory, Filatex Huancayo, grew out of the second location of the first factory. All three factories were owned by the same company, and their total labor force was probably in the region of fifteen hundred workers by 1955.

The development of Manufacturas was not based on local capital nor, for that matter, did it respond to the commitments of locally based industrialists. The original owner was a merchant and his main interests appear to have remained in trade. He spent little time in the factory, moved permanently to Lima after the first few years of the factory's inception, and established a chain of retailing outlets. The expansion of the firms was made possible by bank loans.

It also involved a complicated strategy of indirect financing, provided by the manager of a rival factory, Los Andes. This man, an Italian immigrant well connected with the Italian banking interests in Lima, served as mayor of Huancayo in 1940. He managed Los Andes on behalf of the Lima-based Pardo family, which owned sugar estates and some of the large Lima textile factories. This Italian immigrant owned 51 percent of the original shares of Manufacturas, apparently through obtaining bank loans and through supplying machinery, raw material, and semifinished products from Los Andes. When these maneuvers came to light he ceased to manage Los Andes and moved to Lima, where he became involved in the retailing side of textiles. The machinery that Manufacturas acquired in these ways was secondhand. The bulk of it came from a consignment that was destined for India but had been diverted to Peru because of the Second World War. The Swiss chief technician and manager of Manufacturas, for its entire history as a private enterprise, was awaiting the arrival of that consignment in India and was brought to Peru when the machinery was acquired by Manufacturas.

The economic and political conditions of Peru, at this time, did not permit the financing of enterprise by the issue of public stock; the indirect and informal means of financing an enterprise used in the case of Manufacturas were, consequently, quite common. In the case of Manufacturas, there was no substantial investment of capital from wealthy local families; the money that was being made in Huancayo in this period was being invested in Lima rather than locally.

In the first days of the factory, when the owners were still resident in Huancayo, they took an active interest in the factory. Fearing the growth of unionism among workers, since textile unions were already strong in Lima, the owners treated the workers paternalistically. They provided a locale for recreation, encouraged the formation of football teams and other sports, and sponsored a *Fraternal de Obreros* that provided cultural events, such as film shows and welfare functions. In these years, "exemplary" workers were rewarded by extra payments, workers were often hired directly by the owners, and the owners acquired a reputation for philanthropy in the city and region. One of them donated prizes for sporting events to one of the nearby villages from which many Manufacturas workers were recruited.[18] Union formation was strongly opposed by these owners, and workers attempting to form unions were dismissed. The local political position of the owners as municipal officials and as financial contributors to political parties also safeguarded their interests; their attempts to discipline "troublemakers" received the support of the local authorities.

By such means, the early history of Manufacturas is one of a relative absence of labor conflicts; although raises were granted, wage levels still remained substantially below those of Lima. The advent to power of Odría, a military dictator from 1948 to 1956, enabled Manufacturas to continue the policy of preventing effective worker organization. Indeed, in 1953 a report made to the Peruvian government by foreign economic assessors stressed the favorable conditions for the further development of the textile industry in Huancayo, emphasizing the cheapness of the labor, which, the report remarks, was dependable and not unionized.[19]

These successful strategies to ensure a cheap and dependable labor force were based on the owners' commitments to, and knowledge of, the local context. When these owners became absentee in the late forties, this level of direct involvement dropped sharply. The factory became effectively controlled by the Swiss technician and by a Lima-born member of the Prado family, which had, by this time, acquired a controlling interest in the factory. This management continued previous policies of attempting to weaken worker organization but had little involvement in, or knowledge of, the local political and economic context. Also, the interests of the owners of the factory in the production process diminished as the factory became more tied to banking interests.

The original owners had raised large bank loans to finance the factory's expansion. Also, they made a practice of giving extended credit to retailers, including their own retailing outlets, and they financed these credits by bank letters of credit. The involvement of the Banco Popular (the bank of the Prado family) in the factory became so great that the bank took over a controlling share of the factory. With banking interests in control, the emphasis on credit financing intensified. This was due partly to the relatively high cost of Peruvian textiles, protected from competition by a high tariff and inefficiently produced by antiquated machinery, so that retailers required extended credit to finance their operations. The factory provided this and was covered by the bank credit. In this situation, the profits of the enterprise appeared in the banking and retailing operations rather than in the production process. Given the high cost of the loans it furnished, the factory could not expect to make a profit, and so long as the factory kept producing the goods to be sold, profits would be guaranteed to those other parts of the same enterprise engaged in finance and retailing. The situation became even more complex when the enterprise began to use the factory and its machinery as guarantee for loans raised abroad that were used not to finance technical improvements but to extend the credit operations.

The absentee ownership, the dominance of banking interests, and the emphasis on production per se rather than on a realistic assessment of the cost of production, meant that the industrial capitalism that developed in Huancayo was orientated not to production but to commerce and finance. This development was not accidental, but reflected the organization of dependent capitalism. Sources of finance were based in Lima or abroad and access to this financing depended on having relationships with the dominant capitalist groups; provincial entrepreneurs were foreign immigrants who by kinship or common origins could develop easy lines of credit with the major foreign-dominated Lima financing houses.

Another factor limiting the local commitments of the industrialists was that the factory was part of commercial operations that did not depend on the control and development of local markets. The cash incomes provided by the large-scale mining operations and, to a lesser extent, by other wage-labor opportunities tied to plantations and construction meant that the selling of textile products did not depend upon local agrarian development. The supply of town-made textile products did not displace rural artisans and create needs among a rural population that could be satisfied only by migration to the town and by industrial work. The economy of the villages did not change under the impact of industrialization; equally, the industrialists had no particular ongoing interests in maintaining a political and economic control of either the city or its hinterland as a means of guaranteeing their labor force and ensuring their markets. Since neither workers nor factory owners were totally committed to industry as a source of livelihood, there was considerable flexibility and ambiguity in the relationship between the two parties. Out of this situation emerged the "successful" deindustrialization of what was once an industrial city.

The Union and the Deindustrialization of Huancayo

In discussing the closure of Manufacturas, I am concerned with three main issues. One of these is to understand how it is that an industry was able to lay off some two thousand workers over a period of ten years between 1958 and 1968 without more disturbance and conflict than, in fact, occurred. The relative ease with which this was done is the more surprising when it is remembered that textiles represented the only industry in Huancayo and that employment in the textile industry was not replaced by employment in other industries. Nor was migration to Lima or to the mines a solution. In these years, employment opportunities were scarce everywhere and there was a decline in the rate of outmigration from the valley area.

The second and related issue is the persistence of some workers in hanging onto their jobs and insisting that the factory become a cooperative. The two hundred workers who were to form the cooperative resisted the closure of the factory to the end. They withstood the harassment of the owners, who kept the factory in short supply of necessary materials and finally locked out the workers. These workers went on a hunger strike and, after constant lobbying in Lima over a period of years, succeeded in having the factory turned into a cooperative. Their success and endurance is the more remarkable since no other body of Huancayo textile workers persisted to this extent and many of their own fellow workers were to leave the factory, voluntarily, under the threat of redundancy and closure. The third issue concerns the behavior in this period of management, who made little effort to modernize or improve factory organization.

These three issues are illustrated by the history of the textile workers' union in Manufacturas. This union is a good example of the benefits gained by cooperative endeavor. Through the course of its history, it expanded its organization from twelve members in 1945 to a position where it became the recognized representative of the workers and was entrusted by management with several important administrative functions within the factory. The union ensured that workers benefited from the wage agreements negotiated nationally by the Textile Workers Federation. These agreements included an automatic wage increase tied to the cost of living index, a fixed bonus based on productivity, and full protection under government-enforced social security regulations covering sickness and health care, severance pay, and pension rights.

By the mid-fifties, textile workers, including those of Manufacturas, were among the highest-paid workers in the country, and in 1955 a weaver managing two looms and benefiting from the normal bonus could earn some $4.70 daily in comparison with the $1 of an ordinary bank clerk, the $1.84 of a semiskilled worker in the gasoline industry, and the $1.50 of a skilled worker in the metal industry.[20] The union organized collections in Manufacturas to help the family of a sick or dead member, ran a sports club for members, arranged financial help for children of members to carry on their studies, and started a consumers' cooperative. The union also enforced safety regulations and ensured that the supervisory staff—which was mainly foreign—treated their workers with more care than had been the case previously.

The first union had been formed in 1945 when workers who had had experience of union activity in the Lima textile mills joined Manufacturas and started pressing for a union. In 1947, the union was destroyed with the coming to power of Odría and the dismissal from the factory of the union leaders. By the end of Odría's period of power a group of seventeen workers had begun to reorganize the union, in 1953. These workers met in secret, often under the pretext of a soccer game, but they were constantly harassed by the management and several were to lose their jobs. Finally, in 1954, after constant trips back and forth to Lima, and despite the harassment of the local police, the committee obtained ministry recognition as a union.

The success of these workers in reorganizing the union was due to the evident weakness of the provincial authorities and to the ability of workers to exploit this weakness by going directly to Lima. Many of the workers had worked previously in Lima and had union contacts. After 1954, and especially after 1956, when the APRA political party gained increasing political influence under the civilian government of Bustamante, the textile unions became increasingly powerful. In Huancayo, the local textile union was affiliated with the national union and became the most powerful element in a departmental workers' union that included both rural and urban workers and such self-employed workers as taxidrivers and barbers.

This union played an important part in local political organization, extending the unionization of workers and gaining representation in provincial government. Several of the Manufacturas union leaders served on the provincial council of Huancayo in these years and one became a member of the Board of Public Works, which was delegated by the central government with distributing public works contracts in the region. The Manufacturas union leaders were also involved in extending unionization to the smaller textile factories and workshops of Huancayo. Though to this day these small-scale industrialists blame the union for the failure of their businesses, it seems that the union drive had only limited success. The small workshops were composed of a predominantly female labor force and the workers were easily intimidated by the owners. In this period most, but not all, of the Manufacturas union leaders were *apristas*. One of them had been an *aprista* union official in the mine center of Oroya before he came to Manufacturas.

Most of the local textile leaders were recruited from among the somewhat more prosperous rural households whose members, whether in village or town, were *aprista* supporters. Indeed, the range of urban and rural work organizations included in the departmental union reflects the labor-migration patterns of the area, in which members of the same household often entered different types of employment in the work centers. In one case from Manufacturas, for example, one brother was an *aprista* metalworker in the Oroya foundry, another an *aprista* textile worker in Huancayo, another an *aprista* shopkeeper in Huancayo, and a parent an *aprista* farmer and mayor in the home village. In this situation, it was not simply the conditions of industrial work that radicalized the workers; the economic organization of the area and the opportunities and limitations it presented to local households also stimulated political organization in the work place. The political ideology of APRA was well fitted to this situation, since it attacked foreign monopolies and the national oligarchy and emphasized the importance of native enterprise. The Huancayo textile workers were confronted with an absentee ownership closely tied to the foreign-linked Peruvian oligarchy, but they were also closely linked to the small-scale economic entrepreneurship of the region.

From 1956 onward, the management of the factory ceased to control worker organization and demands. Worker demands were mainly negotiated at a national level and there was little hard bargaining to be done at the Huancayo end. Relationships at work between management and workers became, in this situation, increasingly harmonious. The union won the right to appoint, on strict seniority, the heads of the different sections of the factory; grievances between workers and supervisors were handled between union and management. In these years, the work force became increasingly stabilized, and the union negotiated with management to restrict temporary recruitment and the putting out of work. These were also the years when the textile industry was suffering the effects of competition from contraband material. Production was restricted and management dealt directly with the union over the question of laying off workers.[21]

In the union minutes for these years, there is a sense that the union became part of management. Indeed, some workers complain in the minutes that the union, through its strict enforcement of the seniority rule, is acting against their interests. When the present-day workers remember the benefits they gained from union membership, they overwhelmingly stress the economic ones—won at the national level—and rarely mention protection against the abuses of the private firm or of its local management. When asked how they had liked the private firm, 64 percent replied that they had liked working for it, over half claimed that their wages had been good, and 70 percent claimed that they had been treated well personally.

The union leaders were equally positive, 68 percent of them claiming that they had been well treated by the private firm. Certain events of the period indicate that these positive reactions are not simply over-fond memories; during the height of the conflict betwen union and management over the closure of the factory, the union made a presentation to the manager to mark the years of his service. The cooperative formed from among these workers was to make this man their first general manager. Their second general manager and current executive head had been one of the general managers of the Lima office of the private firm, Manufacturas del Centro, and had attempted to get the union to accept the closure of the factory.

In the early sixties, the union worked closely with management in arranging for the gradual laying off of the work force. Though the union consistently fought to prevent or diminish the number of layoffs throughout this period, the layoffs that did occur, numbering some five hundred workers, were implemented with the union's agreement. This agreement was obtained on the understanding that those laid off would receive indemnities over and above those prescribed by the law, would be given gifts of blankets, and would be those who had entered the factory last. The only exception made to this seniority rule was that of the last layoff, when one whole section was closed. This section— *peinados* (finely finished cloth)—produced articles in little demand, but their workers had been some of the most active in denouncing the abuses of the firm and in attempting to obtain better wages by go-slow and other devices. In the union minutes, when it is finally agreed that the whole section should be laid off (1967), the union leaders justify their decision by commenting on the irresponsibility of this section, stating that they had brought the situation on their own heads.

We can understand these developments by first recalling the earlier description of the labor force. It was a highly mobile labor force linked closely to other sections of the regional economy. For many of these workers, the opportunity to obtain an indemnity and set themselves up in small business or buy land was an attractive proposition. For others, it was clearly an acceptable proposition. Thus, one of the union leaders, who stayed on to become a leader of the cooperative, commented as follows in recalling the last years of the factory: "I didn't like resting and I wanted something to do because I didn't have much faith that I would continue working in the firm or coop, especially since the firm began to lay off workers from about 1963, so I took up tailoring in my spare time." Other of the union leaders also recalled making their contingency plans; a group of them intended to set up a weaving workshop and another had already set up his wife in dressmaking after she lost her job in the factory. An indication of the extent to which the nature of the regional economy allowed for the absorption of this industrial labor force is the degree to which the firm's reduction of its labor was accomplished voluntarily; about 20 percent of the reduction was accounted for by the normal process of mobility, and a further 20 percent consisted of workers who accepted the offer of an indemnity, irrespective of their seniority.

Another indication of the nature of this absorption is given by considering what happened to the workers of another Huancayo textile factory (Los Andes) when it closed in 1969. These data must be treated with caution since they are based on the recollections of the contemporary Manufacturas workers of people whom they knew and are likely to be biased toward those who stayed locally and who were active in the Los Andes union. Of the 150 Los Andes workers cited by respondents, 55 percent stayed in Huancayo and 24 percent went back to their villages of origin. The most frequent occupation cited as the present job of these former textile workers was trade (28 percent), with a further 20 percent working in agriculture and 13 percent in craft work. Many of those who chose to go into trade or agriculture and used their indemnity for these purposes later regretted their choice. Former Los Andes workers organized themselves in 1972 to petition the government to reopen the factory, claiming that they found it hard to make a living. Yet the diversity of small-scale economic possibilities available regionally and forming part of the experience and expectations of workers is a very important factor in the acceptance of redundancy in a situation where there is no other industrial work available.

The behavior of the union becomes more understandable when the characteristics of the union leaders are compared with those of the labor force as a whole. It is the weavers who tend to dominate union office. They formed a cohesive group that came frequently to meetings and were well organized in defense of their interests. They were the best paid of the workers and had the greatest seniority. Apart from being protected by the rule that said that union officials could not be laid off, those who were active in the union, whether holding office or not, had sufficient seniority to escape redundancy. Other of their characteristics made it more likely that they would be committed to industrial work. They were better educated than the bulk of the work force, with 76 percent having attained some secondary education. Their social background in other aspects appears to have been somewhat superior to that of their fellow workers, with only two of them having fathers who had not completed primary school. They and their fathers were born in or near Huancayo. It also seems that they had more of an industrial tradition in their backgrounds: 52 percent of them had been industrial workers prior to joining Manufacturas and only 8 percent had had no previous job or had worked in agriculture. Those whose fathers were farmers formed 24 percent, while 32 percent had fathers who had been craftsmen.

The closure of the factory was more of a threat to the way of life of the union leaders, because of their age and previous work experience, than it was to that of many of their fellow workers. The leaders' social life had become heavily orientated toward the factory. They report many more friendships with other workers inside and outside the work place than do the other cooperative workers.

The final stages of the factory's life were part of the national textile crisis; indeed, the local circumstances of Manufacturas were subordinated to these national issues. By the early 1960s, the textile industry had reached a stage of acute crisis, brought on by the readiness of management and workers to seek in tariff protection the solution to the industry's problems. Confronted by wage demands and the burden of social security provisions, textile management gave way to union demands rather than suffer strikes, and recouped by raising prices and protecting their product from competition by securing discriminatory tariffs against imported textiles. As the price of textiles rose, it became increasingly difficult to find an internal market for them without resort to exaggerated devices of credit finance. Also it became more and more profitable to risk importing contraband textiles. Some managements did attempt to solve the problem by modernizing their factories and installing more automatic equipment. The strength of the unions made this a difficult operation, however, since it became difficult to make workers redundant. Savings on automatic looms were offset by agreements whereby their operators would care for fewer than was logistically possible and be paid considerably more for their labor. Some managements took to setting up new factories alongside their old ones, using the flexibility given by recruiting a new labor force to negotiate more favorable working conditions. The old factory would be kept with its large labor force, but it would be increasingly, if surreptitiously, run down so that it could be declared bankrupt and closed without incurring crippling obligations to the workers.

It was this last strategy that was being used in the case of Manufacturas. As the owners (the Prado family) recognized that the strength of the local union prevented profitable operations, they began to remove the better machinery, some of the material, and even newly imported machinery and place it in their newer factories. The extension of credit to retailers also contributed to increasing the operating debt of the factory. By 1966, the private firm was declaring losses of some $900,000 compared with a paid-up capital of some $1,500,000; these losses were finally to rise to some $4,000,000.[22] Much of this loss was, however, attributable to the devaluation of the Peruvian *sol*. The firm had contracted foreign credits of some $3,000,000 to cover its credit operations and, with devaluation, found these obligations increased by half.

The major interest of the firm remained that of having at hand a supply of goods. This policy was apparent in a suggestion of the owners that the factory should be cooperativized and placed in the hands of the workers. The reasons why a capitalist firm should wish to see itself turned into a cooperative are not difficult to find. The cooperative ensured the supply of goods but did not involve the heavy financial obligations involved in running the factory. When it put forward the proposal, the private company was prepared to hand over the stock, machinery, and buildings and let the workers control the operations, but the owners wished to keep control of the retailing and financing of the operation. These, of course, were the parts of the operation that had always been the most profitable. By giving the workers control of the production, the firm got rid of the most unprofitable part.

Nothing more clearly demonstrates the failure of industrial capitalism in Peru. Their inability to come to terms with worker organization or to take a direct interest in the productive process meant that these capitalists could succeed only by persuading their workers to take on full responsibility for production. Equally, the workers had placed themselves in a situation in which the only way to keep their work going was to become small-scale capitalists by investing their social security and indemnity rights in the purchase of their industry.

The Formation of an Industrial Cooperative

The private firm became a cooperative in November of 1968. The terms of the final agreement were that the firm valued the factory, its land, and its machinery at $26,000 and the material in the factory at a further $13,000. This served as a partial payment to the workers in respect to their pension and indemnity rights. The rest of the amount owed to the workers—some $130,000—was to be made available as a bank credit within two months. The risk the workers took was that if their enterprise failed they would lose the individual compensation they would otherwise have received (an average of some $680 each). The white-collar employees of the factory, whose compensation was much higher, chose to settle directly with the firm and did not enter the cooperative; twenty of the workers made the same decision.

In retrospect, the agreement was a highly favorable one for the workers, since the valuation of the factory was extremely low. This agreement was reached after months of intense negotiations with the aid of the national textile union, the congressional representatives of the province, and the minister of labor. The firm insisted on a much higher valuation for the factory. The official agencies, including the national textile union and the government's cooperative agency, discouraged the idea of the cooperative on the grounds that (a) it would not have sufficient working capital, and (b) the workers were not sufficiently experienced to run such a complex enterprise. What broke the impasse was the military take-over of October 1968. The Manufacturas union leaders confess that, at first, they were worried that a military government would not be sympathetic to their demands; however, they decided to offer their support immediately to both the new provincial and the new national military authorities and to outline their case. In fact, they received strong support from both these authorities; the military officer who was vice-minister of labor personally attended the meetings with the private firm and finally forced a solution. The same officer became head of the government cooperative agency and pushed through the official recognition of the cooperative. The workers' representatives who took part in these negotiations attribute the collaboration of the military government to a desire to avoid both social and political problems in the first months of power.

Despite the difficulties over the negotiations with the private firm, the workers still chose to work closely with some members of the management. The factory manager was asked to stay on as manager of the cooperative, as were several of the technical supervisors; the wife of one of the general managers of the Prado enterprises became, with the vice-minister, the patron of the cooperative at its inauguration. Indeed, the cooperative immediately entered into a contract with several former managers of the Prado enterprises who had formed a private business firm. This firm handled the commercialization and financial negotiations of the cooperative in the first years of its existence. The salaries of the business managers were paid directly or through commission and were some ten times greater than the initial wage of the workers.

The cooperative workers were conscious of their interests and skillful in their defense, but they did not define their interests as threatened by direct exploitation on the part of management. The capitalism to which the workers were opposed was viewed as a distant, impersonal force that many of them saw to be beyond not only their control but also that of management and government.

The history of the cooperative from the moment of its inception is one of remarkable success both socially and economically. By 1972, the cooperative was making a gross profit of some $1,900,000, had taken effective steps to modernize its machinery, was expanding its sales to such an extent that it had difficulty in supplying its customers, and felt itself capable of competing not only nationally but also within the Andean common market. Also, despite the problems that I outline below, the workers have had little difficulty in managing their own enterprise, extending its welfare services, and remaining on good terms

with each other. I want now to consider the problems that the cooperative faced in the four years of its life until 1972.

The first issue is a familiar problem in the organization of a production cooperative—the possible conflict between members' interests
as shareholders in the cooperative and their position as wage earners.
In the case of Manufacturas, this conflict appeared in the tendency for
cooperative members to place their individual interests as owners of
capital above their interests as workers committed to the production
process. Indeed, the cooperative showed the same tendency as private
enterprise to neglect production and overemphasize the commercial
aspect of the enterprise. One indication of these problems was the reluctance of cooperative members to agree to the reinvestment of their
profits in the modernization of the plant. This reluctance was overcome
by 1972, but it remained as an undercurrent of discontent among
members.

This problem of a conflict of interests can be analyzed in two separate
cases. The first concerns the increasing interest of members in the private advantages that they could derive from the cooperative. Members
were allowed to take cash loans from the cooperative; they also had a
right to take goods from the cooperative warehouse on credit and at
a discount that was significantly better than that given to wholesale
merchants. Since there was a demand for the goods of the cooperative,
the discounts and credits represented a charge on the profitability of
the cooperative. The extent of these credits was, moreover, of such a
scale as to make it probable that they were being used to further members' private commercial interests. The outstanding indebtedness of
members to the cooperative by the end of 1971 was 1,319,000 *soles*
($31,000), or an average of $185 per member—about one-and-a-half
months' salary per member. Some members were in debt up to $480.
More significant than this, however, was that this indebtedness was
mainly in the form of credits with the warehouse (70 percent of the
indebtedness) and indicated a scale of private transactions in the firm's
goods that, in many cases, must have been the basis of quite thriving
commercial enterprises run by wife or kin. These practices are good
examples of some of the ways in which formal enterprise is linked to,
and makes possible, the informal economic activities that give employment to much of the working population of cities like Huancayo and
Lima.

Many cooperative members regarded the factory as a resource they
were entitled to exploit individually. In the beginning, members tended
to remove material from the factory for their own use. They also de-

manded loans from cooperative funds to promote private interests, such as establishing a transport enterprise. In 1972, one of the cooperative leaders was discovered to have been systematically, though indirectly, removing funds from the cooperative. This man had entered into partnership with a prominent local wholesale and retail merchant and was supplying him with goods on credit, without entering these in the accounts. By 1972, goods totaling some $480,000 were involved; the official's defense was that he was merely operating a form of extended credit and that the money would have been repaid. The significant element in this case was that this particular official clearly believed that he had done nothing that would harm the cooperative. He had always been an energetic and perceptive member of the cooperative administration. Even after his case became public, he received support from a group of cooperative members. The case did serve, however, to make members more conscious of the dangers of letting private interests intrude into their cooperative responsibilities.

From the first year of its operation, the cooperative made a practice of contracting workers to work in the different sections of the factory. These workers did not become members of the cooperative and were paid at a rate that was less than half that of the regular workers. Also, they were not registered under the social security system and had no rights either to social security benefits, including those of health and pension, or to indemnity on being laid off. Such arrangements are legally possible in Peru in the case of temporary workers who stay less than three months; in practice, however, the contracted labor stayed much longer and was used as a normal part of the work force. This use of contracted labor was against both the cooperative spirit and the government's regulations.

Also, with the introduction, by the military government, of the "industrial community" (*comunidad industrial*), workers with more than three months of service would be entitled to a share in the enterprise's profits, put aside as capital for them. As this capital grows, workers in the industrial community become entitled to representation in the administration of the enterprise. In the case of Manufacturas, the anomalous situation arose that the cooperative should by law have contained a *comunidad industrial*, with the cooperative members standing to the contracted workers as capitalist employers of their labor. The cooperative administration was careful to conceal its use of contracted labor to avoid this outcome, but in 1972 the situation came to the notice of the ministry of labor and the government's organization for social and political mobilization, SINAMOS. At first, the government agencies insisted that the industrial community be established; they later relented, on the understanding that those contracted employees who were left should be incorporated as full members of the cooperative.

Thus cooperative members, despite their long experience of defending their interests against employers, disregarded the rights of other workers. It would be easy to use this case as an example of worker elitism or of the tendency of those placed in positions of power and advantage to adopt bourgeois values. Yet this is not the sense that I obtained through interviewing and talking with the cooperative members. They regarded their actions as favors to others: one remarked that he sponsored a contracted worker because the worker came from the same village and needed work; the cooperative members said that even the wage paid to contracted workers was better than that obtainable in casual employment in the city. Also, the hiring of contracted labor was part of the household and family economy of cooperative members. Of the seventy-one workers under contract to the cooperative, fifty-three were close kin of cooperative members, mainly sons, daughters, or sons-in-law. Indeed, the cooperative administration was quite explicit in encouraging members to recruit their close relatives as contracted workers. It avoided complaints, since their sponsors would take responsibility for the contracted workers, and it helped out a family's economy. Some of the contracted labor were using the job as a means of financing their studies.

The cooperative also faced the dilemma that its members were an aging group of workers; in 1972, 54 percent of the members were forty-six years of age or older. Given the exhausting nature of textile work at high altitudes, many of the older members were beginning to feel the strain of keeping up production. At the same time, they had little confidence that the period of high production through which the cooperative was passing would last for long. They were aware of, and constantly told about, the dangers of competition from abroad when Peru became a full member of the Andean common market. They feared that it would mean a period of lower income as they made sacrifices to invest in machinery and to modernize. In this situation, the cooperative framework produced an acute dilemma: the cooperative needed to increase its production to meet demand and the quickest way to do this, in the absence of more modern machinery, was to expand the labor force. Yet taking on new members represented a permanent addition to the labor force under cooperative rules—an addition that could be made superfluous by market competition or by increased mechanization.

The difficulties of this dilemma are more apparent when the productivity of members and contracted labor is compared. The contracted labor was dispersed throughout the factory; among the weavers, for whom data are available, the productivity of contracted labor using the same looms was consistently higher than that of members, being about 21 percent higher in 1971 and 8 percent higher in 1972. The contracted workers were more productive despite a greater percentage of machine stoppage, due mainly to their absenteeism. Contracted labor also tended to be assigned the more arduous shifts, such as the night shifts.

Though most of the contracted workers were kin, members did not view them as being replacements who would carry on the family tradition of textile work. Though almost all the cooperative members had children, only 48 percent wanted a child to follow in their footsteps in the cooperative. Many members had encouraged their children to study, and, of those members with children eighteen years or older, 53 percent had children who were either studying in, or had finished, higher education. Among the leaders of the cooperative (the old union leaders), 75 percent had a child in higher education. The range of jobs held by the children of members also indicates the absence of a strong family commitment to industrial work: of eldest sons with a job, 22 percent were professionals, 25 percent were white-collar workers, and 13 percent worked in commerce. Of the remaining eldest sons 20 percent had skilled or semiskilled jobs in craft or industry. Most of these eldest children had migrated to work and live in Lima.

In these respects, the characteristics of the cooperative families were no different from those of other families in the region with sufficient resources to help their children begin careers. Regionally, the emphasis on education and obtaining a professional or stable clerical job is a strong one, reflecting not only the prestige of these occupations but also an assessment of the opportunities offered by the expansion of government and associated services. Industrial work was important to these cooperative members because it offered a high and steady income, could provide work for some family members, often on a temporary basis, and was a stepping-stone to other occupational opportunities.

There were specific elements in the Manufacturas situation that gave rise to organizational difficulties in the cooperative. First, the origins of the cooperative in the struggles of a labor union against management and the origins of the cooperative leadership in a union leadership produced specific problems. We have already reviewed some of the characteristics of the union leaders. The leaders were among the better educated and most skilled of the cooperative members; they also had developed a very personal sense of having achieved the formation of the cooperative. One consequence was that they saw themselves as the natural administrators of the new enterprise; they did not merely serve on the committees but took on the office jobs. They became divorced from the rank-and-file members to a greater extent than had been the case in the union, and frequent complaints were made by members that the leaders had secured for themselves the easiest jobs. Moreover, there was a tendency for some of the leaders to continue to act as union leaders rather than as cooperative officials. This was especially true of the president of the administrative council; he had been active both in the metallurgical union in the mining center and in the textile union. He was an astute union politician who proved himself very skillful in negotiations with management. As cooperative leader, he continued with his union style, defending what he saw as the cooperative's interests against the interference of government and professional administrators. Internally, he was constantly on the shop floor, supervising and intervening in disputes and acting, personalistically, to solve them. None of this was necessarily to the detriment of the cooperative, but it hampered the development of stable administrative and managerial policy both internally and externally. Also, the president kept his permanent home in his village of origin, where he had held all the highest municipal offices and still farmed land. When he resigned in 1972, he refused to return to his old post as a weaver, claiming his age and administrative qualifications as reasons, and preferred to withdraw from the cooperative. He made this decision at a family reunion in his village, with the encouragement of his wife and children, of whom one is in college, another in trade, and another a craftsman.

One of the evident difficulties of the cooperative leadership and its membership was that of adjusting themselves to the changing national economic and political context. Since 1968, the importance of the state had grown, especially with respect to business and industry; agrarian reform had made wool production, and pricing, a government matter rather than a question of market supply and demand. The textile industry, including Manufacturas, found itself harmed by government policy prohibiting wool imports despite the high domestic price of wool. Also, the introduction of the *comunidad industrial* and other forms of government intervention in industry emphasized the role of the state in production. With government take-over of certain banks and strict control of foreign exchange, finance became heavily dependent on government management. Above all, the expansion of the bureaucracy, nationally and in the provinces, was making government one of the biggest employers of labor and sources of local income.

In this context, the skills and perspectives that workers and their leaders had developed to deal with private enterprise were no longer

appropriate. It is this that, in part, accounts for the increasing dominance of the professional managers in the life of the cooperative. By
the end of 1972, the cooperative's general manager—who had been the
general manager of the Prado firm—had consolidated his authority and
had been confirmed in his post and high salary. He insisted on the cooperative's being reorganized to permit management more executive
independence from the cooperative committees. The skills he offered
the cooperative were management of finance and of external relations
and managerial expertise. He traveled abroad to look at new technology
and potential markets, and he negotiated the lines of credit that made
the cooperative viable from its inception. He also negotiated with the
government over the supply and price of wool. An efficiency study by
a private firm of consultants was commissioned by the cooperative in
1972. This study supported the general manager's policies and his
proposed reorganization of the cooperative. The manager's position
was further consolidated because the cooperative was increasingly
catering to a complex national market. The bulk of its sales were in
Lima, although it had marketing relationships throughout Peru and
especially in the southern highlands, in Cuzco and Puno.

Conclusion

Though the industrial cooperative represents an interesting experiment in forms of participation and worker control, it is also the compromise product of an industrialization process that failed. Huancayo
did not develop either an industrial capitalism or an industrial labor
force. The industrial development of Huancayo was a temporary expedient representing the meeting of two rather different sets of interests.
First, there were local people involved in a diversified economy in both
urban and rural areas, seeking to maximize their economic opportunities. To these people, factory employment was, in the main, a short-
term source of income and capital to finance other enterprises. There
were, second, Peruvian and foreign migrants with no regional commitments who viewed industrial production as a useful but subordinate
activity to their commercial and financial interests. Both sets of interests
were formed as a result of the uneven development of a national economy dependent on foreign capitalist interests.

In such a provincial and national context, understanding the behavior of industrial workers requires a prior questioning of the significance, and universality, of the process of industrialization. These
textile workers, like many before them, had no reason to think that
the future lay with industrialization, and their assessment was a correct
one. Their cooperation and achievements represent not a response to

industrialization but a further example of the initiative and relative autonomy permitted by the kinds of regional and national development occurring in Peru.

NOTES

1. These factories were Manufacturas del Centro, Manufacturas de Seda, Filatex Huancayo—all three owned by the Prado financial interests—and Los Andes, owned by the Pardo family. These four factories employed some 2,500 workers in total.

2. The literature on the modernization process is immense. See Wilbert E. Moore and Arnold S. Feldman, eds., *Labor Commitment and Social Change in Developing Areas*. A useful comparison with the present study is David Chaplin, *The Peruvian Industrial Labor Force*.

3. This was Fernando Calmell del Solar, minister of labor in the Belaúnde government and prominent Huancayo landowner and businessman.

4. One of the explicit aims of our study of regional development in this region was to compare the nature of the regional commitment of different occupational groups. We did not anticipate the extent to which the different occupations were linked by their common origins.

5. For comparative material on these issues, see Torcuato Di Tella et al., *Sindicato y comunidad: Dos tipos de estructura sindical latinoamericana*; Henry A. Landsberger, "The Labor Elite: Is It Revolutionary?" in *Elites in Latin America*, edited by S. M. Lipset and A. Solari, pp. 256–300; Aníbal Quijano, "Redefinición de la dependencia y proceso de marginalización en América Latina," in Francisco Weffort and Aníbal Quijano, *Populismo, marginalización y dependencia*, pp. 171–329.

6. Peter M. Worsley, "Introduction," in *Two Blades of Grass: Rural Cooperatives in Agricultural Modernization*, edited by Peter M. Worsley.

7. J. Gianella, *Marginalidad en Lima metropolitana*; Aníbal Quijano, "The Marginal Role of the Economy and the Marginalised Labour Force," *Economy and Society* 3, no. 4 (November 1974): 393–428.

8. Quijano, "Marginal Role of the Economy."

9. Chaplin, *Peruvian Industrial Labor Force*.

10. These figures derive from my stratified sample survey of the adult male population of Huancayo in 1972. It included a life-history schedule that I have used to estimate the relative incidence of migration from the different villages.

11. Chaplin, *Peruvian Industrial Labor Force*.

12. Ibid., pp. 131–145.

13. Carlos Samaniego, "Location, Social Differentiation and Peasant Movements in the Central Sierra of Peru," Ph.D. dissertation, University of Manchester, 1974.

14. Chaplin, *Peruvian Industrial Labor Force*, p. 135.

15. Ibid., p. 141.

16. Unfortunately, the factory's records on whether separation was voluntary or not were incomplete, and I neglected to record those that were recorded. This means that no direct comparison is possible with Chaplin's data on cause of separation. The assertions above are based on interviews and on our knowledge of the general patterns of migration in the region.

17. Production in these woolen mills tends to be seasonal because of the

greater demand for wool products during the Lima winter and the decline in demand during the summer.

18. This village, Sicaya, is described in Winder's chapter in this volume.

19. This report was made by the International Development Service in 1953.

20. *Boletín del Comité Textil de la Sociedad Nacional de Industrias*, 1st Trimester, 1955, Lima.

21. Rafael Manrique P., "La transformación de una empresa industrial textil del sistema capitalista al sistema cooperativo," *Bachiller* thesis, Universidad Nacional Mayor de San Marcos, Lima, 1972.

22. Ibid., pp. 20–25.

6. Some Factors Contributing to Peasant Land Occupations in Peru: The Example of Huasicancha, 1963–1968

GAVIN A. SMITH AND PEDRO CANO H.

This chapter describes how a community of peasants and their migrant kin carried out a land occupation as part of their campaign to regain control of land they felt was rightly theirs. We do not address here the question of why this community, rather than another, successfully occupied the land, nor do we assess the national and international economic factors contributing to the right conditions for land occupation.[1] In an effort to remedy what we feel to be a paucity of available material on the detailed internal dynamics of this kind of small "rebellion," we put aside the question, Why? and ask only the question, How?—How was the land occupation carried out?

We draw few conclusions, except where we feel that our own material so conflicts with prevailing views that we ourselves doubt those views. One example will suffice here. Many political scientists, writing on peasant "leagues," "federations," "organizations," and so on, have suggested that their effect is to politicize the peasant: they introduce him to a "modern" kind of politics that enables him to voice his grievances and to affect policy.[2] We would contend that, insofar as these kinds of messages are conveyed to peasants by such organizations, they are invariably belied by reality and hence only politicize "negatively." We would also contend that, at least in the case that concerns us, a dynamic and politically experienced peasant community soon extricates itself from political organizations based on docile followers with opportunist politicians at their head.[3]

One final point: it is often stated that, as a result of the incursions of capitalism into rural society, polarization occurs such that exploitation of one villager by another shatters their identity of interests.[4] While polarization undoubtedly occurs once the capitalist economic rationale takes hold, this should not blind us to the fact that most peasant communities have contained within themselves internal economic differences for extended periods of history. A homogeneous peasantry, as Mintz, Shanin, and numerous others have pointed out, is almost a contradiction in terms.[5] The evidence presented here suggests that interaction among the differing groups within a peasant community provides much of the energy and initiative for eventual political activity vis-à-vis the larger world outside the community. Moreover, as returned migrants and the city-based colonies of peasant communities come to play their role, too, in this type of "peasant politics," so this internal dynamic becomes more potent. Thus, while Professor Hobsbawm's suggestion that "at some point of economic differentiation 'the peasantry' as a political concept disappears because conflicts within the rural sector now out-weigh what all peasants have in common against outsiders" [6] is indisputably true, the period prior to such an occurrence may be quite protracted and especially volatile.

The 1960s, up to the military coup of 1968, witnessed widespread rural unrest in Peru.[7] This took a variety of forms, each of which merged into the other, but all of which for the sake of clarity can be divided into three kinds: the initiatives taken by the peasants themselves that led to the alliance of a number of groups, the best known example of which is that of La Convención Valley of Cuzco; the guerrilla campaigns that reached their apogee in 1965; and the occurrence of land "invasions" undertaken by individual peasant communities throughout this period.[8] The Lima press reported over a hundred such land invasions between 1959 and 1966, and there were certainly far more than this.[9] In some cases they involved conflicts between one community and another, but the vast majority of the cases occurred between an estate and its bordering peasant communities. Land occupation was invariably only one part of a total campaign on the part of the peasants concerned. As well as occupying estate lands, communities withdrew their labor services to the haciendas (if they had any) and opened legal proceedings against the owners for illegal possession of land belonging to the community.

Events of this kind were especially intense in the central Andean departments of Pasco and Junín. In this paper, we are concerned with one such event that occurred in the high grazing lands located where the departments of Junín, Lima, and Huancavelica meet. It is here, at an altitude of fourteen thousand feet, that hacienda Tucle and the bordering peasant community of Huasicancha are located. In relation to Huancayo and the Mantaro Valley complex, the area we are speaking of lies some five hours—by an unreliable dirt road—to the southwest.

The relationship between the hacienda and the community in 1963 was roughly as follows: The hacienda had moved increasingly from a system of mixed farming to predominantly sheep ranching. To do so it had expanded on to pastures claimed by the community. The hacienda employed labor from Huasicancha on both a permanent and a temporary basis. The community, consisting of roughly four hundred families, relied for subsistence on small household plots of arable land located on the steep sides of river valleys near the village. Villagers also had sheep that were pastured in varying ways, as we shall show later. Finally, a large number of villagers had migrated, in varying degrees of permanence, to Huancayo and Lima, but they maintained a lively interest in the village.

The area occupied by the hacienda was some 100,000 acres of high land devoted predominantly to sheep grazing. In some of the lower zones, there was cattle pasture and some arable farming. Bordering this area on the north and west is the Río de la Virgen, on whose steep banks there was a patchwork of tiny arable household plots farmed by the people of Huasicancha. Fallow land and areas of scrub, as well as grazing zones suitable to the peasants' llamas but unsuited to the hacienda's sheep, provided the only secure grazing land for the community.

The Río de la Virgen also served to isolate Huasicancha from neighboring communities, and a practice of village endogamy served further to emphasize this isolation. Nevertheless, the village was by no means an autonomous unit whose members were unambiguously and uniformly all villagers of the same kind and to the same degree. As Bloch noted of the feudal village: "The majority of peasants . . . belonged at one and the same time to two groups constantly out of step with each other; one of them composed of subjects of the same master, the other members of the same village community."[10] And the same was true for Huasicancha, with the difference that the differing "masters" included, besides the hacienda administrator, those of the various livelihoods of the migrants.

In our discussion, *hacienda-village complex* refers to the entire region of "manor" and village. *Hacienda* refers only to the ranch operation itself, its owner, and its salaried staff. *Village* refers only to those people making Huasicancha their year-round home, while *community* refers to all those who call themselves "sons of Huasicancha"—that is, it includes migrants, villagers, and some of the low-level hacienda employees.

Two tasks remain before we concentrate on the events of the land occupation. First we must give a very brief outline of recent history, and second we must outline the dramatis personae of the events to be described.

Historical Background

We begin by describing Huasicancha's political initiatives prior to 1963. We then discuss the emergence of peasant "leagues" in the central Andes in terms of how they affected Huasicancha. Finally, we discuss the instance when the workings of national politics became a firsthand experience for Huasicanchinos, in the form of the election campaigns of 1961 to 1963 as they took shape in Huancayo.

During the Peruvian war with Chile in the early 1880s, peasants of the high *puna* around Huasicancha were recruited as guerrillas (the *montoñeros*) against the Chileans. In the event, the force that had as its base the village of Huasicancha did not confront the invading foreign forces. Instead this force of roughly four thousand *montoñeros* sacked the Tucle, Antapongo, and Laive haciendas, dividing the spoils among themselves. On at least two occasions the guerrillas besieged the provincial capital of Huancayo, until, in 1884, the leaders were shot by order of the general who had originally recruited them. By 1886 the haciendas were not only back in the hands of their original owners, but also many of the owners had taken the opportunity to expand their boundaries at the expense of the neighboring villages.

This situation prevailed, although by no means without incident, until the 1930s. In 1933 the new constitution eased the way for Peru's estimated 4,500 "Indian communities" to acquire official recognition from the government. Since such recognition reaffirmed the inalienable nature of community lands, it became the sine qua non for any confrontation between opposing claimants to disputed lands. Huasicancha initiated proceedings toward recognition on 8 April 1936, following a circular distributed by the Department of Indigenous Affairs. According to this procedure, claims to land should be based on what legal documents the community possessed. Few communities in fact possessed very convincing documents (Huasicancha was exceptional), and in the event de facto possession became a government rule of thumb, and it anyway constituted the most convincing claim in the eyes of the Huasicanchinos themselves.[11]

In a move Bismarck might have admired, the community concentrated attention on land that was currently being disputed—between hacienda Tucle and another small hacienda in one case, and between Tucle and the nearby community of Chongos Alto in the other. From 1937 to 1940 this land was occupied by Huasicanchinos. This occupation was undertaken less by the community as a whole, however, than by one of its authorities, Sabino Jacinto, and his relatives. When the hacienda agreed to part with this small plot of land, Jacinto and his immediate kin were the direct beneficiaries, rather than the community as a whole.

In 1947–1948, the community occupied the area of hacienda pasture closest to the village, about three miles long and one mile wide. The entire village participated, setting up huts on the occupied land and grazing their animals there. After some haggling and much bloodshed —both animal and human—the hacienda "sold" a piece of land to the community in return for the digging of a trench to divide this land from the hacienda property. The conflict took place out of court and the "sale" was never registered in the Huancayo Registry of Properties since, under the constitution of 1933, such exchanges were not recognized in law.[12]

Nevertheless, the community had documents that it claimed went back to 1607, indicating that it had exclusive rights to the use of virtually all the pasturage of hacienda Tucle. But the heavy hand of the Odría regime, following the 1948 campaign, postponed any overt "invasions" until the 1960s.

It was against this background of discontent with the prevailing balance of land between the "indigenous communities" and the large estates that the Movimiento Comunal del Centro (Communal Movement of the Central Sierra) arose in 1958.

The founder and popular leader of the Movimiento was Elías Tacunan Cahuana, the then *personero* of Huasicancha.[13] But by this date Tacunan had become a political figure with stature extending well beyond Huasicancha, so we must pause for a moment to say something about him.

In the flourishing and commercial villages on the floor of the Mantaro Valley, it was not uncommon for sons of the village to enter the ranks of the professions and achieve success beyond the village. Indeed, Tacunan's right-hand man, Véliz Lizarraga, a doctor of law, was from one such village. But it must be remembered that Huasicancha was on the extreme periphery of this market nexus. Tacunan was one of the very few young men who, in order to acquire a high school education, left the village and began to live in Huancayo. He was able to do this primarily through the support of his father, who was a *mayordomo* (senior foreman) on the nearby hacienda of Antapongo. Tacunan eventually apprenticed as an electrician. While in Lima, he met and then joined the early organizers of APRA. He soon introduced to the party another son of Huasicancha with a background similar to his own, named Elías Yaurivilca. Tacunan became APRA's chief organizer in the refining town of La Oroya and founded the union of metallurgical workers in 1948. Yaurivilca became a key figure in APRA's organization in Huancayo during the 1950s and 1960s.

Huasicancha's history of protest extends back to well before the rise to prominence of these two men, of course. It seems less likely that their charisma inspired Huasicancha than that the community's long history of successful protest, coupled with these two men's additional educational advantages, led them to develop a more aggressive approach to rural politics than that of some of their Mantaro peers. Nevertheless, the demands of a career in national politics are rarely the same as the goals of a peasant community, and the goals of the "peasant organizations" headed by Tacunan became increasingly compromised.

According to Tullis, Tacunan's ultimate organization, the Federación Departmental de las Comunidades de Junín (FEDECOJ) (Federation of the Communities of the Department of Junín) epitomizes the most successful of the organizations, acting to bring the peasants into the mainstream of national politics.[14] Supposedly, it bridged the gap between the massive and bureaucratic peasant organizations organized on a national scale and the smaller local federations of a few communities. In fact FEDECOJ was continually hampered by Tacunan's inability to satisfy all his constituents—the wide variety of rural dwellers at the base, as well as the powers of the different national political parties at the apex.[15] After the elections of 1963 (see below), when Belaúnde took power, Tacunan began to see his own Federación as a pressure group within the arena of legitimate politics.

This was not the intention back in 1958, when Tacunan, acting as the leader of a community well known for its aggression toward the *gamonales*—the owners of the means of production—called together the five different districts of Huasicancha, Chongos Alto, Chicche, Yanacancha, and Colca to form the Movimiento Comunal. These constituted a concentrated core of peasant communities all with some history of past conflict with the haciendas, all surrounded by these haciendas, and all loud in the voicing of their grievances. Tacunan made quite clear at this stage that he was not interested in making any affiliations with existing political parties in Lima, and within a year he publicly broke his ties with APRA.[16]

But, from the beginning, these poorer peasant communities on the periphery were only to act as the figurehead for the Movimiento. Tacunan hoped to attract the prosperous peasants of the Mantaro Valley through the formation of a Universidad Comunal, which was begun in 1959 with the support of many middle-class members of APRA in Huancayo. Also, the focus of peasant pressure shifted to the jungle on the opposite side of the Mantaro Valley. Tacunan therefore turned his attention there, forming another federation, Federación de los Campesinos de Satipo, in the jungle.

Communities reacted to Tacunan's federations in very different ways, depending on the degree to which they perceived that they could act successfully alone. Chongos Alto, Huasicancha's neighbor, had attempted action on its own and failed. So had Chicche and Yanacancha. And it was these three communities that showed greater commitment to the federation. In contrast, their successes made Huasicanchinos hesitant to ally themselves with villages that had failed to regain land. One Huasicanchino, a delegate in 1964–1965, told us that the village had more faith in small, localized, intensive confrontations than in diverse and often ineffective bargaining. He stated emphatically that the Federación of Tacunan played no role at all in Huasicancha's campaign. But he went on to emphasize that Tacunan was a conscientious and clever supporter of the peasant's cause.

The various federations that sprang up at this time were not types of peasant unions; in their activities there was a notable absence of direct confrontation with the *gamonales*. Nor did the federations try systematically to politicize the peasants through national and departmental meetings stressing the problems shared with others of their class. Instead, they negotiated directly with government agencies, seeking grants of land for their members, and were prepared to counsel moderation in return for promises of agrarian reform. We can say emphatically that in the area of Junín, where field work was undertaken, it was precisely those villages most radical in their attitudes to land occupation, such as Huasicancha, that took the federations least seriously.

As the Prado administration came to an end toward late 1961, the various political parties prepared themselves for a campaign in which they all recognized that the peasants of the highlands held the balance of the votes and that the only way to get their support would be through promises of land reform.

There were three candidates of national repute running for the presidency: former dictator General Manuel Odría was one. The perennial Haya de la Torre, head of APRA, was another. And the Kennedy-style, American-educated architect Fernando Belaúnde was the newcomer. The campaign took a particularly competitive turn in the Huancayo area, each candidate raising ever higher his promises for land reform. There were abundant grievances to tap: the Mantaro Valley was experiencing something of a depression. Production costs, particularly fertilizer and animal medication, were rising, while potato prices were falling off. In the higher *puna* area there had been outbreaks of hoof-and-mouth disease for two years running, and 1962 witnessed an unusually bad drought. In Huancayo, commercial interests were being damaged by the effects of the national economic slowdown.

There was every chance, moreover, that the elections would be close, and the Huancayo area, hitherto an APRA stronghold, appeared to hold the balance. The unaligned Movimiento Comunal was thus a focus of interest for all the candidates, and the Huasicancha migrants in Huancayo were constantly exposed to the campaign. The Movimiento Comunal was absorbed into Tacunan's peasant federation, FEDECOJ, which Tullis estimated to represent about 30 percent of the communities in Junín.[17] Even the villagers in Huasicancha, through visits to Huancayo and through reading the occasional paper that found its way to the village, were aware of the opportunities presented by this situation.

But not all Huasicanchinos were unitedly behind Tacunan's organization. Haya de la Torre's APRA had an older peasant federation that had less grass-roots support than Tacunan but nevertheless offered its members a greater access to the corridors of power than could Tacunan. This was the Federación Nacional de Campesinos del Perú (FENCAP) (National Federation of Peruvian Peasants). FENCAP drew its greatest strength from the plantations of the coast, where much of APRA's support lay, and control was notoriously centralized in Lima.[18] Nonetheless, FENCAP was paying increasing attention to the Sierra, even though its secretary in Huancayo complained of being hamstrung by the Lima *políticos*, possibly including in this category one of APRA's leading national figures, the Huancayino Ramiro Prialé. The local secretary was Tacunan's old colleague Elías Yaurivilca. So Huasicancha's personal interest in affairs was twofold: Tacunan and Yaurivilca.

Campaigning for the national elections had begun by mid-1961 and went on through the following year. Belaúnde attempted to stress his close friendship for Tacunan and his support for all that he represented. In his platform Belaúnde emphasized the ability of the Indian communities to take their own initiative, and one of his slogans emphasized past evidence of this: *El pueblo lo hizo*—the people did it. But in fact he could not risk endorsing Tacunan's most important demand at this time, which was expropriation of large landholdings without indemnity. Ultimately, Tacunan, publicly scorning all the national parties, put himself up as an independent candidate.

His decision effectively prevented Haya de la Torre from becoming president. The number of votes Tacunan received in the old APRA strongholds of the central highlands would have been enough to give Haya the third of the national vote he needed for election. In effect, the elections served to give Tacunan a political bargaining position that he was unlikely to relinquish easily.

An interim military junta ruled Peru from July 1962 to July 1963 to prevent Odría and Haya from forming a coalition and taking power. During that time a number of pilot land reform projects were carried out, while repression of rural unrest was intensified. In January 1963 there was an anti-Communist campaign in an attempt to "round up the agitators" in the provinces. During the canvassing for the 1963 elections, Tacunan was again the focus of much political bargaining; however, anticipating that Belaúnde would carry all before him, he instructed the members of FEDECOJ to vote for Acción Popular, which won the election.

The Groups Involved in the Campaign to Recover the Land

The factor that most affected the livelihood of a villager was migration. The community of Huasicanchinos immediately offers us three groups of people in terms of migration: those living permanently in the village with little or no experience of migration; those living in migrant "colonies" of Huasicanchinos in Lima, Huancayo, or one of the work centers; and the returned migrants. We should add that there were also close ties between one household and another that served to crosscut these differing groups in the community. Within each of these groups there were a number of variations significant enough to warrant mention. To begin with, if we turn first to the villagers themselves, we are immediately faced with the varying strength of their ties to the hacienda; some were full-time employees, while, at the other extreme, others only worked on the hacienda when the village worked as a communal work force for the hacienda or when they were paying off a "fine" in labor service for having illicitly grazed their animals on hacienda land.

It was virtually impossible to maintain a household in Huasicancha without paying almost daily attention to the presence of the hacienda nearby. Apart from the trespassing "fines" just mentioned, the nature of the labor contract of those working more permanently on the hacienda served to tie them into reciprocal arrangements with other households in the village. The bulk of the jobs held by villagers on the hacienda involved shepherding, often in the remoter parts of the hacienda and always including all the active members of the contractee's household. These men were the *pastores* of the hacienda. In return for their work on the hacienda they were permitted to graze a specified number of their own animals—*huacchas*—on the hacienda pasture. The shepherd, who held his or her position on an annual or biennial contract, made up and often exceeded this complement of animals not just with his own sheep but also with the animals of others in the village. These were referred to in Huasicancha as the *michipas*, but the hacienda forbade this practice and refused to acknowledge that it existed. The hacienda thus had a somewhat distorted picture of the degree to which its shepherds were in fact crucially tied into the village economic network. In return for the *michipas*, the shepherd was able to have villagers care for his plot of arable land in the village, which, owing to the heavy demands of his job, would otherwise be left in fallow. To complicate matters further, many contracted shepherds got others to fulfill their obligations to the hacienda while they concentrated on their affairs in the village. Needless to say, this practice too was condemned by the hacienda administration. The intricacies of these kinds of arrangements were immense, but the point to note is that the line between hacienda *peones*, or employees, and members of the peasant community was a very hazy one indeed.[19]

While economic differentiation within the village in 1963 had not reached such an extent that any villagers permanently hired the labor of other households to operate their own farms, there was nevertheless some variation in the size of the economic enterprises in the village. There were no villagers without arable land and the major differences lay in the number of livestock the household possessed. But such a measure of differentiation is often misleading, since the viability of the household was greatly dependent on its reciprocal and kin ties to others within and outside the village. Reciprocal arrangements with migrants, in which the village household tilled the absentee's arable plot and tended any sheep he might have, were especially significant for the economic rationale of the village enterprise.

Among the migrants still resident away from the village, the largest proportion (50 percent) were to be found in Lima. Virtually all these migrants were in the business of selling fruit, but there were variations in their businesses according to the size of capital involved. Many of those who had been in the city for as long as twenty years had acquired some capital outside the village—a house in one of the *barriadas* (squatter settlements), a *puesto* (stall) in a good location in one of the markets, a truck, and so forth. Others had left Huasicancha more recently and intended to return before making any great financial commitment in the city. Thus, to give two extreme examples, one Huasicanchino lives in a concrete house built over a number of years, has teen-aged children at school, owns an old truck, and has his wife running a stall, while he works a plot of land sharecropped just outside Lima. Another rents quarters in the inner city slums, has no offspring living in the city, and gains his livelihood as a street vendor.

In Huancayo, the variations among Huasicanchino migrants were, if anything, more accentuated. The first migrants had arrived earlier than their Lima counterparts and in many cases were more firmly entrenched, owning perhaps a shop or a garage. At the other end of the economic spectrum, some Huasicanchinos could be found in the Huancayo market acting as unskilled labor, shifting heavy loads. Between these extremes the great bulk of Huasicancha migrants were to be found; these included younger men who, having arrived for high school training, then stayed on as apprentices, and older men working as shop assistants or stall owners in the market. Huancayo offered greater security to Huasicancha migrants through the presence of stable family networks and through the proximity of the village as a resource in time of crisis; however, this latter factor served also to reduce the commitment of the migrant to Huancayo itself. The nearness of the village and the daily intermingling with people from similar villages made Huancayo almost an extension of Huasicancha itself. On the other hand, from the viewpoint of the more permanent migrants to Huancayo, Huasicancha was increasingly seen as an extension of their Huancayo enterprise.

Finally, there existed in the village an increasing number of people who had had quite extensive experience of migration but had returned to set themselves up in the village. The margins between this group and the other two were indistinct—some people planning to migrate again, others "trying out a year or two in the village," and so on. And the group itself contained a number of quite different kinds of households, the most distinct of which were those of migrants returning because of their age, that is, for retirement in the village, and those in their thirties who were in the village as a result of the high job instability in the urban centers.

The internal differentiation of the Huasicancha peasantry created a situation in which the economic rationale of a household in any one of the groups might be quite different from that of a household in another group. Yet, in each case, there were aspects of the enterprise that tied it ineluctably to others quite different in operation. These aspects included the ways in which families found it necessary to spread risks between the hazards of the city economy, on the one hand, and those of the unpredictable highland climate, on the other; the fact that upward mobility for an adult man was most feasible at different times of his life cycle in the village and in the city (i.e., in the city when young and in the village when older); and the changing structure and composition of each household over time. All these served to cut across the differences in the economic goals of each of the groups.

In fact, it is quite possible to trace a set of reciprocal economic arrangements between households, beginning with those already referred to for the hacienda shepherd, through the village household, to ties to a wage-earning migrant in Huancayo (for example) and a small petty capitalist enterprise in Lima. Smith has referred to these arrangements elsewhere as "household confederations."[20] Arable farming at high altitudes has one thing in common with making a living in the margins of a volatile "Third World" urban economy: they both are high-risk undertakings. Here the similarity ends, but this one factor leads all groups of Huasicanchinos to one goal: to increase their investment in livestock. The kinds of events against which sheep ownership may act as a hedge will vary from one group to another, of course, and thereby affect their economic decisions; inflation, for example, may force city dwellers to sell livestock in order to meet daily living costs, while in the village it may be a bad harvest owing to local climatic conditions that leads the peasant to sell a number of his livestock.

Here there is no space to elaborate on the effects such extended ties have on the internal dynamics of each of the enterprises that make up such a "confederation." Suffice it to say that, although the seeking of profit and the strategic investment of accumulated surplus characterizes the economic rationale of Huasicancha migrants, in 1963 this kind of rationality was only in its earliest form of development in Huasicancha itself. There, the farm continued to perform the role of the specifically *peasant* farm: security for its members, production for subsistence, commitment to employ and feed the entire household, and so on. Each of these two extremes was modified, as we have already said, by the very ties it had, directly and indirectly, to its opposite through the "confederations."

The differing economic rationales within the community of Huasicancha meant that the various household heads attached often-contradictory meanings to livestock ownership and to the control of the pasture. Yet the different groups were crucially bound together. The heat generated out of conflicting views of methods and of goals to be attained, when combined with this symbiosis, gave the Huasicancha land occupations their particular form and dynamic.

Formal Beginnings

In this section we consider the reactions of the Huasicanchino groups to one specific event of the land reclamation campaign—a petition to the president of Peru. Throughout the narrative the villagers (those resident in Huasicancha) appear as the central characters, but it will become clear that each of the various groups played crucial parts in the unfolding of events.

On 2 September 1963, Demetrio de la Cruz Lazo, *personero* of the community of Huasicancha, drew up a petition to the president of the Republic on behalf of all the members of the community. Having done so, he journeyed by mule and bus to Huancayo, where he read the petition to the Huasicancha migrants working there. After listening to their suggestions, he continued his journey to Lima and read the document to a number of gatherings. No lawyer had been employed to draw up the petition and it is very plainly worded; it begins by introducing the two delegates chosen to present it. It goes on: "As special delegates of the Community of Huasicancha, we beg you to put in order the reclamation of our lands, which have been stolen from us by the hacienda Tucle, and which are of vital importance to our survival, being good pastures that are indispensable for the upkeep of our livestock and therefore of special economic and social importance . . ."[21]

The petition states that the land was taken violently, with consequent costly legal battles over the past hundred years that destroyed the village economy and resulted in little recovery of land; reclamation is vital to the survival of the community, since the high altitude makes arable farming very risky and more and more arable land is having to be devoted to livestock farming; increasingly *comuneros* are being forced to migrate to the cities and mines, where they contract fatal illnesses; the litigants should be indemnified for the extensive wealth the landowner has managed to accrue from lands that were not his; and the landowner has been able to diversify into other businesses in Huancayo as a result of the labor of *peones* from the village. Finally, the petition outlines the titles in the possession of the community, which it claims date back to 1607.[22]

Having read the petition to various gatherings of Lima residents, de la Cruz had to defend his case against strong attack. There were very few Lima residents in favor of presenting such a document to the president. They suggested that it implied a lack of faith in government promises to deal with the overall problems of the *campesinos*. At the meetings, city residents were at pains to emphasize the unity of the Huasicanchinos, "weighted down by the misery of extreme poverty"; however, they urged that the presentation of the petition should be postponed until such time as all the clubs of former residents of Huasicancha in the different mining and work centers had been given the chance to approve it. De la Cruz would not bend. He pointed out that the villagers had sufficient access to the national press and were as capable of judging the tempo of the national situation as were the city residents. He added that the villagers considered that it was precisely the present state of rural unrest that would move the government to take action on land reform.

Eventually, his insistence that he would not postpone the presentation of the petition was successful. But it was agreed that the petition should be presented by the Lima residents rather than by the villagers' delegates. President Belaúnde did eventually see a delegation of these city residents, who were suitably dressed in ponchos and felt hats. The president thanked the *comuneros* for not resorting to violence, as others had done elsewhere, and he assured them that he would do everything in his power to see to it that their land was returned to them.

These formal and legal antecedents to the actual land invasions were similar to those in many other communities engaged in disputes over land. Attempts to go through lengthy, costly, and time-consuming legitimate channels preceded resort to any other methods.[23] And by 1963 the public discussion of land reform gave a greater impetus to these kinds of petitions.

The Villagers and the Lima Residents

As de la Cruz and a number of the better-off villagers saw it, Belaúnde had himself advocated peasant initiative. They agreed that land reform was bound to come in the present political climate; indeed, they argued that their petition had stemmed from reading newspaper reports of the coming plans. However, they were as suspicious of the communities surrounding Huasicancha and of the claims that they might make under land reform as they were of the landlord himself. De la Cruz's hurry was motivated less by a desire to get on the bandwagon of land reform than by a desire to get ahead of it. Furthermore, the petition and subsequent events reveal a belief on the part of the villagers that "land reform" was not so much an improvement of conditions as a straightforward righting of wrongs. Villagers constantly remarked that "the law is not political" and insisted that politicians must not be allowed to distort it.

The Lima residents, on the other hand, saw the situation very differently. They too were anxious that Huasicancha regain the community pastures so that they could invest more capital in livestock, but they were not willing for the village residents to take the initiative themselves. Many of the villagers already had flocks of sheep, however poor the quality, while the migrants would have to build up their flocks more slowly. Moreover, the Lima residents knew that a government-administered land redistribution would be more susceptible to influence from city dwellers, who were close to bureaucratic channels; in contrast, a self-initiated occupation would make it hard for the city residents to keep control. In a pastoral economy where land is—at least nominally—owned communally, the area of land a family can use is largely a function of the number of animals it can place on the land at a given moment. The city residents wanted to play for time in order to build up flocks. They therefore suggested that all the clubs of Huasicancha migrants be canvassed—a lengthy and almost impossible task. One spokesman even advocated a general meeting in the village on the next *fiestas patrias* (Peruvian national day), that is, ten months hence.

Right from the beginning of the campaign, then, there was a diversity of goals and a series of conflicting interests. In taking over the role of delegates to the president, the city residents wanted to assert their importance to the village; they were afraid and suspicious of attempts to cut them out of village affairs if Huasicancha should recuperate its extensive pasturage of seventy thousand acres purely through village initiative. De la Cruz, as the village representative, had no intention of losing the initiative by bowing to pressures not to present the petition. But he was still aware of the need for financial support from the city residents in the event of a drawn-out struggle. Consequently, de la Cruz was prepared to let the city residents gain the prestige of going to the palace and to let them mobilize the support of Tacunan to do so. The villagers were quite aware of Tacunan's friendship with Belaúnde and the possible advantages that this implied.

The system of political patronage that the city residents used—in the person of Tacunan—effectively tied them to negotiations aimed at "getting the best possible deal," the emphasis being placed on what was conceived to be "possible." But Tacunan was never the unquestioned leader of the Huasicancha land reclamation campaign. In the process he acted as the figurehead for one of the many groups whose activities during the period of the land invasion contributed to its goals and methods.

What we are suggesting is that when Demetrio de la Cruz read out his petition to the Huasicancha migrants in Lima, the contrast was not between sophisticated city leaders and ignorant, passive peasant followers. Indeed, de la Cruz's agreement that it should be the city residents who should approach Tacunan and the president stemmed from a situation five months earlier in which the villagers had ousted Tacunan from the position of village *personero*. Since it had been de la Cruz who had replaced Tacunan, he knew that the city residents would have more influence on Tacunan than he would. Also, it was the initiative displayed by the villagers in throwing out a cosmopolitan *hombre grande* like Tacunan that now made the Lima residents so particularly sensitive about this new village initiative in regard to the petition.

De la Cruz knew how important it was for a man like Tacunan, whose political reputation was built on his peasant origins, to maintain good relations with his village.[24] But by late 1963 Tacunan was unable to exert paternalistic pressures on the villagers because he could offer them few concrete advantages. The kinds of compromises that Tacunan made to increase his influence in the capital were acceptable to less radical peasant communities than Huasicancha and often to city residents whose interests were broader than just land reclamation. But compromises over the extent of land reclaimed and over indemnity were unacceptable to the villagers of Huasicancha, who claimed that *all* the disputed pasture belonged to the community and were not prepared to pay indemnity. The goals as perceived by the village were only at certain very specific times in accord with the goals of various other *comuneros* outside the village.

The Villagers and the Hacienda

We have explained earlier that throughout 1961 and 1962 tension was mounting in the departments of Pasco and Junín. On at least two occasions constitutional guarantees had been suspended by the government. Now we turn to the local events that led to the formulation of the petition to the president in 1963. Throughout the earlier part of that year, and also in the previous year, relations between Huasicancha and hacienda Tucle became increasingly tense. Correspondence of this period includes complaints from Huasicancha authorities to the hacienda administrator regarding the bad behavior of his senior employees. The letters concerning Huasicancha infringements of hacienda property—mostly in the form of illegal grazing—far outnumber either the correspondence of the hacienda with other neighboring communities or its correspondence for previous years with Huasicancha itself.

The violence of the supervisors employed by the hacienda was heightened because the local *guardia civil* (national police force), stationed in the nearby community of Chongos Alto, were more often than not very unwilling to take strong action against the Huasicanchinos. Either offenders were never apprehended by the police or, if they were, they were frequently charged with offenses much smaller than those for which the hacienda had requested their arrest. Policemen, themselves often sons of peasants—though never from the local area—were located in the center of a peasant community. Their daily social encounters took place with peasants and not with hacienda personnel, least of all the administrator. The sanction the hacienda could bring to bear on the police was to deprive the post of luxury items, such as butter. But the police were dependent on the villagers for far more basic necessities.

The difficulties faced by the police can best be illustrated by their experience during an earlier time of tension. Overdiligence in applying the laws in 1947, when there had been a police post in Huasicancha itself, had resulted in the drying up of all supplies of basic foodstuffs for the police staff and the termination of the provision of fodder for their horses. Attempts on the part of the hacienda, whose headquarters were some distance away, to fill this deficiency were so unsuccessful that the police were almost forced to move the post from the village.

The ability of the local police to play a useful role in the relations between a community and its neighboring hacienda was largely contingent on the two parties' coming to some accord of their own. If one or other of them was particularly recalcitrant, the futility of police control quickly became apparent. In the case of Huasicancha, the continuing friction with the hacienda led to so many demonstrations of the powerlessness of the local force that the entire post was withdrawn in 1959. This in turn served to place considerably more emphasis on the substitute authorities within the two conflicting institutions. The *mayordomos* and *caporales* (foremen) of the hacienda were increased in number, particularly from 1963 on. In the village, the *gobernador* and his lieutenants became increasingly involved with defending the community rather than with settling internal conflicts.

One month before the village drew up the petition, the hacienda called on the *personero* of Huasicancha to come to a meeting to discuss the division of responsibilities. The hacienda also wanted Huasicancha to clarify its position on the land claims. The authorities of the community declared that the trouble was being caused by "various *comuneros*," to the detriment of the community as a whole. There is plenty of evidence to suggest that, at this stage, both the hacienda and the authorities of the village saw the conflict in terms of individuals rather than in terms of the expansion of the community as a single unit. Sabino Jacinto, the leader of an old conflict with the hacienda, was in fact actively involved in helping the hacienda to control infringements of its property, having himself been rewarded with a plot of land some years earlier.

Following the meeting of late July, however, the hacienda staff escalated their campaign against illegal grazing on the hacienda, shooting some animals and often burning down the peasants' makeshift huts constructed for shepherding. In many cases, the effects of the repression extended beyond the individual peasant caught on hacienda land, since, invariably, he also shepherded the animals of other *comuneros*. It was the larger stock owners who most needed to make use of hacienda land, and threats to their ability to use pasture reverberated on the smaller holders. Moreover, since it was these large stock owners who tended to hold the positions of authority in the village, they were able to mobilize village support.

Although increasing the pasturage available for livestock affected, actually or potentially, all village members, the payoffs for reaching that goal were not equal. For example, there were some in the village who possessed so few livestock that a continuation of the old policy of illegal trespassing would have seemed a quite viable possibility. And there were others who, through their experience as migrants, had alternative ways of investing their capital, for example, in small shops.

Some of the younger villagers were well aware of the negative effects that the investment of capital outside Huasicancha by migrants or residents would have on the future of the village economy; a village meeting earlier in the year had dealt with this issue. It was felt that pending plans for land reform would serve to persuade people to delay capital outflow. It was also pointed out at the meeting that, as a result of lack of pasture, Huasicanchinos had long since been diverting their capital from the village to other places. By rapidly drafting the overtly high-handed petition to the president, de la Cruz, as *personero* of the community, was in effect crystallizing the situation. If it was not interpreted by either Belaúnde or the hacendado as a declaration of intent, the migrants in Lima were not so deceived.

In January of 1964, the civil judge of Huancayo made an inspection of the land under dispute. The landlord, who was often resident in Huancayo, was well situated to bring social pressure to bear on provincial authorities in the town of Huancayo itself. Therefore the hacienda did not trouble to send representatives to accompany the civil inspectors on their journey round the disputed boundaries. The community, on the other hand, provided the following entourage: the *personero*, the *alcalde*, and the *gobernador*, three other members of the local government, and three special representatives who had been elected to deal with all legal aspects of the dispute. There were two delegates from the migrants in Lima and two from Huancayo. Also present were one cook and three assistants, plus a waiter and two people to look after the horses. Two more went along as experts on where the landmarks were and another two went to carry the beer. The whole job took two days, and on the second day the judge was entertained· by the representatives of the migrants at the neighboring Cercapuquio mine, from which he could return to Huancayo.

A combination of deference, bribery, and show of force appears to have been the *comuneros'* policy on this occasion; however, the net result was a feeling of disappointment on the part of the villagers. In the meeting that followed, it was decided that henceforth the dispute would have to be a community affair organized under the leadership of voted representatives working with the aid of a lawyer. There was much disagreement as to tactics, and at least two of the community authorities resigned on the explicit grounds that they were not prepared to undertake an open confrontation with the hacienda. The migrants pleaded for some caution but offered to raise money by *copa* (a form of head tax) in the work centers.

Soon thereafter the hacienda found many of its shepherds either officially resigning or, more frequently, simply disappearing. The *guardia civil* post in Chongos Alto was informed on each occasion, but it was either unable or unwilling to do much about it. For example, one shepherd who quit his position took with him a horse and eleven sheep and left an outstanding debt of 450 *soles* (about $15).

The Villagers, the Returned Migrants, and the Huancayo Residents

On 12 January 1964, a small invasion of land was undertaken. It differed from the usual trespassing in that instead of a single shepherd with a few animals there were teams of peasants with sizeable flocks of animals. This invasion was in essence a test run, primarily meant to see what kind of reaction would be forthcoming. It was organized by de la Cruz and other elected members of the community, but individual *comuneros* were able to initiate their own actions. For example, many villagers took individual action in bringing social sanctions to bear on relatives who were employees of the hacienda to persuade them to leave their posts. In the event, the two policemen who happened to be at the hacienda at the time of the invasion retired to Chongos Alto, saying that they were not equipped to deal with such a large problem; the administrator of the hacienda urged that the owner take up the matter in the provincial capital.

The Huancayo authorities were reluctant to get involved at this stage, perhaps because Huasicancha's invasion was only one of an extensive number of incidents. The situation throughout the department was getting difficult to control; the military probably wanted to deal with one situation at a time, in the hope that in some cases the land-owners would be able to settle the problems themselves. The January headlines of the Huancayo papers give some idea of the climate: "Invasions and Violence in Satipo and Chacapalca," "Outbreaks of Fighting in Chanchamayo." The government is frequently quoted as ascribing the responsibility to "outside agitators." Yanacancha, a community just one hour from Huasicancha, attempts an invasion, but many are captured and the invasion fails. Then on 26 January a meeting of peasant leaders in Huancayo, attended by de la Cruz, demands government action in support of community claims on land. The government replies by sending forty "Communist leaders" to the jungle prison colony of Sepa. The government then organizes its own peasant meeting in Huancayo, but this meeeting is no less demanding than its predecessor.

The owner of Tucle, a relatively isolated hacienda, was left to look after himself at this stage. He armed his men, and they shot a number of animals and burned down peasant huts. De la Cruz attempted to bring legal action in Huancayo against the hacienda but got no response. On 24 April, impatient with the inactivity of the commission that the president had assured them would deal with their grievances, the *comuneros* of Huasicancha marched onto the hacienda land in force. Leadership was now divided among a number of groups. There were three villagers in charge of the front line of the invasion itself. They were never publicly identified as leaders, and the hacienda, anxious to identify to the Huancayo authorities the outside agitators responsible, either made up the names or were given false ones by the villagers. Once on the hacienda land, the peasants built huts, appointed guards, and organized an assembly. A school was set up for the children.

The *personero* of the community, de la Cruz, was in Huancayo at this stage, attempting to accelerate a legal case against the hacienda. With him were the three delegates elected to take charge of the invasion's legal ramifications. These were all older villagers. Then there were the presidents of the various migrant clubs, of which the most important were those in Lima and the two in Huancayo. The two latter clubs were divided by their support of Tacunan and Yaurivilca respectively. But it is important to remember that, although these two men had some influence with the *comuneros* of Huasicancha, they by no means had control of the situation or even majority support.

The invasion of 24 April made the headlines. The usual story was presented: outside agitators, threats of violence from the peasants, the hacienda building defended by only (*sic*) forty men, and an exaggerated estimate of the number of animals involved. One article ends: "As of ten o'clock last night Manuel Duarte [the hacendado] had not been able to contact the prefect of the department for protection." Duarte turned to the army while the peasants brought pressure on the courts.

The immediate result was that another inspection of the situation at Tucle was made by the government. The huts the peasants had placed on the invaded land were built of old straw and stones in order to give the impression that they had been there "from time imme-morial," the key term in Peruvian land legislation, meaning prior to the 1919 constitution. Children in the open-air school were given lessons in the misnaming of prominent landmarks and were told how to talk to strangers: your father's name is "Papá," your uncle's name is "Taita," and your last name is "Chiquito" ("little one").

The struggle was seen by the Huasicanchinos to be one of legal title and just possession. This is to say, at the level of discourse with out-siders, their claim was always made in strictly legal terms. Questions of the economic need for pasture were dropped and the fact that the land had been invaded was either denied or avoided. The hacienda owner, on the other hand, emphasized peasant involvement in politics, specifically subversive politics, and his own commitment to economic order and efficiency. He said: "The occupation of the ten thousand hec-tares is simply a matter of chaos and subversion. . . . The Tucle Live-stock Company is one of the most important in the region, raising over twenty thousand Corriedale sheep, but the aggressors have put parasite-ridden animals among the company's pure breed stock, with great dan-ger to our own sheep."

The 27 April inspection was a hurried job, and it was not until 7 May that a proper inspection was made. Meanwhile the hacienda had managed to obtain a peace-keeping force of soldiers for the *fundo*, the central farm itself, although the owner and his employees claimed that the soldiers were reluctant to journey far from the hacienda buildings. At an early point of the 7 May inspection, de la Cruz and the lawyer employed by the community began to suspect that Duarte had already come to some agreement with the officials. They therefore left the party of inspectors.

At this time, Belaúnde had become increasingly embarrassed by the situation in Junín and elsewhere in the Sierra and had decided to harden his tactics. On his way back to Huancayo from the inspection, de la Cruz and one of the elected official delegates of the community were captured by the police and jailed. Albino Yaranga, one of the invasion leaders, was captured in his mountain *estancia* (sheepfold). Another official delegate was caught while talking in the lawyer's office in Huancayo, and a fifth, who pretended to be deaf and got away with never giving his name, was also captured. No city residents were captured or jailed. All those captured were accused of being Communist insurgents stirring up otherwise contented and law-abiding peasants. They were kept in jail for most of the remainder of the year, although none went to trial.

From the government's point of view there now appeared to be a possibility of negotiation. The "agitators" had been removed. As the government saw it, the peasants, deprived of their irrational but charismatic local figureheads, would fall apart. Belaúnde announced that no land occupied by peasant invaders would be considered for land reform. In many areas of Peru, peasants, putting great stock in the law, dismantled their huts and returned home to wait. Most of them had to wait until long after Belaúnde had been dispatched to Paris before they got back to the position of 1964.

This new state of affairs served to emphasize the differences between two other interest groups within Huasicancha's protest movement. Once the land invasion policy had replaced political pressure in the capital, the Lima residents had a less active part to play than did the Huancayo residents. The courts, the army, and public opinion were all to be manipulated, if at all, in Huancayo, the provincial capital. Alternatively, if pressure was to be brought on the invaders on behalf of all the out-migrants from Huasicancha, it was the Huancayo residents who were nearest at hand to do it.

In the village, the new leaders replacing those who had been jailed were younger men who had recently returned from a period of migration away from the village. Where their predecessors had tended to be older men whose wealth was largely measured in terms of the traditional local peasant economy, these new men had acquired what capital they had through migration and participation in the national cash economy. A few of them had cash to invest in 1964, but the majority were the victims of the national recession of the early sixties and had returned to the village with just enough to get started there. They differed, therefore, from the migrants in Lima and Huancayo who had managed to weather the economic storm without returning to the village.

The important difference in strategy between these returned migrants and the more traditional permanent residents of the village was one of timing. The discussions in the village meetings of this period revolve around a debate over the urgency of some form of settlement or other. Those families most committed to the raising of livestock for largely subsistence purposes were quite willing to carry on the confrontation indefinitely, safe in the knowledge that time worked against the (relatively) capital-intensive hacienda. The arable plots of these households were usually sufficient to support the household and absorb its labor without recourse to migration. The returned migrants, however, had a different perspective. They may have entered office determined not to negotiate, but they could not afford to allow what little capital they had accumulated through migration to seep away over time. By this time the costs of the land campaign had already reached large proportions and were being met by taxes on each head of family. Consequently, the new leadership tended to fall somewhere between the older leaders and the urban residents in their goals: they were committed to land occupation but did not wish to sustain a long-drawn-out conflict.

By the end of 1964, it was decided in the village that there would be no withdrawal from the invaded land. During the following months, there was growing pressure from some of the better-off Huancayo residents for Huasicancha to settle with the hacienda out of court, along the lines set by the 1948 precedent. In this situation, perhaps the most emphatic difference among the Huancayo residents was between migrants who, in investment decisions, choice of residence, and education of their children, were committed to permanent residence in Huancayo and those who saw Huancayo as a means of gaining sufficient surplus to allow them some upward mobility back in the village. Both groups were interested in investing in Huasicancha, but the first group was seeking safe investment for their surplus capital in the form of easily saleable and relatively stable sheep. The second group was looking to their eventual occupation as peasant farmers, involving house, arable land, and usually a small shop in the village.

Of course, since very few of this latter group ever achieved their ambition the important point here is the intention. Since this intention tended to change over time as commitments to Huancayo increased, it was the more recent arrivals or those who had not been particularly successful in the provincial capital who fell into this category. This difference was reflected in the activities of the two migrant clubs in Huancayo at the time. De la Cruz's diary, written in jail, records the name of every *comunero* who gave support to the imprisoned group. He complains strongly about the older and more established of the clubs in Huancayo: this club had been founded by Tacunan and showed no support for the imprisoned men. He records his gratitude to the other club.

The more established Huancayo residents shared a view of events similar to that held by the more powerful Lima residents. If their past ties were to Huasicancha, their present ties were to Huancayo and, increasingly, to Lima, where they sent their sons to be educated and where some were increasing their investments. In this respect, these Huancayo residents were following the path of some of their Lima counterparts who had first migrated to the provincial capital before moving to Lima. So the pressure from this particular Huancayo club was for Tacunan to use his influence to obtain a reasonable settlement with the government while it was still possible.

The close ties of the other Huancayo club with the village are reflected in the fact that some of the new village leaders were still members of this club. The intransigence of the villagers provided this club with the opportunity to reduce the power of the hitherto more influential older club. The younger group was often composed of the unmarried members of families that were still resident in the village; for the time being, at least, they were overtly in favor of continued attrition.

In September, an interministerial commission was set up to enquire into invasions of land, and its representatives made a visit to Huasicancha. This is how one of the villagers described the visit in the village records:

> It was set up at the request of Augusto Duarte, who bribed [había comprado] the two delegates of the ministries who went to Huasicancha. The community received them with the band and then a general assembly was summoned by the guests, in which the two officials took over the entire speaking. The official delegates of the community were not permitted to speak. Señor Elías Tacunan, who represented FEDECOJ as general secretary, was, however, allowed to address the assembly, which he did entirely in favor of the *gamonal* and for expropriation by Reforma Agraria, and not in favor of the demand that is being made by the community. He was for the "limited settlement" solution. From that date on, Tacunan lost all prestige as a representative of the community.

Subsequent bargaining with this interministerial commission revealed the growing split between the traditional villagers and the returned migrants, who acted as delegates and sought a compromise solution.

The picture was complicated by the return of a number of the previously jailed leaders, which gave added weight to the policy of non-compromise. On a number of occasions lengthy negotiations in Huancayo were followed by announcements in the press that a solution had been reached. The elected delegates then returned to the village for ratification, to have everything rejected by the villagers. On two such occasions the new leaders were thrown out of office and replaced by others, some of whom met with the same fate.

Throughout this period, de facto occupation of hacienda pasture was becoming sufficiently successful for the head of the community to begin, by 1967, to allot sheepfolds far into what was, officially, hacienda land. Infrequent official visits to the area occasioned halfhearted attempts by the villagers to remove themselves from the points of deepest encroachment. The court decision of 1968 that recognized Huasicancha's claims in full was, in part, a consequence of the difficulty—both political and physical—of removing the peasants from their positions. The validity of the community's titles was acknowledged by the land-disputes court (*Juez de Tierra*) in Huancayo, and Huasicancha obtained rights to seventy thousand acres of land.

Conclusion

Hobsbawm writes, "The widespread Peruvian peasant movement in 1962–64 produced unrest rather than revolution." [25] As such it produced a wide range of examples of just the kind of peasant protest activity that occurs frequently in the "Third World," albeit in less widespread form. It is not therefore an entirely fruitless exercise to ask questions about these kinds of protest activities. What does an experience like the one we have described, especially when it is a successful experience, contribute to "peasant politics"?

In the Mantaro area the Huasicanchinos are seen as a community exhibiting unusual solidarity, and they themselves look back on the 1960s as a period of great unity. This kind of intense experience involves the participants in a common separation from others. If the separation is as much from similar communities or groups as it is from the opposition, then it is put forward as a conservative component of peasant protest. If the emphasis is placed on the experience acting to clarify the line between the peasants and their nonpeasant enemy— the landlords or the government—then a more optimistic conclusion is drawn. [26] It is only in restrospect, however, that such nice lines can be drawn around the protesting group. Inconvenient friends outside (like the lawyers) can be forgotten and doubting Thomases within overlooked.

But the protest is only part of the ongoing experience of making a living, both in the larger world and in the community itself. Despite Huasicancha's solidarity against hacienda Tucle and the various government commissions, the experience of the land recuperation campaign revealed internal differences emerging from differing economic rationales. These differences led to varying interpretations of the goals to be attained and the methods for attaining them. This in turn gave the villagers, through their interaction with the migrants, a broader perspective on national political issues. It would be incorrect to suggest that the Lima residents and their Huancayo counterparts were simply "more developed persons [who] naturally became the leaders of the movement."[27] Rather they were foils against which the process of political awareness was played out. While the villagers were perhaps better located to assess the hacienda's weaknesses and the migrants to assess changes in the provincial and national political climate, it also appears that many of the older villagers viewed the issues more as the righting of wrongs than as political bargaining. And perhaps it is at this point that traditional peasant politics cannot be insinuated into "modern" politics: wrongs cannot be only partly righted. Justice must be untarnished by compromise.

Finally, a word about the implications of this kind of village-level unrest for peasant federations and peasant political parties. Both polarization within the small-scale farming sector and the differing demands arising from regional disparities often restrict such national-level organizations to a short life. But the evidence presented here would suggest that even when internal exploitation between one peasant household and another is still not yet powerful enough to make irrelevant more "primordial loyalties," such large organizations find it difficult to appeal to *all* their peasant constituents.[28] The penalty for assuming there to be such a thing as a homogeneous peasantry is far heavier for politicians than for academics. In fact the question that perhaps most needs more narrow definition is just what we mean when we talk of the "leadership" of peasants, in the context of an ongoing political protest like the one described here.

NOTES

1. This chapter forms part of a larger work by Smith, in which more attention is paid to factors not dealt with here. See Gavin A. Smith, "The Social Basis of Peasant Political Activity: The Case of the Huasicanchinos of Central Peru," Ph.D. dissertation, University of Sussex, 1975.

2. See, for example, Susan Bourque, "Cholification and the Campesino," Latin American Studies Program Dissertation, Cornell University, 1971, and F. Lamond Tullis, *Lord and Peasant in Peru: A Paradigm of Political and*

Social Change. The analogy of a "triangle without a base" to illustrate the condition of peasants prior to such organizations, and the joining up of the base—i.e., communication between the peasants—to represent politicization after the arrival of the organizations, is used by Tullis and many others. For a critique of the approach, see Norman Long, "Structural Dependency, Modes of Production and Economic Brokerage in Rural Peru," in *Beyond the Sociology of Development*, edited by Ivar Oxaal, Tony Barnett, and David Booth.

3. What looks like opportunism, from the viewpoint of the peasant community, may, from the retrospective viewpoint of the historian, appear to be no more than the necessary maneuvers of a wise man.

4. See, for example, Karl Kautsky, *La Question agraire*, and V. I. Lenin, *The Development of Capitalism in Russia*.

5. See the various discussions in the first issues of *The Journal of Peasant Studies*.

6. Eric Hobsbawm, "Peasants and Politics," *The Journal of Peasant Studies* 1, no. 1 (October 1973): 18.

7. Aníbal Quijano, "Contemporary Peasant Movements," in *Elites in Latin America*, edited by S. M. Lipset and A. Solari; J. Cotler and F. Portocarrero, "Peru: Peasant Organizations," in *Latin American Peasant Movements*, edited by H. Landsberger; Gerrit Huizer, "Land Invasion as a Non-Violent Strategy of Peasant Rebellion: Some Cases from Latin America," *Journal of Peace Research*, no. 2 (1972); Howard Handelman, *Struggle in the Andes: Peasant Political Mobilization in Peru*, pp. 62–99.

8. For La Convención, see H. Neira, *Cuzco, tierra o muerte*, and *Los Andes, tierra o muerte*; Wesley Craig, "Peru: The Peasant Movement of La Convención," in *Latin American Peasant Movements*, edited by H. Landsberger. The guerrilla campaigns are dealt with by Héctor Béjar, "Peru: entrevista a dos guerrilleros," *Pensamiento Crítico*, no. 6 (July 1970), and *Peru 1965: Notes on a Guerrilla Experience*; L. Campbell, "The Historiography of the Peruvian Guerrilla Movement," *Latin American Research Review* 8, no. 1 (Spring 1973): 45–70; Richard Gott, *Rural Guerrillas in Latin America*.

9. Eric Hobsbawm, "Peasant Land Occupations," *Past and Present*, no. 62 (February 1974); Handelman puts the figure at between 350 and 400 land invasions and argues that: "The peasant mobilization of the early 1960's was unquestionably one of the largest peasant movements in Latin American history" (*Struggle in the Andes*, p. 121).

10. Marc Bloch, *Feudal Society*, I, 242.

11. Carlos Samaniego, "Location, Social Differentiation and Peasant Movements in the Central Sierra of Peru," Ph.D. dissertation, University of Manchester, 1974, p. 242.

12. This conflict is dealt with in more detail in Smith, "The Social Bases of Peasant Political Activity," pp. 85–92.

13. The *personero* was the elected leader of the legally constituted *comunidad indígena*. The *comuneros* are the legal members of the community and at this time included both villagers and migrants.

14. Tullis, *Landlord and Peasant in Peru*, pp. 197–199.

15. The use of the term *constituents* to include those above, as well as those below, the politician is a little idiosyncratic, but see Michael Lipsky, "Protest as a Political Resource," *American Political Science Review*, no. 2 (1968), pp. 1144–1158.

16. Much of this information comes from discussions with the man who was then Tacunan's second-in-command, Dr. Jesús Véliz Lizarraga of the Universidad Nacional del Centro. The interpretation is, however, our own.

17. Tullis, *Lord and Peasant in Peru*, p. 199.

18. Bourque, "Cholification and the Campesino."

19. The complex relationships these shepherds have with other villagers is discussed in Smith, "The Social Bases of Peasant Political Activity."

20. Gavin A. Smith, "Internal Migration and Economic Activity: Some Case Studies," Center for Developing Area Studies Working Papers, no. 14, McGill University, 1975. In this paper, Smith discusses the differences in the economic rationalities of the peasant farm in Huasicancha and the urban enterprises of Huasicancha migrants.

21. These documents are drawn from the village records, notes, and diaries of *comuneros*, records of the *Juez de Tierra* in Huancayo, and the collected documents of hacienda Tucle in the archives of the Reforma Agraria in Lima. At this stage, no lawyer had been employed to draw up the petition.

22. Inspection of the document indicates that the correct date was in fact 1707. For an account of the commercial activities of the owner of Tucle, see Bryan R. Roberts, "The Social History of a Provincial Town: Huancayo, 1890–1972," in *Social and Economic Change in Modern Peru*, edited by R. Miller, C. T. Smith, and J. Fisher, p. 162.

23. Gerrit Huizer, *Peasant Rebellion in Latin America*.

24. Tacunan had lost his position as *personero* under the unlikely charge of having taken a small sum from the community coffers. It was the kind of accusation that a national political figure would be most uneasy about, especially when it came from his own village.

25. Hobsbawm, "Peasants and Politics," p. 11.

26. Huizer, *Peasant Rebellion in Latin America*.

27. Perrie, quoted in Hobsbawm, "Peasants and Politics," p. 18.

28. Hamza Alavi, "Peasant Classes and Primordial Loyalties," *Journal of Peasant Studies* 1, no. 1 (October 1973).

7. From Cooperative to Hacienda: The Case of the Agrarian Society of Pucará

JUAN SOLANO SÁEZ

The village of Pucará,[1] situated at the southern end of the Mantaro Valley nine miles from Huancayo, has a recent history of cooperative enterprise that includes a livestock cooperative, a transport cooperative, and the communal exploitation of arable land.[2] Like Muquiyauyo, farther to the north, Pucará has been identified as among the most progressive of the valley communities in terms of its history of communal work and its provision of educational services.[3] By 1971, some 90 percent of male heads of households and 70 percent of female heads of household were literate.[4] The development of education in the village commenced in the early part of the century and accelerated rapidly after 1940 with the construction of new schools; in 1945, for example, the villagers constructed a school with their own labor.[5] Many children continued their education in the secondary schools of Huancayo and Chupaca, and after 1960 Pucará students began to attend the newly founded national university at Huancayo.

This "progressive" character of Pucará is often linked to its economic structure, which exhibits less marked differentiation than is the case with many other Mantaro communities. The pattern of landholding is relatively evenly distributed, with most households possessing between 1 and 2 hectares of privately owned land, broken up into a large number of small plots. Out of a total of 850 hectares of arable land, 230 hectares are dedicated to horticulture, mainly for the Huancayo market, and this land is divided into 825 separate plots. The re-

191

maining 620 hectares is divided into 1,735 plots and is used for cultivation of staple crops (potatoes, cereals, beans).

This relative homogeneity and scarcity of land has made communal resources, both pasture and arable, of strategic interest to most village households. This strategic interest is in part a result of the high level of the commercialization of agriculture in Pucará. Pucarinos specialize in the marketing of a wide range of vegetables to the Huancayo and Chupaca markets. This market gardening was directly initiated by returning labor migrants who had worked for commercial farmers on the outskirts of Lima. Indeed, from at least the end of the last century, villagers had been involved in migration to Huancayo, Lima, and other work centers.

It is the aim of this chapter to explore the significance of formal cooperative institutions in a context where there exists a greater degree of socioeconomic homogeneity than in most valley villages and in which agriculture is still a major part of the domestic economy, but where, in addition, external linkages through trade and migration continue to constitute important components in the local economy. The material presented is intended to serve as a comparison with similar organizations of the cooperative type found, on the one hand, in such villages as Matahuasi and Sicaya, in which there is greater internal socioeconomic differentiation than in Pucará, and, on the other hand, with Muquiyauyo, in which agriculture is no longer the major focus of the domestic economy.[6]

This theme is examined by reference to one particular example of cooperative enterprise, which led indirectly to the formation and development of a small hacienda owned by a group of peasants. This hacienda was organized along the lines of a traditional highland hacienda with *colonos* (workers) who provided various labor services; the peasants, as owners, assumed the role of the hacendado, acting as patrons of fiestas, becoming godparents to the children of workers, and attempting to keep salaries to a minimum level. This apparent contrast between the hacienda and the cooperative form of organization that preceded it provides yet another illustration of the ways in which commercially oriented farmers use available institutional resources and models to meet the twin problems of scarcity of land and scarcity of labor.[7]

A further important dimension is that the formation of the hacienda represented an attempt at lessening the control of government over local agricultural activities and development. In the situation of increasing land fragmentation in Pucará, government extension agencies played a major part in providing the technical and credit facilities necessary to encourage larger-scale farming, often through the utilization of communal land.[8] However, this entailed close supervision by government experts and consequently, from the perspective of the individual, less flexibility in the management of resources. Hence a commercial group who previously had manipulated communal institutions to advance their economic interests found it necessary, under the new constraints imposed by central government, to convert their joint resources into a private enterprise.

The History of the Agrarian Society of Pucará

In 1953, the Agrarian Society of Pucará (*Sociedad Agrícola Pucará*) was formed as a cooperative to administer government agricultural credit. The government's program of supervised agricultural credit had among its main aims the creating of credit-worthy *comuneros*, the introduction of new agricultural techniques, and the consolidation of fragmented land holdings into more efficient units of production. Agricultural and administrative techniques were to be introduced through the local agency of SEAP (Servicio de Extensión Agrícola del Perú).[9] The capital was provided by the provincial branch of the national Agricultural Development Bank (Banco de Fomento Agropecuario del Perú).

The stated aim of the founders of the Agrarian Society was that of "making money." In the early meetings, there was frequent reference to the profits to be made from the cooperative experiment. For many there was also the interest of receiving training in new agricultural methods. As one of the first members of the society stated to me in an interview, "Just as the big producers know how to produce efficiently in agriculture and how to produce so much and so well, so in contrast what we produce has little value . . . It is for this reason that I joined the project so I could learn their techniques."

From the beginning, the government technicians received strong support from the *personero* of Pucará community, one of the highest authorities of the village. This man is now one of the co-owners of the hacienda. The *personero* was not one of the largest landowners in Pucará, owning only about two hectares of land, but he owned a shop in the village and traded agricultural products. He had studied in Huancayo and finally established himself in Pucará in 1925, inheriting land from his parents. In 1945, he organized a group of villagers into a sheep cooperative (*granja comunal*) with the aim of protecting part of Pucará's communal pasture from the incursions of the nearby hacienda, Sociedad Ganadera del Centro. This cooperative was successful, and nine of its original members were to join this man in the new agricultural project. He was one of the first villagers to begin trading directly with Lima in vegetables (e.g., peas and beans), and in 1950 he had begun a cooperative scheme to organize the production and sale of these products. It was he, then, who first approached the official agencies to initiate the new project.

The idea of the project was as follows: twenty-one hectares of communal land would be sown with potatoes; the national Agricultural Development Bank would provide the necessary capital; and the extension agency would technically direct the project. The original plan was to work most of the arable land of the community as one unit of production. Consequently the village authority responsible for communal property (Comité de Administración de Bienes Comunales) had to cancel the rental of twenty-one hectares of communal land; this land had previously been worked as individual plots by approximately one hundred *comuneros*. One initial problem was that, under the existing legislation, communal lands were inalienable and could not be mortgaged.[10] This meant that such lands could not be offered as a guarantee against a bank loan; to get around this difficulty the cooperative rented the communal land and took responsibility for the loan. The bank loan was made initially for a year only but was renewable for a second and third year.

The bank provided a loan of 150,000 *soles* at the usual interest rate of 9 percent. The community agreed to rent the land to the cooperative for five years and was to receive, in return, some 20 percent of the profits. A similar return was offered to those farmers who decided to rent their private lands to the cooperative. All profits remaining after the bank and the community were paid were to be shared equally among members of the cooperative.

In the first year, because of the late date of the initiation of the project, work was begun immediately; there was no time to discuss the advantages of the cooperative with the villagers. The *personero* met a series of difficulties from a group of *comuneros* opposed to the project. These, in the main, were people who previously had rented small plots from the community. There was also conflict with the school authorities, who objected to the use of land that had been ceded to them by the community. These arable communal lands had originally been church land, controlled by religious fraternities (*cofradías*), which in 1941 were taken over by the village when it gained legal recognition as a *comunidad indígena*. From the beginning, these lands had been rented to individual households, and a part of them had been given to the school to cultivate as a source of revenue.

The original plan of recruitment for the cooperative had been to include two representatives from each of the five *barrios* of the village and to delegate to them the task of recruiting other members from their *barrios*. Yet many persons refused to take part, some for lack of interest, others fearful of failure; others were turned down by the bank because of previously unsatisfactory credit repayments. Finally, ten members were recruited.

The cooperative had a *junta directiva* (executive committee) made up of the *personero* of the community, who was president, a secretary, and a treasurer, with the remaining seven members acting as committee members. The extension agent organized each of the members to take charge of one area of land, and instructed them in the use of insecticides, fertilizers, and machinery and in the recruitment and supervision of the paid work force.

An initial difficulty was that the bank, contrary to the wishes of the extension agency and of the cooperative, demanded that the cooperative should have a full-time administrator. It also proved difficult to recruit a paid work force for preparing and sowing the land because of local opposition to the project; this opposition came to a head when the bank's representative persuaded the police to imprison various individuals who were thought to be attempting to disrupt the scheme. Consequently labor was recruited as much from neighboring communities as it was from Pucará itself. There were also problems of internal organization. Individual members did not carry out the tasks assigned to them. The manager of the cooperative had a series of personal conflicts with the members; they felt that he left them with no responsibility. According to Alers-Montalvo, the members complained that the administrator had no experience of potatoes, having worked on the cotton estates of the coast.[11] The manager also quarreled with the extension agency and at the end of six months he had to leave the project with an unresolved charge of homicide against him. The extension agency took charge of the project's technical direction, and, during the period of cultivation and harvesting, its technicians frequently came to inspect the work. The bank also maintained close supervision, checking that the money was used as stipulated and compiling accounts of the costs of sowing, harvesting, and so on.[12]

Compared with the normal level of productivity in Pucará the harvest of the cooperative was excellent. However, due to the low price of potatoes in the first year the final net profit to each of the ten members of the cooperative was only six hundred *soles*, after they had paid the 20 percent share to the community and covered other costs, such as the hiring of machinery.

In the second year there was much greater interest in the cooperative.

Twenty-five members joined, including representatives of the *barrios* and some of the political authorities. But the opposition to the bank and to the extension agency grew. Once again the bank demanded that the extension agent take full charge of the technical direction of the project, and this was seen by members as an imposition of control upon them. Members complained that they were not trusted with responsibility, that they were treated like children, and that they were being experimented with to give prestige to the extension agency.

A significant change was made during this year in the renting of communal land; instead of paying the community 20 percent of the profits, it was agreed that 5,000 *soles* would be paid annually. Half of this money was to be raised in advance from among the members. When members learned of this, many of them resigned from the cooperative, leaving only twelve active members. This eliminated those with less resources. During the second year the farm was divided between ten hectares of potatoes and ten of peas. The yield was higher than in the preceding year, giving a net profit of some 76,000 *soles*.

In the third and fourth years, the cooperative had eleven members. Increasingly, the members took responsibility for the cultivation of crops and for the technical side of the enterprise. One of the members was nominated as "manager" to take overall responsibility for planning and direction. This person also subsequently became a co-owner of the hacienda. In both these years profits were high, averaging over 100,000 *soles*.

These eleven members were men who had higher than average extensions of private land, but they were not among the largest of the local farmers. Many in the group combined farming with other economic activities, such as trade and transport, and one of the members was a bank clerk in the neighboring village of Huayacachi. Several of them had held office in the village and all but two had been among the thirty-two founder members of the village's sheep cooperative, which was formed in 1945. What is perhaps most striking about the leaders of the group, however, is the nature of their migration and work experience. As mentioned earlier, the *personero* was a commercial entrepreneur. Another leading member, who owned about five acres of land, had a shop in the village and was a trader in agricultural products. This man had been born in Huancayo in 1894 of a mother who was from Pucará and a father from Huancavelica. He settled in Pucará in 1930 and had gradually bought land in the village. Another member, who became manager of the cooperative in 1958, had studied in Huancayo for four years; he then worked as a clerk in a store in the mining center of La Oroya for twelve years, until 1940. He came to

Pucará in that year to establish a large grocery store and to farm some five acres of inherited land. Another of the early leaders, who was president of the cooperative in 1956, was a large-scale trader and trucker who lived most of the time in Huancayo. He had spent a great deal of his time away from Pucará as a young man and had inherited only a very small plot of land.

The leaders of the group, then, were not primarily locally committed farmers but men who had established themselves in Pucará after labor migration experiences. In several cases, the initial capital had been derived from savings accumulated during migration; the experience and contacts made during this work experience were also evidently related to their present enterprises. They were a group already oriented to external opportunities and to seeking new entrepreneurial possibilities. Although several had held or were holding political office in local government, they were not a traditional elite in the sense of controlling or being committed to exploiting local resources, particularly land.

The Formation of the Hacienda and Village Reactions

In 1957, with the profits obtained in previous years and with the financial and technical help of the extension agency and the bank, the cooperative members decided to buy the hacienda Callacasa. This hacienda was owned by one of the established hacienda families of the region; it consisted of fifteen hundred hectares of land situated in a warmer climatic zone than Pucará.[13] The hacienda was sited at two-and-a-half hours by car and a further one-and-a-half hours by foot in the province of Tayacaja in the neighboring department of Huancavelica. The price of the hacienda was 220,000 *soles*, which was provided, in equal individual shares, by the twelve founder members. All these men were members of the cooperative.[14]

The purchase of the hacienda gave rise within the community to accusations that the cooperative members had become "hacendados," and a movement developed in the village for the community to "recover its own lands" and to exploit them itself. Under these pressures the cooperative decided to give up its exploitation of communal land, but it continued with the name of Sociedad Agrícola Pucará Callacasa, functioning now as a joint-stock company rather than as a cooperative. The company exploited the hacienda and also a total of ten hectares of land in the village owned by its members. It continued, however, to make use of loans from the bank.

The community of Pucará took over the direct exploitation of its land, organizing the work by *barrio* and through *faenas* (collective work parties). Profits were destined for expenditure on public works projects.

The extension agencies continued to supervise the project, but the *junta comunal* took over the responsibility for the organization of the work. In the first year a profit of some 88,000 *soles* was achieved, which was subsequently invested in such public works as a new cemetery, an electricity plant, and the village transport cooperative.

The transport cooperative had originated in an earlier conflict between private and communal interests.[15] A group of villagers had established a bus company to provide services between Pucará and important centers; this company had raised its tariffs despite strong village resistance. The company was supported by the provincial authorities, and, in retaliation, the leaders of the village decided to create a bus service operated by the community authorities, named *Cooperativa Comunal de Transportes*. The community's decision to reclaim control of its lands held by the agricultural cooperative followed the same strategy of attempting to limit private monopolies by concerted village action. In both cases, however, the community failed to maintain a pattern of cooperative organization. The buses of the transport cooperative became increasingly private in nature and the cooperative was later renamed Empresa de Transportes Huracán.[16]

In 1958 the profits of the agricultural cooperative were divided between the community and the *barrios* and amounted to 77,000 *soles*. During this time complaints were made by *comuneros* against the nonwage system of work; in the third year this disaffection reached a point where it severely reduced the productivity of the project. By 1960, only one of the village's five *barrios* continued to participate enthusiastically in the project; though this *barrio* obtained a good return from communal cultivation, the profit went to offset the losses made on the remainder of the community land. In 1961, the Extension Agency took a less direct interest in the communal lands in Pucará, leaving it to the initiative of the *comuneros* to organize production. This led to a return to the previous system of renting out communal land to individual households. With this decision, the community broke off its relationships with both the Extension Agency and the bank, leaving such contacts to the initiative of individual households.

The hacienda company had, by this time, adopted a similar course. By 1961, the company had cancelled its debts with the bank and from that year worked as a private company with its own capital. The company is now, in effect, a hacienda in which there can still be found all the traits of semifeudal exploitation characteristic of haciendas of highland Peru.[17] The means of production are in the hands of the twelve owners, and workers have usufructuary rights only so long as they provide labor service to the hacienda. In return the owners fulfill certain social obligations, providing gifts of coca, cakes, clothes, and so forth to workers and their families.

The major result of the nine years of government supervision of co-operative agriculture was the introduction of new farming techniques. Approximately 50 percent of our sample of those who had participated in the experiment mentioned that they had learned new methods, such as the use of insecticides and fertilizers or new ways of producing vegetables, from the extension agencies present during the project. Also, the project did introduce new credit-worthy farmers to the bank; eleven farmers currently receiving loans from the bank have done so since the initiation of the project. It is also evident that the joint cultivation of communal land influenced other communities in the valley to adopt similar experiments.

Yet, despite these general gains for the community, the history of the cooperative and the formation of the hacienda is fundamentally one of internal conflict. In order to understand the nature of these conflicts and the relationship between the villagers and government agencies, it is necessary to examine the social and economic characteristics of Pucará.

The Basis of Socioeconomic Differentiation in Pucará

Pucará is a village of about nineteen hundred inhabitants divided into 385 households. Of these, some 91 percent of heads of household consider themselves to be primarily involved in agriculture as a means of livelihood. The major nonagricultural occupation is shopkeeping, but, in addition, some 28 percent of the population complement farming with work as traders, carpenters, transporters, tailors, and so on. Migration has been, and still is, an important component of the village economy. Of the male heads of household, 78 percent have had migration experience outside the village, and migration is used by men at specific periods of their life cycles to build up resources within the village. Often younger men will migrate in order to acquire sufficient capital to marry; at a later stage in their careers, they may once again migrate to meet the necessities of a growing family. Migration has the general significance of being both a source of cash and a stimulus to innovation in local productive and commercial activities. The possibilities of marketing products and the contacts for doing so often arise out of a migration career. What limits enterprise in Pucará is the scarcity of local productive resources: this forces individuals to continue to explore a range of external opportunities.

Let us now compare the characteristics of the owners of the hacienda with those of the two other major social groupings in the village, namely, the farmers and the shopkeepers (table 1). From this it emerges that the members of the hacienda company have considerably more years of migration experience than do the other two groups; they also, on average, have higher levels of education and larger village landholdings. They are, on average, older than either of the other two groups, and almost all of them have migrated at one time or another to Lima. These statistics suggest that they constitute an elite group wih sufficient material and cultural resources to take advantage of economic opportunities.

However, these overall comparisons between groups in Pucará obscure important dimensions of the economic structure. Some 20 percent of the farming population have larger areas of village landholding than do the members of the hacienda company. Also, many of these farmers are involved in other economic enterprises, such as large-scale transport businesses operating on a regional basis. The most striking example is the one mentioned earlier of the Mariscal Cáceres Bus Company, which operates a fleet of about ten buses linking Huancayo, Lima, and other provincial capitals. This was first established by a group of individuals in Pucará, who used savings from migration and profits from agriculture. The buses remain individually owned by the members of the company, but the company has its headquarters in Huancayo.

It is within this context that we can better understand the resistance to the agricultural project and to government control. Members of the agricultural cooperative were neither so politically nor so economically dominant as to be able to consolidate their control over communal

TABLE ONE

SUMMARY OF THE SOCIOECONOMIC CHARACTERISTICS OF FARMERS, SHOPKEEPERS, AND OWNERS OF THE HACIENDA (HEADS OF HOUSEHOLD)

Socioeconomic characteristics	Farmers	Shopkeepers	Owners of the hacienda
Average level of education	3rd Year primary	5th Year primary	2nd Year secondary
Average number of dependents	3	2.5	3
Average number of years spent away from Pucará	2	4	8
Average holding of arable land	3 acres	4 acres	7 acres
Number of cases	372	23	11

resources. Also, their rival groups did not wish to commit the time or resources to exploit them themselves; indeed, for many of them it was more advantageous to rent communal land individually as a complement to their other activities.

Making use of external opportunities and manipulating government agencies has long been a way of life for households in Pucará. At the same time, given the relative homogeneity of Pucará's social and economic structure, no one group is able to monopolize such contacts; the wide range of migration and trading ventures in which they are involved have made such contacts accessible to most heads of household. Hence, constant political play takes place in the village in which small groups seek out particular external contacts to help them in their local economic opportunities, while other groups, using rival contacts, mobilize political parties or institutions in opposition.[18] What is significant is not who is successful in any particular conflict, but rather the circumstance that no group is able to consolidate its control over the local scene. For this reason, the more successful of local entrepreneurs have expanded their enterprises outside of Pucará and are not dependent on local labor or institutions; such is the case with both the hacienda and the bus company.

To all groups, government supervision and control was an irritant, because they already had considerable economic and organizational experience. Also, the formal mechanisms of credit allocation and management introduced by government constrained individual entrepreneurship and manipulation. For example, it has long been a practice in the Mantaro Valley for agricultural credit loans to be used surreptitiously to finance other enterprises, such as purchasing trucks or underwriting trading ventures.

Social Relationships and Economic Enterprise

Cooperative organization in Pucará is also hampered because the economic survival of households has depended on relatively exclusive exchange groupings that provide each other with aid and complementary services. Interhousehold cooperation is differentiated by such factors as the amount of labor available to the household, where households are involved primarily in agriculture or other ventures, and the types of links maintained outside the village. Households with well-established relationships of exchange tend to form the basis for formal organizations, such as cooperatives; in turn, this leads to a certain exclusiveness as positions of authority are monopolized and other groups become wary of entering.

I want now to analyze, in detail, the social relationships of the members of the Hacienda Company of Pucará in order to explore these suggestions and relate them to the economic structure of the village.

The members of the company are a group closely interconnected not only by common experience but also by friendship and kinship ties. They are also a group with a variety of interests other than agriculture, including commerce, public employment, and transport.

Exchange of labor by this group outside the hacienda occurs mainly over livestock and agricultural tasks but also includes help with irrigation and house construction. For example, I recorded the following conversation between two members of the company: "Do me a favor and help me turn over my plot in Huallpahuay tomorrow, because time is passing and I am way behind, due to the trip I made to my brother in Chanchamayo. In return, I will help you in moving your timber from Rumi-Chaza." Help with respect to illness usually occurs between relatives and does not imply a direct economic return. Loans, like help during illness, occur mainly between relatives. If we consider these three types of exchanges among members of the company a clear difference emerges between two subgroups (see diagram).

The first group (M. Espinoza, Flores, Díaz, G. Espinoza) maintains relationships based mainly on assistance during sickness and on the giving of loans, whereas the second group (Iparraguire, Ambrosio, Ureta, Chahua, Chamorro) is characterized by exchanges of labor. The loan connecting Flores and Chahua was made on a single occasion at Chahua's request and has not been exchanged, unlike the loans between members of the first group. The isolated Inga is an immigrant to Pucará, is a bachelor, and has insufficient resources to enter into such exchanges.

The differences between the subgroups are explained, first, by the socioeconomic position of the members and, second, by the nature of their participation in the company. In the group that is united by exchanges concerning problems of health and loans, all are related by kinship. Three of the group have occupations in addition to agriculture: two are shopkeepers, one is a trader. The remaining member lives with one of the shopkeepers, his brother. This group is economically able to hire agricultural laborers, a practice made necessary by the lack of an available large household labor force. It is impractical for these men to exchange labor with other relatives, since they would find it difficult to return the obligation. It is this group, then, that contracts laborers for their village plots from the hacienda labor force. Since they have occupied leadership positions in the hacienda, they are easily able to organize the recruitment of hacienda workers for sowing

Networks of Exchange of Work, Help During Illness, and Loans

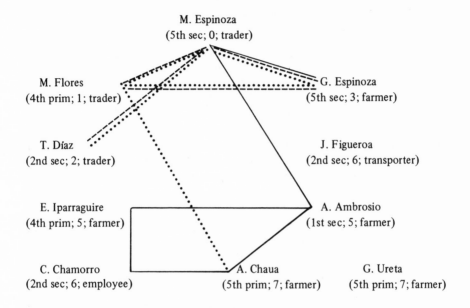

NOTES: Exchange of work   _____
         Exchange over health   ─ ─ ─ ─ ─ ─
         Exchange of loans   ················

The data in parentheses refer, first, to level of education, second, to number of additional members of household and, third, to principal occupation.

and harvesting, paying them a daily wage of between thirty and forty *soles*.

Members of the first group have occupations that give them common interests in maintaining external contacts; indeed, the work relationship between the transporter, Figueroa, and G. Espinoza is based on mutual help with information and with the collection and transportation of produce and goods, since Figueroa lives in Huancayo. In contrast to the members of the second group, the men of this first group are more likely to have members of their immediate family resident outside Pucará. Of Flores's six children, one lives in Iquitos, another in Lima, and the rest in Huancayo. Four of G. Espinoza's children live permanently outside Pucará and only one lives with him. Also, their levels of education attest to the educational progress in Pucará, for three of their children have finished college and now hold professional jobs.

In contrast, the other group depends mainly on agriculture and, because it lacks economic resources, must depend more heavily on the exchange of labor services among themselves. The only exception is Chamorro, who is a public employee in Huancayo. This man works in Huancayo and is therefore unable to spend much time in the hacienda; thus he has to depend on the other members. The members of this second group have households of between five and seven members, of whom three or more are of adult status. These larger households enable them to maintain closer relationships of work exchange, and they have no need to contract laborers either within or outside Pucará.

The level of education of the first group is, in general, higher than that of the second group, with more members having obtained some secondary education. It is the men of the first group who have been the administrative officers for the company. The only member of the second group who has occupied a leadership post is Chahua.

Despite their common situation as owners of the same hacienda, these social differences among the members affect the working organization of the company. For example, a conflict emerged during the election of the present administrative officers of the hacienda. The second group had presented a member of their group as candidate for the post of manager. This man was not accepted by those in the first group, who claimed that the only person suitable was Díaz, because he knew a great deal about the administration of the hacienda and was also familiar with the current agrarian reform law. They pointed out that his appointment was necessary to ensure an adequate defense of their interests should the government decide to intervene in the hacienda. And, on the basis of similar arguments, two other executive positions were filled by members of the first group. The only member of the second group to be elected was Chahua, who owned the largest extension of village land. Once the meeting was over, members belonging to the second group complained bitterly, proclaiming that they had never held any important office, and they threatened to refuse to supervise the work on the hacienda.

This analysis of exchanges between members of the company illustrates the types of economic situation that lead to differentiation between groups of peasant households. At the time of the formation of the company, all members had sufficient in common to wish to cooperate in the extension of their family enterprises. The two groups were linked indirectly through ties of occupation, such as their participation in the sheep cooperative, economic exchange, and some degree of kinship. After the establishment of the company, however, the different demands of their household economies led to conflicts within the company and to the emergence of two separate internal networks.[19]

This case serves to highlight the problems attendant on cooperative organization at the community level. The economy of Pucará has become increasingly diversified as it has been drawn into the urban orbit. There has also been pressure on available arable land. This has meant the increasing involvement of families in non-agricultural activities that generate cash income. This practice has tended to undermine traditional forms of labor exchange, but it has also stimulated experimentation with new forms of cooperative alliance. Small shopkeepers in Pucará, for example, assist each other in purchasing products and supplying products not in stock. This group of shopkeepers is made up predominantly of immigrants from Huancavelica, who have married into the village and are closely united through kinship bonds. Households involved in transport activities have developed similar alliances based on complementary economic interests and cemented by formal association and by bonds of friendship and kinship.[20]

These cooperative alliances are restricted in regard to both the numbers of those involved and the status position of the participants; for example, traders have more possibilities of useful exchange with fellow traders than, for example, with relatives whose need is for extra labor on their farms. One of the bases for such alliances is interpersonal trust developed out of long association; this trust is an important component in the extension of economic enterprise beyond the immediate household. This means, however, that the workings of formal cooperative organizations are unlikely to follow universalistic principles of management and election to office. People in Pucará trust officeholders with whom they have particular relationships of exchange. Thus, because of the fragmentation of interests and alliances, formal organizations that attempt to cater to the needs of the whole population tend to be subverted to the ends of particular economic interests.

It is interesting that in Pucará there are no significant village-wide fiestas, whereas, in other villages of the Mantaro, such fiestas have often served to consolidate economic and social alliances.[21] Also, the degree of social and economic fragmentation has impeded the development of clear class divisions within the community. Some observers have interpreted the situation of Pucará as one of internal solidarity; I would prefer to emphasize the shifting pattern of alliances that, situationally, may provide the basis for collective action on the part of particular interest groups. Such a pattern of alliances does not, however, encourage the consistent development of cooperative forms of organization. This lack of consistency results from internal social and economic differentiation, combined with increasing dependence on external economic resources. The differences that exist between households may be small economically, but they are highly significant for understanding differences in household strategy and cooperation.

Conclusion

The difficulties encountered by the cooperative agricultural project in Pucará were based on such differences among members as their forms of income, additional occupations, and possession of private landholdings. These problems were accentuated by the tendency of the government agencies to make unilateral decisions with respect to the functioning of the cooperative. In the early days, these agencies paid attention only to technical considerations and took little account of the social factors influencing the success of the cooperative. These social factors, such as local unwillingness to provide labor without payment, restricted cooperative possibilities.

The organization of the hacienda outside the Mantaro Valley enabled its owners to more easily exploit a labor force without being restricted by either community or government norms of exchange. But the establishment of the hacienda did not solve the problems of cooperative farming. Differences in access to resources led to competition among the owners. The main factors relevant to an analysis of this process were differences in the size of private landholding, in migration experience, in levels of education, and in political ambition.

The case of Pucará illustrates the difficulties of attaining community-wide cohesion in the face of the fragmentation of interests created, in part, by the external orientation of the local economy. This external orientation is reinforced by the interests of government and other formal agencies in mobilizing local economic and social resources to promote regional and national development. Despite the relative homogeneity of the village, it has become increasingly socially fragmented over time, and this fragmentation has inhibited the emergence of a united front on such issues as the implementation of agrarian reform and the development of local resources and institutions.

NOTES

1. This chapter has been translated and amended by the editors from Solano's professional thesis presented to the Universidad Nacional del Centro del Perú in 1973 and entitled "Un estudio caso de la Sociedad Agrícola Pucará." The study is based on participant observation and interview material collected as part of the British SSRC project in Pucará between 1970 and 1972.

2. Other accounts of Pucará that deal more fully with this cooperative tradition are Manuel Alers-Montalvo, *Pucará: Un estudio de cambio*, and G. Alberti and R. Sánchez, *Poder y conflicto social en el valle del Mantaro*.

3. Harry Tschopik, *Highland Communities of Central Peru*; José María Arguedas, "Evolución de las comunidades indígenas," *Revista del Museo Nacional* 26 (1957): 102.

4. These data are taken from a random sample of interviews with 127 heads of household in Pucará.

5. Alberti and Sánchez, *Poder y conflicto social*, p. 79.

6. Compare the chapters by Winder, Long and Sánchez, and Grondin in this volume.

7. The strategies adopted by Pucará entrepreneurs show a similar logic to those of the "independent farmers" described by Samaniego in this volume.

8. Government and international agencies have, for many years, attempted to promote programs designed to combat land fragmentation in the Mantaro area. The Pucará experiment was one of the first, and, currently, the German Technical Mission in the valley is experimenting with other village-based agricultural schemes.

9. Manuel Alers-Montalvo, "Social Systems Analysis of Supervised Agricultural Credit in an Andean Community," *Rural Sociology* 25, no. 1 (1960): 51–64. This program was sponsored by the Servicio Cooperativo Interamericano de Producción de Alimentos (SCIPA) as a demonstration project.

10. See Winder in this volume for the legal origins of the *comunidad campesina*. Pucará had originally been an annex of Sapallanga and it was only with its recognition as a *comunidad* that it gained control of its communal resources.

11. Alers-Montalvo, "Social Systems Analysis," p. 57.

12. Alers-Montalvo, *Pucará: Un estudio de cambio*. My discussion of the performance of the cooperative relies heavily on Alers-Montalvo's material collected during the period of the extension project.

13. This family was the Tovar family, who owned various properties in Huancavelica, though most of them lived in Huancayo. They had acquired it in 1915 from the Giráldez family, another important Huancayo-based hacendado family.

14. One of the twelve later died, so my subsequent discussion refers to eleven owners. The eleven cooperative members of 1956 had recruited an additional partner who had participated in the early years of the cooperative.

15. This type of conflict between private and communal interests over exploitation of local resources is comparable with the situation of Huayopampa in the upper Chancay Valley (Fernando Fuenzalida et al., *Estructuras tradicionales y economía de mercado: La comunidad de indígenas de Huayopampa*).

16. Alberti and Sánchez, *Poder y conflicto social*, p. 90.

17. Julio Cotler, "The Mechanics of Internal Domination and Social Change in Peru," *Studies in Comparative International Development* 3, no. 12 (1967–1968); Henry Favre, Claude Collin Delavaud, and José Matos Mar, *La hacienda en el Perú*.

18. Alberti and Sánchez, *Poder y conflicto social*, pp. 110–122. My interpretation is different in that I find that the rival groups have less consistency of interest as a consequence of the complex, externally linked nature of the local economy.

19. See Smith and Cano in this volume for an analysis of the significance for internal conflict of the different rationalities of household economies in Huasicancha.

20. Such alliances between transporters have been noted for other parts of the valley. See Bryan R. Roberts, "The Interrelationships of City and Provinces in Peru and Guatemala," in *Latin American Urban Research,* vol. 4, edited by W. A. Cornelius and F. M. Trueblood, pp. 224–228; and Long and Sánchez in this volume.

21. Roberts, "The Interrelationships of City and Provinces."

8. The Impact of the *Comunidad* on Local Development in the Mantaro Valley

DAVID WINDER

The military government's peasant community statute, implemented during General Velasco's regime, is a less well known part of its agrarian reform than is the establishment of large agricultural cooperatives to replace haciendas and coastal plantations.[1] The implementation of the 1970 statute deserves attention partly because it explicitly aimed at revitalizing communal systems of land ownership and exploitation. It is an example of those agrarian reform policies that seek to achieve greater social and economic equality and increased productivity, using indigenous traditions of political and economic organization. Both the collective *ejido* of Mexico and the *Ujamaa* villages of Tanzania are examples of such attempts to develop new agrarian institutions on the basis of supposedly collectivist traditions.[2] The peasant community statute in Peru had as one of its principal stated aims the development of production or service cooperatives based on existing peasant communities (*comunidades indigenas*); the government considered the restructured *comunidad* a viable corporate organization capable of extending its control over new resources and managing them effectively.[3]

The use of traditional institutions as a means of structural reform raises the issue of whether a government's conception of the functioning of such institutions corresponds to their historical reality. It is unlikely, for example, that communal institutions remain unaffected by the capitalist penetration of an underdeveloped country or by centuries of colonial or neocolonial domination. Also, the effectiveness of a communal reform policy is likely to be extremely limited when the eco-

209

nomic organization of society remains based, as in the case of Peru, on market principles of assigning value and allocating resources. The study of the implementation of the community statute is one means of assessing the internal transformations of the agrarian structure produced by capitalist penetration and the limitations these transformations entail for a centrally directed policy of reform.

My analysis concentrates on two of the most economically developed villages of the Mantaro Valley; both of these were *comunidades indigenas* with a long history of communally achieved development in installing agricultural improvements, such as irrigation, and such services as water, sewage, and education. Their high level of both economic development and communal achievement makes them interesting, if exceptional, opportunities to study the contradictions implicit in the peasant community reform. To preface my analysis of the contemporary situation, I examine the changing role and functions of the *comunidad* since Spanish colonial times; this overview provides background information that is complemented by the accounts of Grondin (1974) and Samaniego (in this volume) of the ways in which, historically, the idea and organization of the *comunidad* were used for particular ends by different rural social strata.

Historical Origins of *Comunidades Campesinas*

Although Peruvian writers of the early part of this century idealized the precolonial social system, locating the origins of the *comunidad* in Inca culture and in primitive communism, recent writings have emphasized the central role of the household in precolonial society.[4] While land rights were vested in *ayllus*,[5] plots were allocated to each household according to the number of dependents, and the household was the basic unit of labor. Other lands were collectively worked for the Inca emperor, the Sun God, and the *curacas* (local caciques or chiefs), who exercised control over a number of *ayllus*.[6] Members of *ayllus* were also obliged to give their labor in the construction and maintenance of irrigation works and other public services. This obligation was termed *mita*.

Colonial agrarian policy can, to a large extent, be understood in terms of the dilemma of Crown officials who needed to reward the *conquistadores*, encourage Spanish settlement, and, also, protect the lives and traditions of the indigenous population; the interest of the Crown in the Indian population was that they were potential converts to Christianity and provided labor and tribute.

The interests of the Spanish colonizers were met through the *repar-*

timiento (grant of land) and the *encomienda*. The *encomienda* conferred on its holder the right to receive tribute and free labor from the Indian population. This institution encouraged the exploitation of the local population and threatened to create alternative bases of power to that of the Crown. The *encomienda* was suppressed in the early seventeenth century, but the Crown was unable to control effectively the large landholders, or hacendados, as they subsequently were called. The hacienda often originated in the *repartimiento* system and was a landholding to which the owner had legal title. It was the ownership and control of land that guaranteed the hacendado his labor force and his production; in return for subsistence plots of land or for a share in the animals or crops, Indian households and, sometimes, whole villages provided a specified number of days of service to the hacienda. The position of the landed elites was strengthened by their alliance with the local authorities of the Crown—the *corregidores*.[7]

The protection of the indigenous population was the subject of a series of royal ordinances throughout the colony; these ordinances attempted to safeguard land belonging to *indígenas*, regulated their hours of work, wages, and tribute to be paid. The ordinances also made it difficult for an *indígena* to own private land. One of the most important results of this policy, especially for the development of the *comunidad indígena*, was the establishment of *reducciones* or *pueblos* by Viceroy Toledo in 1569.

The *reducciones* emerged from the Crown's attempt to create a more efficient administrative system, facilitating the control of the labor and other resources of the local community and, also, promoting conversion to Catholicism through the setting up of parishes and religious brotherhoods. Carlos V, in 1551, decreed that the indigenous population should be concentrated in *pueblos* (towns) and not live isolated by mountains and deprived of the spiritual guidance of priests. The following year, Felipe II issued an ordinance in which he requested the viceroy to ensure that the Indians held their property communally.

In these townships the indigenous population was given land that they were to hold collectively as a *común de indios*, later called *comunidad de indígenas*.[8] Individual households could be given the usufructure of this land, but according to the Ordinances of Toledo the land could not be disposed of without the permission of the viceroy. The concept and practice of communal land use was not alien to the Spanish colonizers; Arguedas describes how the system of communal use of pasture and the granting of parcels of arable land to each community member had long been the practice in Spain.[9] The pattern of land tenure that the Spanish colonizers developed in the *reducciones* contained features of both Inca and Spanish systems. Pasture land was for the communal use of the *indios*, or *comuneros*, as they came to be called. Arable land was usually divided out annually, according to Spanish or Inca tradition. Only members of the *común* (i.e., *comuneros*) were entitled to participate in this division.

Arguedas cites the case of the community of Mollapata de Apurímac, where the Inca method was followed, namely, that the land was shared out in accord with the increase or decrease of family size.[10] Special provisions were made for the allocation of land parcels to those who had recently gained *comunero* status by becoming heads of household. In addition to this community land, land was allocated to cover the expenses of the town council (*municipio*), to provide for a community grain store that was used to supply the poorer members of the community in times of need, and to support the *cofradías*.[11] These *pueblos* were governed by *curacas* who were made responsible for the collection of taxes and the organization of the *mita*.

In the 614 *reducciones* with their communal landholding system we find the origin of the present-day *comunidad*, a corporate landholding institution recognized by law.[12] Not all the indigenous population was brought together with the *reducciones*; many *ayllus* were allowed to remain on their lands and were given legal title to these lands.[13]

Under colonial rule we see the emergence of the two contrasting socioeconomic systems in the Peruvian agrarian structure—the hacienda and the *comunidad indígena*. The former expanded at the expense of the latter. The usurpation of community lands by Spaniards and local caciques occurred most rapidly in the coastal valleys and some of the richer intermountain valleys, where soil fertility was high and ample irrigation was available. The *comunidad indígena* became increasingly a phenomenon of the sierra (mountain area) and the traditional *ayllu* organization survived only in the more remote parts of the country.

The achievement of independence from Spain brought a change in the legal status of *comunidades*. Bolívar's decrees of 1824 removed the limited protection afforded them under colonial law by abolishing the communal landholding system. This policy of ordering community lands to be redistributed as private property was intended to stimulate the economic recovery of rural areas. While the policy encouraged the further development of a class of large landholders from among those responsible for implementing the government decision (caciques, village notables, lawyers), the general socioeconomic condition of *comuneros* failed to improve.[14] A process of increasing differentiation occurred, and "indeed by the 1850s the old *comunidades* had become something of a microcosm of the surrounding countryside, containing within their old boundaries a general mix of large and small, privately-owned holdings." [15]

Matos Mar described how Bolívar's decrees affected the Chancay Valley communities. [16] By decreeing that communal lands should be shared out among heads of household with the right of sale, the legislation led to the disintegration of large corporate family groups and to the decline of the power of communal organization. Throughout the nineteenth century the continuing transference of communally controlled land resources into private hands produced a new system of social stratification at the local level. This comprised—

1. a small group of rich elders who controlled scarce irrigated land and because of their control over resources tended to monopolize the positions of authority in the community;

2. the majority of peasants, who were *minifundistas* (microplot holders), mainly due to the inheritance system that divided land among all male and female heirs;

3. the young landless peasants, who, through lack of means, were unable to perform their duties within the politicoreligious system that had developed under Spanish rule. [17]

With the opening up of lines of communication with provincial capitals and Lima, it tended to be the small elite group that benefited by obtaining key political posts and by transferring their surplus into expanding commercial activities. Their emergence as brokers enabled them to strengthen their control over the community.

In the lowland villages of the Mantaro Valley the transference of arable land ownership from *ayllus* to family units had started as early as the latter part of the seventeenth century and was complete by the mid-nineteenth century. The process of alienation took place earlier than in the Chancay Valley due to the spread of the cash economy that resulted from the expansion of the mining sector in the area and the large market that the mines provided for foodstuffs. Early in the twentieth century the improved communications with Lima greatly expanded the market for foodstuffs and encouraged the emergence of groups of commercially oriented farmers within local communities.

It was within this context of the social and economic differentiation of local communities that, from 1900 onwards, *comunidades indígenas* became a subject of interest to many political and intellectual groups. Some groups were concerned with the adverse effect of the expansion of plantations, mines, and urban areas on the indigenous population;

other groups were interested in strengthening community organization as a means of access to a cheap source of temporary labor for road building, plantation harvests, and mine work.[18]

In response to the *indigenismo* pressure groups, President Leguía incorporated a number of articles into the 1920 constitution to protect *comunidades*. The main provisions were the granting of official legal status to *comunidades* and the protection of their communal land resources from the encroachment of private landowners.[19] In 1921 a new Indigenous Affairs Bureau was created within the Ministry of Development to implement the constitutional provisions, and in 1926 the process of official recognition began. In 1926, 59 *comunidades* were registered and, by 1969, 2,337 had been officially recognized.[20] Yet despite this legal protection, the disintegration and despoliation of the communities continued unabated.[21]

I will now narrow the focus to an analysis of the evolution of two *comunidades*, examining events leading to the official recognition of each *comunidad* and describing its role in improving local infrastructure, services, and household incomes. The two Mantaro Valley *comunidades* are those of the villages of Sicaya and Matahuasi (see map 2, p. 00). Sicaya has a population of 5,237 (1972 census) and 3,696 hectares of arable land (approximately 20 percent of which is irrigated). Six percent of the arable land is owned by the *comunidad*.[22] It is situated ten kilometers to the northwest of Huancayo in the province of that name. Matahuasi has a population of 3,972 (1972 census) and 1,575 hectares of arable land (60 percent of which is irrigated). Sixty hectares of arable land are owned by the *comunidad*. It is situated twenty-five kilometers to the north of Huancayo in the province of Concepción.

Sicaya and Matahuasi Seek Official Recognition as *Comunidades Indígenas*

By the early twentieth century, Sicaya and Matahuasi were among the most socially and economically differentiated of valley villages. Relative to other villages they both had ample resources in arable and pasture land; Matahuasi had less land per capita than Sicaya, but a much greater proportion of this land was irrigated. In both villages a group of commercial farmers, owning extensions of twenty hectares and upwards, dominated the local political institutions. Despite these similarities, the two villages have different histories with respect to the development of the *comunidad indígena*. In Sicaya, the *comunidad* was legally recognized earlier than in Matahuasi and was endowed with greater extensions of communal land; in Matahuasi, pressures for the individual partitioning of existing communal resources delayed the

legal recognition of the *comunidad indígena* and resulted in most of
these resources being appropriated by individual farmers. By contrasting the process by which the *comunidad indígena* was legally recognized
in these two villages we can explore the complex functions of the
comunidad.

The village of Santo Domingo de Sicaya was first mentioned in 1583
in a report sent by Viceroy don Martín de Enríquez de Almanza to the
king of Spain. During the colonial era Sicaya appears to have lost extensive land resources in the valley, the highlands, and the hot lowlands, and upon independence the only significant communal lands
remaining were the pastures of Cacchi (11,700 hectares) on the high
plateau west of the village.[23] The small settlement of Cacchi, a dependent annex of Sicaya, had taken the initiative of applying for legal
recognition as an indigenous community in 1931, claiming right to
ownership of all the pasture. Cacchi was inhabited by shepherds who
tended the flocks of Sicaínos in return for the right to pasture their
own sheep and a share in lowland agricultural products. A small group
of Cacchinos had built up sizeable flocks of their own and had started
to grow potatoes, thereby reducing their dependence on the Sicaya
farmers.

Because of the high risks involved in keeping livestock at a distance
(eighty kilometers), most Sicaya farmers had, by this time, concentrated
their investments in lowland agriculture. The exceptions were a group
of farmers who still had significant flocks of sheep, cattle, and llamas
in Cacchi and who were aware of the need to protect these resources
against the expanding haciendas. The owners of the hacienda Laive
used their influence in Lima government circles to obtain a decision
in favor of Cacchi and thereby deprive Sicaya of two-thirds of its total
land. This temporary alliance between Laive and Cacchi developed
because the hacienda considered it to be easier to dominate an independent Cacchi; Cacchi had far fewer political contacts in Lima than
did Sicaya (see Samaniego, in this volume).

Sicaya had sought legal recognition as a *comunidad indígena* as early
as 1931. The promoters of this scheme—the group of commercial farmers in the village—argued that by obtaining the "indigenous" classifica-
tion they would be entitled to more government help through the
Indigenous Affairs Bureau.[24] Apart from the disputed Cacchi lands,
Sicaya did not, however, possess directly any communal land resources;
such resources were a necessary condition of recognition as a *comunidad.*

One potential set of communal resources was the church lands; approximately two hundred and fifty hectares of arable land had been
given to the Sicaya parish by local families for the support of the church

and for the cult of particular saints. Plots of varying sizes were cultivated annually by the sponsors of fiestas to help toward the costs of
these religious festivals. According to Escobar, these lands were worked
communally until the turn of the century; at this time, the system
began to break down under the increasing individualization of social
relations in the village that resulted from increasing trade and improved communication with urban areas.[25] During 1925 and 1926 there
was evidence of increasing tension between the farming community and
the church; this tension led eventually to the invasion of church land
in 1927. Escobar argues that the main factors were the anticlerical
preachings of the liberals and economic conditions.[26] He also cites the
increasing migration into the village and a steadily rising cost of living.
It was also the case that villagers feared that the church intended to
sell the land to individuals.

In contrast to the situation in Matahuasi, however, Sicaya farmers
and their authorities maintained a common front in their negotiations
with the church authorities, which lasted from 1927 to 1931. An agreement was reached between the bishop of Huánuco and twenty-two
villagers, many of whom had held the position of *mayordomo* in the
cofradías, by which the church kept 30 hectares and the remaining 220
hectares were sold for fifteen thousand *soles* to the Junta Administradora de los Bienes de la Iglesia (Administrative Committee for Church
Properties). In order to pay off the debt incurred, this committee sold
20 hectares to a farmer from the neighboring village of Orcotuna. The
remaining 200 hectares (comprising fifty-five scattered plots of irrigated
and nonirrigated land) were rented out to those farmers who could
afford it. In 1933, when the *comunidad* was formally recognized, it
opted to continue with the same policy; this policy has continued ever
since and has provided the *pueblo* with a regular source of income.

Matahuasi was founded as a *reducción* in the late sixteenth century.
The *comunidad* claims to have documents proving that its ownership
of lands dates from 1740.[27] The fact that the documents were kept in
the church implies that the *comunidad* lands in question were originally given to the *cofradías* and worked by *comuneros* to finance the
fiestas and maintain the religious images. As in other valley *pueblos*,
all arable land belonging to the *comunidad* probably became private
property as a result of Bolívar's decrees dissolving the *comunidad indígena*; all that remained in communal hands after the 1820s were the
cofradía lands and a few hectares of pasture near the river.

These *cofradía* lands were administered by the Junta Administradora
Comunal (the predecessor of the *comunidad*), which had no legal standing. The original lands granted to the *cofradías* and the church had

been increased by bequests from richer people in the village. Some of the land, a total of 230 hectares, was worked by communal *faenas* (work parties), and the harvests of barley and potatoes were sold to finance the three principal fiestas in the village—San Sebastián (20 January), San Luis Conzaga, Patron of Youth (21 June), and La Virgen de la Asunción (15 August). Other parts of the land were rented out.

Every year the Junta Administradora Comunal would ask for *mayordomos* to come forward to cultivate the respective *cofradía* plots. Each *mayordomo* would then promise to finance the particular fiesta. The return he got on the harvest would then be his, but he risked losing if the harvest failed. Villagers talk of the enthusiasm with which *comuneros* used to collaborate in these *faenas*. They say that as recently as 1930 most adults resident in the village were *comuneros* and fulfilled their obligations to the *comunidad*.

Following the bishop of Huánuco's decision in 1930 to sell the lands of parish churches, the *comuneros* of many villages mobilized to keep the lands under communal control. The people of Matahuasi took no steps to defend the church land until 1936, when the vicar of Jauja started to sell land in Matahuasi. He did so without consulting the *comunidad* or officially publishing his intention to sell. There was no valuation of the land nor public auction.

The *comunidad* reacted by calling a public assembly, at which they appointed a committee "for the defense of community property." Three members of this committee, led by the *personero* (legal representative), traveled to Lima to petition government ministries on behalf of the *comunidad*, requesting the assistance of government in protecting the communal land. Not only did they fail to fulfill the appointed mission but two of them bought the best lands for themselves and helped members of their families to purchase land. Control over this excellent irrigated land (140 acres or 15 percent of the total irrigated land in the district) has enabled the purchasers and their heirs to improve their economic and social position relative to the majority of small holders.

Displaying belated initiative, the Junta Administradora Comunal eventually moved to defend the remaining ninety hectares of church land. But the junta proved unable to manage this land effectively, and on 27 June 1938 a document signed by ninety-two *comuneros* was sent to the district council, stating: "As there exists grave danger that the community lands may be exploited by other persons, the *comunidad* requests the district council to take over the administration and protection of *comunidad* lands and administer them in benefit of local progress." The district council responded by organizing a consumer and production cooperative society whose small group of members, mainly wealthier farmers and intermediaries, benefited from the usufruct of individual plots of community land for three years. The mayor himself, together with a friend, rented thirty hectares.

During this period more church land was sold by the diocesan priest at Jauja. As late as 1942, 7.5 hectares were sold to one of the original purchasers. The fact that purchases were spread over almost six years highlights how ineffective the Junta Administradora Comunal was at the time. The alienation of land was finally stopped with the reorganization and legal recognition of the community in 1942. At the time of recognition, there were only 209 registered *comuneros*, about 30 percent of total heads of household in the district.[28]

Role of the *Comunidad* in *Pueblo* Development

A number of studies have focused attention on the role of the *comunidad* as the mobilizer of labor through *faenas*.[29] In small-holder zones, such as the Mantaro Valley, where little or no land is worked communally, this constitutes the principal activity of the *comunidad*. The effectiveness of the *comunidad* in initiating projects and organizing labor varies with individual villages. Of particular importance are the aims and objectives of the *comunidad* as defined by its leaders and the means it has at its disposal to encourage participation in communal work projects.[30]

Any one of a number of village institutions can initiate public works projects, call for voluntary labor, and supervise the work. Principal among these is the *consejo distrital* (district council or municipality), and others include the parents' associations (for school construction, extensions, and repairs), the district administration of waters and irrigation, the governor's office, and the *barrios* and *cuarteles*, where these exist.[31] While membership of these institutions usually overlaps, conflicts of interest may develop when different interest groups control different institutions or when there are opposing factions within institutions.

My analysis of public works projects completed between 1935 and 1973 in Sicaya indicates that the *comunidad* has played a leading role in initiating projects; however, these projects have in no way altered the unequal distribution of land and economic resources in the village. For these projects the *comunidad* has provided the major part of the *pueblo* financial contribution, with income from renting community lands. Migrant clubs in Lima have assisted these projects by raising funds and exerting pressure on the appropriate government departments for the allocation of resources and technical assistance.[32] An example of the ability of the *comunidad* to mobilize voluntary labor and sustain interest and participation over a long period (1955–1958) was the installation of the piped drinking water supply. The *comunidad* provided 34,000 man days of voluntary unskilled labor to construct a reservoir in the catchment area, twelve kilometers of pipeline, and a bridge. All *comuneros* were obliged to work one day a week or send a substitute. Those who could afford to do so sent a paid laborer (*peón*) in their place, with the result that the physical work was carried out mainly by the poorer peasant farmers and laborers. The high rate of participation in these work parties is explicable in terms of the total absence of easily accessible water in Sicaya and the promise of piped water to each house.

In addition to labor, all residents were asked to contribute money toward the cost of the project. Only 241 of the 800 heads of family gave the requested monetary contribution. Many non-*comuneros* (tradesmen, craftsmen, and professionals) made no contribution, yet they were the first to benefit from the new service since they could buy pipes to connect their houses with the main grid. A breakdown of financial contributions to the project indicates the heavy dependence on help from government and international agencies, who contributed more than 70 percent of the total cost.

The case of Sicaya provides a clear example of how the richer owner-farmers have made use of the *comunidad* to provide a propitious environment for the expansion of their commercial farming and trading activities. Through their contacts with political leaders, often using migrant villagers as intermediaries, they have been able to gain financial support for local improvement projects, thereby increasing their personal prestige and legitimizing their authority. There is little evidence to suggest that this constitutes part of what would generally be regarded as a community development process. The selection of projects was made by the district council and/or *comunidad* officials and inevitably represented the interests of the privileged sectors of rural society.

When compared with Sicaya, the *comunidad* of Matahuasi appears to have played a less important role in initiating *pueblo* projects. This principally results from its less secure economic base (income derived from renting out thirty hectares of arable land) and the preoccupation of the *comuneros* with attempts to recover the "church" lands. Since 1941, a very significant proportion of its income has been used to finance legal proceedings; the large number of references to this conflict in the *comunidad* records is an indication of the extent to which this issue has dominated community affairs, to the detriment of other projects. The conflict between the *comunidad* and the group of influential farmers who bought the church land accounts, in part, for the difficulties in bringing people together to discuss and solve the problems facing the *pueblo*.

As one way of assessing the extent to which *comuneros* do cooperate with each other in joint ventures and the conditions under which they do so, I examined the records of participation in *pueblo* projects. These data were checked by interviewing 50 percent of the *comuneros*. Table 1 gives the results.

The records indicate that *comunero* participation has been greatest in projects one and three. Both these projects were carried out at a time when there was reasonable collaboration between *comunidad* and district council. In both periods, the mayors were elected by popular vote and villagers were consulted at different stages during the planning and implementation of the projects.[33] The mayor for the period 1964–1968 had been elected in an open assembly, and he had held regular public meetings to report on progress in his negotiations with outside bodies and to ask for ideas and opinions from those present. He was a craftsman and small farmer and able to command the support of a larger sector of the population than did most of his predecessors, who were mainly medium- or large-scale farmers and intermediaries.

Villagers saw both schemes as satisfying a definite need in the village and providing their families with specific benefits. In both cases the *comunidad* provided the necessary land (four hectares in the case of the agricultural college), all the unskilled voluntary labor, and a significant part of the total budget. The government provided technical assistance, tools, and materials at the time when they were required (through *Co-operación Popular*, or Popular Cooperation Program) and, in general, gave encouragement and motivation to the *comunidad*. These two self-help projects came nearer to meeting the requirements of a community development project than any others previously planned or completed in the *pueblo*.

In contrast, the new church building is an example of a project that has received the support of only the minority of villagers; work on this building has been in progress for twenty years. The *comunidad* as an institution has not been involved in calling work parties or collecting funds. Work parties were summoned by the district council, and funds were collected by a special committee (*Comité pro-Templo*). A major reason for the lack of collaboration between *comunidad* and district council on this project has been the close involvement of some of the purchasers of church land in the special committee and the continued antagonism between *comunidad* and church. The majority of *comuneros* see the church building as a project designed and ex-

TABLE 1
PRINCIPAL PUBLIC WORKS PROJECTS CARRIED OUT BETWEEN 1945 AND 1968 IN MATAHUASI

Percentage Responses of *Comunero* Sample (57 Respondents)

Name of Project	Dates	Initiating institution and principal leaders involved [a]	Principal contribution of *pueblo* was in:		Whether there was a contribution from government [b]		Whether there was a nongovernment contribution from outside *pueblo* (migrant clubs)		Nature of contribution of *comunidad*
(1) Agricultural College (*Instituto Agropecuario*)	1967–1972	District council/*comunidad* Carlos Roque—mayor (APRA/UNO candidate) Leonel Valdorama—mayor	Labor Money Materials Don't know Total	53 30 17 – 100	Yes No, or don't know Total	30 70 100	Yes No, or don't know Total	5 95 100	Donated Land
(2) New Church Building	1954 (still unfinished)	District council Carlos Roque—mayor Rodrigo Alvaroz—mayor (large farmer, son of purchaser of church land)	Labor Money Materials Don't know Total	30 28 12 30 100	Yes No, or don't know Total	25 75 100	Yes No, or don't know Total	20 80 100	—
(3) Clinic (*Posta Médica*)	1967–1969	District council/*comunidad* Carlos Roque—mayor Enrique Ortiz—mayor Arturo Ortiz—mayor	Labor Money Materials Don't know Total	65 23 9 3 100	Yes No, or don't know Total	38 62 100	Yes No, or don't know Total	0 100 100	Donated Land
(4) Electricity Generator	1958–1966	District council/*comunidad* Alberto Golan—mayor	Labor Money Materials Don't know Total	14 32 3 51 100	Yes No, or don't know Total	21 79 100	Yes No, or don't know Total	7 93 100	—

[a] These data are taken from the records of the *pueblo* and the *comunidad*.
[b] There is a tendency for *comuneros* to undervalue contributions from the outside.

ecuted by rich members of the *pueblo* with the financial help of wealthy migrants and occasional government grants.

Migrant clubs in Lima have contributed more money to the church project than the three other groups mentioned above. Subcommittees (*pro-Templo*) were formed during the 1940s in Lima, Miraflores (a suburb of Lima), and Casapalca (a mining town) to collect money and materials. Migrant clubs of other valley *pueblos* have also tended to give greatest support to prestige projects. As many migrants still retain land in the *pueblo* and are often fearful that it will be expropriated, they are reluctant to negotiate on behalf of the *comunidad* over the question of recovery of *comunidad* lands. It is significant that the district council has been able to call on assistance from the migrant clubs in Lima, whereas the *comunidad* has lacked the advantages of these contacts.

The migrant clubs were involved in the negotiations over the purchase of an electricity generator (project 4, table 1). In February 1959, the mayor formed a committee of Matahuasinos in Lima (which was in fact the committee of one of the migrant clubs)—*Auxilios Mutuos*—to represent the district council in its dealings with institutions in Lima. This committee accompanied the mayor on his visits to the Ministries of Finance and Development and for talks with the members of the House of Deputies representing the department of Junín. It appears from village records that the committee was misled by the deputy for Junín into believing that it had obtained a new twenty-five kilowatt generator for the cost of only 8,000 *soles*.[34] When they went to collect the generator from the importing house, it turned out that the *pueblo* had to pay 290,000 *soles*. An assembly of the *comunidad* was held in the *pueblo*, attended by only sixty *comuneros*, at which an attempt was made to reverse the decision to purchase the generator in view of the revised cost. The district council, however, on the recommendation of the Lima committee, decided to proceed with the purchase.

Following this unfavorable start, the district council has failed to interest the majority of *comuneros* in the scheme. Forty people assisted in one way or another in putting up the building to house the generator. Some provided money for zinc roofing, others provided nails, some sent paid laborers, carpenters, and bricklayers, while others provided paint or refreshments. There was a noticeable absence of voluntary labor. These forty people were members of the Co-operativa de Consumo de Energía Eléctrica Matahuasi Ltd. (electricity cooperative), which had been formed at the request of the mayor. A total of 140 households joined the cooperative and agreed to pay monthly contributions varying from 15 to 150 *soles* (average 60).

The history of the electricity cooperative is one of mismanagement and increasing indebtedness. The fact that by 1965 only thirty-six people had paid their first membership quota indicates that it was a cooperative in name only. In 1961 a joint meeting of the district council, *comunidad*, and cooperative committee decided to hand over the administration of the electricity generator to the district council. However, the district council was unsuccessful in making the repayments on the generator, and in 1966 the firm in Lima threatened to start legal proceedings in view of the heavy debt. In December of that year it is recorded that the second part of the annual central government subsidy to the village (16,000 *soles*) was to go toward debt repayment on the generator.[35] At the end of 1966, consumers still owed 30,000 *soles* and the district council owed 43,000 *soles* to the Lima firm. There are no records of these debts having been paid, and the generator has lain idle since September 1967 when Matahuasi was connected to the grid of the Mantaro Valley electricity cooperative.

At the turn of the century, it had been possible to achieve a reasonably high turnout at *faenas* by means of fines and coercion, but in recent years *faena* attendance has been sparse. Prior to 1925, the five *cuarteles* (including the three annexes) would be called out regularly to prune eucalyptus trees in the main streets, repair the cemetery and streets, and build the new district council offices. By the 1920s the weakening authority of the mayor was apparent in his failure to force local carpenters to work for nothing on the district council building.[36] District council records of the fifties and sixties give evidence of increasing infrequency of *faenas* and decreasing attendance. Particularly noticeable was the reluctance of inhabitants in the annexes to attend *faenas* in the *pueblo* of Matahuasi. In 1970 the work of repairing the cemetery and bridges was put out to contract.

Because of its inability to mobilize labor and internal resources, the district council has been forced to depend increasingly on obtaining financial help from central government. This has necessitated competing for favors with all the other districts in Peru (there are 120 in the department of Junín alone), involving expenditure on receptions for visitors and frequent journeys to Lima and Huancayo. An examination of the council minutes indicates that the promises of grants and technical assistance given by the government far exceeded the amounts that actually reached the community.

In conclusion, I suggest that the *comunidad* has largely failed to initiate projects involving the mobilization of voluntary labor for mutual benefit. Some of the projects completed have contributed to the provision of improved services, the improvement of infrastructure, and what has sometimes been termed the creation of social capital; however, these projects have failed to act as a mechanism for income redistribution. The *comunidad* has taken no independent steps to improve significantly the incomes of its members, while in most instances government has chosen to bypass the institution.

Government economic assistance to farmers in the form of credit and technical assistance has been channeled through an agricultural cooperative. This cooperative was created to encourage commercially oriented farmers to change their techniques, introduce different crops, and cater to new markets. Government help for public works projects has been granted to the district council as the official authority representing the whole district. As in the case of Sicaya, the *comunidad* of Matahuasi rented its land to the highest bidders. These were frequently non-*comuneros* and related by kinship to the richer commercial farmers who had purchased "church" land.

The lack of unity of purpose and of interest within the *comunidad* reflects the desire of each member to derive maximum benefit for his household from any organized activity. The household continues to be the basic management and economic unit.[37] Each family, through occupational diversification, manipulation of kinship ties, use of migration opportunities, investment in education, and improvement of existing economic activities, evolves a strategy in order to maintain or improve its existing standards of living. Participation in the *comunidad* and in the *faenas* it organizes forms only part of this strategy.

Evidence for a decline in communality associated with increasing individualization is supported by other Peruvian studies.[38] By 1970 *comunidades* controlled very little cultivable land and were only very rarely concerned with productive processes or with working communal land. Frequently, the *comunidad* represented only a minority of villagers and was therefore marginal to the lives of most peasant small holders. Nevertheless, it was this organization that the military government decided to use in 1970 as the basis for the development of cooperatives that would supposedly bring greater equality to Peruvian rural society. We now examine the legislation designed to bring about these changes and the initial reactions of the two communities.

The Statute of Peasant Communities: Aims and Consequences

Since the 1920 constitution, which reinstituted the colonial policy of legally protecting the *comunidades indígenas*, there had been only minor changes in the government organization of local communities. In 1942 the Department of Indigenous Affairs was transferred from the Ministry of Development to the Ministry of Justice and Labor, which in turn became the Ministry of Labor and Indigenous Affairs in 1949. The activities of this ministry were highly centralized and only a limited range of services was provided. Community representatives had to undertake long and expensive journeys to Lima to make use of services, which were mainly of a legal-advisory nature. The process of obtaining legal recognition for the community of Sicaya cost the *comuneros* 2,500 *soles* in subsistence allowances to their representatives, fares, surveyors fees, and so on.

A major change in the status of *comunidades* occurred on 24 June 1969 (*El Día del Campesino*), when their designation was changed from *comunidad indígena* (indigenous community) to *comunidad campesina* (peasant community). As Dobyns notes: "A socio-economic designation has been substituted for one of racial connotation. This corresponds much more to the socio-cultural reality of Peruvian communities."[39] The government also altered its relationship to the *comunidades* by taking their administration out of the Ministry of Labor and placing it under the much more decentralized Dirección General de la Reforma Agraria in the Ministry of Agriculture. Two years later, the Division of Peasant Communities was transferred to the jurisdiction of SINAMOS (Sistema Nacional de Apoyo a la Mobilización Social).

On 17 February 1970 the statute for peasant communities was promulgated.[40] The preamble emphasizes the importance of encouraging the modernization and commercialization of agriculture and of stimulating the development of production cooperatives. It also speaks out against the excessive fragmentation of holdings characteristic of *minifundia* (small-holder) areas. The aims of the statute are given as follows:
1. to increase the participation of peasant communities in the integrated development program of the country as a whole
2. to preserve the territorial integrity of the community and facilitate the better use of its natural resources
3. to revitalize and modernize the traditional form of land utilization, prohibiting the subdivision and fragmentation of resources
4. to rejuvenate traditional norms and values compatible with national development objectives
5. to promote the development of different forms of mutual help and traditional cooperation leading toward the establishment of cooperative organizations

In order to achieve these objectives, communities were to be reorganized so as to become economic units capable of embracing both production and servicing activities and of ensuring the full employment of *comuneros*. Training centers at the local level were to be given the task of developing the managerial and technical skills essential for the successful realization of these goals; they would also run courses in cooperative education.

A critical part of the statute concerns the revised membership rules for the *comunidad,* which aim to limit membership and access to community land to persons of lower economic status. In order to qualify, the following requirements must be met: the person (1) must have been born in the community or be a child of a community member (*comunero*); (2) must be head of a household or of adult status; (3) must have stable residence in the community; (4) must work basically in agriculture; (5) must not be a landowner liable to rural property tax either inside or outside the community; (6) must not have a major source of income from outside; and (7) must not be a member of another *comunidad campesina.* Subsequently, in December 1970, another clause was added that makes it possible for persons whose principal occupation is nonagricultural to become members, although they are not granted access to community land.

The statute leaves it to individual communities, in consultation with the regional office of the Dirección de Comunidades Campesinas, to specify more exactly the economic criteria for membership. In the Mantaro Valley this has been done by fixing a ceiling for membership of four hectares on irrigated private landholding or a maximum income of 2,500 *soles* per month from employment. State employees are specifically excluded from membership.

The administrative structure of the *comunidad* is brought into line with that of existing cooperatives. Maximum authority in the community is vested in a general assembly that meets at least twice yearly; the assembly is responsible for the approval of investment plans and requests for credit and for major decisions that affect the administration of community resources. A *consejo de administración* executes the policies set by the general assembly and is concerned with day-to-day management, while a *consejo de vigilancia* is given the responsibility for internal financial and administrative control. Members of both *consejos* are elected for a two-year period but can be reelected for one further period.

The principal internal constraints on the implementation of the statute in Matahuasi are the limited organizational and technical skills of the new members. At a general assembly in October 1970, only 30 of the 250 who were previously *comuneros* were considered eligible. Of the 120 who attended, 60 percent were women, and in the majority, they were very small scale farmers. By July 1972, another 90 who had not previously been *comuneros* had taken up the option to join.

Comparison of a 50-percent sample of newly registered *comuneros* with a general village sample of heads of households shows that *comuneros* are younger (43 percent under forty-five years), that there are more women (62 percent) among them, and more of them are immigrants (33 percent). The *comuneros* have less education and 65 percent have not completed primary school education (table 2).

Most important are the landholding statistics, which indicate an average holding of about 0.5 hectares for *comuneros* as compared with 2 hectares for the general village sample. Moreover, no *comunero* cultivates 3 or more hectares as against 19 percent for the general sample (for details see table 3).

In Matahuasi, the revised membership rules have achieved the objective of permitting only the poorer peasants to benefit from community

TABLE 2

EDUCATION OF *COMUNEROS* AND HEADS OF
HOUSEHOLD IN MATAHUASI

Level of Education	*Comunero* Sample (Percentages)			All Heads of Household (Percentages)
	Males	Females	Total	
No schooling	4	18	13	10
Incomplete primary	38	61	52	29
Primary	38	13	22	37
Incomplete secondary	12	5	8	11
Secondary	8	3	5	6
Higher	—	—	—	7
Total	100	100	100	100
Number	(24)	(39)	(63)	(105)

TABLE 3

LANDHOLDING OF *COMUNEROS* AND HEADS OF
HOUSEHOLD IN MATAHUASI

Extension of land in hectares	*Comunero* Sample (Percentages) Arable				All Heads of Household (Percentages) Arable			
	Own	Rent	Share-crop	Pasture	Own	Rent	Share-crop	Pasture
No land	38	90	79	78	22	94	91	87
Up to 0.9 hectares	27	8	13	22	26	2	8	5
1 to 1.9 hectares	32	2	6	—	21	4	—	4
2 to 2.9 hectares	3	—	2	—	12	—	1	1
3 or above hectares	—	—	—	—	19	—	—	3
Total	100	100	100	100	100	100	100	100
Number	(63)	(63)	(63)	(63)	(105)	(105)	(105)	(105)

resources. At the same time, these peasants' low level of education, limited experience in clubs or associations, and lack of political consciousness contribute to a low level of active participation in vital policy decisions. The main burden of administration and planning has fallen on one or two individuals who are better educated and better equipped for the tasks. The new system—by which the arable land belonging to the *comunidad* is worked by *comuneros* who are paid a share of the harvest or a daily wage—is managed by the president of the *consejo de administración* (administration committee of the *comunidad*) virtually on a full-time basis. *Comunero* labor is not used intensively, though this is one of the stated aims of the new legislation (Article 9b). Heavy reliance has been placed on the hiring of machinery from individual farmers in the locality at high rates.

Many of the internal problems that have emerged within the new organization are products of the method of labor organization and the lack of participation in decision making. General assemblies are held only about every six months to give formal approval to requests for bank loans and to reports on the financial state of the organization. *Comuneros* treat the *comunidad* as an employer of labor and source of supplementary income rather than as a collective institution based on a communitarian ideology. These problems result, in part, from the differentiated nature of the membership, which, despite the appearance of relative social homogeneity, generates divergent and, at times, conflicting economic interests.

It is significant that the major participants in work on *comunidad* lands and in general assemblies are the landless *comuneros*. These *comuneros* rely on the community and on temporary work for commercial farms in the district for their livelihood, though they tend not to control positions of authority. Positions of authority are mainly the prerogative of the somewhat better-off and better-educated *comuneros* whose income derives primarily from their own small holdings or nonagricultural occupations and who therefore regard the community as a source of supplementary benefits only. An additional difficulty is that the statute permits *comuneros* to retain their own small plots of freehold land, to which they often give priority, especially during peak periods.

In effect, the role of the *comunidad* is restricted to providing varying amounts of supplementary benefits to 14 percent of the village heads of household. Since the surplus generated is distributed among active members or absorbed by loan repayment commitments, the *comunidad* is in no position to initiate or contribute to village improvement projects. Since 1970 the interests of the district council and the *comu-*

nidad have increasingly diverged, until now the *comunidad* plays no part in mobilizing labor for public works projects.

This polarization is due principally to the fact that these two institutions now represent conflicting interest groups. Following the implementation of the new community reforms, a group of landowners, owning, on average, about 8 hectares of land (some of which had been church land) and supported by local businessmen, had managed to gain control of the district council. In interviews, they said that following the agrarian reform and the change in *comunero* membership they feared that efforts to recover the "church land" would increase. Article 121 of the statute declares that all acts of transference of *comunidad* lands into private hands since 8 January 1920 are nullified.[41] For these landowners, the district council served as a useful power base to protect their interests and to prevent the *comunidad*'s gaining access to important channels of communication with government.

To examine the ways in which the larger and medium-size farmers[42] hinder or assist the development of the *comunidad* we need to consider the pattern of control of access to land resources, machinery, credit, agricultural inputs, and markets. In the absence of any obligation on the part of the *comuneros* to work for the *comunidad*, the larger farmers are able to tempt them away by offers of immediate payment and of such extras as cigarettes and lunches. With an open wage market operating, the *comunidad* cannot count on a regular supply of labor at critical times of the agricultural cycle. For this reason, and because agricultural machinery is quicker and more efficient than animal-drawn equipment, the *comunidad* relies heavily on the half-dozen richest farmers in the village for the hire of their tractors and harvesters.

In an effort to overcome problems of labor shortage and high costs for hiring machinery, the *comunidad* has planted 30 hectares of alfalfa. This crop requires relatively low labor inputs throughout the year, can produce approximately nine harvests from one planting, and can be harvested by the purchaser. The *comunidad* is at a disadvantage in marketing its other products since it has no storage or transport facilities. It must sell in the field at harvest time, when the prices are at their lowest. In contrast, the agricultural cooperative, made up of the richest farmers in Matahuasi, receives help from officers of the German Technical Mission, whose principal duties are to improve animal husbandry and milk production, provide organizational support for the development of marketing and service cooperatives in the region as a whole.[43] Recently this mission has initiated a pilot scheme aimed at providing comprehensive farm planning and extended credit facilities to the more "progressive" farmers who are members of the cooperative. Special arrangements exist for cooperative members to obtain pure-bred cattle, producing high milk yields, and the necessary financing for the construction of modern cattle stables.

The community has received relatively little technical assistance. Government aid is confined to the offering of loans to meet the cost of production. The community has received two major loans from the Development Bank (*Banco Fomento Agropecuario*) to cover the costs of cultivating wheat, potatoes, barley, and alfalfa, amounting to some 383,000 *soles*. Due to poor yields, resulting from unexpected frost and hail, and to low prices and maladministration, the community found itself unable to repay the first installment on these loans. The community purchases its fertilizers and seeds from the shop run by the agricultural cooperative in Matahuasi.

These external constraints suggest that, for the *comunidad* to become a viable enterprise and compete in a capitalist market economy, it will need to receive more technical assistance and services from government. Such assistance has a low priority at the present time in Peru, and, despite its reform ideology, government has found it less costly in resources and personnel to encourage small-scale commercial agriculture in small-holder zones.

In Sicaya, unlike Matahuasi, the Statute of Peasant Communities was only partially applied. The new formal structure was adopted, namely, that of the *consejo de administración* and the *consejo de vigilancia*, but the leadership continued to be elected from among the older and more prosperous small holders. Membership rules were not strictly applied: 8 percent of the 469 newly registered *comuneros* own more than the permitted land ceiling of four hectares, while only 5 percent have less than one-third of a hectare. Of the non-*comuneros*, 43 percent own no private land and a further 17 percent own less than one hectare (table 4). The situation is almost the reverse of that of Matahuasi; in Sicaya, the *comuneros* are drawn from those with the greatest access to economic resources.

In our random sample of heads of household in Sicaya, *comuneros* have a somewhat higher education level than do non-*comuneros*. The difference between the *comunero* and non-*comunero* sample is a complex one; the non-*comuneros* appear to be drawn from both the poorest and least well educated sectors of the population and from those with relatively high levels of education. Many of the non-*comuneros* are migrant workers from the neighboring department of Huancavelica who have settled fairly permanently in Sicaya as dependents or share-croppers of the richer farmers.

TABLE 4
LANDHOLDING AMONG *COMUNERO* AND
NON-*COMUNERO* HEADS OF HOUSEHOLD IN SICAYA

| | Comuneros (Percentages) | | | | Non-Comuneros (Percentages) | | | |
| | Arable | | | | Arable | | | |
Land Extension in hectares	Own	Rent	Share-crop	Pas-ture	Own	Rent	Share-crop	Pas-ture
No land	10	56	78	92	43	79	74	91
Up to 0.9 hectares	28	20	13	5	17	14	21	7
1 to 1.9 hectares	30	17	7	3	26	5	5	2
2 to 2.9 hectares	14	3			7	2		
3 and above hectares	18	4	2		7			
Total	100	100	100	100	100	100	100	100
Number	(60)	(60)	(60)	(60)	(42)	(42)	(42)	(42)

TABLE 5
EDUCATION LEVELS OF *COMUNERO* AND
NON-*COMUNERO* HEADS OF HOUSEHOLD IN SICAYA

| | Comuneros (Percentages) | | | Non-Comuneros (Percentages) | | |
Education	Males	Females	Total	Males	Females	Total
No schooling		31	7	23	29	26
Incomplete primary	52	23	46	12	53	32
Primary	28	23	26	12	12	12
Incomplete secondary	16	23	17	29	6	18
Secondary	2		2	6		3
Higher	2		2	18		9
Total	100	100	100	100	100	100
Number	(46)	(14)	(60)	(19)	(17)	(36)

Eighty-seven percent of *comuneros* employ wage laborers on a temporary or permanent basis. Of the 200 hectares of *comunidad* land 180 hectares continue to be rented out on a five-year contract to 150 *comuneros*. Most of them rent between ⅓ hectare and 1 hectare, but one *comunero*, a commercial farmer, rents 14 hectares. They are allowed to sublet to others. From 1965 to 1971, 30 percent of rents were not paid, and by 1972 a rent debt of 250,000 *soles* had accumulated. Despite difficulties in collecting rents, the community still derives about 100,000 *soles* a year from this source. Most of this income continues to be spent on public service projects.

A small group of young *comuneros* in Sicaya attempted to get their leaders to ensure equal access to communal lands by persuading them to give cooperatives priority in the allocation of plots. These younger *comuneros* also wanted to see a move toward communal farming and a limit placed on the amount rented to individual *comuneros*.[44] Further indications of dissatisfaction with the policy of renting out *comunidad* lands were replies to the question in our survey of heads of household, "What do you consider to be the best way of using communal land?" Forty percent favored farming a *cooperativa comunal* (communal cooperative), 18 percent renting out plots on an equitable basis, and 10 percent renting out to those who need it. Thirty percent favored the present policy of renting out to those who could afford it.

The leaders have continued to resist this pressure for change from the membership. Since the *comunidad* was legally recognized, it has principally represented the interests of the group of medium-scale and larger farmers who rent communal land (at present 33 percent of the total membership). It is this group that is opposing the application of the membership rules laid down under Articles 23 and 24 of the statute. If these articles were adhered to, at least 16 percent would lose their *comunero* status and there would be an influx of landless or near-landless immigrants into the organization.

Conclusion

Data and observations on cooperative and mutual aid practices in Sicaya and Matahuasi lead me to question the assumption that it is possible to revitalize existing patterns of traditional cooperation and mutual aid. In many parts of highland Peru institutional systems for organizing labor exchanges and work parties, such as the *mita, faena, minka,* and *ayni,* are now of relatively minor importance. Only rarely are they concerned with the joint exploitation of communal resources. The *comunidad* is seen as an organization representing a minority of village heads of household and having a negligible impact on the lives of the great majority of villagers. It has been concerned principally with the mobilization of labor for public works projects. Frequently, these projects did not satisfy the "felt needs" of the members; as the burden of work and the benefits have been unevenly spread, it has become increasingly difficult to mobilize voluntary labor. The *comunidad* has no way of applying sanctions to non-*comuneros* and to *comuneros* who do not have usufructure of communal lands.

Since the *comunidades* of Matahuasi and Sicaya were legally recognized, they have failed to take any steps to improve significantly the incomes of the majority of small farmers who comprise the membership. There has been little effort to establish joint production activities and no joint action in the marketing, service, and distribution sectors. The only noticeable exception to the latter was the abortive attempt by a group of *comuneros* and teachers to set up a communal bus co-operative in Sicaya. Government assistance, in the form of credit and technical assistance, has not normally been channeled through the *comunidad*. Parallel and often competing "cooperative" organizations have been established, and through them the more commercially oriented farmers have been encouraged to change their techniques, introduce different crops, and cater to expanding new markets.

The Matahuasi *comunidad*, in attempting to introduce communal production with inadequate government assistance, has been placed at a serious disadvantage and continues to be heavily dependent, economically and politically, on influential local groups. In this situation, the existence of a communitarian tradition would appear to be a myth and, if the aims of the 1970 statute are to be achieved, heavy demands will have to be placed on government resources in the fields of training, credit, technical assistance, marketing, and servicing. Instead, scarce technical resources have been diverted to work on the major cooperative enterprises of the government's agrarian reform policy, the SAIS (sociedades agrarias de interés social) and the CAP (cooperativas agrarias de producción).

If *comunidades* are to be transformed into effective local development agencies, the change must be carried out with full appreciation of the social, economic, and institutional structure of each *comunidad* and of the internal and external constraints placed on it. Of particular importance is an analysis of the *comunidad* as an arena within which different groups compete for control over scarce land resources. In Matahuasi, the large farmers were prepared to yield control over the very limited areas of communal land, since this did not adversely affect their interests. In Sicaya, the commercially oriented farmers consider the community land they rent as a valuable asset and are continuing to control the organization and maintain unequal access to this resource. Despite the lack of a local tradition of communal land exploitation or economic action, Matahuasi *comunero* leaders are attempting to use the *comunidad* structure as an instrument of change. In contrast, Sicaya *comunero* leaders see it as an instrument of control. These different responses are inevitable given the ambiguity in the new legislation and the problems of providing adequate supervision of the implementation process. Other difficulties are created because the new organization of the *comunidad* creates a functional specialization between management and policy making by the body of the membership, which is an unfamiliar form of organization for peasant communities.[45]

The other vital factor behind the inability of the government to implement this policy (as of 1974) has been its lack of administrative capacity; government has also been unwilling to take any steps that could result in a decline in marketable surplus and/or an increase in opposition from a politically powerful rural middle class. Given the urgent need to expropriate all large estates and devise new systems of cooperative organization for the beneficiaries, it would certainly appear logical to leave the much more controversial question of small-holder community reorganization to a later stage.

Our study of SINAMOS (the government agency responsible for the program of peasant community reform) shows clearly the lack of administrative and political capability facing the government. SINAMOS was created by merging eight organizations, all concerned with community development.[46] An examination of the literature produced by SINAMOS conveys the impression that it has many parallels with what in other countries would be called a community development ministry. An official publication clarifying the objectives of SINAMOS states that it has "a coordinating and supportive role to play . . . in the process of transferring the decision-making capacity to the people."[47] It goes on to talk of the need to bring about a profound transformation in the economic structure of society and sees its work as constituting a movement toward correcting centralism and encouraging regional development.

In common with other "integrated community development programs," stress is laid on the importance of the local office, from which *promotores* (promoters) visit cooperatives, *comunidades,* and other local-level organizations in order to encourage them to discuss and resolve their own problems. Their role is similar to that of the village-level workers in other countries, but with the emphasis clearly on the promotion of participation rather than the teaching of agricultural techniques and the like. The official functions of the promoters are (1) to stimulate the creative capacity of the population; (2) to encourage the organization of the population; (3) to encourage and stimulate a dialogue between the government and the population; (4) to inform the people about the actions and services of the state so as to ensure their fuller use; and (5) to carry out leadership training.[48]

The employees of SINAMOS have interpreted the role of the organization in many different ways. It is therefore not surprising that villagers, labor union leaders, small-holder farmers, and others have also been confused; in the absence of a clearly defined policy, rumors have circulated and opposition has increased to the point where the government seems ready to wind up the organization. Some people see

SINAMOS as an institution that aims to set up labor unions and peasant federations with the intention of manipulating them, while others believe that its intention is to create a political party to serve the interests of the state.

In a climate of uncertainty about its future, this new government department has been able to achieve very little in its short existence. It has been hampered by a shortage of trained personnel, frequent staff changes, and a lack of unity of criteria; it has also been confronted with resistance from already established government departments. The implementation of the statute has been one of the programs to suffer. SINAMOS has concentrated its attention initially on creating production cooperatives on the expropriated agroindustrial complexes and establishing neighborhood organizations in the squatter settlements on the peripheries of the capital city. These activities constituted both political and economic priorities.[49]

Some organizations concerned with rural development were left outside SINAMOS, and problems of inadequate coordination and duplication of effort continued to limit the effective use of government resources. Every three months an intersectoral committee met in Huancayo, attended by the regional directors of the Ministries of Health, Agrarian Reform, ZAX (Tenth Agrarian Zone—Ministry of Agriculture), and Education, and SINAMOS, together with one of the land judges and a representative of the *guardia civil* (police force).[50] These meetings functioned principally as a forum in which each representative informed the rest of his organization's activities; only limited attempts were made to coordinate their programs in any effective way. For example, it was decided that Agrarian Reform should be responsible for the transference of land, while SINAMOS was to assist in this transference.

Although it supposedly had specialists in cooperative organization, SINAMOS had to rely on extension officers from ZAX for agricultural advice and on the Agricultural Development Bank for credit. When interviewed in Huancayo, the representatives of both these organizations expressed greater interest in working with individual commercial farmers or with groups of small holders than with *comunidades*. While SINAMOS officially accepted the policy of extending communal property and the Agrarian Reform Office spoke of the need to expropriate property in the Mantaro Valley above a ceiling of fifteen hectares, other government agencies were giving priority to work with farmers owning up to forty hectares.

Our observations show that the lack of effective coordination between SINAMOS, ZAX, and the Agrarian Development Bank adversely affected the quality and quantity of service provided to the *comunidades*. Matahuasi failed to receive any more help in community organization and cooperative management than it did before the creation of SINAMOS. SINAMOS appeared to be most concerned with "legalizing" the elections, statutes, and so on (i.e., formal controlling functions). These functions were carried out from the zonal office in Huancayo.

It has not been within the scope of this paper to review the general literature on community development theory and practice or to test our findings against those in other countries. However, we believe that the relevance of this study extends beyond the Mantaro Valley to other situations where governments are attempting to initiate changes in the social and economic structure of rural society. By focusing on the complexities of the implementation of policy related to restructuring small-holder communities I have sought to question some of the basic assumptions underlying government legislation.

The statute of peasant communities was based on a series of false assumptions about the evolution and socioeconomic structure of rural communities. This disharmony between policy and reality produced a number of unintended consequences that limited the effectiveness of the legislation. I suggest that community development legislation in other countries also tends to be based on incorrect assumptions about the nature of the "traditional" community. These usually emphasize its cultural homogeneity, high solidarity, and capacity for self-help and for the generation of local resources. Our analysis has shown that care has to be taken in drawing assumptions from observations of communal work projects. Though they are often considered as indicators of high solidarity and participation, they may constitute part of the system of domination and dependency at the local level. Such assumptions about the nature of rural communities may result in governments' considering that they are ideal units on which rural development planning can be based. We have, however, illustrated the dangers of a piecemeal approach that neglects the need for radical reform at other points in the economic, social, and political system.

Finally, our case study has drawn attention to the dilemma facing development planners in many Third World countries, namely, how to create land tenure systems that will be more just and equitable, will give the state more direct control over the production process, and yet will provide sufficient incentives to the individual farmer. Balancing the needs of the national economy against those of social justice for rural inhabitants inevitably leads to inconsistencies in government policy. Our case studies of Matahuasi and Sicaya illustrate the difficulties of introducing collective modes of agricultural production into highly differentiated communities that are part of a capitalist system.

NOTES

1. See Roberts and Samaniego in this volume.
2. Dore provides a useful discussion of the ambiguities attending such innovations (Ronald F. Dore, "Modern Cooperatives in Traditional Communities," in *Two Blades of Grass: Rural Cooperation in Agricultural Modernization*, edited by Peter Worsley, pp. 43–60).
3. "Peasant community" is hereafter referred to as *comunidad* to avoid any confusion with the village or *pueblo*. Up until 24 June 1969 it was known as *comunidad indígena* ("indigenous" or "Indian" community). I shall only use the pre-1969 term when referring to works written before that date.
4. Hildebrando Castro Pozo, *Nuestra comunidad indígena*, and "Del ayllu al co-operativismo socialista," *Biblioteca de la Revista de Economía y Finanzas*, vol. 2; José Carlos Mariátegui, *Seven Interpretive Essays on Peruvian Reality*; G. Bandelier, *The Islands of Titicaca and Koati*.
5. *Ayllu* has different meanings in different contexts: genealogy, lineage, kinship, group, class, or nation. See Diego González Holguín, *Vocabulario de la lengua general de todo el Perú llamada lengua qquichua o del Inca*. In Inca times, it was most likely a corporate group with localized parentage and synonymous with community.
6. Hildebrando Castro Pozo, "Social and Economic-Political Evolution of the Communities of Central Peru," in *Handbook of South American Indians*, edited by J. H. Steward, pp. 483–499. John H. Rowe, "The Incas under Spanish Colonial Institutions," *Hispanic American Historical Review* 37, no. 2 (1957): 155–199. A collection is now available of Murra's work on Inca and colonial institutions: John V. Murra, *Formaciones económicas y políticas del mundo andino*.
7. Magali Sarfatti Larson and Arlene Eisen Bergman, *Social Stratification in Peru*; John Rowe, "The Incas."
8. A *común* was the minimum unit for the collection of taxes and a reserve of manpower.
9. José María Arguedas, "Conclusiones de un estudio comparativo entre las comunidades del Perú y España," *Revista Visión del Perú*, no. 1, 1964.
10. Ibid.
11. *Cofradías* were religious confraternities or brotherhoods, each one dedicated to the worship of a particular saint. Membership carried with it the responsibility of working the lands belonging to the *cofradía* (the proceeds of which financed the annual fiesta) and the obligation of passing through the hierarchy of offices in the organization (*alférez*, *capitán*, and *mayordomo*). See Robert G. Keith et al., *La hacienda, la comunidad y el campesino en el Perú*.
12. Emilio Romero, *Historia económica del Perú*.
13. CIDA (Comité Interamericano de Desarrollo Agrícola), *Tenencia de la tierra y desarrollo socio-económico del sector agrícola*, p. 13.
14. Peter F. Klarén, *Modernization, Dislocation, and Aprismo*; Jean Piel, "The Place of the Peasantry in the National Life of Peru in the Nineteenth Century," *Past and Present*, no. 46 (1970): 108–133; Castro Pozo, "Social and Economic-Political Evolution."
15. Klarén, *Modernization, Dislocation, and Aprismo*, p. 51, footnote 1.

16. José Matos Mar et al., *Dominación y cambios en el Perú rural.*

17. Ibid., pp. 111–112.

18. This *indigenismo* movement was represented by two organizations, the Sociedad Amigos del Indio (Society of Friends of the Indian) and the Asociación Pro-Indígena (Pro-Indigenous Association), through the medium of two periodicals, the *Sierra* in Cuzco and the *Mercurio Peruano* in Lima. See François Chevalier, "Official *Indigenismo* in Peru in 1920: Origins, Significance and Socio-Economic Scope," in *Race and Class in Latin America*, edited by Magnus Mörner.

19. Jorge Basadre, *Historia de la República del Perú*, vol. 9.

20. Harry F. Dobyns, *Comunidades campesinas del Perú.*

21. Klarén, *Modernization, Dislocation, and Aprismo*; José María Arguedas, *Yawar Fiesta*; Ciro Alegría, *Broad and Alien Is the World*; Chevalier, "Official *Indigenismo* in Peru in 1920."

22. This land had previously belonged to the church of Sicaya. These figures of land extension are only approximate, since it is difficult to obtain reliable information; they are based on Ministry of Agriculture estimates complemented by my local information.

23. The pasture of Cacchi had been sold by the Apoalaya family (the caciques of the area) to the Holy Church of Santo Domingo de Sicaya in 1707. Sicaya lost four-fifths of these pastures when they were invaded by the hacienda Laive in 1836. See Carlos Samaniego, "Location, Social Differentiation and Peasant Movements in the Central Sierra of Peru," Ph.D. dissertation, University of Manchester, 1974.

24. The correspondence between the *alcalde* and the Indigenous Affairs Bureau in Lima, 1930–1933, and data on *comuneros* and ownership of animals for 1931 in the archives of the district of Sicaya, Peru.

25. Gabriel Escobar, "Sicaya, una comunidad mestiza de la sierra central del Perú," in *Estudios sobre la cultura actual del Perú*, edited by L. Valcárcel, pp. 164–165. See, also, Gabriel Escobar, *Sicaya: cambios culturales en una comunidad mestiza andina*, for a full analysis of the social and economic organization of Sicaya with information on family, ritual, and patterns of reciprocity.

26. Escobar, *Sicaya*, pp. 141–169.

27. District Council minutes, 1969.

28. Details concerning the application by the Matahuasi *comunidad* for official recognition and other legal proceedings mentioned are taken from the archives of the Dirección de Comunidades Campesinas in Lima.

29. Dobyns, *Comunidades campesinas del Perú*; Richard N. Adams, *A Community in the Andes: Problems and Progress in Muquiyauyo*; Paul L. Doughty, *Huaylas: An Andean District in Search of Progress.*

30. As far as direct legal sanctions are concerned, up until 1933 all able-bodied villagers could be obliged to contribute their labor or send a substitute for work on roads and bridges under Article 135 of the Law of Municipalities. However, Article 55 of the 1933 constitution overrides this by stating, "No one can be obliged to lend his personal labor without his free consent and without due remuneration."

31. Doughty, *Huaylas.*

32. For literature on migrant clubs of Matahuasi and Sicaya, see Norman Long, "The Role of Regional Associations in Peru," in *The Process of Urbanization*, edited by M. Drake et al., pp. 173–191; Bryan R. Roberts, "The Interrelationships of City and Provinces in Peru and Guatemala," in *Latin Ameri-*

can Urban Research, vol. 4, edited by W. A. Cornelius and F. M. Trueblood, pp. 224–228.

33. Except for brief periods since 1945, mayors of district councils have been nominated by the prefect of the department. In some villages this has meant the confirmation of a decision taken at a village general assembly, whereas, in others, persons with good political ties with regional and national figures were able to secure these posts.

34. The eight thousand *soles* referred to the cost of repair and transportation only. See District Council minutes, 1958–1959.

35. The Belaúnde government introduced a scheme for annual grants to district councils. Previously the only income was derived from licenses on small shops and petty traders, fees for the registration of births, marriages, and deaths, and the occasional sale of eucalyptus trees lining the streets.

36. District Council minutes, 1920–1921.

37. Manning Nash, "The Social Context of Economic Choice in a Small Society," in *Economic Anthropology*, edited by E. E. Le Clair, Jr., and H. K. Schneider.

38. David Winder, "The Effect of the 1970 Reform on the Peasant Communities and on the Community Development Process in an Area of Peru." M. Ed. thesis, University of Manchester, 1974.

39. Dobyns, *Comunidades campesinas del Perú.*

40. The statute (Decreto Supremo No. 37–70–A) brought together all previous legislation relating to *comunidades campesinas*. The most important of these are Articles 207 to 212 of the 1920 constitution, Articles 70 to 74 of the Peruvian civil code, the new statute of *comunidades indigenas* (27 July 1966), Articles 115 to 126 of the Ley de Reforma Agraria (Decreto Ley 17716), and the Reglamento de Co-operativas Comunales (Decreto Supremo No. 240–69–AP).

41. The *comunidad* of Matahuasi has attempted to take advantage of this legal disposition to recover church land, but without any success. The administrative structure of agrarian tribunals in Huancayo is totally inadequate to deal with the demands placed on it. In 1973 there were only two land judges for the whole of the department of Junín.

42. These terms are used comparatively and are related to the average land-holding for the village (table 3).

43. A description of the milk cooperative that is helped by this mission is given by Long in this volume.

44. According to Article 102 of the supreme decree 37–70–A, *comunidades* are permitted to allow individual *comuneros* usufructure of plots of communal lands provided that there is sufficient land available to give each person at least one-quarter of a hectare and that no individual should receive more than the agricultural family unit for the zone (i.e., four hectares of irrigated land in the Mantaro Valley). Under Article 125, the *comunidad* can grant the use of its lands to cooperatives or SAIS (*sociedades agrarias de interés social*) whose members are *comuneros*.

45. Thomas F. Carroll, "Peasant Cooperation in Latin America," in *Two Blades of Grass: Rural Cooperatives in Agricultural Modernization*, edited by Peter Worsley, p. 225.

46. Three of these organizations came from the prime minister's office: The National Office of Cooperative Development (O.N.D.E.L.O.O.P.), National Office of New Towns (O.N.D.E.P.T.O.N.), National Office of Community De-

velopment (O.N.D.C.). One came from the Ministry of Economy and Finance: The National Fund for Economic Development (F.N.D.E.). One came from the Ministry of Housing (General Directorate of Communal Promotion), and three from the Ministry of Agriculture: Directorate of Peasant Organizations (D.O.R.), Directorate of *Comunidades Campesinas* (D.C.C.), and Directorate of Promotion and Diffusion of Agrarian Reform (P.R.O.D.I.R.A.).

47. SINAMOS, 1972, p. 9.

48. SINAMOS, 1972, p. 36.

49. Within two days of the agrarian reform law, 225,000 hectares of irrigated lands on the coast—80 percent of the cultivated coastal land and involving more than fifteen thousand workers—had been expropriated. See Rubens Medina, *Agrarian Reform Legislation in Peru.*

50. As part of the agrarian reform law the government created land judges to deal exclusively with all matters relating to expropriation, revindication, and assignment of holdings.

9. The Evolution of Pastoral Villages and the Significance of Agrarian Reform in the Highlands of Central Peru

BRYAN R. ROBERTS AND CARLOS SAMANIEGO

This is an account of the nature and local meaning of one example of the most extensive and most fully implemented part of Peru's recent agrarian reform—the cooperativization of the large-scale cattle haciendas of the Peruvian sierra. Beginning with the largest of these haciendas, the land and the villages bordering on that land have been reorganized into *sociedades agrarias de interés social* (SAIS). The first of these SAIS is based on the lands of Cerro de Pasco Corporation's haciendas and includes sixteen selected villages; the total amount of land affected is 216,000 hectares.[1] SAIS Cahuide, to which most of our data refer, was the second SAIS to be organized; it borders the SAIS Túpac Amaru and is based on the haciendas of the Sociedad Ganadera del Centro, affecting 269,155 hectares of hacienda land and including twenty-nine villages. This expropriation and reorganization is but part of the agrarian reform program, which also affects the agroindustrial plantations of the coast, agricultural haciendas, small-scale cattle haciendas, and the organization and distribution of land within peasant villages.[2] The SAIS program has characteristics that highlight some of the especial features and problems of agrarian reform in Peru. The haciendas and villages affected are located at heights above 11,500 feet and contain the best natural pasture and about 80 percent of Peruvian livestock; agricultural possibilities are poor and mainly limited to certain root crops. The size of these haciendas is not accidental, for large land extensions are necessary for efficient stock raising; also, pasture represented one of the few means by which foreign and national capitalists could directly extract a profit from the agricultural resources of the Andes. For most of the nineteenth century, wool was Peru's second most important export crop.[3]

It is this agrarian system that in novels and popular comment has often become identified with the most exploitative aspects of landowner-peasant relationships in the Peruvian polity.[4] The gradual and often violent encroachment of haciendas on the lands of villages, the tying of peasants by personal services and labor to haciendas, and the manipulation of legal and political authority by landowners to suit their interests—these are some of the most salient features commented upon in the descriptions given of life in the highlands. This viewpoint has influenced the nature and progress of agrarian reform, associated, as it has been, with invasions of hacienda land by villages claiming it as their own and with lengthy legal and political battles over land rights and land distribution. The problems posed to successive governments by this climate of conflict and by the land-extensive characteristics of profitable cattle raising in the highlands have been major influences not only in promoting agrarian reform but also, as we shall see, in shaping the particular form that SAIS have taken.

Though opposition of hacienda and poor peasant may have influenced governmental policy, it is becoming increasingly evident that this opposition represents an oversimplified view of the dynamics of Andean society. That the haciendas were as directly exploitative of their workers as is commonly supposed has been seriously questioned.[5] In this paper we develop the argument further by documenting the considerable economic differentiation present in even the smallest of highland villages and by placing both villages and haciendas within a wider set of social and ecological relationships that have constantly affected the development of the highland economy. Villages and villagers were never enclosed completely within the hacienda system, and thus it was the contradictory strategies adopted by villagers, lowland farmers, and hacienda owners aimed at increasing production in the early twentieth century that underlay the land conflicts that took place. One of the most important aspects of this conflict, which we detail later, is that it diversified the economic relationships and resources of highland villages and lessened their dependence on the pastoral economy. This points to one of the essential dilemmas of agrarian reform in central Peru: such reform is based on the assumption that its beneficiaries—the inhabitants of the highland villages—are dependent on the improvement of local opportunities, when, in fact, many of the more dynamic

groups within these villages had already ceased to regard such opportunities as relevant to improving their own life chances.

We will first consider the nature of the SAIS organization as an instrument of agrarian reform. This will be followed by an analysis of
the processes that have differentiated the economies and relationships
of highland villages and by an assessment of the impact of present-day
SAIS development aid and policy on the component villages. Our case
material, survey data, and observations concentrate on villages within
SAIS Cahuide and, as points of reference, on the villages and small
towns within the Mantaro Valley to which they are historically tied
by political, economic, and social relationships.

The Organization of SAIS

The basic philosophy and model of organization adopted by the
present Peruvian government in its agrarian reform are based on those
of the cooperative movement.[6] The fundamental principle of this
movement is that those who work within an enterprise are the owners
and are entitled not only to a wage in return for the work they do
but also to a share in profits in proportion to the capital or resources
they have invested in it. A cooperative enterprise is controlled through
periodic assemblies of its members, who elect working committees to
supervise day-to-day operations. In large and complex enterprises, requiring constant coordination and planning, a permanent administrative staff is appointed, subject to the control of the assembly and
elected committees. The basic points to be made about cooperative
organization are: it is autonomous of state control; it is voluntary,
and members may withdraw both labor and capital; it requires the
full participation of members in the work of the enterprise; and its
benefits, as in commercial businesses, must accrue, in direct form, only
to members. It represents, in effect, a decentralized instrument of social
and economic transformation in which the incentives to improve production are based on individual self-interest as well as on an ideology
of cooperation. Hence it constitutes a form of organization that, in
principle, works through capitalizing on the existing efforts of local
people to improve themselves. These local efforts involve individual
economic interests and are often difficult to coordinate and to reconcile
with national social and economic planning. These problems manifest
themselves in the recent Peruvian case.

Faced with difficulties with existing labor unions, the Peruvian government has opposed the continuance of unions in the new agrarian
cooperatives on the grounds that there should exist no conflict of interest between workers and owners. There have been problems in re-

conciling conflicts of interest within the large sugar cooperatives among the different classes of member-workers, technicians, and office staff.[7] An additional problem is how far members have the right to define the goals of their organization vis-à-vis those of national economic priorities.

Such problems have been most fully expressed and institutionalized in the form in which SAIS have been established. A SAIS is not, strictly speaking, a cooperative: it is a form of organization explicitly reserved for those situations that have not yet fulfilled the essential requirements of cooperative organization. From the viewpoint of the Peruvian government, SAIS are designed for situations in which the members of the future cooperative do not own or work the major resources incorporated into the cooperative.[8] Thus the villages included in the SAIS of central Peru did not legally own the hacienda lands, nor did their inhabitants work on the hacienda. The grounds for selection of member-villages were various: they exhibited a predominantly agrarian village economy, bordered the haciendas, were villages officially recognized as "indigenous communities," had not previously benefited from agrarian reform, and evidently had need of pasture land. Since any outstanding claims that villages had to the ownership of hacienda land were not formally considered in the selection process, it is clear that government did not regard them to be owners of the resources upon which the SAIS was mainly based. The purchase of hacienda land from the legal owners is part of the agrarian debt that each SAIS individually must pay off over a period of twenty-five years. In addition, each SAIS is in debt to the government for the purchase of the hacienda stock. These debts must be paid in full before the existing members of a SAIS become the absolute owners of their resources and, until that time, their control over the operations of the SAIS are limited by the extraordinary powers of intervention retained by the government. These powers are delegated to state officers from the Ministry of Agriculture, who participate in the main decisions of the enterprise.

Under the organization of a SAIS, a clear working distinction is maintained between the old hacienda lands, known as *unidades de producción*, which retain their previous unity and organization and, in practice, many of the former administrative staff, and the lands of the villages. The *unidades de producción* are worked by a permanent work force of shepherds, laborers, service personnel, and technicians organized into a service cooperative that is an additional constituent member of a SAIS. Villages and the service cooperative nominate delegates to the general assembly of the SAIS, which considers and approves general policy and elects two standing committees from among its delegates—an administrative committee (*consejo de administración*) and a committee of vigilance (*consejo de vigilancia*)—to supervise the running of the SAIS.

The administrative personnel, including the general manager of the SAIS, are formally responsible to this general assembly and to the standing committee; hence they can be removed from office by votes of this assembly, and SAIS policies and budgets can be and are altered by this assembly. In practice, however, the participation of the members in determining policies is restricted by the existing debts of the SAIS and by the financial obligations and supervision to which it exposes them.

The relationship of the SAIS to village farming and development is channeled in many SAIS, through a development division. This has a permanent administrative staff responsible for carrying out education and extension work in the villages. This division encourages and helps villages to form agrarian or other cooperatives within the villages, arranges for technical assistance from the Ministry of Agriculture, and negotiates loans with national and foreign development banks and agencies. As members of a SAIS, villages are entitled to a share in profits; however, this share is diminished by existing debt obligations and statutory requirements to set aside part of the profits for reinvestment, educational work, and social welfare. The extent of these obligations is such that only about 25 percent of the profits of a SAIS in any year are available for distribution to its constituent members.[9] In the case of SAIS Cahuide, the total available for distribution to the members in 1972 was approximately $72,000 or an average of just over $2,400 per village. The distribution of these funds is supervised by the development division, or by its equivalent in other SAIS, and must be invested in such village projects as schools, road and bridge construction, and the purchase of vehicles for transport.

As constituted, the SAIS represents a middle-of-the-road instrument of agrarian reform; it does not represent the decentralized working autonomy of a cooperative, nor is it a state-run enterprise. It is a gradualistic instrument by which its members slowly take over more control and receive greater benefits from their enterprise. Indeed, it is foreseen that eventually the SAIS will become cooperatives: villages will be fully incorporated parts, working their own lands through cooperative organization, and various industrial, consumer, service, and distribution cooperatives will be established within the overall framework.[10] The setting up of SAIS has enabled government to meet the demands of small-scale farmers for more land by creating the sense of social and economic participation, while retaining, under their close control, the productive efficiency of the large livestock haciendas.[11] This last consideration is important, since government faces evident difficulties in feeding its rapidly growing urban population and in stimulating urban industry.

This model of transformation is one in which change comes from above through the example and supervision of locally based, government technical personnel. It assumes that the best hope of improving the economic situation of villagers lies in their participation in this new organization and in the form of aid that the SAIS can give them. In the following section, we assess the extent to which this represents an accurate picture of contemporary developments in the member villages of SAIS Cahuide.

The Social Differentiation of Highland Pastoral Villages

Every village belonging to SAIS Cahuide is officially registered as an "indigenous community" (recently renamed "peasant community," *comunidad campensina*).[12] In most cases, this official recognition dates to the 1930s and legalizes the village as a land-owning corporation whose resources cannot be sold or otherwise permanently alienated. However, it is important to recognize that, although the concept of "community" implied a series of customary obligations for its members, such as contributing to public works, it did not guarantee common access to water, land, and pasture, since these rights were rented to families or were given in usufruct to households and passed on by inheritance. Consequently, within a village community there developed considerable inequalities in the use of communal resources by households; these inequalities were apart from any that arose from purchase of land or from grants of land by government authority. Hence "community" did not entail any form of collective farming; the household was the basic unit of production and any extrahousehold labor needed was obtained through exchanges with kin and neighbors or by contractual labor of various kinds.[13] More significant for our present discussion is the fact that the definition or registration of an "indigenous community" provided the means by which a village could attempt to demarcate its potential land and labor resources. The legal battles that raged among Peruvian highland villages over rights to land concerned these two basic elements: a definition of the populations from which a village could expect labor for public or private projects, and the restriction of access to lands individual households could farm.

In this context, highland villages have a special place; none of them originated as autonomous villages. They are the outcome of processes of economic development and differentiation in the nearby Mantaro Valley. Many of them—for example, the two villages for which we have intensive data, Cacchi and Yanacancha—originated simply as the abodes of shepherds caring for the flocks of lowland villages. Others were the means by which new lands, including agricultural lands, were brought into cultivation by households belonging to the cadet branches of valley lineages. In both cases, these highland villages remained under the political jurisdiction of valley villages and retained strong economic and family ties with them.[14]

We now want to consider certain sources of differentiation within these highland villages. In their location and political origins highland villages are part of a complex ecological system by which households and wider political units sustain themselves and generate surpluses. This pattern has been analyzed in terms of a system of vertical control whereby households and political units sought to include within their domain the different agricultural and human resources required for survival.[15] In concrete terms, this meant that highland villagers needed access to lowland agricultural resources of different kinds and at various ecological levels; conversely, lowland villagers required access to highland pasture and to root crops. From the beginning, then, there was a two-way movement linking highlands and lowlands: the highlands, through labor services or ownership, had access to lowland agriculture, and they also exchanged products wtih the lowlands. The lowlands, as the original owners of highland pasture and the agricultural lands, had access to both of these, yet they required the services of highland shepherds and additional farm labor.

The most readily available means of ensuring service from shepherds was to give them part of the increase of the flock each year, as well as agricultural produce. These animals become the property of the shepherd but were cared for alongside the flocks of his employer. Over time, considerable private herds were built up by the highland shepherds, and these often outnumbered the sheep kept for lowland farmers. For example, one shepherd from the highland village of Cacchi had accumulated his own herd of over a thousand sheep, apart from the number of alpaca and llama he also controlled. Most highland households, then, were able to build up private flocks of their own, and similar processes were occurring in the neighboring haciendas where hacienda shepherds grazed their own sheep on hacienda pasture. Indeed, the situations of shepherds, whether in village or hacienda, were basically alike. There were relationships between them in their working activities: hacienda shepherds often originated from highland villages; they were often related by marriage to villagers; and they would graze sheep on hacienda land for people from the villages whenever needed (the *michipa* system).

Highland villagers also used the haciendas as opportunities for occasional work as laborers, domestic servants, or shepherds. Within the highland villages, the differential opportunities that arose for accumulating flocks began to create significant differences in the economic position of villagers. Some villagers no longer looked after the flocks of lowland employers but, instead, became employers in their own right, hiring fellow villagers. Others, for example, were originally themselves lowland farmers who had decided to dedicate themselves to stock raising. Thus, for the enterprising and the fortunate, the highlands offered ample scope for the expansion of farming.

In a pastoral economy, there is little elasticity in the demand for labor. Making more effective use of pasture at these altitudes can be achieved only by more extensive herding and the improvement of stock. Neither of these activities necessarily requires additional labor and may, indeed, reduce the need for labor when accompanied by improved techniques. Consequently, stable settlement of population in the highlands and increases in village population can create an excess supply of labor that can be absorbed only through the diversification of economic activities, so that some household members engage in craft production—usually textile—others in trade, and others in labor migration. The economic differentiation of families in highland villages intensified this process: poor families had fewer animals and more limited access to pasture than richer ones, and, in order to meet their subsistence requirements, they had to offer their labor for a variety of activities.

This internal diversification became affected by more general economic processes with the emergence of large-scale, wage labor opportunities in the local economy. From at least the early 1920s there was considerable circulatory migration from highland villages. The most frequent types of work reported are road construction and mining, although work in agriculture in the valley and in neighboring highland villages and haciendas is also reported. Pastoral activity permits more flexibility in the timing of seasonal labor migration than does agriculture. Highland villagers appear to have migrated for short work periods at almost any time in the year: in the valley this kind of short-term migration is confined to the slack period after the harvest. These labor opportunities meant that households in highland villages could complement stock raising by additional sources of income, and the income could be reinvested locally. Returning migrants built houses, set themselves up in trade and crafts, bought animals, and improved their production. Thus, those families who did not own sufficient stock to subsist could continue to farm locally only by diversifying their economy.

Ecology and farming practice created opportunities for individual betterment. This was not a situation in which local improvement occurred through group mobility. Indeed, in both the highland and the lowland villages, customary "communitarian" practices, such as *faenas* or communal work parties, were often a means by which the larger farmers, who were also the local political authorities, gained access to free labor: the labor might be directed to public works, but these works (irrigation ditches, roads, and agricultural facilities) generally benefited the larger farmers (i.e., those who owned the irrigated land, needed to transport their products to market, or had most animals).

This suggests that many of the intervillage conflicts and even those between village and hacienda must be interpreted, primarily, in terms of competing individual economic interests. Also, the political subordination of highland villages to lowland ones meant that lowland farmers had access to highland pastures and that highland farmers were not in complete control of their own labor and pastoral resources. This pattern emerges from cases of political protest from the highland villages of Cacchi and Yanacancha—the former taking place in the 1930s and the latter in the late nineteenth century. These movements, which were aimed at undermining lowland domination, were in each case led by the better-off local farmers, who were among the few literate members of their communities. Their economic self-interest is clearly and explicitly expressed in the documents they wrote during the struggles. They complain, for example, of the way in which their growing needs for pasture are being hampered by the political and economic control exercised by lowland villages. Later, after attaining independence for their villages, these leaders appropriated large tracts of communal land for personal use, which they justified on the grounds that they had done most of the work in achieving independence. There is no evidence that the poorer families of the locality either derived much benefit from political independence or were particularly involved in the struggle for it. During these struggles there are interesting cases of alliances between the large haciendas and highland villages. For example, Cacchi sought the protection of the vast Ganadero del Centro Company, which owned the neighboring hacienda Laive. This Lima-based company was sufficiently powerful to counter the considerable political influence of the lowland village of Sicaya, which had controlled the land and settlement of Cacchi. In return for its support, the hacienda received a favorable settlement by the villagers of a long-standing border dispute, and, in the years that followed, the village received material aid from the hacienda and favorable opportunities for work on it.

These temporary alliances between highland villages and haciendas were more frequent than is often supposed, and they were based on the recognition of common interests against lowland political jurisdictions. However, they were temporary, because haciendas restricted the possibilities of expansion available to highland villages. It is also clear that, once again, it was the larger highland farmers who led the opposition to the haciendas. In interviews with household heads carried out in Cacchi—a village with a long history of conflict with the hacienda Laive and a reputation for radicalism—the only people to denounce the hacienda and to regret not having recovered land from it were the largest farmers. In one case, the farmer explicitly linked this attitude to the shortage of pasture in the community and to the difficulty of expanding his own herd. In these conflicts, the leaders of the village received support from the whole community, for freedom from political interference by haciendas had indirect benefits for everyone, as did the possibility of obtaining more pasture land. The mobilization of support, however, was initiated by the larger farmers, who held key political posts in the village and used their positions to obligate people to take part.

Despite the conflicts with haciendas and lowland jurisdictions, the highland villages needed to develop and maintain individual relationships with each of these places. The development of these relationships, often based on marriage and *compadrazgo* (ritual co-parenthood), led to an internal diversification of households. A brother or a sister, for example, would move to a different place, marry and settle there, but continue to maintain close social and economic relationships with the highland village of origin. The equal inheritance of family property among all siblings strengthened relationships between kin in different locations; furthermore, the custom whereby women, especially the mother, had to care for the animals enabled males to seek work elsewhere. We do not argue that this economic diversification by household was necessarily a conscious economic strategy for highland villagers; similar processes are reported for the lowlands. Nevertheless, the nature of pastoral activity, as we have already suggested, encourages some family members to leave home and find employment elsewhere. Under these circumstances, and given the economic conditions of the region, it was highly probable that widespread networks of economic and social exchange would develop.

This fact can be better appreciated if the variety of possible exchanges are detailed. One very important exchange for highland villagers was help with educating children in lowland schools. These were the best schools of the area, and in this, as in other areas of Peru, there has been a long educational tradition.[16] Almost half of our present informants in Cacchi and Yanacancha spent part of their early years being educated outside the community—usually in the lowland marketing town of Chupaca. Apart from education, households need help with the marketing of produce. Although exchange relationships can be developed on a personal basis between highland farmers and their lowland clients, anxieties are constantly expressed about selling crops directly in lowland markets. We recorded frequent accounts of the abuses to which highland villagers have been subject by market authorities or rival traders from the lowlands.

One way highland villagers have protected themselves against these abuses has been to establish alliances with lowland traders or set up their own stalls in the market towns. Highlanders living in the lowlands assist visitors from the highlands with information on market conditions, often provide accommodation, and act as intermediaries with local authorities. Also, during the day prior to a busy market day, more information can be obtained in Chupaca about events in the highlands than could normally be obtained in the highland villages themselves, given the dispersed nature of their settlement. Likewise, migrants established in the mines and in the provincial and national capitals are used to lobby higher-level political authorities on behalf of highland communities. Thus, for example, all the negotiations with the Ministry of Agriculture to obtain a loan for Cacchi to set up a cooperative were conducted by villagers resident in the provincial capital of Huancayo.

Highland migrants resident in the lowlands also receive benefits from these relationships. Such relationships provide them with a sense of identity in the towns and cities where they now live. Soccer teams are organized by place of origin, and there are frequent social gatherings among migrants and visitors from the villages. City residents from the highlands often express anxiety about the doings of their kin in city and village and about how these doings might reflect on their own social positions. In this sense, they are closely integrated into a social field that spans both city and village. Those migrants who are traders often profit directly from exchanges with the highlands by having ready access to wool or meat. In all cases recorded, lowland residents from the highlands received food from their home villages, and, even when they were not professional traders, they would occasionally trade or barter with these products. It is worthwhile remembering that, in the informal economic conditions that prevail in Peruvian towns and cities, every household tends to have at least one foot in some kind of trading activity.

The expansion and improvement of livestock farming—the earliest expression of these processes of diversification—ended as increased population pressure on pasturage led to overgrazing. We have some partial data from the village of Yanacancha to illustrate this process. By 1928, the village was overgrazing its lands, and between then and 1972 stock had drastically declined (see table 1). A similar process is described by farmers in Cacchi, who link it with their desire to capitalize on their stock resources in order to educate their children or settle in the lowlands.

So far, we have seen how the development of highland enterprise produced conflicts with haciendas and lowland towns; the other side of the coin is the way in which economic surplus was directed toward investment in the lowlands. This has taken two forms. In the first, stock or other highland assets are sold off to pay for the education of children, often to university level. This was the case of the three largest farmers of Cacchi, whose herds were reduced from just over one thousand sheep to something around three hundred or four hundred, so that their sons might be educated to secondary level and beyond. The second pattern is for houses to be purchased in lowland towns and economic enterprises established there. This generally involves the movement of most of the family to the town, leaving only one or two members to look after their continuing highland interests.

These processes entail the decapitalization of highland agriculture, insofar as highland capital is realized in order to reinvest in the lowlands, where the farmers perceive the greater economic opportunities to lie. However, they retain their interests in the highlands, claiming rights to pasture or land they have always held and leaving kin to protect it for them. This process is illustrated in table 2, which gives details on migration from Cacchi. The largest stockholders are those with most children and siblings outside Cacchi: these absent members

TABLE 1

DECLINE OF LIVESTOCK IN YANACANCHA

Year	Number of households	Area of pasture (in hectares)	Total sheep that pasture can support	Total sheep	Sheep over-grazing	Average sheep per household
1928	205	14,848	45,000	66,500	21,500	324
1972	396	11,062	33,186	35,640	2,454	90

TABLE 2
PLACE OF RESIDENCE AND OCCUPATIONS OF CHILDREN AND SIBLINGS OF CACCHI HEADS OF HOUSEHOLD

Actual Place of Residence of Children and Siblings (Percentages)

Number of Sheep Owned by Head of Household	Cacchi	Other Highland Village	Huancayo	Chupaca	Other Valley Village	Outside Mantaro Area	Lima	Mine	Total
200 or more (80 respondents)	34	12	16	19	–	5	5	9	100
100 to 199 (89 respondents)	66	8	9	7	–	2	2	6	100
99 or less (157 respondents)	60	4	11	10	2	3	3	7	100

Present Occupations of Children and Siblings (Percentages)

Number of Sheep Owned by Head of Household	Agriculture	Trade	Other Service	Artesan	White Collar	Study	Domestic	Total
200 or more (80 respondents)	29	10	3	7	7	26	18	100
100 to 199 (89 respondents)	40	11	5	5	5	12	22	100
99 or less (157 respondents)	51	1	3	8	2	18	17	100

are often engaged in valley trade or are undergoing higher education, thus necessitating their permanent absence from the village. Also, it is the larger stockholders whose children and siblings show the greatest economic diversification. The kinsmen who remain in the village to look after the animals have a right to part of the product: this tends to re-create the situation with which these villages began. However, the resources are now distributed among a large number of households, and local opportunities for improvement are much reduced.

We conclude this section by discussing two highland families that have diversified their interests both spatially and economically. The first is from the village of Yanacancha. The father of the family, Pedro Cangalaya, was a leader during the 1920 struggle against the lowland village of Ahuac; at that time Yanacancha was seeking its independence, complaining of the rents and labor services exacted by the village authorities of Ahuac. Pedro Cangalaya was one of the largest farmers of Yanacancha, holding about eight hundred sheep, apart from llamas and alpacas. It was, in effect, he and the other larger farmers who paid the rents to Ahuac, since they were the only local farmers with a regular cash income. The Ahuac authorities accused Pedro of having appropriated for his personal use considerable extensions of communal pasture and of having profited from the settlement of a border dispute with the neighboring hacienda.

After independence, Pedro extended his control over pastures in Yanacancha, justifying this action on the grounds that he had suffered considerable personal difficulties during the struggle. At the height of his farming career he possessed over one thousand sheep. He also held the highest political offices in Yanacancha, and during his period of office he allowed his supporters to extend their own pasture rights. In addition, he engaged in trade, transporting his products to markets in Chupaca and Huancayo, and educated his children to primary level in Chupaca. He had five children: three went away to work—two to the mines and a daughter to marry a lowland farmer; two remained in Yanacancha, dividing the pasture and animals between them. The two brothers remaining in the village now possess fewer animals between them than did their father, but they are still considered to be the richest farmers. Their reduced resources have encouraged them to diversify: one of them is a part-time musician, and the other takes on a variety of jobs. Both brothers have sold off stock to educate their own children, who are now for the most part permanently away from home.

The second family comes from Cacchi; their father was also a large farmer and a leader in the independence movement. He died, leaving the eldest brother to take care of the rest of the family, consisting of three more brothers and a sister. The eldest brother has held all the important offices of the village and, this last year, was the village delegate to the new SAIS organization. He owns the largest shop in the village and has large flocks of sheep, llamas, and alpacas. However, his wife takes responsibility for these activities, as he himself spends much of his time trading meat and wool in the valley. He also owns a house in Chupaca. The second brother is a full-time market trader in Huancayo; however, the large ironmongery stall he runs is essentially a family enterprise, and other family members help in and profit from it. The youngest brother is studying at the university in Huancayo. His brothers have assisted in financing his education and, in return, he runs a second market stall for them. A fourth brother farms in Cacchi, and takes responsibility for looking after the animals belonging to the rest of the family. The family's resources in Cacchi have been used to establish the various members in the valley, and the economic exchanges among these different members remain intense. They visit back and forth frequently, delegate to each other different economic activities, and help each other when problems arise.

These two cases illustrate the general points we made earlier. The dynamic elements in the economies of the highland villages have become increasingly focused on outside activities. This focus involves permanent residence outside, though the relationship with the village is maintained and the village has, in various ways, become subordinated to the valley economy. Although, as a unit, the village may suffer economically from this relationship, it is clear that villagers, especially some of the more influential ones, are tied by personal self-interest to these external activities. These activities are often trading ventures or involve levels of education that make it unlikely that the migrant will ever return to the highland village. Thus villagers have become involved in economic and social fields that make them less concerned with the opportunities available in pastoral agriculture and more concerned with the exploitation of a wide range of existing resources to further their individual careers. In the following section we examine the implications of this fact for the present-day functioning of the SAIS.

The Impact of the SAIS on Its Members: Contemporary Case Studies

We have already indicated many aspects of the relationship of SAIS to its members; we now need to detail some of the ways in which SAIS is being used to develop the highlands. The characteristics of the organization are such that initiative in planning and development comes chiefly from within the administrative organization of the SAIS or from its foreign and national technical advisors. Such factors as government's direct responsibility for the efficient functioning of the SAIS, the emphasis placed on productivity to pay off existing debts, the infrequent nature of general assemblies, and the responsibilities carried by full-time technical personnel all ensure that the representatives of the villages have very little chance of participating actively in decision making. This lack of participation is strongly felt by representatives and communities and was one of the most frequent complaints made to us against the organization.

This lack of integration is illustrated by the case of the workers, including the technical staff, on the *unidades de producción*. The 535 employees have been organized into a *co-operativa de servicios* that has two representatives in the general assembly. In contrast, the communities have 58 representatives. Yet, since the inception of the SAIS, the lower-paid workers (shepherd, workers in the dairy units, et cetera) have constantly petitioned for improvement in their wages and material conditions, claiming that they were, in fact, better-off under the old hacienda structure. Also, the employees, through the cooperative, receive 2.3 percent of the net profits of the SAIS, whereas some communities receive, singly, more than 4 percent of the profits.[17]

Employees argue that their right to pasture their own animals freely has been curtailed now that the number of livestock and area of pasturage are strictly controlled. They also complain that they no longer have an accessible authority to which they can direct their claims and problems. Whereas, under the old hacienda structure, the administrator of the hacienda had clear authority to settle disputes, under the present organization of the SAIS the different levels of administrative personnel avoid direct responsibility, alleging that it belongs to higher-level bodies. The situation of the lower-paid workers is more difficult since their representatives in the SAIS assembly (the two cooperative representatives) have usually been drawn from the administrative and technical personnel.[18]

The workers feel that the communities and senior staff alike are unsympathetic to their claims to better conditions and do not support them in the general assembly. In fact, in 1972, the assembly rejected a petition of 120 workers for (1) equalizing pay between shepherds and operatives, (2) the right to pasture twenty-five animals of their own (*huacchas*), (3) a 2 percent increment per child, and (4) a 5 percent bonus to foremen, skilled workers, and shepherds with more than five years of service. The assembly also voted to restrict the privileges of the administrative staff, removing the right to an annual bonus, freezing salaries above ten thousand *soles* a month, and eliminating their right to personal service. Community representatives have continued to see a conflict of interest in spending a greater part of the profits of SAIS on remuneration for the workers, technicians, and administrators.

One outcome of this situation has been the attempt by the workers of SAIS Cahuide to form a labor union. This move has been opposed by the senior administrative staff, who have themselves become a target of hostility from both workers and villagers for the excessive salaries they receive, given the ideology and social development policies of SAIS. This hostility has undoubtedly been aggravated by their receiving higher salaries than were common under the old hacienda, for which many of them had worked. The assembly of the employees' cooperative finally agreed to set up a defense committee to look after the interests of all the employees on the SAIS; however, the members of this committee were drawn disproportionately from the administrative staff.[19]

In 1972 and subsequently, the community representatives lobbied for abolition of the agrarian debt; this illustrates one of the persistent limitations of the type of aid that SAIS gives to its communities. Analysis shows that aid is mainly concentrated in social welfare. Under SAIS, medical services in the member communities have been improved to provide regular visits by doctors, dentists, and public health specialists. There is also a team of social workers and educational extension officers who regularly tour communities. While free transport is occasionally provided for community use, material aid is mainly confined to projects financed out of profits they receive. But since, as we have seen, these profits have been small, material aid has largely consisted of such things as a new bridge, improved roads, better school buildings, a pickup truck, equipment for a cooperative building, and improvements in irrigation works. The most substantial projects in these communities have been initiated and financed through the good offices of the SAIS: thus, in Cacchi, a substantial loan has been negotiated with the aid of SAIS personnel to initiate an industrial and agricultural cooperative. The loan was obtained from the national development bank and backed by an international development agency. Although this kind of help is important, it is little different in kind or extent from that which these communities received from government agencies in the past—in particular from the public works department and from the regional offices of the Ministries of Agriculture and Public Health. The limited nature of the aid given to communities is explicitly recognized by development personnel working for SAIS, who state that lack of funds means that they cannot initiate the necessary programs for transforming infrastructure and encouraging local industry.

In practice, the most concerted attempt made by the SAIS administration to introduce change has been its efforts to change the social and economic structure of communities. Hence, development officers of the SAIS have been active in trying to persuade community members to initiate the more radical aspects of agrarian reform by equalizing access to pasture and agricultural land, developing cooperative modes for exploiting local resources, and bringing the commercialization of products within the SAIS organization. Since they are limited in the material assistance they can give, development personnel are led to stress such changes in local structure as some of the most important benefits that SAIS can bring. This program is restricted not only by lack of personnel and money but also by internal opposition from economic interest groups within the community. This opposition was acknowledged by development officers of the SAIS: "There exist certain *comuneros* who are opposed to the application of the community statute because of their established interests. We note the existence of a system of internal domination akin to that of small *gamonales* [exploitative landowners] within the communities." [20] Given that the community delegates to the SAIS come predominantly from those farmers with most animals and rights of pasturage—which they consider as private family property—then the weight of this opposition is likely to be formidable. Moreover, our data also show that it is these same larger farmers who are most interested in, and know most about, the SAIS and its organization. The majority of community members evidence little interest in or knowledge of the SAIS. According to interviews conducted by SAIS Cahuide's development division, 49 percent of community members had no knowledge or understanding of what SAIS was, and a further substantial proportion had only a little understanding.

This contemporary situation can be set within our previous historical discussion by considering the case of Yanacancha. Yanacancha village has received special attention from the development officers and technical personnel of SAIS; it includes the most extensive pasture of any community in SAIS Cahuide and a large proportion of this is high grade, being a continuation of the best lands of the former hacienda Laive, one of the most efficient and productive of the SAIS's *unidades de producción*. Technical officers have been attempting to persuade Yanacancha to extend its agrarian cooperative to include more sheep owned by community members. These sheep would be pastured and supervised jointly to permit improvements in animal husbandry and breeding that would increase community revenue. In practice, their efforts have so far proved a failure and have given rise to considerable intracommunity acrimony. One section of the village (Huayllacancha), which forms a semi-independent neighborhood and which seeks full independence, accuses the official leaders of the village of wishing to protect their own interests and those of their friends, and of depriving Huayllacancha of its communal pasture. Behind this dispute lie the processes we have described earlier. Of the total pasture of Yanacancha, all the best pasture and some 60 percent of lesser quality pasture is in the hands of individual households. The distribution is extremely uneven: some 40 households out·of a total of 212 claim grazing rights to almost 60 percent of grazing land. This unevenness of distribution is less marked in the neighborhood of Huayllacancha, where a lesser proportion of grazing land is in private hands. However, farmers in Huayllacancha have been attempting to extend their grazing rights over the communal pasture close to their neighborhood, which they have customarily farmed. A possible restriction on their ability to do so is that this land formally belongs to the village as a whole and they cannot legally restrict access to it. Apart from this issue, they argue that their neighborhood, which is located at some distance from the central neighborhood, needs its own school, and they complain of giving labor to public works that benefit the central neighborhood most.

The efforts of the Huayllacancha farmers to form an independent community represent an attempt to define their boundaries so that they can restrict access to their lands and labor. Though they accuse the central neighborhood officials of being exploitative, rich farmers, they do not question the principle of private ownership of land: indeed, the leaders of the Huayllacancha movement are the middle- to larger-scale farmers of the locality. Huayllacancha borders on the hacienda Laive and its independence would bring into question Yanacancha's own claim to SAIS membership as a bordering community. The Yana-cancha leaders see the Huayllacancha movement as a threat to their potential for economic expansion both individually and within the SAIS.

Thus, the economic interests of individual farming households interfere with attempts to rationalize local farming and to distribute its benefits more evenly. This being the case, it may appear surprising that poorer families in the locality have not shown themselves more active in support of SAIS development policies: SAIS representatives continue to be elected from among the larger farmers and elections are not marked by intraneighborhood acrimony. To understand this, we must remember the characteristics of these poorer families. They are often linked by kinship to the richer families and work for them. More significantly, poorer families have been most subject to temporary labor migration. They contain the highest proportion of unmarried household members away working in mines, in construction work in the cities, and in agricultural labor. These migrants send remittances home and intend to return; they do not have the skills and resources that would make it easy for them to establish themselves permanently in town. In this respect, their migration contrasts with that of the larger farmers, who are more likely to migrate by household and permanently. These factors—the temporary absence of many members of poorer families and the individual opportunities they have to make a living and begin to accumulate property—divert the attention of the poorer families from the inequalities in local farming. They are not constantly confronted by them and have few opportunities to recognize the possibilities offered to them by SAIS organization.

This case study illustrates the contemporary dilemma of SAIS organization, that its member communities continue to be differentiated internally and in ways that continue to individualize their economic relationships. Each household develops its particular strategies for economic survival; these involve migration and the diversification of economic activities. These factors make the finding of a local basis for communal activity more problematic, since villages become broken into smaller units. Also, within each farming household, increasing reliance is placed on other economic activities. The common interests that households have in pastoral activity are consequently reduced, and there are increasing signs of cash payments replacing communal obligations and those of mutual aid. Farmers prefer to pay fines for not participating in communal work parties—a fine amounts to considerably less than what their labor can bring elsewhere. This affects the local commitments of the larger farmers also; a substantial section of their revenue now comes from ancillary occupations that depend on individual relationships outside the highlands. Their flocks are less numerous than those of their fathers, both because of population expansion and subdivision of inheritance and because of the practice of converting resources into lowland investments.

Conclusion

We have concentrated on the problems posed to agrarian reform in the highlands and have described the particular social and economic processes that have differentiated constituent villages and brought their individual members into the wider social and economic organization of Peru. In one sense, the SAIS reform comes too late to help these communities: the increasing focus of their interest in the cash economy and their diminished economic commitment to pastoral activity does not create a natural community of interest within the SAIS. The capacity of the SAIS to interest its member communities must lie in developing a substantial provision of new work opportunities, many of which could be in industry and service occupations. The limitations imposed by the agrarian debt make this possibility a remote one, though there have been suggestions that the SAIS should take over ancillary town-based industries, such as the declining Huancayo textile industry. Without the provision of work opportunities linked to the working structure of the SAIS, there is a danger that the needs of households to continue to develop individual strategies of survival will, first, prevent communal development projects being effectively initiated and, second, increasingly serve to subsidize, on an individual basis, the development of urban areas through investments in education, housing, trade, and the like. We argue that the problems these villages and the SAIS face in organizing themselves communally are not attributable to their economic backwardness or to traditional orientations. Rather, these problems emerge because villages have been exposed to and have become incorporated into the kinds of capitalist development that occurred in the central highlands. Since these forms of capitalist development still continue and no alternative work opportunities are provided, it is to be expected that villagers generally regard the SAIS with indifference. This is to repeat the familiar theme that any agrarian reform, to be effective, must include a comprehensive plan for regional and national development. Unless this is done, the partial solutions to the problems outlined above, contained in the setting up of some few industries or other work opportunities within the SAIS, are likely to benefit only sections of the village population. It is within the framework of a more comprehensive reform that more effective and extensive participation of members will occur, as it becomes evident to them that their personal and group interests coincide within the same organizational structure.

NOTES

1. The Cerro de Pasco haciendas, which belonged to the mining company of that name, had been included in the agrarian reform measures of the government previous to the present military government. However, until the Agrarian Reform Law of the military government there did not exist any clearly defined plans for the reorganization of expropriated land. The only previous experience of reorganizing expropriated haciendas had been the Belaúnde government's parcelization of the Fernandini hacienda, Algolán, among the communities that had long-standing legal claims to its pasture. As we will see, the disruption of cattle production consequent to this measure and the breakdown in the overall organization of the hacienda influenced the search for a different type of agrarian reform reorganization for this type of cattle hacienda.

2. See Ramón Zaldívar, "Agrarian Reform and Military Reformism in Peru," in *Agrarian Reform and Agrarian Reformism*, edited by D. Lehmann;

Carlos Fonseca, "Comunidad, hacienda y el modelo Sais," *América Indígena* vol. 35, no. 2 (April–June 1975); Rodrigo Montoya et al., *La Sais Cahuide y sus contradicciones.*

3. Jean Piel, "The Place of the Peasantry in the National Life of Peru in the Nineteenth Century," *Past and Present*, no. 46 (February 1970): 108–133.

4. See José R. Sabogal-Wiesse, "Gamonalismo en Los Andes," paper presented at symposium on "Landlord and Peasant in Latin America and the Caribbean," Cambridge University, December, 1972.

5. This is the viewpoint being developed by Juan Martínez-Alier, through his work on the archives of the expropriated haciendas. See his *Los huacchilleros del Perú.*

6. The data on which we base this analysis are taken from the Texto Único de la Ley de Reforma Agraria, Edición Official, Diario Official *El Peruano*, Lima, 1970; also, "Las Comunidades integrantes de la Sais Túpac Amaru," Documentos no. 1, COMACRA, Dirección General de Reforma Agraria, Ministerio de Agricultura, Lima, 1971; "Jatari" División de Desarrollo, SAIS "Cahuide" Ltda., no. 6, Huancayo, 1972; Montoya et al., *La Sais Cahuide.*

7. See Colin Harding, *Agrarian Reform and Agrarian Struggles in Peru.* This study concentrates on the conflicts taking place in the coastal region.

8. See Reglamento de Cooperativas Comunales y Sociedades Agrícolas de Interés Social, Oficina Nacional de Desarrollo Cooperativo, Apr. 5593, Lima, p. 39.

9. For a general overview of current reforms, including the SAIS, see Michael Anderson, "Nuevas formas de participación de los trabajadores en la economía del Perú," *Report to the Ford Foundation*; see also Fonseca, "Comunidad, hacienda y el model Sais"; and Zaldívar, "Agrarian Reform."

10. There is a specific part of the Agrarian Reform Law designed to reform the *comunidades campesinas* (see Texto Único, p. 38). This reform has not been fully implemented. For an analysis of its impact on the Mantaro Valley, see David Winder in this volume, and Norman Long and David Winder, "From Peasant Community to Production Cooperative: An Analysis of Recent Government Policy in Peru," *Journal of Development Studies*, 12, no. 1 (October 1975): 75–94; G. Alberti and R. Sánchez, *Poder y conflicto social en el valle del Mantaro.*

11. See Zaldívar, "Agrarian Reform."

12. See Winder in this volume.

13. For a description of these practices see Richard N. Adams, *A Community in the Andes: Problems and Progress in Muquiyauyo*; and G. Alberti and E. Mayer, eds., *Reciprocidad e intercambio en los Andes peruanos.*

14. A similar situation exists in other areas of highland Peru. See, for example, Favre's analysis of the separation of highland from valley villages in the department of Huancavelica (Henri Favre, "Le peuplement et la colonisation agricole de la steppe dans le Pérou central," *Annales de Geographie* 84 [July–September 1975]: 415–440).

15. John Murra, "El 'control vertical' de un máximo de pisos ecológicos en la economía de las sociedades andinas," *La visita de la provincia de León de Huánuco, (1562)*, vol. 2.

16. We have records dating from the end of the nineteenth century of children from highland villages being sent to board in the neighboring towns to attend secondary schools. The frequent legal disputes in which these villages were involved as corporations and the self-interest we have described on the

part of local farmers in these proceedings must be major reasons why, in even the smallest village, there has long been an evident desire to have children educated at least to literacy and to have a school of its own. The leading role taken by local schoolteachers, often in private schools, in helping communities in their disputes reinforced this respect for the potential of education.

17. For a full exposition of these points, see Montoya et al., *La Sais Cahuide*, pp. 45–60, 99–102.

18. "Jatari," División de Desarrollo, p. 41.

19. Montoya et al., *La Sais Cahuide*, p. 58.

20. Ibid., p. 60.

10. Peasant and Entrepreneurial Coalitions: The Case of the Matahuasi Cooperative

NORMAN LONG AND RODRIGO SÁNCHEZ

Introduction

This chapter analyzes the history, functions, and social composition of one marketing and servicing agrarian cooperative situated in the Mantaro Valley.[1] The account focuses on three related aspects: the cooperative's objectives and performance, the role of various promotion agencies sponsored by the state, and the location of the cooperative and its members within the structure of socioeconomic relationships characteristic of the zone.

The discussion of economic cooperation requires that we distinguish initially between different basic forms: cooperation in the process of production, in the marketing of products, and in the acquisition of commodities and essential inputs. Cooperation in production entails the joint use of some or all of the factors of production, such as land, tools, or labor; cooperation for marketing signifies an agreement by farmers to accept a uniform pricing system for the product or products they sell. This latter type is frequently combined with that of the provision of various technical services and with the supply of seeds, fertilizers, and insecticides.

The most systematically organized form of agrarian cooperation in production is that of the production cooperative or collective farm in which all factors are communally owned and/or controlled. This type has proved difficult, if not impossible, to establish in contexts where private ownership of the means of production and capitalist financial institutions predominate, that is, in small-holder peasant and capitalist systems.[2] In these contexts we find that, unless a radical program of land expropriation and consolidation has been implemented, it is the marketing and servicing cooperative that is the characteristic form.[3]

The next dimension to consider is whether or not cooperation occurs within the context of formal associations, like cooperative societies or farmers' associations, or whether it functions through the use of networks of an informal kind that bring farmers together to carry out specific tasks. The analysis of economic cooperation must perforce take account of both formal and informal organization. Unless this is done it becomes difficult to arrive at a balanced assessment of the role and performance of formally organized cooperative institutions, since the latter normally constitute only one out of a range of possible alternatives open to farmers for solving the problems they face.[4] Literature on modern cooperatives often fails to take sufficient account of this aspect and thus does not fully appreciate the ways in which behavior within the formal framework is affected by other types of commitment and by cooperative arrangements outside the institution.

A further important consideration is how far the formal institutions themselves are the result of intervention by the state or outside agencies, or how far they represent a relatively spontaneous development by the farmers themselves in the attempt to solve particular problems. Obviously most cooperative organizations are an outcome of the interaction of these two processes. However, the degree to which government agencies continue to be or become involved in the running of these institutions is important for understanding why it is that certain organizations persist despite their manifestly poor economic and administrative performance. They often cannot, it seems, be dismantled by the membership or declared bankrupt and voted out of existence.

As we have indicated, marketing and servicing cooperatives are typically found among small-holder peasants, like those of the Mantaro Valley. The main functions of cooperative marketing have been described in terms of strengthening the bargaining position of farmers vis-à-vis the market and of affording them the opportunity to benefit from certain economies of scale and from various organizational advantages they would not otherwise enjoy.[5] Both these aims, of course, are usually subsumed under the more general one of obtaining higher farm incomes and a more equitable distribution of wealth. The marketing cooperative may help farmers to resist the unfavorable deals offered by private traders; without a cooperative farmers frequently have no alternative but to market their produce through such intermediaries. Also, if the cooperative has storage or processing facilities, farmers may be able to hold back their produce from the market until later in the season, when prices are better. It is in these ways, then, that marketing cooperatives increase the bargaining power of the farmer himself.

Normally, we find that the marketing of crops or livestock is combined with various servicing functions. The cooperative society provides seeds, fertilizers, insecticides, and farm implements at low cost to members. It is able to do this because it negotiates directly with import agents and firms and makes purchases in large quantities at reduced price. Most such cooperatives also provide technical assistance with new forms of technology and give advice on agricultural and livestock practice. In addition, through their contacts with government and banks, they undertake to support farmers in their applications for short- or long-term credit.

Much of the literature on rural cooperatives in the Third World concentrates on isolating factors that inhibit the development of viable cooperative institutions,[6] for, while there are several examples of highly successful cooperative experiments,[7] a great deal of discussion has been devoted to explaining the reasons for the "failures." The types of explanation offered range widely. They include the cataloguing of various organizational and administrative deficiencies that result from a lack of technical and other skills among members; a consideration of the ways in which "traditional" or individualistic value orientations generate interests that are basically incompatible with cooperative goals; and questions concerning the negative effects of existing power structures and of the role of the state. Some studies have attempted to link this discussion to a more general assessment of peasant forms of economic and social organization; they have tried to explain why peasants face difficulties in establishing enduring and dependable modes of cooperation. Thus, George Foster argues that Mexican peasants involved in small-holder family production do not develop corporate groupings above the level of the household; instead, they evolve a highly individualistic network of dyadic ties based on kinship, *compadrazgo* (ritual kinship), and patronage.[8] These interpersonal networks are constantly shifting in composition as the content and meaning of particular relationships are renegotiated. Such a structure, he maintains, is associated with the image of the "limited good," which regards all resources as finite and unexpandable and which, therefore, depicts social life as a competitive game whereby one man's gains are always at the expense of others. Because of this, Foster argues, peasant attempts at setting up modern cooperative forms of organization often fail.

Although Foster clearly recognized that the notion of peasant society entails the existence of ties of dependency with metropolitan powers, both national and international, it was left to others to analyze in detail this structure of domination, or what has been called "internal colonialism." Writers emphasizing the structure of domination argue that the fragmented and competitive nature of peasant societies arises *precisely because of* their incorporation into colonial and postcolonial society. It is not explicable solely in terms of internal sociocultural processes. This wider structure is characterized by marked inequalities that emerge from the control exercised by various nonpeasant groups, who are primarily interested in the appropriation of economic surplus from the peasantry.[9] Several studies have shown that rural cooperatives have so far achieved little in effecting significant structural change.[10] Indeed, most formal organizations of this type have tended to reinforce existing patterns of socioeconomic differentiation and have provided an arena within which members of a local economic elite (e.g., commercial farmers and traders) have sought to extend their control and influence over economic and social matters.[11]

This chapter explores these dimensions through a discussion of one marketing and servicing cooperative in the Mantaro Valley: the Matahuasi cooperative (Cooperativa Agraria de la Margen Izquierda del Mantaro). Although based in Matahuasi, this cooperative now serves many other communities to the east of the Mantaro River. A fuller analysis than can be attempted here would necessitate a detailed study of existing types of cooperation and competition, both within and outside the boundaries of formal institutions. The cooperative, in fact, is only one of several types of social framework within which horizontal and vertical relationships are developed and maintained. Moreover, since its members operate simultaneously in several different frameworks at once, it becomes somewhat artificial to isolate actions that take place within the cooperative from those outside.

The Socioeconomic Setting

As has been indicated in an earlier chapter,[12] Matahuasi is situated in the center of the valley, to the east of the Mantaro River. It is well connected by road and railway to Huancayo, at the southern end of the valley, to La Oroya, the nearest mining town, and to Lima and the coast. In 1972, Matahuasi had a resident population of about four thousand people. Its economy is primarily based on agriculture, although it also has an important commercial and transport sector. Table 1 gives a breakdown of the occupational structure. From this it can be seen that 54.3 percent of adult heads of households are involved in agricultural production. The rest are engaged in a variety of occupations and range from teachers and other professionals (7.6 percent) to shopkeepers and traders (11.4 percent) and small-scale craftsmen (9.5 percent) or unskilled workers (7.6 percent).

The agricultural sector is highly differentiated. Table 2 shows that while 14.3 percent of the population control four or more hectares of private land, the vast majority (68.5 percent) control less than two hectares. There is also a growing category of landless laborers and persons with uneconomic holdings who must work for other farmers or seek a living in some nonagricultural occupation. In fact, census statistics tend to underestimate the number of landless laborers, since most

TABLE 1

DISTRIBUTION OF PRINCIPAL OCCUPATIONS
IN MATAHUASI DISTRICT, 1971

Occupation	Number	Percentage
Farmers	57	54.3
Shopkeepers/traders	12	11.4
Craftsmen	10	9.5
Teachers/skilled employees	8	7.6
Nonagricultural workers	8	7.6
Agricultural laborers	3	2.9
Timber merchants/truckers	3	2.9
Retired/unemployed	4	3.8
Total	105	100

NOTE: This is a random sample of heads of households.

TABLE 2

DISTRIBUTION OF PRIVATE LANDHOLDINGS
IN MATAHUASI DISTRICT, 1971

Size of Landholdings	Number	Percentage
Landless sector	23	21.9
Less than 1 hectare	27	25.7
1 to less than 2 hectares	22	20.9
2 to less than 3 hectares	13	12.4
3 to less than 4 hectares	5	4.8
4 and more hectares	15	14.3
Total	105	100

NOTE: This is a random sample of heads of households.

of them live under the same roof as their employers and, for all intents and purposes, count as dependent members of the latter's households.[13]

The commercial sector is represented by twenty-five shopkeepers, four timber merchants who buy, process, and sell timber to the mines to be used as pit props, four large-scale agricultural middlemen, several livestock traders, milk intermediaries, and smaller agricultural middlemen. There is also a small professional group made up of teachers and government employees, plus a handful of skilled and unskilled urban workers who travel each day to work in Huancayo.

Since the opening of the Cerro de Pasco mines and the expansion of Lima, the national capital, there has been a steady out-migration of Matahuasinos for work and education. Matahuasi, together with Sicaya, now has one of the largest number of village-born members living outside the valley. There are over one thousand persons from the village currently living in Lima, and many others are scattered throughout the towns and cities of Peru. In addition, ten families who still have roots in Matahuasi have members living overseas, in the United States or Europe.

The Formation of the Matahuasi Cooperative

The establishment of the cooperative in Matahuasi resulted indirectly from increased agricultural extension work in the Mantaro region during the late 1960s. During this period the Belaúnde government, with the assistance of various foreign aid programs, set up a number of training schemes for small-scale farmers throughout Peru. In 1966 the Instituto de Capacitación Campesina, later called ALPACA, based in Huancayo, organized a series of short courses for farmers of the area, and two or three persons from Matahuasi and the nearby hamlet of Huanchar attended. At about the same time, SIPA (Servicio de Investigación y Promoción Agraria) began opening extension offices in the villages of the valley and offering technical aid to local farmers. These projects were part of a general strategy, which included the now-famous program called *Co-operación Popular*, to encourage greater participation by peasants in rural development and to help them to cooperate in local development.

One of the farmers from Huanchar who attended the ALPACA course was later offered a six-month scholarship in the United States to learn modern methods of agriculture. He spent his period there living on farms in South Dakota and Wisconsin seeing how American farmers organized and managed their farms. On his return, he immediately set about exploring the possibility of forming a local agrarian cooperative.

His idea of forming a cooperative was initially well received. The cooperative model was familiar to many villagers, as they had firsthand knowledge of the recently inaugurated valley-wide Mantaro electricity cooperative and also knew of the earlier experiments in Muquiyauyo and other villages. Discussions concerning the cooperative quickly centered on the question of setting up an association that would have as its primary aim the elimination of the milk intermediaries who, since the 1930s, had controlled the marketing of milk and cheese. Milk producers were generally dissatisfied with the way these traders operated; it was alleged that they used no standard measure for buying milk and that their prices were artificially low. The producers claimed that the intermediaries made huge profits, which they invested in property and businesses in La Oroya and land in Matahuasi.

Writing of Maravilca, a hamlet of Matahuasi, Flores describes how, in 1935, there were three main milk traders. These men were later to become three of the largest landowners and businessmen in the zone.[14] This and other evidence suggests that, during the opening up and expansion of the mining towns of the central highlands, trading in milk and livestock products constituted an important source of entrepreneurial profit.

Having decided on the broad objectives of the proposed cooperative, the group of farmers sought the advice of the agricultural officer attached to the SIPA office in Matahuasi. This man showed immediate interest in the project and in April 1967 assisted them in forming an organizing committee; in the following month the association started marketing milk. The agricultural officer put at their disposal the government vehicle in his charge and provided contacts with clients in Huancayo, where he lived. Several of these customers were the owners of restaurants and cafes. He also took great interest in the campaign to attract new members and frequently traveled with the farmers to visit families in the vicinity in order to persuade them to join the new association. In addition, he guided them in drawing up a formal constitution, which was essential if they were to become registered legally as a cooperative society.

After the constitution was formulated, setting out the basic objectives and membership criteria for the association, SIPA was asked by government to undertake an independent feasibility study. The main conclusion of this study, however, was that the cooperative should not base its operations solely on the marketing of milk but should also be concerned with the supply of fertilizers, insecticides, seeds, and other products for the general farming population. It was further recommended that the association open membership to all persons residing on the eastern bank of the Mantaro River and not confine itself to people from Matahuasi and nearby villages.

Following this, in October 1967, the cooperative was formally established with an initial membership of 103 persons and a capital sum of some 10,300 *soles*. The membership rules specified that each member should pay an entrance fee of 100 *soles* and agree to make twenty additional contributions over the next few years up to a total of 2000 *soles*. Since 1967, membership has steadily grown and, by 1972, it had reached a figure of 360 registered members. Whereas most of its first members were from Matahuasi and its immediate environs, later the membership was distributed throughout many of the villages along the eastern bank of the river and even spread out to include farmers living in the higher *puna* areas to the east on the road to Satipo.

During the early years, the cooperative faced the difficult problem of not having its own vehicle and had to use the truck provided by SIPA. It also had relatively little capital with which to purchase the fertilizers for the store it had opened in Matahuasi. It finally solved these problems by securing a government loan of 1,100,000 *soles*, which was earmarked for major capital outlay. On behalf of the cooperative, SIPA arranged for the society to take out membership in the Livestock Owners Association of Peru (Asociación de Ganaderos del Perú), from which good quality cattle feed was obtainable at a reduced price. In addition, the government attached a group of Peace Corps volunteers to help with the accounting system and with demonstration work. Later, an agreement was signed with the West German government to secure technical assistance in the agricultural sector of the Mantaro region; from 1968 onward, several German livestock specialists began to work closely with the cooperative in Matahuasi.

The German Technical Mission quickly assumed a major role in the running of the cooperative. With funds from the German government, a pasteurization plant capable of processing ten thousand liters of milk daily was constructed, and went into operation in June 1973. Although this was the most visible impact it had, the mission also set up a central association of cooperatives and worked strenuously on improving animal husbandry and increasing the quantity and quality of milk production.

By 1969 the operational capital of the cooperative amounted to about three million *soles*. This enabled it to establish two additional service stores in Jauja, at the northern end of the valley, and in Comas, in the hills to the east of Matahuasi. There were also plans to open stores in two other valley villages—Concepción and San Lorenzo. Most of the capital for financing these developments derived from government loans, for, aside from the initial payment of membership dues, the cooperative found it was increasingly unable to persuade members to invest their private capital in it. Hence the cooperative rapidly became a largely government-subsidized enterprise with a massive input from overseas technical staff. Also, its main source of revenue came not from the sale of milk but from fertilizers and other farming items.

Milk Marketing and Production

As we suggested earlier, the impetus for the formation of the co-operative came from a group of farmers who were dissatisfied with the price they received from intermediaries for their milk. At this time traders were purchasing milk for 2.30 *soles* per liter and selling it in La Oroya and Jauja for nearly 4 *soles*. There were also, as we indicated, complaints that they were cheating farmers with short measures.

The cooperative responded to this situation by raising its buying price to 3 *soles* and introducing the use of proper liter measures and milk churns. The milk was sold in Huancayo for 3.50 *soles*. This action initiated a sequence of competition with the traders whereby the latter first raised their buying price to 3.20 *soles* and the cooperative then topped that, and so on, until 1969, when the cooperative found that it was forced to hold its price at 4.20 *soles* but, as an incentive, offered a fixed price throughout the year rather than a fluctuating price de-termined by demand and supply. This, it was hoped, would win the support of the milk producers, for it provided a security private dealers did not offer. However, the strategy was not entirely successful, because the traders themselves raised their lowest price level to meet the 4.20 paid by the cooperative and, in addition, paid anything up to 5 *soles* per liter when the demand for milk was high. During the 1971–1972 period, the cooperative once again raised its price but was unable to go beyond 4.50 *soles*; this left the private dealers in a position to outbid them whenever they wished.

In discussing with farmers the problem of why the cooperative was never able to compete effectively with the intermediaries, it was often stated that the traders were able to give higher prices because they watered down milk·and mixed poorer with better quality products. While this may be true, other reasons are the high operational costs and product inflexibility of large-scale as against small-scale commerce. In comparison with the cooperative, all present-day milk traders are relatively small operators who combine the milk and cheese business with other farming or trading interests. Also, whereas the cooperative runs a vehicle and employs a driver and assistant, the milk trader often does not possess transport other than a tricycle used for collecting the milk and delivers his milk to La Oroya by bus. He is also more interested in the production of cheese for sale than in milk per se and utilizes unpaid family labor in its preparation.

Table 3 gives a breakdown of the average weekly income and expenditure for milk marketing in July 1971 for the cooperative as compared with a small-scale trader based in Matahuasi. These data show that, while the net profit per liter for the cooperative is only about 0.22 *soles*, for the trader, who sells the product as cheese that he has processed himself, the profit is 2.30 *soles*. This difference is the more striking since the trader marketed his cheese in La Oroya, some two hours away by

TABLE 3

A COMPARISON OF THE AVERAGE WEEKLY INCOME
AND EXPENDITURE ON MILK TRADING FOR THE
COOPERATIVE AND A PRIVATE TRADER (JULY 1971)

THE COOPERATIVE

Liters collected per week	Buying price	Selling price	Total profit
3500	4.50 *soles*	5.00 *soles*	1750 *soles*
		Gasoline expenses (daily round trips to Huancayo)	350 *soles*
		Wages of driver	630 *soles*
		Net weekly profit	770 *soles*
		Profit per liter	0.22 *soles*

SMALL PRIVATE TRADER

Liters collected per week	Buying price	Selling price	Total profit
300	4.70 *soles*	7.50 *soles* (sold as cheese, 2.5 per liter: each cheese at 3 *soles*)	840 *soles*
		Transport expenses (3 round trips by bus to La Oroya per week at 50 *soles* each)	150 *soles*
		Hired labor costs	—
		Net weekly profit	690 *soles*
		Profit per liter	2.30 *soles*

road, and not in the nearby regional city of Huancayo, which is only twenty kilometers' distance.

Cheese production, then, appears to be a more profitable line. Yet the cooperative is constrained from moving into cheese processing because of the additional costs and administrative problems it would entail. Whereas the small-scale trader can draw upon unpaid family labor, the cooperative would have to recruit extra paid hands, since its members would be unlikely to offer free labor, given the precedent set by the employment of a driver and assistants. It would also, because of the larger scale of the operation, probably need considerable capital outlay in order to purchase the necessary cheese-making equipment and to cover operating costs.

The viability of small-scale milk and cheese trading must, in addition, be related to the fact that these traders combine this trading with other complementary forms of economic activity. For instance, the man in the above example produces alfalfa as fodder for livestock, cultivates potatoes, maize, and beans partly for susbsistence and partly for marketing, and also raises chickens and pigs. The sale of cheese in La Oroya is combined with the marketing of chickens to restaurants, of pigs to various butchers, and of eggs to a number of retail shops. In fact, he has a regular trading network in La Oroya based on kinship, *paisano*, and friendship ties, which he had built up when he worked in La Oroya as a milk vender for a well-known shopkeeper. His father had also worked in the milk business for a number of years and was for a time an assistant to various agricultural intermediaries based in Matahuasi itself.

Milk marketing has always presented the cooperative with difficulties. In 1969–1970 serious deficits were discovered in the cooperative's accounts that pointed toward embezzlement by the driver. Although nothing was conclusively proved, the driver was forced to resign his position; however, immediately on leaving the job, he purchased a van and set himself up as a competitor to the cooperative. Another problem arose because of the need to control milk quality. In order to retain its regular customers in Huancayo, it was essential for the cooperative to supply a rich and clean product. This required the careful vetting of milk purchased from members so that standards were maintained. Several members had their membership suspended for adulterating milk. In August 1970 four members were expelled for watering down milk, for concealing the fact that their cows were diseased with mastitis, and for selling to intermediaries after having promised to market through the cooperative. Prior to this the cooperative had attempted to fine individuals one *sol* per liter of poor quality milk, but when this system failed to achieve the desired result it was decided to withdraw membership. Two of those expelled had held positions of leadership in the society.

Yet despite the fact that the cooperative has been beset by various administrative problems, it has, together with the German mission, played a significant role in promoting increased milk production in the valley. Income from milk sales rose from 865,832 *soles* in 1969 to 1,300,000 *soles* in 1971, an increase of 50 percent. Matahuasi is especially well suited to dairy farming, as about 60 percent of its land is under irrigation and there are extensive areas devoted to alfalfa. In 1971, there were twelve hundred cattle in the district.

Nevertheless, the number of farmers marketing their milk through the cooperative remains small. In 1970–1971 there were about forty-five households in the Matahuasi district who produced regularly for the market, but of these less than half sold to the cooperative. By far the majority of milk producers who sell to the cooperative live in Matahuasi or Huanchar; with the exception of two farmers who own large farms of twenty-two and forty-four hectares respectively, they are medium-scale farmers controlling between about five and ten hectares each. According to an evaluation carried out by the German Technical Mission, it becomes economically viable to engage in commercial milk production with a few head of good quality cattle only at the level of about five to eight hectares of land, since one needs to combine pasture and fodder cultivation with food crops for subsistence.[15] This land should not be broken into a large number of scattered plots. These ecological and other factors (e.g., personal job preferences and other opportunities for making cash) mean that commercial milk production is confined to a relatively small sector of the population: those farmers possessing approximately five or more hectares of land (about 12 percent of the total Matahuasi population) who have dairy cattle.

The pasteurization plant, constructed at Concepción in 1973, illustrates the difficulties facing a cooperative based on small-scale producers. Members of the cooperative had hoped that they would receive preferential treatment for the milk they sold. However, the opening of the plant has led to much stricter quality control and to the larger producers' being preferred, since only they can guarantee regular supplies. This latter aspect is particularly important because, although the plant was planned to process some ten thousand liters daily, in June 1973 it was operating at well below one-sixth of its capacity.

From time to time, the cooperative and the German mission have tried to persuade the various local district councils in the valley to help restrict the activity of milk intermediaries by passing local government ordinances prohibiting the sale of milk to buyers other than the cooperative. But so far nothing along these lines has materialized. It is now hoped that the newly formed Central Cooperative—an association of cooperatives based in Huancayo—may be able to achieve more positive results. The Matahuasi cooperative has also been unsuccessful in securing contracts for the supply of milk to large companies like the Cerro de Pasco Mining Corporation. For example, in 1971, the corporation put out to tender a contract for the weekly supply of two thousand liters of milk for their work force at the smelter in La Oroya. However, the contract was captured by three local traders who had long-standing political contacts in the corporation and in local government in La Oroya and who had previously shown themselves to be reliable suppliers of produce.[16]

The Provision of Fertilizers and Other Products

The cooperative's other important function is that of supplying fertilizers and seeds to the general farming population. This function was built into the scheme right from the start, when government intervened to persuade it to undertake this in addition to milk marketing.

Guano de isla (fertilizer made from bird droppings) was first introduced into the Mantaro Valley in the 1930s, but synthetic fertilizers were not used until the 1960s, when there was much more intensive agricultural extension work in the zone. At about the same time, several commercial farmers had begun using tractors instead of oxen for ploughing, and the malt company (*maltería*) from Lima had introduced threshing machines for harvesting barley, which they required for brewing beer. The cooperative, then, commenced operations at a time when the agricultural technology had already begun to shift toward more mechanized forms and when a number of farmers were already using fertilizers and improved seeds. One measure of technological advancement in Matahuasi can be judged by the fact that, by 1971, 22 percent of the farming population was using modern machinery (tractors, threshers, et cetera), 59 percent traditional techniques (i.e., oxen and plough, hand tools), and 19 percent a mixture of both.

The major difficulty these farmers faced, especially the smaller operators, was that of obtaining fertilizer. Its distribution was controlled by various firms (*casas comerciales*) in Huancayo and it was uneconomic to transport it in small quantities to Matahuasi. The one advantage the *casas comerciales* had, however, was that they offered credit to clients they trusted. This system enabled farmers to reserve cash they might otherwise have spent on fertilizers for expenditure on labor or other items later in the growing season. But it also entailed the establishment of close bonds with personnel in the *casa comercial* and a willingness to repay one's debts at the end of the season or face continued indebtedness and a rising interest rate.

The formation of the cooperative was designed to solve these problems. A couple of years or so before, SIPA had opened a store in Matahuasi from which a limited amount of fertilizer was distributed. The cooperative was to take over and expand this service. During the first year, SIPA worked closely with the cooperative in organizing the purchase and transport of fertilizers from Lima; in the second, however, the cooperative obtained a loan of 1,100,000 *soles* from the Agricultural Development Bank. This loan enabled them to make arrangements with a wholesale dealer to deliver directly to Matahuasi, thus cutting out the *casas comerciales* of Huancayo. This tactic had the effect of causing the various wholesaler firms to compete against one another in order to offer the best terms and led to a substantial reduction in the price charged for bulk purchase, although, in addition, the cooperative had to meet the transport costs.

There is no available information on the amount of fertilizer purchased in Matahuasi by local farmers prior to the formation of the cooperative. However, since its establishment, the expansion of fertilizer sales has been considerable. Table 4 shows revenue from fertilizer and other similar items during the first four years of operation. The drop in takings for 1970 is explained by the fact that a large amount of stock was unsold from the previous year. The significance of this branch of business is further emphasized when it is realized that some 90 percent of total revenue derives from these sales.

The expansion of fertilizer sales has resulted partly from the gradual extension of the cooperative's field of action from Matahuasi to other valley villages between Jauja and Huancayo and to the higher altitude zone of Comas. Comas and its nearby settlements specialize in the production of potatoes that come onto the Lima market a month or two before those of the valley region. The zone is at too high an altitude

TABLE 4

SALES OF FERTILIZER BY THE MATAHUASI
COOPERATIVE, 1968–1971

Year	Value in Peruvian *Soles*
1968	3,036,012
1969	6,938,371
1970	5,525,630
1971	8,700,000

for dairy farming, but people there use the cooperative to buy fertilizers and insecticides for their crops.

Sales have also increased because fertilizers, insecticides, and other products are sold to nonmembers as well as to members of the cooperative, although the latter of course have first option on supplies when they are short. Moreover, nonmembers do not receive the same facilities and support when applying for government loans, nor do they share in any dividends that might be available. The main advantage of the cooperative to them, as also to members, is that it offers somewhat lower prices than the *casas comerciales* and maintains a network of fertilizer stores throughout the zone that are easily accessible to most farmers. Nevertheless, sales in Matahuasi make up 40 percent of all fertilizer sold (table 5); the rest goes to the Jauja, Huancayo, and Comas areas. The table also shows the relatively large amount of fertilizer (some 23 percent) purchased by cooperative members living in the central village of Matahuasi. The latter constitute only 4 percent of the total number of buyers. This suggests that, despite the general expansion in sales, the bulk is still purchased by the larger farmers living in Matahuasi. On the other hand, about 36 percent of the fertilizer is sold to nonmembers, so the cooperative provides a useful service for the farming population as a whole.

The cooperative solved the problem of transporting supplies from Lima by inviting a group of truckers from Matahuasi to join it. None

TABLE 5

SALES OF FERTILIZER TO MEMBERS AND NONMEMBERS OF THE MATAHUASI COOPERATIVE, 1970

Place of Residence	Cooperative Members Number (Percentage)	Percentage of Fertilizer	Nonmembers Number (Percentage)	Percentage of Fertilizer	Totals Number (Percentage)	Percentage of Fertilizer
Matahuasi (central village)	48 (4.3)	23.2	315 (28.2)	7.9	363 (32.5)	31.1
Matahuasi (hamlets or *anexos*)	40 (3.6)	5.0	150 (13.4)	4.3	190 (17.0)	9.3
Other localities	103 (9.2)	36.2	461 (41.3)	23.4	564 (50.5)	59.6
Totals	191 (17.1)	64.4	926 (82.9)	35.6	1117 (100)	100.0

of them have much interest in agriculture per se (they own little land), but they now form a subcommittee concerned with transport (La Comité de Transportes de San Sebastián, named after the Club San Sebastián, which takes its title from the patron saint of the village). These truckers are controlling members of the Club San Sebastián and maintain a close-knit network of work and nonwork relationships with each other. The agreement was that they would transport fertilizers and other products from Lima to Matahuasi for a charge of 0.25 *centavos* per kilo (now raised to 0.28 *centavos*). This arrangement apparently worked well, and in 1970 they earned a total of about 500,000 *soles*.

The deal was originally planned and worked out by leaders of the cooperative and the Club San Sebastián, who are close friends and can often be found drinking together in local bars and gossiping in the cooperative office. The truckers have experienced certain difficulties with commercial and wholesale agencies in Huancayo and elsewhere, as a result of being members of the cooperative and carrying the cooperative symbol and the San Sebastián insignia on their trucks. Dealers do not necessarily like contracting work to truckers who are members of a cooperative, as they see the cooperatives as competitors.

Some of the bigger farmers in the vicinity make their own arrangements for the supply of fertilizers directly from firms in Lima. Indeed, on one occasion a local big farmer offered to sell the cooperative some of his own stock of fertilizer when the cooperative ran short. A member and official in the cooperative, he was seen by some as "wishing to control its activities" and by others as supporting the movement, renting them equipment at low cost and selling his milk to them.

Other Investments

The cooperative invested in a small retail shop in Huanchar. This project was initiated by a group of enthusiasts whose hamlet is poorly served by shops. A sum of six thousand *soles* was voted for this venture, but after two years it had to be closed down. Huanchar is a small settlement of about a thousand people, close to Matahuasi, where there are excellent shops. As in milk marketing, the cooperative found that it was unable to compete with private shopkeepers whose operating costs were lower and who apparently did not find it difficult to obtain goods on credit from wholesale dealers. In fact, there appears to be a general reluctance to sell on credit to cooperative organizations: as one salesman put it, "cooperatives and communities [*comunidades*] have a bad reputation and virtually no guarantees because their assets cannot easily be appropriated if they run into debt."

A major investment of the cooperative was the purchase of land on which to build the cooperative center, which consists of offices, garages, and a warehouse. The land for this center was obtained from a member of the cooperative who agreed to sell approximately 31,321 square meters at a cost of 399,647 *soles*. The amount was to be paid in one lump sum of 200,000 *soles* and the rest in three payments over the following two years. In order to raise the necessary capital for land and building, the cooperative allocated one year's net profits (valued at 80,000 *soles*) and managed to secure a government loan of 500,000 *soles*. The clearing of the land for the new buildings and the preparation of the foundations were to be organized through *faenas* (work parties). However, despite the large membership of 360 persons, few seemed willing to participate. In August 1972, a *faena* was organized for collecting stones for the foundations but only 15 people turned up.

Although it is not within the scope of this discussion to analyze in detail its financial problems, it is important to emphasize that, throughout its short history, the cooperative has incurred heavy capital investment in transport, in equipment for milk marketing and office use, and in land and materials for building; it has also faced high administrative costs for staff salaries and office materials. With very little initial working capital provided by the members and a general unwillingness on their part to make further contributions, the cooperative has had to seek large government loans. This situation, together with certain irregularities in the account books, has meant that the cooperative has faced high debt repayments; as a result, so far there have been no dividends to share among members. It is for this reason that many small farmers see little advantage in membership.

The Role of Promotion Agencies

From its inception, the government, through the Ministry of Agriculture and other departments, has been involved in supporting the cooperative. It has provided large loans for the purchase of fertilizer and equipment, offered technical assistance, and attempted to control the accounting procedures. It has also been a major influence on policy, in that the initial decision to expand the servicing function was the result of direct government intervention.

At the time the cooperative was founded, there was already in Matahuasi an extension service office (SIPA) that gave technical help to farmers in the vicinity and distributed fertilizers and seeds. This office was closed down and transferred to Concepción once the cooperative was running effectively. The cooperative took over its functions and was placed under the supervision of the German Technical Mission.

One of the paradoxes of this situation, however, is that since its arrival the German mission has been systematically attempting to bring the cooperative into closer relations with government. This is illustrated by the way in which the mission recommended that the cooperative office be moved to Concepción—to be located within the new Ministry of Agriculture substation building—and went ahead assuming that the members would concur with this plan. It was only when the office accommodation had already been arranged and the rent paid in advance that the mission discovered that the cooperative members were bitterly opposed to this scheme and refused to move. There were two main reasons for rejecting the plan. In the first place, the leaders of the cooperative, who were mainly from Matahuasi, wished, for reasons of control and prestige, to retain Matahuasi as the administrative center. Second, the cooperative members did not like the idea of being a satellite of a government department and thus losing the little autonomy they had gained.

A new dimension has recently been added to this complaint by the formation of the Central Cooperative in Huancayo. This organization was the brainchild of the German mission, which has taken the view that the major solution to financial and organizational problems is the development of more centralized control over various essential services. The Central Cooperative is formed of representatives from the three marketing cooperatives of the region—the Matahuasi cooperative, the Chupaca cooperative on the western side of the Mantaro River, and the Yanamarca cooperative located to the north of the valley—together with officials from the German mission and the Ministry of Agriculture. Its main functions are to provide specialized services, such as accounting and information on market prices for crops and fertilizers; to assist with the commercialization and industrialization of the products handled by the affiliated cooperatives; to supply them with fertilizers, equipment, machinery, and credit essential for production; to sell various consumer necessities; and to offer technical assistance.

The Central Cooperative was set up in 1970 but has not yet achieved much, due to various internal organizational difficulties. According to some observers, these difficulties have resulted from the actions of a group of APRA politicians from Chupaca and Huancayo who have used the institution as a platform from which to advance their political, commercial, and professional interests. The response of the Matahuasi cooperative to this situation has been on two levels. In 1973 they maneuvered one of their own members into the executive committee of the Central Cooperative in an attempt to protect their own interests. This man, a large-scale farmer based in Matahuasi, is a member of APRA and has an extensive network of political allies in the region.

The second tactic has been to send delegations to the Ministry of Agriculture and to SINAMOS (Sistema Nacional de Apoyo a la Movilización Social) in Lima to solicit direct aid from central government when needed.

The Social Composition of the Cooperative

Since its founding, the cooperative has trebled its membership and expanded its geographical scope to cover the whole length of the Mantaro Valley from Jauja to Huancayo and up into the hills as far as Comas. Table 6 gives the geographical location of members in 1970. This increase in membership has led to a broadening of the social base to include many different categories of farmers specializing in the cultivation of different crops and operating in different ecological niches and at various scales of enterprise. From being a cooperative set up to handle the marketing of milk, it has become an organization primarily concerned with the sale of fertilizers throughout the region.

The original founders were a group of farmers practicing dairy and arable farming in the Matahuasi-Huanchar area; it is this group that has tended to monopolize the positions of responsibility during the first five years of its existence. As table 7 shows, many of them have held more than one post in the cooperative, and several have had experience in local government as well. All of them control above the average landholding for the district, which is two hectares: most possess over five hectares and some have very large extensions. The rest of those who have occupied leadership positions also come from Mata-

TABLE 6

GEOGRAPHICAL LOCATION OF COOPERATIVE
MEMBERS, 1971

	Number	Percent
Matahuasi (central village)	50	15.3
Matahuasi (hamlets or *anexos*)	14	4.3
Huanchar	21	6.4
Apata	32	9.8
San Lorenzo	15	4.6
El Mantaro	9	2.8
Concepción and nearby villages	49	15.0
Comas	38	11.7
Jauja and nearby villages	70	21.5
Huancayo and nearby villages	28	8.6
Total	326	100.0

TABLE 7
COOPERATIVE LEADERS, 1967–1972

Place of residence	Main occupation	Offices held by year					Amount of land owned (in hectares)	Milk production
		1968	1969	1970	1971	1972		
Huanchar	Farmer	√	√	√	—	√	7	√
Matahuasi	Farmer	—	√	√	—	—	12	—
San Lorenzo	Farmer	√	√	√	—	—	10	√
Matahuasi	Farmer/shopkeeper	—	√	—	—	—	22	√
Matahuasi	Farmer	√	√	√	—	—	44	√
Concepción	Farmer	√	√	√	√	—	6	√
San Lorenzo	Farmer	√	√	—	—	—	?	—
Santa Rosa	Farmer	√	√	√	√	—	3	—
Huanchar	Farmer	—	√	√	√	—	9	√
Matahuasi	Farmer	—	√	—	√	√	3	√
Apata	Farmer	√	√	√	—	—	12	√
Matahuasi	Farmer/miller	—	√	√	√	—	5	√
Matahuasi	Farmer	—	—	√	√	√	5	√
Matahuasi	Farmer/intermediary	—	—	√	—	—	7	—
Matahuasi	Farmer	—	—	√	—	—	?	—
Matahuasi	Farmer	—	—	√	—	—	?	—
San Lorenzo	Farmer	—	—	√	—	—	?	—
?	Farmer	—	—	√	—	—	?	—
Matahuasi	Farmer	—	—	—	√	√	4	—
Matahuasi	Farmer	—	—	—	√	—	3.5	√
Concepción	Farmer	—	—	—	√	—	?	—
Concepción	Farmer	—	—	—	√	—	?	—
Matahuasi	Farmer	—	—	—	—	√	13.25	√
Matahuasi	Farmer	—	—	—	—	√	15	—
Matahuasi	Farmer/shopkeeper	—	—	—	—	√	4	—

huasi or from the nearby villages of Concepción, San Lorenzo, Apata, and Santa Rosa. One or two of them have dairy cattle, but the majority practice only arable farming.

Despite the pressure from other groups that have joined the cooperative more recently and now represent a sizeable part of the membership, there has not yet been any successful bid for leadership by them. For example, Jauja, which makes up 21.5 percent of the total membership and now outnumbers Matahuasi, has no committee member; Comas and Huancayo are also unrepresented. As we explained earlier, the Comas group joined primarily to obtain fertilizer for its potato crop and has since acquired its own substore, as have Jauja, Huancayo, and Concepción. In 1971, Comas was exploring the possibility of setting up its own independent servicing cooperative as an alternative to control from Matahuasi, which it strongly opposed.

An analysis of the social characteristics of cooperative members residing in the Matahuasi district shows that, in comparison with the general population and with members of the *comunidad* (i.e., *comuneros*),[17] they constitute an economically privileged group. Average arable landholding for householders in the district is 2 hectares, for *comuneros* only 0.5 hectares, but for members of the cooperative 3.6. Moreover, if to private arable land we add land that is rented or sharecropped and private pasture land, the average amount available to cooperative members increases to 5 hectares as against 0.8 for *comuneros*. Table 8 gives details on land held by cooperative members and *comuneros*, who represent, respectively, the "top" and the "bottom" of the agricultural hierarchy. As the table shows, several cooperative members (some 11 percent) own holdings of 9 or more hectares. The majority of them have occupied leadership positions.

Cooperative members in Matahuasi, then, form a category of farmers producing some surplus of food crops (in some cases a very substantial surplus) for marketing; sixteen (or 30 percent) of them produce a regular supply of milk for sale. The majority operate their farms using some mechanization (17 percent own their own tractors and others hire them) and employ seasonal wage labor (81 percent hire *peones* on a temporary basis). Moreover, while most depend upon farming for their livelihood, others (mainly the smaller operators) practice additional occupations as craftsmen or small shopkeepers. The cooperative does not contain within it the larger commercial entrepreneurs, but it has close contacts with them through the personal networks of its leaders and through the group of truckers that forms the transport committee.

The cooperative is also notable for the relatively high education of its members. It possesses something like three times as many persons with secondary education as does the general population, and its illiteracy rate is very low. Eight percent of members in fact practice professional occupations in addition to running their farms. The most striking example is that of a medical doctor who works in the hospital in Huancayo but lives and farms on a large scale in Matahuasi.

One of the consequences of the high economic and educational status of cooperative members in Matahuasi is that the cooperative is not faced with a scarcity of persons with organizational and technical skills, as is the *comunidad*. Forty percent of cooperative members have held office, some of them several times, in voluntary associations concerned with sports and recreational activities, the running of local fiestas, or

TABLE 8

A COMPARISON OF PRIVATE LANDHOLDING FOR A
SAMPLE OF COOPERATIVE MEMBERS AND *COMUNEROS*

Land Extension in Hectares

	0	less than 1	1–2	2–3	3–4	4–5	5–6	6–7	9	10	12	13	20	Total
Cooperative members	4 (8)	4 (8)	14 (26)	6 (11)	5 (9)	7 (13)	4 (8)	3 (6)	2 (3)	1 (2)	1 (2)	1 (2)	1 (2)	53 (100)
Comuneros	24 (38)	17 (27)	20 (32)	2 (3)	0	0	0	0	0	0	0	0	0	63 (100)

Percentages in parentheses.

the administration of local institutions like schools. Also, several cooperative members have previously occupied positions of responsibility in the *comunidad* (9 percent) and in municipal government (30 percent). Hence members bring to their organization, and to the other positions they hold, the benefits of their experience and contacts in various associational and professional fields of activity.

Increasing Heterogeneity and Conflicts of Interest

Yet, despite the comparative advantage the cooperative has over other local associations, it continues to be beset by numerous organizational and financial problems. The cooperative has never been able to persuade its members to fulfill the membership regulation of contributing two thousand *soles* a head, for, having paid the initial fee of one hundred *soles*, many individuals made no further contributions. In 1973, when the membership had risen to 470 individuals, only 70 (or 14.9 percent) were fully paid up. A substantial number of persons were merely interested in using the cooperative as a source of cheap fertilizer and had taken out membership for this facility and in the hope that perhaps one day they might receive some dividends as well.

This orientation toward the cooperative is most evident in the responses to the question we asked of members in Matahuasi, "Why did you join the cooperative?" Only 10 percent made reference to cooperative ideals; most emphasized the services it offered (39 percent) and the rest stressed general economic benefits (20 percent), milk marketing (12 percent), the influence of agricultural officers (10 percent), and other, non-specific reasons (9 percent). This attitude appears to have been characteristic also of the truckers who joined to organize the transport committee: none of them viewed their membership as entailing any commitment to the organizaion itself, beyond that of fulfilling their contract. With the exception of the manager, a similar attitude was expressed by the various employees. Indeed, as the case of the first driver illustrates, a few of them probably used their positions to embezzle cooperative funds.

In the eyes of the leaders, the "progress" of the cooperative was measured mainly by the expansion of the membership. It was for this reason that considerable effort was given to publicizing the work of the cooperative throughout the zone. Several subcommittees to deal with cooperative education were set up, and seminars and discussion groups were organized to draw in new members. The cooperative became so enthusiastic about its educational role that, in 1971, it proposed the establishment of a scholarship scheme for members to train in cooperative matters and a library and radio program through which its work could be advertised. The recruitment of new members tended to have priority over the consolidation of the existing membership, and it led to increasing heterogeneity and to diverging interests that affected the running of the organization.

The expansion of membership has produced a more geographically dispersed pattern. This makes it difficult for members living in outlying districts to attend the general assemblies and participate in decision making in Matahuasi; as a result, the Matahuasino leaders continue to control positions of leadership and policy decisions. Nevertheless, so long as the group from the highland village of Comas remains in the Matahuasi cooperative, there will be a clash of basic interests between them and the Matahuasinos over the relative importance of various branches of the cooperative enterprise.[19] For the controlling group in Matahuasi, the expansion and improvement of dairy farming continues as a priority, since they stand to gain from the development of the pasteurization unit at Concepción. But for the Comas and other groups this is a matter of no economic significance.

Conflicts of interest, however, are not confined to Matahuasi vis-à-vis other localities: social differentiation among the members of the cooperative in Matahuasi also generates differences in objectives. For the larger farmers wishing to expand and develop their farms, the cooperative offers a valuable way of acquiring government credit and technical aid. It is this category of farmer who tends to control the organization and who emphasizes the wider benefits of cooperative effort. For example, in 1969, the president of the cooperative declared:

> We farmers alone will never get progress. Alone we will never get aid from government and other institutions. Yet with the cooperative the small farmer is no longer alone: we are hundreds of thousands with the means to make government listen and give us technical assistance and financial help. The cooperative is also able to solve our difficulties by buying fertilizers and seeds of good quality and at low prices. When we sell our produce through the cooperative we can escape from the intermediaries who always try to take advantage by buying goods at a lower price than is paid in the market.

In another context, he pointed out that the cooperative movement is "one of the solutions to our standard of living, but we must leave behind the traditional system, which each time continues to prejudice our economy and social and cultural life."

Such statements highlight the contradiction between publicly expressed cooperative ideology and the achievements of the cooperative.

While the president and others talk in general about neutralizing the power of the intermediaries, who operate not only in the field of milk marketing but also in the more important sectors concerned with the export of grains, potatoes, and timber, no concerted efforts have yet been made other than the rather ineffectual control of milk distribution. Indeed, it is highly unlikely that the cooperative would attempt to take over the marketing of agricultural products, since several of its more prominent members, or their close kinsmen, are themselves agricultural middlemen. Also, their alliance with the Matahuasi truckers is tacitly based on an agreement that the cooperative will not interfere with the truckers' freedom to transport for whomever they please.

The claim that the cooperative provides credit and technical facilities for small farmers tends not to be true in practice. The larger farmers are better placed to receive loans, having assets to offer as security. Also, it has been the policy of the German mission to encourage the development of a "progressive" or "yeoman" farmer class specializing in dairy farming.[20] This necessitates the farmer's having at least five to eight hectares of good land, and thus again gives support to the medium- and large-scale farmer. In this regard, it is particularly interesting that, at meetings called to discuss cooperative policy, the smaller farmers have shown more interest in discussing the need for consolidating land holdings, and the difficulties involved in attempting this, than they have in the problems of increasing milk production. The only real benefit the cooperative provides to the smaller farmer is the offer of cheaper fertilizer and the convenience of being able to buy it without traveling to Huancayo.

The low level of participation and commitment by the bulk of the membership was explained by one leader in terms of "members' not yet being adjusted to a cooperative style of living. They place too great an emphasis on being independent. Cooperatives run along socialist lines," he claimed, "are an impossibility in the Mantaro Valley with its *minifundia* system and major differences in wealth."

While there is some validity to this view, a more significant factor affecting participation is the differential rewards to be gained by various sectors of the membership. The leaders, who are economically better placed to start with, participate in the management of the enterprise "on behalf" of the membership, while at the same time protecting and developing their own private concerns. They see no necessary incompatibility between their personal and cooperative interests. Indeed, the cooperative increases the range of entrepreneurial possibilities and resources open to them, and it also provides them with some ideological justification for assuming positions of control, since they possess the necessary skills and experience. Hence the cooperative ideology serves to create and reinforce the image that the leaders are concerned with promoting the public good because they occupy positions of responsibility in a people's organization. This enables them to enjoy some degree of social support from the middle peasantry. A further consequence, however, is that less favored groups regard the cooperative as an extension of the private entrepreneurial or political interests of these leaders, as the main benefits accruing from the cooperative are seen to flow into their hands. These less favored categories adopt an opportunistic attitude toward the institution and derive whatever they can in the way of benefits too. But, lacking essential economic and organizational resources, few of them are in a position to challenge or join the leadership group. It is for this reason that they manifest a low level of participation in meetings and express little commitment to the organization as a whole.

Relations between the Cooperative and the *Comunidad*

A more hostile attitude toward the cooperative exists among the peasants of the poorest sector of the population, none of whom are members. This sector is made up of landless peasants and small holders whose economic resources are so minimal that they cannot make use of the technical and other services provided by the cooperative. Many of these individuals are involved in working either temporarily or permanently for medium- and large-scale farmers of the district, who are members of the cooperative and who often hold positions of leadership. Because of this work relationship, the poorest peasants tend to see the cooperative as being intimately related to the economic interests of their employers and thus basically antagonistic to their own. Only recently, however, has this opposition begun to express itself openly and collectively. The catalyst for this expression has been the implementation of the new Statute for Peasant Communities, which, in Matahuasi, has led to a reorganization of the membership of the *comunidad*.

As Winder has shown earlier in this volume, the main aim of the new legislation is to revitalize community institutions based on control of communal resources and to allow only the poorer peasants access to these resources. It is envisaged that the new organization, having successfully limited membership to persons possessing small plots or none at all, will develop collective forms of agricultural production leading to the establishment of fully fledged production cooperatives, which may later be extended to embrace marketing and servicing functions as well.

The new statute, then, constitutes a potential threat to the Mata-huasi cooperative, as the community could usurp its functions and develop equally close links with government. This possibility arises because government has, at least on paper, pledged itself to provide communities with the kinds of credit and technical services previously offered only to cooperative members and large farmers. Futhermore, the new agrarian law encourages communities to initiate litigation to recover land originally alienated from the community by private individuals. This latter aspect is a particularly delicate issue in Matahuasi, since land disputes have been a major and continuing concern since the sale of *cofradia* land in the 1930s and early 1940s. In fact, several of the purchasers of this land (which had been attached to various Catholic saints for the celebration of religious fiestas and worked by the people of the village) are now leaders in the cooperative and clearly identified as some of the biggest landowners in the district.

Given this background, it is perhaps not surprising that the implementation of the new statute has led to a certain polarization of the cooperative and the *comunidad* in Matahuasi. The new community organization affords a secure political platform from which the poorer peasants can rally support against the better-off farmers of the district. From their point of view, the cooperative is an association of capitalist farmers who have robbed the community of land and extracted labor from the poorer strata of the population. This process, then, has produced increased hostility between these two government-sponsored types of cooperative within the village and has led to the recent alliance of the cooperative with the district council, which is seen as offering a possible counter to any moves that the *comunidad* might make to recover land.

This situation indicates that, over the next few years, the Matahuasi cooperative could face difficult political problems at village level, now that *comuneros* are better able to organize themselves. On the other hand, the present government continues to give priority to the more economically advanced sectors of the rural population and to encourage the development of small-holder and capitalist farming. Within this program the marketing and servicing cooperative will continue to play an important part in stimulating commercialized forms of production and in providing infrastructural support at relatively low cost to government itself. It seems likely therefore that the Matahuasi cooperative will remain a permanent feature and that the *comunidad* will face a long and probably unsuccessful struggle, unless government is prepared to back it with enormous support in production, marketing, finance, and technical expertise.

Conclusion

The main aim of this chapter has been to examine the various activities of the Matahuasi cooperative and to characterize the nature of the membership. In doing so, however, we have confronted a range of problems concerned with the internal and external relations of the institution. This has required us to consider, albeit briefly, the patterns of internal differentiation based on locality and on differences in economic status and types of production. We have also examined the ways in which different social categories utilize the services of the cooperative and accord it a different significance in the pursuit of economic goals. The external relations of the cooperative introduce two other important dimensions: its articulation with government and the German Technical Mission, and its relationship to other local-level organizations. These relationships suggest that an analysis of the Matahuasi cooperative cannot be adequately achieved without some appreciation of the wider politicoeconomic structure of the region within which it is located.

The cooperative can be viewed as an arena within which contradictory tendencies and structural oppositions become apparent. It shows the coexistence of peasant and capitalist forms of production and the effect of this coexistence on households of differing size and economic level; it also reflects the struggle between rich and middle farmers. It highlights the opposition of the cooperative as an institution to other locally controlled institutions and interest groups that compete for control over aspects of the local economy and for any new resources that may become available. It depicts the struggles between different localities, such as those between villages within the valley region and those between valley and highland. And, finally, it reflects the tension between provincial groups wishing to retain their autonomy and control over development in the face of the centralizing power of the state and its promotion agencies.

Other associations concerned with local-level development exhibit similar tendencies. What is distinctive about this type of organization, however, is that such social-structural oppositions manifest themselves at the ideological level too. The ideology of cooperativism espouses egalitarianism and participatory democracy, while at the same time it adheres to the notion of economic progress tied to individual achievement.

People join the cooperative for different reasons and with different resources, and the rewards, too, are greater for some than for others. The cooperative does little to equalize these differences, and for some individuals it is a further opportunity for them to expand their entrepreneurial interests and consolidate positions of power. Even though the cooperative may fail in its basic economic objectives (in this case, milk marketing), it may still offer the possibility of enrichment through the assumption of bureaucratic office and the development of strategic outside contacts. The cooperative, then, represents an unequal coalition of individual households and interests that enables members to pursue their own household strategies while incurring few obligations. But their success in manipulating and utilizing the institution is basically determined by their command over socioeconomic resources and relationships that originate from outside the cooperative itself.

NOTES

1. Material for this paper was collected by Norman Long during field work in 1971. The authors would like to acknowledge the assistance of Teófilo Altamirano and Juan Solano, who acted as research assistants throughout the project, and the help of a group of students from the University of Huancayo who conducted interviews in Matahuasi.

2. Two important exceptions appear to be the Hutterite collective settlements of Canada and the kibbutzim of Israel (see John W. Bennett, *Hutterian Brethren*, and Melford E. Spiro, *Kibbutz: Venture in Utopia*). The relative success of these experiments seems related to the fact that they were initiated by movements of a strong socioideological nature. For Third World examples, see the *ujamaa* policy of Tanzania (Norman Long, "Cooperative Enterprise and Rural Development in Tanzania," in *Rural Co-operatives and Planned Change in Africa*, edited by Raymond Apthorpe, pp. 333–361; and David Feldman, "The Economics of Ideology: Some Problems of Achieving Rural Socialism in Tanzania," in *Politics and Change in Developing Countries*, edited by Colin Leys); and the collective *ejido* system of Mexico (Susana Glantz, *El ejido colectivo de Nueva Italia*; Raymond Wilkie, *San Miguel: A Mexican Collective Ejido*).

3. See John S. Saul, "Marketing Cooperatives in a Developing Country: The Tanzanian Case," in *Two Blades of Grass: Rural Cooperatives in Agricultural Modernization*, edited by Peter Worsley, pp. 347–370; and David Metcalf, *The Economics of Agriculture*, pp. 105–107.

4. Analyses of informal patterns of agrarian cooperation are found in John W. Bennett, "Reciprocal Economic Exchange among North American Agricultural Operators," *Southwestern Journal of Anthropology* 24 (1968): 276–309; and in Charles J. Erasmus, "Culture, Structure and Process: The Occurrence and Disappearance of Reciprocal Farm Labor," *Southwestern Journal of Anthropology* 12, no. 4 (1956): 444–469.

5. R. Shickele, *Agrarian Revolution and Economic Progress*, pp. 323–327; and Metcalf, *Economics of Agriculture*, pp. 105–107.

6. See Ronald F. Dore, "Modern Cooperatives in Traditional Communities," pp. 43–60; and Peter Worsley, "Introduction," in *Two Blades of Grass: Rural Cooperatives in Agricultural Modernization*, edited by Peter Worsley.

7. For example, Denmark (F. Skrubeltrang, *Agricultural Development and Rural Reform in Denmark*) and Japan (T. Ogura, ed., *Agricultural Develop-*

ment in Modern Japan). Interesting case studies dealing with the growth of marketing cooperatives in East Africa are: G. A. Maguire, *Towards "Uhuru" in Tanzania,* which discusses the Sukuma cotton cooperatives; Goran Hyden and Edward Karanja, "Cooperatives and Rural Development in Kenya," in Apthorpe, *Rural Cooperatives,* pp. 157–220; and Saul, "Marketing Cooperatives."

8. George Foster, *Tzintzuntzan*. For a summary of the main criticisms see Sutti Ortiz, "Reflections on the Concept of 'Peasant Culture' and Peasant 'Cognitive Systems'," in *Peasants and Peasant Societies,* edited by Teodor Shanin, pp. 322–336.

9. Rodolfo Stavenhagen, "Classes, Colonialism and Acculturation," *Studies in Comparative International Development* 1, no. 6 (1965): 53–77; Julio Cotler, "The Mechanics of Internal Domination and Social Change in Peru," *Studies in Comparative International Development* 3, no. 12 (1967–1968): 229–246; and Eric R. Wolf, "Aspects of Group Relations in a Complex Society: Mexico," *American Anthropologist* 58, no. 6 (1956): 1065–1078.

10. See Thomas F. Carroll, "Peasant Cooperation in Latin America," in Worsley, *Two Blades of Grass,* pp. 199–252; and Orlando Fals Borda, ed., *Estudios de la realidad campesina: cooperación y cambio,* vol. 2.

11. Carroll, "Peasant Cooperation," pp. 240–244; Orlando Fals Borda, ed., *Cooperatives and Rural Development in Latin America: An Analytic Report,* vol. 3, pp. 87–94.

12. For further background information on the history and setting of Matahuasi, see Winder, in this volume, and also the same author's M.Ed. thesis, "The Effect of the 1970 Reform on the Peasant Communities and on the Community Development Process in an Area of Peru," University of Manchester, 1974, chapters 3–5.

13. These make up what Mintz calls "the hidden proletariat" in peasant society (Sidney W. Mintz, "The Rural Proletariat and the Problem of Rural Proletarian Consciousness," *The Journal of Peasant Studies* 1, no. 3 [April 1974]: 304–306).

14. E. Flores, *La comunidad de Maravilca,* p. 122.

15. One agricultural officer estimated that farmers would need a minimum of four hectares of grazing land with good water points to keep eight cows, and this does not take into account the household's food crop requirements.

16. The Matahuasi tie-up with traders and businessmen in La Oroya and other towns and cities is discussed in Norman Long, "Multiple Enterprise in the Central Highlands of Peru," in *Social Relations of Confidence in Enterprise,* edited by Arnold Strickon and Sidney M. Greenfield. See also Norman Long, "The Role of Regional Associations in Peru," in *The Process of Urbanization,* edited by M. Drake et al., pp. 173–191.

17. A discussion of the meaning and functions of the *comunidad* (community) in the Mantaro area is contained in Winder in this volume.

18. Figures on educational levels for members of the cooperative as compared to *comuneros* are given in Norman Long and David Winder, "From Peasant Community to Production Cooperative: An Analysis of Recent Government Policy in Peru," *Journal of Development Studies* 12, no. 1 (October 1975): 75–94. This paper also provides data on the age/sex structure.

19. The interrelations of valley and highland (*puna*) villages at different historical periods are dealt with in Samaniego's paper in this volume.

20. In 1971, the German mission set up a series of experiments in supervised farm planning. This program focused on a small number of carefully selected dairy farmers, who were given close technical advice and offered special credit facilities so that they might acquire purebred livestock and build modern stables.

11. Peasant Cooperation and Underdevelopment in Central Peru

NORMAN LONG AND BRYAN R. ROBERTS

This concluding chapter considers the theoretical implications of the foregoing studies and examines the relevance of the Mantaro case for discussions on the role of peasantries in national development. In particular, we explore three interconnected themes: the nature and significance of household and interhousehold cooperation, both economic and political; the importance of internal differentiation in a peasant-based economy; and the role of the state. We focus on how the different rural classes use customary and new forms of cooperative institutions to defend or advance their interests, under changing national and regional economic conditions. The discussion will, we hope, highlight some of the mechanisms by which, in the Mantaro region, a mainly peasant economy becomes "depeasantized" through commercialization and economic diversification, without the disappearance of household enterprise and without the development of a substantial permanent wage-labor force.[1] Though we base our argument on material presented in previous chapters, we also introduce additional data, especially on forms of reciprocity and distribution at the village level.

The Analysis of Cooperation and Collective Action among Peasants

In this first section, we review literature dealing with the question of peasant participation in national economic and political development. While in the past many studies of the peasantry concentrated on their cultural and economic conservatism and on the difficulties this entailed for modernization, the recent upsurge in specifically peasant studies is based on the assumption that peasants can and do play an

297

active part in national development.[2] The role of the peasants may
vary from a willing collaboration with government-sponsored programs
of agricultural reform to a hostility expressed through a reinforcement
of "traditional" practices; however, in neither case are peasants re-
sponding passively to external initiatives.

Anthropologists and other social scientists have argued that peasant
society is a "part-society" whose viability depends on peasants' finding
ways of "making do" with the scarce resources allocated to them by
the more powerful, culturally dominant groups.[3] In this type of situation the characteristics of peasant social organization can be understood
only in terms of the nature and strength of its economic and political
links with the wider society.

An apparent exception to this is Wolf's concept of the "closed corporate peasant community," which describes a relatively undifferentiated peasant economy.[4] He argues that such a community maintains
its identity by resisting external influences and by discouraging individual accumulation of wealth, through commitment to various communal institutions and practices involving redistribution. However, it
seems very unlikely that this model, in its purest form, applies to any
Peruvian or even Latin American situation. Moreover, as Keatinge
points out, communities may have some of the features of the closed
corporate community, such as thriving communal institutions, but
communal identity serves as a means of securing concessions from government or of furthering members' economic interests against encroaching outsiders.[5] Thus, the vitality of community-based forms of cooperation depends not on isolation but on a community's external economic
and political relationships.

Internal patterns of cooperation and community-based enterprise are,
at times, inhibited by the household-based nature of peasant organization. In a situation in which resources are perceived to be limited and
expansion prevented by a hostile external environment, social relationships at the village level tend to be individualized and competitive.[6]

This "limited good" perspective stresses the essential atomism of
peasant social structure.[7] In this situation, peasants will compete among
themselves for the different types of resources and prizes available;
outside the family they will set up relatively short-term coalitions with
other individuals and households. This analysis implies that peasants
operate within a social matrix composed of a fluctuating set of dyadic
relationships. Hence, collective action, even among fellow villagers or
kinsmen, is inherently unstable and will reflect a coalition of interests
and goals. This type of social organization, it is argued, is embedded
in a cultural framework that includes normative assumptions stressing

the fundamentally competitive and hazardous nature of life. These sociocultural patterns are said to account for the persistence of certain traits like fatalism, suspiciousness, envy, and conservatism among peasants, even when they are confronted by such a major environmental change as that of the movement to the city for work.[8]

The above characterization of peasant society has had a persisting impact on the way in which peasant participation in national development has been viewed by anthropologists, community development workers, and economic development experts. The difficulties of getting peasants to work together to develop local resources have been attributed to the socially fragmented nature of peasant organization and to the essentially parochial nature of values and attitudes. The basic problem is identified as one in which the characteristics of local organization and its associated cultural forms inhibit effective participation in modern society, even when external conditions are relatively favorable.

A somewhat different approach emphasizes class or ethnic patterns of exploitation as accounting for the so-called backwardness and resistance to change shown by peasant groups. The dominance of a hacienda over its workers and neighboring villages and the exploitation of Indian villagers by mestizo traders are factors that have been cited as producing and perpetuating patterns of fragmentation and cultural conservatism.[9] Within these systems of exploitation, villagers compete for access to sources of power and influence; furthermore, access to information has been shown to be tightly controlled by dominant individuals and groups who act as brokers to the wider politicoadministrative system.[10] Though this perspective offers a different interpretation of the sources of peasant backwardness from that of the Foster model of the "limited good," its emphasis on the powerlessness and atomism of peasant groups is similar.

In the field of applied anthropology, this emphasis has manifested itself in two main ways. First, there has been a stress on improving the access to information and the level of skills present in the local community. In the Peruvian case this is illustrated by the stress on literacy campaigns at the local level and by attempts to institutionalize direct channels of access to government, bypassing such traditional gatekeepers as local merchants and hacienda owners.[11] Second, anthropologists and other development workers have focused on the reform of local structures of power and authority, such as the Vicos experiment described in the Introduction.

The limitation of the above approaches is their tendency to concentrate on the community or hacienda as the basic unit of peasant life. By so doing, they neglect the effects on local processes of the national, politicoeconomic system. This tendency has also led, in the applied literature, to an emphasis on the need to direct change from the outside, since peasant communities or hacienda workers are seen as not possessing the capacity to organize themselves to make effective use of external opportunities. Even those writers who analyze the macrostructure of inequality in Peru have at times, in our view, placed excessive emphasis on the fragmentation of underprivileged local groups and on their reliance on outsiders to organize resistance.[12] Hence, there are numerous references in this literature to the key roles played by townsmen, village migrants, and students in stimulating collective organization at the local level.

The first of our objections, then, is one that is most clearly expressed in the analysis of A. G. Frank of the implications of Latin America's economic dependency on Europe and the United States.[13] Frank emphasized the necessary interconnection of the processes of development and underdevelopment, arguing that the dynamic of growth of the advanced industrial countries has depended on the exploitation of colonial and neocolonial peripheries.[14] Third World countries were used as sources of cheap, primary materials and, for certain basic industrial processes, as sources of cheap labor.

In terms of the internal organization of underdeveloped countries, a major consequence is the chain of exploitation that links the metropolitan centers to their provincial satellites. These exploitative relationships can be visualized, for example, as manifest in the way in which large city traders are linked to traders in smaller towns or to large landowners. The basic point is that even the most remote village and poorest agricultural laborer have been fully integrated into a hierarchical system whereby, at successive points, the metropolitan centers siphoned off economic surplus. As Frank points out, peasant communities since the earliest colonial times have provided labor for mines and workshops and have participated in the urban market through purchase of manufactured goods and the sale or exchange of agricultural products. Much of this participation was enforced by colonial laws concerning labor service or the compulsory purchase of goods.

The remoteness of many of these peasant communities and their "traditional" characteristics, rather than isolating them from the dominant economy, can, in fact, be viewed as entailing their greater exploitation. Urban merchants and landowners could use the subordinate status of villagers and their relative lack of information concerning the workings of the wider market system to extract greater economic and political gains for themselves. From this perspective, the fragmentation of peasant society and even the partial survival of forms of local cooperation result from the integration of local groups into the wider market and political system. Hence, far from representing basic and unchanging forms of organization, peasant communities are constantly adapting to the demands and vicissitudes of the dominant polity and economy.

In other analyses of Latin America's external dependency, more detailed attention has been given to the forms of articulation of the peasantry with other social groups. In particular, dependency has been analyzed as an internal structure of class relationships that inhibits the independent organization of each class, reinforcing its dependence on the metropolitan centers.[15] Such an approach has focused attention on the differentiation of peasants; it emphasizes the internal mechanisms of exploitation that prevent peasants and other social groups from recognizing and pursuing common political and economic objectives. This view is consistent with the notion that class formations among peasants are poorly developed; this notion derives, in part, from the prevalence of networks of particularistic relationships, based on kinship or patron-client ties, that crosscut socioeconomic categories. Consequently, peasant cooperation and collective action are impeded by the ill-defined nature of class interests and the shifting patterns of class alliance. Political mobilization among peasants over specific grievances rapidly disintegrates under the pressure of individual and competing interests. The opposition of peasants is bought off by governments through the granting of short-term concessions. Likewise, the diversity of peasant situations militates against coordinated action at a national or even regional level. As one of the best documented of recent peasant mobilizations in Peru shows, the effectiveness of mobilization depends on the prior existence of some degree of organization and awareness among peasant groups.[16]

For these reasons, commentators have stressed the importance of nonpeasant groups in providing a consistent direction and ideology for revolutionary struggle, even within predominantly peasant nations. The industrial proletariat is generally regarded as the leading force in revolution, even when numerically weak, because the homogeneity of its class position develops class consciousness and the capacity to organize itself and others.[17] Similarly, intellectuals (e.g., students and teachers) may assist in disseminating coherent programs of political action. For these reasons, the central highlands of Peru may appear at first sight to be a potentially revolutionary situation, given the close proximity of factory, mine, and village populations suffering from acute land shortage; also, the rapid spread of education at village level has meant the presence of intellectuals aware of radical political philosophies.[18]

This analysis does not apply, however, because the industrial workers of the central highlands are not a homogeneous proletariat.[19] As we have seen in earlier chapters, the miners retained a lively interest in village land, often leaving their families to subsist there and returning frequently during the year. Likewise, as Roberts shows, the textile workers of Huancayo represented an unstable labor force that also retained interests in land and commerce. The retention of these interests meant that both miners and textile workers had opportunities for investment and entrepreneurship outside the industrial situation. Indeed, many of the leaders of the mine unions and the textile unions were rich peasants in their villages, with interests opposed to those of poorer groups. Such a diversity of interests did not prevent miners and textile workers from organizing into effective unions and engaging in ferocious opposition to the owners of their enterprises, but it did diminish the coherence and persistence of class opposition.[20]

It is not within our scope to provide an exhaustive review of the literature of political action among peasants, yet we want to indicate the complexities of such actions in a situation in which there is a blurring of class boundaries. In the central sierra, there are neither "pure" peasants nor a "pure" industrial proletariat.

One way of understanding the changing pattern of alliances and conflicts within the peasantry and between peasants and other social groups is to focus on the articulation of peasant production with that of other economic sectors. Such a focus offers a means of explaining how apparently incompatible class alliances are formed.

An example of this type of analysis is that of Laclau, who argues that underdevelopment is produced because modern capitalism has reinforced precapitalist forms of economic and social organization.[21] Laclau focuses on the hacienda system, rather than the peasantry; nevertheless, his analysis has implications for our discussion. Certain types of haciendas produce commodities at low cost only in so far as they have access to tied labor, and this form of production may contribute to the expansion of production in the modern capitalist sector.[22] Thus, cheap foodstuffs are provided for urban consumption, and the profits of agricultural exports may be invested in industry. Consequently, the hacienda system may survive through the alliance of "traditional" landowners and "modern" urban economic elites. This form of analysis is related to earlier Marxist writings on the role of noncapitalist forms of production in capitalist expansion.[23] In particular, the discussion of primitive accumulation centered on the ways in which the capitalist sector exploited the peasant sector, using the isolation, "traditionalism," and so on of this sector to extract surplus. Thus Lenin, in discussing the development of capitalism in Russia, characterizes the rural community in terms similar to those we apply to the Peruvian community. He writes: "The facts point precisely to the development of capitalist agriculture among 'community members' and to the complete adaptation of the notorious 'communal ties' to the farms of big crop growers that employ labourers."[24] He goes on to characterize the peasant community in the following way: "The Russian community peasantry are not antagonists of capitalism, but, on the contrary, are its deepest and most durable foundation."[25] Taxation, inflation, the unequal pricing of urban vis-à-vis rural products, and control of markets are among the many means by which capitalism appropriated surplus necessary to its own expansion and maintained peasant "backwardness."

In contrast to the process of primitive accumulation in some parts of Europe, the articulation of the capitalist mode of production with noncapitalist forms of production has been generally weak in Peru and in many other Third World contexts.[26] By weak articulation we mean the situation in which capitalism utilizes noncapitalist forms of production for its own expansion but does not undermine the viability of these other forms for a considerable period of time.[27] As earlier chapters have shown, this entails the use of peasant labor and production by such capitalist enterprises as mines and plantations while, at the same time, political support is given to peasant economic and social institutions.

The maintenance of the "traditional" organization of peasant communities, based on small-holder farming, can be interpreted as functional for the development of dependent capitalism. Mines and plantations profited from the continued existence of a labor supply "cheapened" by its retaining a subsistence base.[28] Village land maintained the families of migrants and offered security in times of economic recession, and wage labor supplemented the household economy and permitted it to survive. From this standpoint so-called traditional values and institutions cease to constitute impediments and barriers to capitalist development; instead they are functionally useful for the form that this development takes in underdeveloped countries. As Bradby points out, there is a strong case for arguing that the continued exploitation of noncapitalist forms of production is *convenient*, if not actually *necessary*, for capitalist expansion.[29]

This approach—relating peasant production to that of other economic sectors—enables us in later sections to focus attention on the internal economic transformations in village economies consequent upon the different stages of capitalist penetration. For example, urban-industrial capitalism and agromining capitalism "require" different types of articulation with the village economy. These differences in articulation are expressed in changes in the village economy, such as a shift from subsistence agriculture to cash crops for urban consumption or from domestic craft production to transport and service occupations based on the village. Differences in articulation are also reflected in population changes, such as changes in village sex and age structure consequent on different types and rates of migration. Such an approach also enables us to account for the changing significance of the fiesta system and of customary patterns of reciprocity in the central highlands. The increasing participation of nonresidents in fiestas and greater cash investments in the celebrations reflect the attempts of entrepreneurial groups to take advantage of the new forms of articulation between the village and the national economy.[30]

However, we do not wish to overemphasize the extent to which capitalism controls and organizes local-level and mainly noncapitalist processes. There is a centralist bias in much writing on underdevelopment; local-level processes are given little independent significance in determining the course of a nation's development and are interpreted as mere responses to external stimuli. This centralist bias is evident in the non-Marxist and applied anthropology studies that treat change as an exogenous factor, neglecting such factors as the development of small-holder production and demographic processes.

A similar centralist bias is detectable in some Marxist studies on the peasant economy; these studies have sometimes exaggerated the capacity of the dominant capitalist economy to organize the rural sector. Although we accept that the dominant capitalist mode determines the viability and potential of the peasant sector, in most underdeveloped countries the limited penetration of modern advanced capitalism allows considerable scope for variation in the way in which the rural sector is structured economically. This implies significant differences between neighboring villages in their internal social and economic differentiation, in their potential for political action, and in their economic diversification.

These variations provide rich opportunities for locally based political and economic entrepreneurship, to which, on many occasions, the modern capitalist sector and the state have had to "respond." This vitality and internal dynamism makes the peasantry an important, if somewhat unpredictable, force in national development. An appreciation of this point means that peasants cannot be considered to be either economically or politically marginal.

This line of argument leads us to give serious analytic weight in the following sections to differences in the social and cultural, as well as economic, resources available to different peasant groups.

Household and Interhousehold Cooperation

We have characterized the region as one containing many of the features of a peasant economy. Until the end of the nineteenth century, only a small percentage of the total rural population was directly or indirectly dependent upon nonpeasant forms of production, such as haciendas, capitalist farms, or large-scale industry.[31] As we noted in the introduction, however, labor migration was common from at least the colonial period and linked the village economy with the vicissitudes of the national and even of the international economic system. Nevertheless, the Mantaro area remained throughout this period predominantly a zone of small-holder agriculture complemented by pastoral activities, craft industry, and small-scale trading.[32]

In the contemporary period, it is more difficult to characterize the region as a peasant economy. In many valley villages, half or more of the resident, economically active population may depend on nonagricultural occupations. The proportion of wage and salary earners in the villages is often high. Certainly, the area's economy is fully integrated into the national economy, and villagers are increasingly oriented to urban employment and to urban patterns of consumption. Yet despite these trends, capitalist relations of production are not a pervasive feature of the village economy. Also, the household and interlinked households remain basic units in the management of resources and in the control of labor.

How, then, do these trends in the local economy relate to patterns of family and community-wide cooperation? In the Mantaro area the major unit of collaboration is the family household that controls property and organizes production activity. Generally, this consists of a nuclear family or a three-generation extended family made up of a senior generation that owns the basic resources of the family, together with one or more married sons or daughters and their children. Frequently, especially in the contemporary period, the de facto resident household will vary somewhat from this ideal model. We found many cases of households managed by a senior woman whose husband was either working permanently away or had died.

Though communal property exists at village level and the majority of villages in the zone have been officially registered as *comunidades campesinas*, almost all arable land and all animals are inherited on an individual basis and managed by the household itself. The inheritance system is, in theory, one that allows for equal partition of the property among both female and male offspring; in practice, however, arrangements exist whereby it is possible for certain heirs to take over the farming unit, recompensing their other siblings through cash, animals, or a share in the harvest. These others must often find work outside the agricultural sector as craftsmen, traders, or wage laborers.

The inheritance system is further complicated by the fact that property passes through both the paternal and maternal sides of the family. Also, among certain families it is customary for children to receive some share of their inheritance before the death of their parents: this share is frequently given at marriage, when the new couple will set up house by themselves. This constitutes a form of anticipatory inheritance that encourages neolocal residence.

These household characteristics conform to those that analysts have identified as constituting peasant forms of social and economic organization.[33] As a production unit, the peasant household operates primarily to meet its own consumption needs and, in addition, produces a small surplus for market trading or exchange in kind; this surplus is required both to supplement the domestic economy and to meet tax or other obligations imposed by the political authorities.

The degree of fragmentation of landholding has increased in recent years; in some of the villages studied, the average size of a family's landholding was three hectares at the beginning of the century, but by 1972 this had dropped to approximately one hectare per household. The minimum holding of land that is sufficient for the subsistence needs of a five-member household is estimated to be in the region of three to four hectares of valley-bottom, irrigated land.

The characteristics of peasant farming mean that such farming operates according to principles of management and allocation of resources different from those of the capitalist enterprise. In the peasant enterprise, decisions as to the extent and type of crops or livestock and as to the purchase or sale of land depend on three prime considerations: the consumption needs of the household, the available family labor, and the availability of alternative supplementary income sources.[34] Labor availability and consumption needs are intimately related to the biological cycle of the growth and decline of family units; for example, new members are added to the consumption unit by birth or marriage and labor is gained or lost by similar processes.

This focus on the internal processes of the household unit does not exclude consideration of the effects of market price fluctuations. Peasants are likely to take all these factors into account when allocating available labor to meet consumption needs with the least possible drudgery. In slack periods of the agricultural season, peasants seek to utilize their labor in activities off the farm; land may be left unused once other forms of labor provide the peasant household with more advantageous conditions. What differentiates the peasant farm from the capitalist undertaking is not simply the relative absence of wage labor but also the interdependence and mutual commitments of the members of the peasant household. As Manning Nash argues, the peasant household "is a multi-purpose social organization which, unlike a firm, cannot liquidate if it makes poor calculations." [35]

These commitments impede the creation of a permanent wage-labor force for capitalist enterprises, even when relatively high wages are offered. Thus, in Peru, the mining sector had to resort to a system of debt bondage (*enganche*) in order to recruit its first workers. In subsequent years the *enganche* system was discontinued, but the bulk of the mine labor force in the Mantaro area remained temporary, averaging only from three to five years of employment. Likewise, the seasonal timing of migration to the coast for work on the sugar and cotton plantations complemented the production cycle of the peasant household and, as a consequence, was relatively insensitive to the state of the labor market as reflected in wage levels. [36]

Peasant economic behavior is an intrinsic part of social and cultural organization; the consumption needs of a household and, to a certain extent, the availability and use of labor are defined by social and cultural practice. [37] For example, in the Mantaro Valley, religious commitments have played an important role in the operation of peasant economic organization. As Samaniego puts it: "The household in the Chupaca zone of the Mantaro Valley has to produce sufficient to maintain its members and to give in exchange for the products and services with which it could not cope alone. It has to conserve some seed and livestock for future production. In addition to these essentials, it has to find sufficient to provide for the religious festival celebrated corporately." [38]

This type of economy helps us to understand the special characteristics of interhousehold and community-wide cooperation in the Mantaro region. No one household is likely to be able to satisfy its consumption needs over a long term on the basis of its own labor and land resources; ecological factors may restrict the range of products grown, and climatic uncertainties may lead to the destruction of crops or animals. Also, cultural expectations and political or social pressure may set levels of production above those that are readily achievable by the household's existing land and labor resources. These imbalances are likely to be increased the more involved the household becomes in the money economy. Under these conditions, the household must seek to mobilize external resources, but in such a way that it does not jeopardize, through irreversible commitments, its basic means of subsistence (i.e., through the sale of land or a large proportion of livestock or the permanent employment of its members). We can expect, then, that forms of interhousehold cooperation within a village will be mainly informal and flexible in content; this cooperation will be set within an enduring set of reciprocities based on such factors as kinship, religion, and locality. So long as such exchanges continue to meet the necessities of households and so long as they have access to a basic minimum of land, peasants are likely to resist market pressures toward becoming permanent wage laborers and to be wary of being incorporated into formally organized cooperative or collective enterprises.

This perspective on interhousehold cooperation enables us to comprehend why it is that in the Mantaro Valley there are both a rich variety of informally organized cooperative endeavors and, also, as the papers in this volume demonstrate, a history of difficulties with formally organized cooperative enterprise. These difficulties are relative ones, since formal cooperation has served, and continues to serve, the economic and political strategies of certain groups within the peasantry and outside it. In the Mantaro Valley, cooperation and collective action has always been double edged; at times it has advanced the interests of the peasant producer and allowed him to retain a certain independence; at others it has reinforced his dependent status and led to an increase in his exploitation.

Thus, the persistence of customary forms of peasant cooperation is best explained not because such forms represent remnants of "traditional" behavior or of primitive communism but because they are some of the basic means by which the continuity and survival of the peasant household system is ensured. As such, these forms of cooperation are also important points, articulating the peasant with the wider economy; it is through changes in the forms of interhousehold cooperation that the transformation of the local economy first occurs. It is often through the manipulation of the various institutions of peasant cooperation that entrepreneurs can pursue their interests, forming coalitions with peasant producers and acting as brokers between the local economy and external capitalist enterprises. The study of the changing forms of peasant cooperation therefore enables us to understand the direction, variation, and sources of change in the regional economy.

The ecology of the Mantaro Valley and the nature of its agrarian

structure have, historically, given rise to different forms of interhousehold and community-level cooperation. From precolonial times, a
characteristic pattern of agrarian organization was that described as
vertical control of ecological levels.[39] Variations in climate, soil, and
topography in the Andean region have meant that the subsistence
needs of the village populations could be best met by access to land
situated on different ecological floors.

The most important floors were: the "hot" lowlands, situated to the
east of the Mantaro Valley and stretching down to the Amazonian
basin, for early crops of corn and tropical products; the valley bottom
floor, suited to a range of temperate crops and especially wheat, potatoes, and vegetables; the "intermediate" zone on the slopes of the
valley mountains, with somewhat poorer soil that is mainly restricted
to the growing of tubers and some cereals; and the pastoral highlands
above the valley, mainly devoted to livestock but with the possibility
of some cultivation.

Access to land on these different floors enabled families and villages
to produce the combination of crops and livestock that ensured subsistence the year round; for example, different varieties of tubers, with
different maturation periods and conservation periods, could be grown
on different floors. The agricultural situation was further complicated
by the presence of microclimates within each floor determined by such
factors as ravines, prevailing winds, forest, and so on; Samaniego identifies five major microclimates on the valley floor that permitted farmers to plant at different times and with a variety of crops.[40]

In the Inca period, it seems that access to these ecological zones was
controlled by the *ayllu* and *saya* organization; with the Spanish conquest, there was a progressive disintegration of this politicoecological
structure as *ayllus* were relocated to form new settlements (*reducciones*)
and as Spanish landowners appropriated extensive tracts of land.[41] One
of the consequences of this reorganization was that households and
villages were confined increasingly to one ecological floor; it was exceptional for households, and even villages, to possess land that included
the range of soils and climates that ensured an easy subsistence. In the
Mantaro area, many interhousehold exchanges of services and products
could, in fact, be interpreted as attempts to gain access to the products
of different ecological floors.[42]

The basic types of exchange that prevailed between households in
the Mantaro area provided for (1) exchange of products, (2) access to
agricultural and pastoral land, (3) access to labor for farming, house
construction, and so on, and (4) access to products or to a money wage.
These types of exchange varied in their specific content according to

such factors as zone, local custom, and the status of the parties involved.[43] The existence of such exchanges enabled households to meet their consumption needs without becoming dependent on wage labor or the market.

Sharecropping (al partir) first developed in the Mantaro area when landlords were unable to obtain sufficient cheap labor to farm profitably. These landlords preferred to let out substantial tracts of their lands and in return receive part of the harvest and labor services. In the livestock haciendas there existed a similar practice by which shepherds were recruited and partly remunerated by being allowed to pasture their own sheep and retain a proportion of the offspring (the huaccha system). In the "traditional" hacienda system, it was to the economic advantage of neither landlord nor peasant worker to operate with wage labor.[44] The hacienda provided a product with a relatively low market value, and its commercial viability depended on its not paying a full subsistence wage to its workers.[45] Since the hacienda had ample land, it used this to obtain a "free" or low-cost labor force through al partir or the huaccha system. From the standpoint of the worker, access to land or animals provided a higher annual income. than could be gained in wage labor; it also allowed him to utilize household labor more effectively.

The geographical area covered by these exchanges was often considerable; in trueque (the barter system), households would often travel considerable distances to the tropical lowlands to exchange highland-produced meat and hides for corn, tubers, and fruits. Trueque is still practiced in certain of the highland villages of the Mantaro area, such as Cacchi. Such exchanges were often reinforced by kinship relationships between the exchange partners, resulting from previous intermarriages or migrations, or by compadrazgo (ritual coparenthood).

The significance of cooperation for peasant economic organization in the Mantaro area is most clearly illustrated by the systems of labor exchange existing at the village level. Traditionally, a household's first recourse in mobilizing extra labor was kin and affines. These relatives were expected to provide labor for such tasks as house construction, the opening up of new fields, or harvesting; they were also expected to give material assistance with such problems as lawsuits, illness, and religious obligations. This exchange system was underpinned by the common interests of both kin and affines in property, and siblings normally had first option when family land was sold or rented. Also, the geographical proximity and ecological complementarity of land divided by inheritance encouraged the continuing cooperation of the heirs. In this situation, affines of the same generation were often crucially important in developing stable interhousehold cooperation; unlike consanguineal relatives, they did not compete over inheritance but simply shared a common interest in their spouses' plots.[46]

This system of kinship exchange was flexible since, in practice, households could choose relatively freely among kin; their stable exchange partners tended to be those with whom they had a series of overlapping interests both economic and noneconomic. In general, interhousehold exchanges in the Mantaro area were between families of roughly equivalent socioeconomic status.[47] This practice was modified by generational differences among kin, as when a father retained control of the family land and his children provided labor services although married and separately resident. Also, at times, very poor or orphaned kin would become dependent workers for their richer relatives, a phenomenon recently described by Mintz as a "concealed proletariat."[48]

Between nonkin or distant kin, the most general form of cooperation was between status equals. In the *uyay* system "incomplete" subsistence households obtained the loan of extra members for such tasks as sowing, weeding, and harvesting in return for providing similar labor for the other households. This labor did not have to be returned immediately but could be provided at a later date, depending on the needs and labor availability of the two households. These relationships of labor exchange were sometimes continued even where there was no objective necessity on the part of either household; they provided a network of enduring relationships that gave some security to the peasant household in face of the uncertainty of future needs. Such relationships were also a basic element in village solidarity. In the contemporary period, this network of labor exchanges has been utilized for such purposes as the mobilization of political support and the organization of fiestas. The *minka* system was an exchange by which households received payment in kind or money for their labor and, in return, other households or the community obtained that labor for specific tasks. *Minka* did not usually set up enduring relationships of exchange between households; it was used either for urgent or specialized tasks, such as carpentry or a quick harvest, or when the needs of a household were themselves unusual, as in the case of those producing a surplus for market. In the central highlands of Peru, it has typically been the *minka* that has enabled the richer peasants to develop "unequal" relations of exchange with their poorer fellows, extracting the labor required to market their agricultural surplus.[49]

At the turn of the century in the Mantaro area, payment within the *minka* was generally in kind, but nowadays it is usually paid in money, together with food and the customary coca and *aguardiente*. *Minka* is not, strictly speaking, wage labor, partly because some subsistence is provided, but also because *minka*, like *uyay*, is part of a community-wide set of reciprocal obligations. Unlike *uyay*, *minka* involved obligations of the patron-client type. In some cases, the patron was the community as a whole and the *minka* was the means whereby labor was obtained for public works and other communal projects. In other cases, a richer peasant obtained labor through *minka* and this implied that his labor force could expect certain favors of him; he would, for example, patronize the village fiesta, providing free drinks for all, or be the godparent of a worker's child, providing some clothing and educational expenses.

Communities of the Mantaro area have also developed modes of cooperation at the community level. These modes of cooperation function to deal with those facets of peasant economic and social life that cannot be handled on an individual household basis. One of the most important of these has been the organization of religious observances, the maintenance of the church, and religious festivals. Since the conquest, the parishes of the area had accumulated lands through private endowments; these lands were cultivated through a *cofradia* (religious brotherhood) system by which individual peasants, as officeholders (sometimes called *mayordomos*) and members, were responsible for financing and celebrating festivals (fiestas) attached to particular saints. Each *cofradia* utilized the unpaid labor of the community.

This form of collective organization was a source of tension at the village and regional level; to many of the peasant households, the continued collective exploitation of these lands reduced the amount of resources available to them locally. There was continuous pressure to allow individual households to rent these lands and to exploit them individually.[50] The following extract from the proceedings of the Huancayo Provincial Council in the year 1875 indicates the nature of such disputes:

> The work on the *cofradia* lands, which is called the *faena* by the communal organization of the villages, is the source of the corruption of these communities, because, the work neglected, it normally becomes the basis of orgies that last until late at night . . . When these lands are put under the care of religious organizations, they daily suffer important deterioration, because, apart from the abuses of those called the *Priostes*, they do not enjoy the care that only a private and direct interest can provide to increase the wealth

of the land using fertilizer and cultivating crops . . . Put out to rent on the condition of improving the land, they can provide for both the religious ceremonies and the repair of the church.[51]

Despite these tensions, the fiesta system has remained an important focus of community organization in the Mantaro area. Though they are usually financed not by *cofradía* land but by the individual contributions of the officeholders, week-long fiestas still occur in most villages of the Mantaro area. They are attended not only by residents of the village but also by migrants and outsiders. Indeed, in the fiestas we studied, migrants resident outside the community often held office and financed the fiesta. The persistence of the fiesta system is partly explained by the fact that fiestas continue to play an important role in the reproduction of the local economy: they provide an organizational and ideological framework for the development of various kinds of economic and political relationships among households. They allow individuals to pay off their social debts by financing fiestas and by according others positions of prominence in these activities. They provide a context in which individuals create new alliances and consolidate economic and other partnerships, and they also enable individuals and social groups to cement important external social relationships.[52]

In these ways, the fiesta system, like the *minka*, allows certain social groups to consolidate, and symbolically express, their positions of economic and political dominance, while couching this expression in terms of a communitarian ideology. The evolution of fiestas in the Mantaro area reflects the changing relationship between peasants and the wider economy. Around the turn of the century, it appears that individuals were unwilling, in some communities, to take on responsibilities for the fiestas; returns from *cofradía* lands were insufficient to meet the costs of fiestas, and individuals were reluctant to invest their savings in holding office. Indeed, Samaniego claims that, in Ahuac, richer members of the village persuaded poorer villagers to take office in the fiesta as a strategy to gain control of the latter's land. The debts incurred in financing the fiesta forced poorer peasants to mortgage their land and, often, led them to seek wage labor outside the village. Castro Pozo reports similar pressures in Acolla in 1916.[53] In this same period, the increasing costs of fiestas in Matahuasi led to the demise of the system for several decades. The revival of the fiesta system in Matahuasi and other valley villages comes later and is connected with the increasing dependence of the village economy on the urban-industrial sector through migration and economic exchange.

This perspective can be applied to the other forms of community-wide cooperation, namely, the communal work party (*faena*) and the communal institution itself (the *comunidad indígena*, now called the *comunidad campesina*). Though, as Winder shows, the origins of these communal institutions may be traced to the precolonial period, their present form is directly related to the development of state authority in Peru.

During the early Republican period, there was increasing socio-legal pressure to eliminate the vestiges of communal institutions and property. It is not until the earlier part of the twentieth century that communal institutions were consolidated and given legal form in the recognition of the *comunidades indígenas*. This revival of the communal form owed something to ideological currents of the time, in particular to the "pro-indígena" movement.[54] The practical effect of the legal recognition of the *comunidad* was to provide mechanisms for obtaining labor and financial resources to construct public works serving the village and linking it to the wider economy. The building of roads, the construction of irrigation channels, the building of schools, and so on were made possible by communal *faenas*, by the use of communal land, and by levies on households in the community.

These public works contributed to the development of the local economy; also, they served to integrate that economy into the national capitalist economy and provided further opportunities for certain local groups to diversify and develop new entrepreneurial roles. Communal institutions contributed to the differentiation of the village economy; for example, such infrastructural works as irrigation and roads benefited most those who held the more extensive and better situated lands and who marketed their surplus. In turn, this situation created more opportunities for trading and transport, and members of richer households took advantage of them.

At this point, we can expand on our earlier contention that cooperation and collective action in the Mantaro area has been double edged. In an economy in which capitalist relations of production have not been historically dominant at the village level, cooperative institutions both serve the survival needs of subsistence households and provide important resources that enable market-orientated peasant farmers and traders to expand their enterprises. In this situation, these two classes of peasant "actors" approach cooperation from a different standpoint. The rich peasant wants to utilize cooperative relationships as a means of appropriating the labor power of others; the poor subsistence peasant wishes, where possible, to use his labor power to generate forms of balanced exchange.

Differences in interest are a source of tension both within dyadic relationships of cooperation and within cooperative institutions. Yet this emphasis on conflicting uses of cooperation among a peasant population should not obscure the complementarities of interest that frequently bind partners to such unequal exchanges. The security provided by the framework of mutual obligations and expectations allows for the development of vertical ties and alliances that crosscut class differences within the peasantry. In Peru, as in other parts of Latin America, *compadrazgo* and patron-client relationships frequently form the basis for the vertical integration of the rural population.[55] Such factors as the expansion of local economic opportunities or the possibilities of gaining access to externally located resources may lead to alliances for mutual benefit between households of unequal social and economic position. Moreover, the existence of such sociocultural frameworks as the fiesta system or community institutions facilitates such alliances and provides ideological legitimations for them.

Cooperative strategies at the village level are also influenced by the extension of central government authority aimed at promoting the growth of the capitalist sector.[56] As the Peruvian government became interested in village production and organization as a means of obtaining local labor and material resources, so cooperation, in various forms, had its payoff at the village level; it protected village resources from the threats of haciendas and other external interests and provided access to government financial and technical assistance. Yet, such formalization also strengthened government control over localities. The recognition of *comunidades indigenas* enabled government authorities to deal directly with the lowest-level political units; this facilitated the conscription of labor for public works, especially road building. The subsequent formation of peasant unions and cooperatives fulfilled similar functions, enabling government to monitor and, if necessary, to intervene in local economic and political processes. Formalized cooperation entailed written rules and regulations and made office holders accountable both to their membership and to government. Communal institutions and cooperatives thus serve increasingly to reinforce unequal exchanges between the village population and regional and national centers.

Internal Differentiation and Cooperation

In the Introduction we outlined the major changes in the pattern of social and economic differentiation in the Mantaro area. For the present purposes, the significant changes were, first, the increasing political and economic importance of a class of richer peasant farmers toward the end of the nineteenth century, and, second, a further shift in the process of differentiation during the first half of the twentieth century, as, increasingly, individuals and households looked to external possibilities to maintain or expand their domestic economy. Over time, as we noted, this process led, in many villages, to land ceasing to be the primary criterion for social and economic status. With increasing demographic pressure, landholdings fragment and, beginning with the rich peasants, there is a tendency for household members to move permanently to the large urban centers, often as a result of educational and commercial success.

One important analytic issue is why these processes did not lead either to the disintegration of village organization or to a polarization of peasants into opposing classes. For example, the rich peasant farmers of Russia exploited the poorer farmers of their villages, but these poorer farmers still remained loyal to them in the face of government intervention. This peasant inconsistency in the eyes of government and of other external interests led Shanin to label peasants an "awkward class."[57] Although the Russian commune had greater control over a village's land resources than was usually the case in Peru, the Russian peasant situation is comparable in many ways to that of the Mantaro area.

In both the Peruvian and the Russian cases, the composition of the peasant village can be analyzed in terms of three broad farming strata. The richer peasants have sufficient good land to produce a surplus for the market, but they do this mainly through using their own family labor. On the average, the land owned by these farmers is not extensive in size when compared with the hacienda or capitalist farm; however, their landholding enables this category to maintain a standard of living that sets them apart from other households and facilitates their social and political domination of community life. Such factors as the hospitality this group is able to offer, its generally higher levels of literacy, its external contacts and experience, and the organizational skills acquired in the management of its enterprises explain the dominant position of this group. In both the Mantaro area and Russia, the richest members of this class of peasants tend not to hold office at the communal and district level, but the officeholders are usually allied to them by kinship or economic interest.

In the Mantaro area, we calculate, on the basis of our landholding and livestock data from a sample of villages, that in the contemporary period this class of peasants composes approximately 15 percent of total households. As a proportion, it is unlikely to have changed considerably since the turn of the century, but the economic basis of this class is now different, due to the more intensive use of agricultural land

and to the development of nonagricultural specialisms. We estimate that nowadays upwards of four hectares of good irrigated land will provide a basis for permanent market production; this landholding will be complemented by livestock grazed on additional pasture and, often, other sources of income. For highland pastoral communities, we use an approximate estimate of upwards of two hundred head of sheep. Other sources of income are widespread among the rich peasant class and nowadays include trading ventures, transport, and, among some members of the household, wage labor.

The second peasant stratum is that which we label the subsistence-orientated peasants; this corresponds to the middle peasant stratum of the Russian studies. An essential defining element of this category is that their land or livestock holding alone does not provide a regular surplus beyond basic household necessities, thus preventing them both from systematically extending their enterprise and from undertaking prestigious and high-cost political and social activities. It is among this group of peasants that supplementary activities, such as craft work and petty trading, are often found. In the Mantaro area, the size of land-holding necessary for the survival of this group is between one and four hectares; at the lower end of the scale, supplementary activities, including sharecropping, are essential to maintain relative economic independence. In the livestock villages, we estimate that between one hundred and two hundred animals, providing wool, meat, and hides to market in exchange for foodstuffs, is the usual holding of this stratum of peasants. The proportion of this group varies considerably from village to village; in most villages nowadays they make up the largest stratum of households, with between 40 and 50 percent of households.

The third stratum consists of the poor peasants whose land or animal holding is never sufficient to provide a basic subsistence. Members of this group must seek local and extralocal employment as a regular feature of their household strategy. Unlike the subsistence households, they often do not have the resources to engage in supplementary independent economic activities or even to set up long-term sharecropping arrangements. Their disadvantage is a cumulative one, for their lack of resources makes them inappropriate partners for the various types of labor and land exchange. The low levels of literacy of this group bar them from lucrative wage-labor employment, and they are usually not regarded as suitable marriage partners by more prosperous households. It is among this class of peasants that richer households recruit their servants, shepherds, and other permanent dependent labor.

The estimates of the proportions of households falling into the three broad strata serve merely to indicate the structure of the peasant economy in the Mantaro area. The figures we have given are notional and would, in any event, require a more careful specification for different localities, soil types, and varieties of household composition. The analytic importance of these distinctions is to point to the coexistence of qualitatively different economic rationales within a peasant population. Differences in the land or livestock ownership of these different strata may appear statistically marginal, yet their significance is manifested in the different internal economic, social, and political strategies open to different classes of peasants. These strategies, in turn, reproduce the overall structure of relationships. We have, for example, already noted in a schematic way how the different classes of peasants in the Mantaro area participate in and use cooperative institutions in qualitatively different ways.

Our division of the farming economy in the Mantaro Valley into three broad strata does not imply that individual households remain fixed in any one category. Indeed, the existence of high levels of social and economic mobility for individual households is, as the Russian and other literature demonstrates, one of the principal factors explaining why the existence of marked social and economic inequality at the village level does not necessarily lead to a politically disruptive and polarized situation.[58] The system of partible inheritance in the Mantaro Valley has resulted in a certain degree of mobility within villages; households with large landholdings but with a large number of offspring have been reduced, in the second generation, to much smaller units. Though these units may be individually sufficient to maintain a rich peasant level, the heirs, for social or occupational reasons, will frequently decide to sell, rent, or sharecrop the land and may themselves reside in the urban centers. A dramatic example of this process is that of the Guerra family of Chupaca, which had once been the dominant landowner of the zone; in the course of forty years at the turn of the century, repeated division of the land among the heirs (mainly urban professionals) led to most of the original landholding of some eight hundred acres being put on the market. Such opportunities for renting or purchasing land enabled households who were originally of the subsistence class to become rich peasants.[59]

The model of household economic mobility in the Mantaro area is different from that of the Russian example discussed above, in several important ways. In the Russian case, it is argued that the tendency of richer peasants to have larger families, combined with fixed land resources and the permanent out-migration of the poorest households, produces a process of cyclical or multidirectional mobility.[60] The out-

migration of the poorest enables households with few members to consolidate landholdings and to rent or purchase additional property,
while rich households gradually descend in the social scale as their land
becomes partitioned. The historical and demographic data for the
Mantaro area are not adequate for an assessment of whether or not
the different strata of peasants varied in household size; a more important factor in the mobility process of our area is the pattern of
outmigration.

Our own data suggest that, from at least the late nineteenth century,
there has been a steady flow of permanent out-migration from the villages of the area; this out-migration appears to have been concentrated
among the richer peasant class of the area. It was this class of peasant
that was able to use its resources to educate its children, establish them
in trade or the professions, and, in short, take advantage of the types
of permanent employment opportunities that were being created by
the development of the urban-industrial sector. The migration pattern
of poorer households was seasonal or short-term migration into unskilled jobs in agriculture and construction.

These migration patterns had the consequence of increasing demographic pressure on the land by maintaining, through temporary migration, poorer households on plots that were insufficient for subsistence.
Though the out-migration of the richer peasants did make available
some land for upwardly mobile subsistence households, the exploitation of this land was limited by the difficulties of obtaining labor in
face of alternative opportunities. In this context, all strata increasingly
diversified their household economy in order to maintain or improve
their position. This process was well established by the turn of the century; by the 1970s, diversification of the village economy had reached
a point at which, in some villages, more than half the economically
active population were engaged in nonagricultural activities as their
principal source of income. These families continue to retain and work
land and regard it as an essential component of their household economy; at the same time, it is often the opportunity for external work
that enables them to continue in the village.

We will reserve a detailed examination of these processes for the
subsequent volume; their significance for the present analysis is to
emphasize that the understanding of peasant social structure and mobility in the Mantaro area cannot focus simply on the internal process
of land allocation and demographic variability. For most of the present
century, external economic opportunities have formed part, directly
or indirectly, of the economic rationales of the three peasant strata in

the area. These opportunities have enabled certain households to save and purchase land and animals. Other households, through their external relations, have been able to maintain a prosperous level of living in the village without building up a substantial land base.

The importance of external opportunities to this economy affects the strategies of the various peasant groups; the provision of local education becomes an important economic asset and so do those forms of association, such as migrant clubs, fiestas, and cooperatives, that link the rural locality to urban centers. The prevalence of migration as part of the local economy also means a reduction in the tensions produced by internal differentiation. Not only do all households have access to economic opportunities through migration, lessening their perception of internal exploitation, but also differences in the rewards that the different strata receive are likely to be attributed by other local people to chance features of their migration careers.

However, as several of the papers in this volume show, new forms of tension are produced by migration and the incorporation of the local economy into the national one. These appear in struggles for the control of institutions, such as cooperatives, migrant clubs, or the *comunidad*, that have become identified with particular occupational groupings. Nevertheless, villages in the Mantaro area have maintained a certain solidarity in the face of government intervention, often including the support of migrants resident in urban and other work centers. The most striking recent example of this village solidarity that we documented was the resistance to the program of SINAMOS (the government's political mobilization agency), which explicitly aimed to reform village institutions and land tenure for the benefit of the poorer peasant strata.[61]

The final part of our explanation of the relative absence of polarization despite differentiation requires us to reiterate briefly our comments on household interdependence and cooperation. As Alavi has shown for Punjabi villages, the conflicting economic interests of the different peasant strata are masked by primordial loyalties and sentiments and overlapping interests and relationships.[62] In the Punjabi situation, as in that of the Mantaro area, economic relationships are embedded in social and cultural relationships; the same ties that enable one group to exploit another are those that provide for a household's social security and identity. The poor peasant who labors for a richer relative has claims on his employer's patronage in times of need, on behalf of his children, and, even, to share in the increase of his wealth.

In the absence of a developed labor market, the richer peasant needs to maintain, through his generosity and patronage, a network of kin and fellow villagers who will provide labor or other assistance. He will also need such relationships to develop a political clientele. These interdependencies are especially important within a village-based economy, because such an economy is subsumed within a wider politico-economic order; to articulate effectively with external powers, both poor and rich peasants must collaborate. The poorer peasant needs support to interpret and relate to the outside forces and uncertainties; the richer peasant needs a show of solidarity to increase his bargaining power in face of the centralizing tendencies of capitalism and the state. In the Mantaro Valley, community ideology has often been an effective device in uniting villagers against external forces; its effectiveness derives from the different, but complementary, ways in which the various strata in the villages benefit from the forms of social, political, and economic security offered by community-wide cooperation.

Government and Cooperative Organization

Our preceding account of cooperation in the Mantaro area has shown that many of the specific forms of local-level cooperation have either evolved in response to changes in the structure of government or been directly initiated by government and its agencies. This relationship between village-level cooperation and changes in government is not fortuitous; changes in the Peruvian economy have entailed changes in the characteristics of the state and, consequently, in local institutions. The advantage of this perspective is that it provides us with a means of relating the changes occurring at the village level in the Mantaro area to changes occurring in the national economy. The nature of Peruvian economic dependency changes as it moves from the mercantilist stage, when foreign (mainly British) trading interests were important but did not directly control productive activity, then to the agromining stage, when foreign capital directly controlled important sectors of production, and, finally, to the stage based on an urban-industrial economy. Each stage of dependency generates a particular set of class relations based on the dominant forms of economic exploitation. In none of these stages have capitalist relations of production been sufficiently widespread to include most parts of the village economy or, for that matter, the majority of the economically active population.[63] It is this context that makes nonmarket means of securing labor or extracting surplus production important for locally and nationally dominant classes. The ways in which this appropriation is achieved depend upon the prevalent system of class relations; the implications of changes in this system for cooperative organization in the Mantaro area can now be outlined.

In the Mantaro Valley the rich peasant farmers emerged during the second half of the nineteenth century as the dominant social group; this dominance was made possible by the economic opportunities created by the expansion of the mercantile economy and, subsequently, by the development of the agromining economy.[64] These rich peasants, like similar groups in other parts of the country, organized themselves to take control of the local economy; to achieve this they needed to free themselves from the political constraints imposed by the existing provincial power structure. This structure was composed of landowners, mine owners, and large traders resident in the important towns and villages of the region. In the first place, the rich peasant farmers sought and obtained the political independence of their own villages, multiplying thereby the number of local administrative units (districts). Further restrictions on the power of the independent farmer class were manifest in the scarcity of infrastructure and in the difficulty of mobilizing labor. These restrictions were partially overcome by making existing traditions of communal cooperation part of the local government apparatus. The formalization of the *comunidad indígena* in place of the *común* is an example of this process.[65]

These movements at the local level took place when there was little effective central government control of the provinces. However, the development of an agromining economy meant an expansion of central bureaucracy in the first half of the twentieth century and the growth of a commercial bourgeoisie interested in the sale of manufactured products throughout the country. This class was committed to opening up communications at the provincial level and to developing a market economy at the local level. Their interests coincided with those of the large-scale mining and agricultural enterprises, which needed a large and available labor force. In this context, central government actively sponsored the development of communications and other infrastructures and took more direct control over provincial administration.. Government at the district and community level was, however, left mainly in the hands of the rich peasant and his allies.

In the development of the *enganche* system, the complementarity of interests between dominant local and national classes was manifest: the rich peasant farmers acted as agents in labor recruitment for mines and plantations, enforcing labor contracts through their control over local administration. The nationally powerful mining, commercial, and agricultural class supported the petitions of these local groups to secure independent jurisdictions for their villages; in some cases, such national figures helped the rich peasants and their communities in their fights with the traditional haciendas.

In the agromining stage of dependency, increasing centralization and the extension of the railway network begin to limit the local possibilities of small-scale economic enterprises. Urban growth tends to concentrate in the larger towns of the region, notably Huancayo. Also, the rationalization of the large haciendas may have restricted the commercial and agricultural possibilities of village traders and farmers. This stage corresponds to the period during which village institutions branch out and establish migrant associations in the mining centers, provincial cities, and national capital. These associations are active in lobbying government and in raising funds for village projects.

The energies of the more economically powerful villagers turn increasingly from controlling village institutions to participating in the national political arena through membership in APRA, trade unions, and migrant clubs. This class of villagers no longer uses existing patterns of household and village-level cooperation to develop the local economy; as Grondin shows, they sponsor the development of local services, such as schools, electricity, and public buildings, that improve the image and comforts of the village rather than develop its productive base.

In the urban-industrial stage of Peruvian capitalism, the interests of the dominant social and economic groups are increasingly confined to the large urban centers; the villages are less important as a source of temporary wage-labor, and their significance to the dominant groups becomes that of providing a cheap supply of foodstuffs for the urban market. In this situation, there are no evident complementary interests relating the market-oriented peasant farmers to the dominant urban-industrial groups. The latter rely, increasingly, on the development of a strong state authority to guarantee the stability necessary to advance their interests.[66] Central government seeks to extend its control over local agricultural production to plan more effectively the supply of foodstuffs and to maintain prices at a reasonably low level. Also, agrarian reform and the payment of the agrarian debt accelerate the transfer of capital from agriculture to industry. Cooperative and governmental institutions at the local level become, increasingly, means of extending this bureaucratic control; such institutions no longer can be used by the locally dominant peasant strata as relatively autonomous means of advancing their interests.

There is a transition period in which central government continues to delegate community development work to those groups dominant in the villages, but this work is increasingly geared to developing the infrastructure of the national state. The village becomes more and more dependent on central economic and political initiatives. Much of the community development work of the Belaúnde government (1962–1968) was of this kind; the government stress on "popular action" was, in effect, a means of carrying out infrastructural improvements needed to develop the national economy at the expense of the local community.[67]

This discussion of the changing significance of peasant cooperation presents only one side of the picture; it suffers somewhat from that centralist bias we discussed earlier. As Laite and as Smith and Cano point out in this volume, the interests of powerful economic and political groups are not always well defined and their strategies are often inconsistent. Lack of information about local conditions or possibilities of agricultural development inhibits even the best-laid plans of government; when that government is dealing with a heterogeneous peasant population its attempts at regulation are even more likely to have unintended consequences. Even those groups, such as the richer peasant farmers, who could be expected to have greater local knowledge are often hoodwinked by their poorer and supposedly less capable neighbors.

It is one thing to describe, as we have done above, the strategies available to powerful groups to exploit the peasant population; it is quite another thing to demonstrate that these groups were successful in their endeavors. Attendance at communal *faenas* in the Mantaro Valley was often minimal, especially when the work did not seem to directly benefit those summoned to work; at other times, as one exasperated authority commented, the value of the work was nullified by the tendency of work parties to get drunk at public expense. There are, then, a multitude of ways in which the "exploited" can express their truculence and subvert the most ingeniously devised plans to extract their labor or their surplus. The persistence of flourishing small-scale enterprises in all sectors of the Mantaro area's economy is itself evidence of a successful resistance to the centralizing and homogenizing impact of capitalist development on agrarian society.

Our brief outline of the relation between the evolution of the Peruvian state and village-level cooperation is intended to indicate the kinds of pressures to which cooperative practices are subjected. The various forms of peasant cooperation that we have analyzed constitute the field in which local and extralocal alliances are achieved. These forms help to explain the persistence of the peasantry in the face of the centralizing tendencies of modern capitalism. They are also convenient for a state seeking to extend its control in an unevenly developed country.

NOTES

1. Bartra uses the concept "permanent primitive accumulation" to describe a similar process in rural Mexico; in the Mexican situation, however, there are greater numbers of large-scale farming enterprises and a larger rural proletariat in comparison to Peru (Roger Bartra, *Estructura agraria y las clases sociales en México*).

2. See the various articles in the first volume of *The Journal of Peasant Studies*: Eric Hobsbawm, "Peasants and Politics"; Hamza Alavi, "Peasant Classes and Primordial Loyalties"; Teodor Shanin, "The Nature and Logic of the Peasant Economy: A Generalization"; Claude Meillassoux, "The Social Organization of the Peasantry"; and Sidney W. Mintz, "A Note on the Definition of Peasantries" (*The Journal of Peasant Studies* 1, no. 1 [October 1973]).

3. See Clifford Geertz's review of the literature that conceptualizes peasant society as "part-society" ("Studies in Peasant Life: Community and Society," in *Biennial Review of Anthropology*, edited by Bernard Seigel); also Eric R. Wolf, *Peasants*.

4. Eric R. Wolf, "Types of Latin American Peasantry: A Preliminary Discussion," *American Anthropologist* 57, no. 3 (1955): 452–471.

5. Elsie B. Keatinge, "Latin American Peasant Corporate Communities: Potentials for Mobilization and Political Integration," *Journal of Anthropological Research* 29 (1973): 37–58.

6. George Foster, "Peasant Society and the Image of the Limited Good," *American Anthropologist* 67 (1965): 293–315, and *Tzintzuntzan*.

7. Arthur Rubel and Harriet J. Kupferer, "Perspectives on the Atomistic-Type Society: Introduction," *Human Organization* 27, no. 3 (1973): 189–190.

8. Edward Banfield, *The Moral Basis of a Backward Society*; Everett Rogers, *Modernization among Peasants: The Impact of Communications*.

9. F. Lamond Tullis, *Lord and Peasant in Peru: A Paradigm of Political and Social Change*, pp. 39–51; compare also Rodolfo Stavenhagen, "Classes, Colonialism and Acculturation," *Studies in Comparative International Development* 1, no. 6 (1965): 53–77.

10. These perspectives have often been based on Frank W. Young's model of "information-processing" at the village level (Young, "A Proposal for Cooperative Cross-Cultural Research on Inter-Village Systems," *Human Organization* 25, no. 1 [Spring 1966]: 46–50).

11. Oscar Núñez del Prado, *Kuyo Chico: Applied Anthropology in an Indian Community*.

12. See Julio Cotler, "The Mechanics of Internal Domination and Social Change in Peru," *Studies in Comparative International Development* 3, no. 12 (1967–1968): 229–246; José Matos Mar et al., *Dominación y cambios en el Perú rural*.

13. Philip J. O'Brien, "A Critique of Latin American Theories of Dependency," in *Beyond the Sociology of Development*, edited by Ivar Oxaal, Tony Barnett, and David Booth. See also Fernando Henrique Cardoso, "Dependency Revisited," The Charles W. Hackett Memorial Lecture, Institute of Latin American Studies, The University of Texas at Austin.

14. André Gundar Frank, *Capitalism and Underdevelopment in Latin America*, pp. 27–44.

15. Aníbal Quijano, "The Marginal Role of the Economy and the Marginalized Labour Force," *Economy and Society* 3, no. 4 (November 1974): 393–428.

16. Eric J. Hobsbawm, "A Case of Neo-Feudalism: La Convención, Peru," *Journal of Latin American Studies* 1, no. 1 (1969): 31–50; Wesley Craig, *El movimiento campesino en La Convención, Perú*; Eduardo Fioravanti, *Latifundio y sindicalismo agrario en el Perú*.

17. For a full discussion of this issue with respect to Peru, see Aníbal Quijano, "Redefinición de la dependencia y proceso de marginalización en América Latina," in *Populismo, marginalización y dependencia*, edited by Francisco Weffort and Aníbal Quijano, pp. 171–329.

18. For comparative material on Chile, see James Petras and Hugo M. Zemelman, *Peasants in Revolt: A Chilean Case Study, 1965–1971*.

19. Thomas C. Greaves describes the importance of the rural proletariat but underestimates the degree to which groups, such as miners, remain part of the village economy ("The Andean Rural Proletarians," *Anthropological Quarterly* 45, no. 2 [1972]: 65–83).

20. Julian Laite, "Trade Union and Political Organization among Miners in the Peruvian Sierra," mimeographed, Department of Sociology, The University of Manchester, 1975; A. DeWind, "From Peasants to Miners," paper presented to the American Anthropological Association, New Orleans, 1973.

21. Ernesto Laclau, "Feudalism and Capitalism in Latin America," *New Left Review* 67 (May–June 1971): 19–38. See also Cristóbal Kay, "The Comparative Development of the European Manorial System and the Latin American Hacienda System," *The Journal of Peasant Studies* 2, no. 1 (October 1974): 69–98. Kay shows that the hacienda system was very much affected by the nature of dependent capitalist development.

22. See Shane Hunt, "The Economics of Haciendas and Plantations in Latin America," Discussion Paper no. 29, Research Program in Economic Development, Princeton University, 1972.

23. Rosa Luxemburg, *The Accumulation of Capital*; V. I. Lenin, *The Development of Capitalism in Russia*; E. Preobrazhensky, *The New Economics*.

24. Lenin, *Capitalism in Russia*, p. 93.

25. Ibid., p. 176.

26. We deliberately use the term noncapitalist *form* of production to avoid suggesting that there exist in Peru production systems that have a logic of operation and an institutional superstructure independent of the dominant capitalist *mode* of production. These noncapitalist forms are subsumed within capitalism and are shaped by the expansion of capitalism. We are grateful to Cristóbal Kay and Bernardo Sorj for helping us to clarify our position on this issue.

27. A discussion of the articulation of modes of production in Peru is found in Barbara Bradby, "The Destruction of Natural Economy," *Economy and Society* 4, no. 2 (May 1975): 127–161; also Norman Long, "Structural Dependency, Modes of Production and Economic Brokerage in Rural Peru," in *Beyond the Sociology of Development*, edited by Ivar Oxaal, Tony Barnett, and David Booth. This type of analysis has been applied to South Africa by Harold Wolpe ("The Theory of Internal Colonialism: The South African Case," in Oxaal et al., *Sociology of Development*).

28. Ernesto Yepes, "Some Aspects of Recent Peruvian Socio-economic History," Ph.D. dissertation, University of Manchester, 1974.

29. Bradby, "Destruction of the Natural Economy."

30. Norman Long, "The Role of Regional Associations in Peru," in *The Process of Urbanization*, edited by M. Drake et al., pp. 173–191; Carlos Samaniego, "Location, Social Differentiation and Peasant Movements in the Central Sierra of Peru," Ph.D. dissertation, University of Manchester, 1974, pp. 331–337.

31. Even within the hacienda the peasants were able to develop a household economy, controlling small plots and animals and using unpaid family labor. See Juan Martínez-Alier, *Los huacchilleros del Perú*; Long, "Structural Dependency," pp. 268–271.

32. Samaniego, "Location, Social Differentiation," pp. 51–112.

33. "Introduction," in *Peasants and Peasant Societies*, edited by Teodor Shanin, pp. 11–18.

34. A. V. Chayanov, *The Theory of Peasant Economy*; S. H. Franklin, "Systems of Production: Systems of Appropriation," *Pacific Viewpoint* 6, pp. 145–166; Teodor Shanin, *The Awkward Class*.

35. Manning Nash, "The Social Context of Economic Choice in a Small Society," in *Economic Anthropology*, edited by E. E. Le Clair, Jr., and H. K. Schneider, p. 318.

36. Christopher Scott, "Issues in the Analysis of the Labour Market for Sugar Cane Cutters in Northern Peru: 1940–1969," *The Journal of Peasant Studies* 3, no. 3 (1976).

37. Nash, "Economic Choice," pp. 311–321.

38. Samaniego, "Location, Social Differentiation," p. 30.

39. John Murra, "El 'control vertical' de un máximo de pisos ecológicos en la economía de las sociedades andinas," in John Murra, *Formaciones económicas y políticas del mundo andino*, pp. 59–116.

40. Samaniego, "Location, Social Differentiation," pp. 395–403.

41. John H. Rowe, "Inca Culture at the Time of the Spanish Conquest," in *Handbook of South American Indians*, edited by J. Steward, pp. 183–330. Also John H. Rowe, "The Incas under Spanish Colonial Institutions," *Hispanic-American Historical Review*, 37, no. 2 (1957): 155–199.

42. Samaniego, "Location, Social Differentiation," p. 80.

43. A general review of exchange systems in the Andean region is given in G. Alberti and E. Mayer, eds., *Reciprocidad e intercambio en los Andes peruanos*.

44. Martínez-Alier, *Los huacchilleros del Perú*.

45. Hunt, "Economics of Haciendas."

46. Norman Long, "Commerce and Kinship in Highland Peru," and Billie Jean Isbell, "Kuyoq–Those Who Love Me: An Analysis of Andean Kinship and Reciprocity in a Ritual Context," in *Andean Kinship and Marriage*, edited by R. Bolton and E. Mayer.

47. Samaniego, "Location, Social Differentiation," p. 154.

48. Sidney W. Mintz, "The Rural Proletariat and the Problem of Rural Proletarian Consciousness," *The Journal of Peasant Studies* 1, no. 3 (April 1974): 304–306.

49. Carlos Fonseca, "Modalidades de la Minka," in *Reciprocidad e intercambio en los Andes peruanos*, edited by G. Alberti and E. Mayer, p. 109.

50. See the chapters by Samaniego and Winder in this volume.

51. Actas de Concejo Provincial de Huancayo, 15 March 1875.

52. Long, "The Role of Regional Associations"; Hans C. Buechler, "The Ritual Dimension of Rural-Urban Networks: The Fiesta System in the Northern Highlands of Bolivia," in *Peasants in Cities: Readings in the Anthropology of Urbanization,* edited by William Mangin, pp. 62–71.

53. Cited by William Baxter Hutchinson, "Sociocultural Change in the Mantaro Valley Region of Peru: Acolla, a Case Study," Ph.D. dissertation, Indiana University, 1973, pp. 254–255.

54. François Chevalier, "Official *Indigenismo* in Peru in 1920: Origins, Significance and Socio-Economic Scope," in *Race and Class in Latin America,* edited by Magnus Mörner.

55. Wolf, *Peasants.*

56. See Yepes's discussion of the development of government under President Leguía (1919–1930) ("Recent Peruvian Socio-economic History").

57. Shanin, *The Awkward Class.*

58. Ibid.; see also the case of Turkey in Paul Stirling, *A Turkish Village.*

59. Samaniego, "Location, Social Differentiation," pp. 259–260.

60. Shanin, *The Awkward Class.*

61. Norman Long and David Winder, "From Peasant Community to Production Cooperative: An Analysis of Recent Government Policy in Peru," *Journal of Development Studies* 12, no. 1 (October 1975): 75–94; also G. Alberti and R. Sánchez, *Poder y conflicto social en el valle del Mantaro,* p. 189.

62. Hamza Alavi, "Kinship in West Punjab Villages," in *Contributions to Indian Sociology,* New Series, no. 6, edited by H. Madian, pp. 1–27.

63. Richard Webb, "Government Policy and Distribution of Income in Peru, 1963–1973," *Discussion Paper* no. 39, Research Program in Economic Development, Woodrow Wilson School of Public and International Affairs, Princeton University, 1974.

64. See Yepes, "Recent Peruvian Socio-economic History," for a discussion of the difference between the mercantilist (British) stage of imperialism in Peru and the agromining stage (based mainly on North American capital).

65. Marcelo Grondin in this volume.

66. Aníbal Quijano, "Imperialismo y capitalismo de estado," *Sociedad y Política,* no. 1 (June 1972).

67. François Bourricaud, *Power and Society in Contemporary Peru,* pp. 322–343.

Bibliography

Adams, Richard N. *A Community in the Andes: Problems and Progress in Muquiyauyo.* Seattle and London: University of Washington Press, 1959.

Alavi, Hamza. "Kinship in West Punjab Villages." In *Contributions to Indian Sociology,* New Series, no. 6, edited by H. Madian (December 1972): 1–27.

———. "Peasant Classes and Primordial Loyalties." *The Journal of Peasant Studies* 1, no. 1 (October 1973): 23–62.

Alberti, G., and E. Mayer, eds. *Reciprocidad e intercambio en los Andes peruanos.* Lima: Instituto de Estudios Peruanos, 1974.

———, and R. Sánchez. *Poder y conflicto social en el valle del Mantaro.* Lima: Instituto de Estudios Peruanos, 1974.

Alegría, Ciro. *El mundo es ancho y ajeno.* Buenos Aires: Editorial Losada.

Alers-Montalvo, Manuel. *Pucará: Un estudio de cambio.* Lima: Instituto Interamericano de Ciencias Agrícolas, O.E.A., Oficina Regional de la Zona Andina, 1967.

———. "Social Systems Analysis of Supervised Agricultural Credit in an Andean Community." *Rural Sociology* 25, no. 1 (1960): 51–64.

Anderson, Michael. "Nuevas formas de participación de los trabajadores en la economía del Perú." *Report to the Ford Foundation,* Lima, September 1972.

Arguedas, José María. "Evolución de las comunidades indígenas." *Revista del Museo Nacional* (Lima) 26 (1957): 78–151.

———. *Yawar Fiesta.* Lima: Librería-Editorial J. María Barca, 1958.

Astiz, Carlos. *Pressure Groups and Power Elites in Peruvian Politics.* Ithaca: Cornell University Press, 1969.

Banfield, Edward. *The Moral Basis of a Backward Society.* Glencoe, Illinois: Free Press, 1958.

Bartra, Roger. *Estructura agraria y clases sociales en México.* Mexico City: Era, 1974.

Basadre, Jorge. *Historia de la República del Perú.* 10 vols. Lima: Peruamérica, 1964.

Béjar, Héctor. "Perú: Entrevista a dos guerrilleros." *Pensamiento Crítico* (Havana) no. 6 (July 1970).

———. *Peru 1965: Notes on a Guerrilla Experience.* London: Monthly Review Press, 1970.

Bennett, John W. *Hutterian Brethren.* Stanford, California: Stanford University Press, 1967.

———. "Reciprocal Economic Exchange among North American Agricultural

Operators." *Southwestern Journal of Anthropology* 24 (1968): 276–309.

Bloch, Marc. *Feudal Society.* London: Routledge and Kegan Paul, 1962.

Blumer, H. "Early Industrialization and the Laboring Class." *Sociological Quarterly* 1, no. 1 (January 1960).

Bollinger, W. S. "The Rise of the United States Influence in the Peruvian Economy, 1869–1921." M.A. thesis, University of California, 1972.

Bourque, Susan. "Cholification and the Campesino." Latin American Studies Program Dissertation, Series No. 21. Ithaca: Cornell University, 1971.

Bourricaud, François. *Power and Society in Contemporary Peru.* New York: Praeger, 1970.

Bradby, Barbara. "The Destruction of Natural Economy." *Economy and Society* 4, no. 2 (May 1975): 127–161.

Buechler, Hans C. "The Ritual Dimension of Rural-Urban Networks: The Fiesta System in the Northern Highlands of Bolivia." In *Peasants in Cities: Readings in the Anthropology of Urbanization,* edited by William Mangin, pp. 62–71. Boston: Houghton Mifflin, 1970.

Campbell, L. "The Historiography of the Peruvian Guerrilla Movement." *Latin American Research Review* 8, no. 1 (Spring 1973): 45–70.

Cardoso, Fernando Henrique. "Dependency Revisited." Charles W. Hackett Memorial Lecture. Austin: Institute of Latin American Studies, The University of Texas at Austin, 1975.

————, and J. L. Reyna. "Industrialization, Occupational Structure and Social Stratification in Latin America." In *Constructive Change in Latin America,* edited by C. Blasier. Pittsburgh: Pittsburgh University Press, 1968.

Carroll, Thomas F. "Peasant Cooperation in Latin America." In *Two Blades of Grass: Rural Cooperatives in Agricultural Modernization,* edited by Peter Worsley, pp. 199–252. Manchester: Manchester University Press, 1971.

Castillo, Hernán. "Chaquicocha: Community in Progress." *Socioeconomic Development of Andean Communities,* Report No. 5. Ithaca: Department of Anthropology, Cornell University, 1964.

————. "Mito: The Orphan of Its Illustrious Children." *Socioeconomic Development of Andean Communities,* Report No. 4. Ithaca: Department of Anthropology, Cornell University, 1964.

Castro Pozo, Hildebrando. "Del ayllu al co-operativismo socialista." *Biblioteca de la Revista de Economia y Finanzas,* vol. 2. Lima: P. Barrantes Castro, 1936.

————. *Nuestra comunidad indigena.* Lima: Editorial Lucero, 1924.

————. "Social and Economic-Political Evolution of the Communities of Central Peru." in *Handbook of South American Indians,* edited by J. H. Steward, vol. 2, pp. 483–499. Washington, D.C.: Bureau of American Ethnology Bulletin 143, 1946.

Censo Nacional de Población y Ocupación, 1940. Lima: Ministerio de Hacienda y Comercio, Dirección Nacional de Estadística, 1944.

Cerrón, A. S. *Breve historia de Ahuac.* Huancayo, Peru, 1956.

Chaplin, David. *The Peruvian Industrial Labor Force.* Princeton: Princeton University Press, 1967.

Chavarría, Jesús. "The Intellectuals and the Crisis of Modern Peruvian Nationalism: 1870–1919." *Hispanic-American Historical Review* 50, no. 2 (May 1970): 257–278.

Chayanov, A. V. *The Theory of Peasant Economy.* Edited by D. Thorner, R. E. F. Smith, and B. Kerblay. London: Irwin, 1966.

Chevalier, François. "Official *Indigenismo* in Peru in 1920: Origins, Significance and Socio-economic Scope." In *Race and Class in Latin America*, edited by Magnus Mörner. New York: Columbia University Press, 1970.

Comité Interamericano de Desarrollo Agrícola (CIDA). *Tenencia de la tierra y desarrollo socio-económico del sector agrícola, Perú.* Washington, D.C.: Unión Panamericana, 1966.

Cotler, Julio. "The Mechanics of Internal Domination and Social Change in Peru." *Studies in Comparative International Development* 3, no. 12 (1967–1968): 229–246.

————, and F. Portocarrero. "Peru: Peasant Organizations." In *Latin American Peasant Movements*, edited by Henry A. Landsberger. Ithaca: Cornell University Press, 1969.

Craig, Wesley. *El movimiento campesino en La Convención, Perú.* Lima: Instituto de Estudios Peruanos, 1968.

————. "Peru: The Peasant Movement of La Convención." In *Latin American Peasant Movements*, edited by Henry A. Landsberger. Ithaca: Cornell University Press, 1969.

Denegri, M. A. *La crisis del enganche.* Lima, 1911.

Dew, Edward. *Politics in the Altiplano: The Dynamics of Change in Rural Peru.* Austin and London: University of Texas Press, 1969.

De Wind, A. "From Peasants to Miners." Paper presented to the American Anthropological Association, New Orleans, 1973.

Di Tella, Torcuato, et al. *Sindicato y comunidad: Dos tipos de estructura sindical latinoamericana.* Buenos Aires: Editorial del Instituto, 1967.

Dobyns, Harry F. *Comunidades campesinas del Perú.* Lima: Editorial Estudios Andinos, 1970.

————; Paul L. Doughty; and Harold D. Lasswell, eds. *Peasants, Power and Applied Social Change: Vicos as a Model.* Beverly Hills, California: Sage Publications, 1971.

Dore, Ronald F. "Modern Cooperatives in Traditional Communities." In *Two Blades of Grass: Rural Cooperatives in Agricultural Modernization*, edited by Peter Worsley, pp. 43–60. Manchester: Manchester University Press, 1971.

Doughty, Paul L. "Behind the Back of the City: 'Provincial' Life in Lima, Peru." In *Peasants in Cities: Readings in the Anthropology of Urbanization*, edited by William Mangin, pp. 30–46. Boston: Houghton Mifflin Co., 1970.

————. *Huaylas: An Andean District in Search of Progress.* Ithaca: Cornell University Press, 1968.

Erasmus, Charles J. "Culture, Structure and Process: The Occurrence and Disappearance of Reciprocal Farm Labor." *Southwestern Journal of Anthropology* 12, no. 4 (1956): 444–469.

Escobar, Gabriel. *Sicaya: Cambios culturales en una comunidad mestiza andina.* Lima: Instituto de Estudios Peruanos, 1973.

————. "Sicaya, una comunidad mestiza de la sierra central del Perú." In *Estudios sobre la cultura actual del Perú*, edited by L. Valcárcel. Lima: Universidad Nacional Mayor de San Marcos, 1958.

Espinoza, S. Waldemar. "Los Huancas, aliados de la conquista." *Anales Científicos* (Universidad Nacional del Centro, Huancayo) 1, no. 1 (1972).

Fals Borda, Orlando, ed. *Cooperatives and Rural Development in Latin America: An Analytic Report*, vol. 3. Geneva: United Nations Research Institute for Social Development, 1971.

————. *Estudios de la realidad campesina: Cooperación y cambio*, vol. 2.

Geneva: United Nations Research Institute for Social Development, 1969.

Favre, Henri. "Le peuplement et la colonisation agricole de la steppe dans le Pérou central." *Annales de Geographie* 84 (July-September 1975): 415–440.

———; Claude Collin Delavaud; and José Matos Mar. *La hacienda en el Perú*. Lima: Instituto de Estudios Peruanos, 1967.

Feldman, David. "The Economics of Ideology: Some Problems of Achieving Rural Socialism in Tanzania." In *Politics and Change in Developing Countries*, edited by Colin Leys. London: Cambridge University Press, 1969.

Fioravanti, Eduardo. *Latifundio y sindicalismo agrario en el Perú*. Lima: Instituto de Estudios Peruanos, 1974.

Fisher, John, "Silver Mining and Silver Miners in the Viceroyalty of Peru, 1776–1824: A Prolegomenon." In *Social and Economic Change in Modern Peru*, edited by Rory Miller, Clifford T. Smith, and John Fisher, pp. 13–26. Monograph Series, No. 6. Liverpool: Centre for Latin-American Studies, 1976.

Flores, E. *La comunidad de Maravilca*. Lima: Instituto Indígena Peruano, 1967.

Fonseca, César. "Comunidad, hacienda y el modelo Sais." *América Indígena* 35, no. 2 (April–June 1975).

———. "La economía 'vertical' y la economía de mercado en las comunidades alteñas del Perú." In Íñigo Ortiz de Zúñiga, *Visita de la provincia de León de Huánuco* (1562), vol. 2. Huánuco, Peru: Universidad Hermilio Valdizán, 1972.

———. "Modalidades de la Minka." In *Reciprocidad e intercambio en los Andes peruanos*, edited by G. Alberti and E. Meyer. Lima: Instituto de Estudios Peruanos, 1974.

Foster, George. "Peasant Society and the Image of the Limited Good." *American Anthropologist* 67 (1965): 293–315.

———. *Tzintzuntzan*. Boston: Little, Brown and Company, 1967.

Frank, André Gundar. *Capitalism and Underdevelopment in Latin America*. New York: Monthly Review Press, 1969.

———. *Latin America: Underdevelopment or Revolution*. New York: Monthly Review Press, 1969.

Franklin, S. H. "Systems of production: Systems of Appropriation." *Pacific Viewpoint* 6 (1971): 145–166.

Fuenzalida, Fernando. "La matriz colonial de las comunidades de indígenas andinas." In *La hacienda, la comunidad y el campesino en el Perú*, edited by Robert Keith et al. Lima: Instituto de Estudios Peruanos, 1970.

———. "Poder, raza y etnía en el Perú contemporáneo." In Fernando Fuenzalida et al., *El indio y el poder en el Perú*, pp. 15–87. Lima, Instituto de Estudios Peruanos, 1970.

———; José Luis Villarán; Jurgen Golte; and Teresa Valiente. *Estructuras tradicionales y economía de mercado: La comunidad de indígenas de Huayopampa*. Lima: Instituto de Estudios Peruanos, 1968.

Geertz, Clifford. "Studies in Peasant Life: Community and Society." In *Biennial Review of Anthropology*, edited by Bernard Siegel. Stanford, California: Stanford University Press, 1962.

Gianella, J. *Marginalidad en Lima metropolitana*. Lima: Cuadernos DESCO, 1970.

Glantz, Susana. *El ejido colectivo de Nueva Italia*. Mexico City: SEPINAH, Centro de Investigaciones Superiores, Instituto Nacional de Antropología e Historia, 1974.

Godelier, Maurice. *Rationality and Irrationality in Economics*. London: New Left Books, 1972.

González Holguín, Diego. *Vocabulario de la lengua general de todo el Perú llamada lengua Qquichua o del Inca*. Lima: Universidad Nacional Mayor de San Marcos, 1952.

Gott, Richard. *Rural Guerrillas in Latin America*. Harmondsworth, England: Pelican, 1970.

Greaves, Thomas C. "The Andean Rural Proletarians." *Anthropological Quarterly* 45, no. 2 (1972): 65–83.

Grondin, Marcelo. "Un caso de explotación calculada: La comunidad campesina de Muquiyauyo, Perú." Ph.D. dissertation, Universidad Iberoamericana, Mexico City, 1975.

Handelman, Howard. *Struggle in the Andes: Peasant Political Mobilization in Peru*. Austin and London: University of Texas Press, 1975.

Harding, Colin. *Agrarian Reform and Agrarian Struggles in Peru*. Working Paper No. 15. Cambridge: Centre for Latin American Studies, University of Cambridge, 1974.

Hilliker, Grant. *The Politics of Reform in Peru: The Aprista and Other Mass Parties of Latin America*. Baltimore and London: The Johns Hopkins Press, 1971.

Hobsbawm, Eric J. "A Case of Neo-Feudalism: La Convención, Peru." *Journal of Latin American Studies* 1, no. 1 (1969): 31–50.

———. "Peasant Land Occupations." *Past and Present* no. 62 (February 1974): 120–152.

———. "Peasants and Politics." *The Journal of Peasant Studies* 1, no. 1 (October 1973): 3–22.

———. "Peru: The Peculiar Revolution." *New York Review of Books*, 16 December 1971, pp. 29–36.

Holmberg, Allan. "Changing Community Attitudes and Values in Peru." In *Social Change in Latin America Today*, edited by R. Adams and R. Gillin. New York: Vintage Books, Random House, 1960.

Horton, D. E. *Land Reform and Reform Enterprises in Peru*. Report submitted to the Land Tenure Center and International Bank for Reconstruction and Development. Madison, Wisconsin: University of Wisconsin, 1974.

Huizer, Gerrit. "Land Invasion as a Non-Violent Strategy of Peasant Rebellion: Some Cases from Latin America." *Journal of Peace Research* no. 2 (1972).

———. *Peasant Rebellion in Latin America*. Harmondsworth, England: Pelican, 1973.

Hunt, Shane. "The Economics of Haciendas and Plantations in Latin America." Discussion Paper No. 29. Princeton: Research Program in Economic Development, Princeton University, 1972.

Hutchinson, William Baxter. "Sociocultural Change in the Mantaro Valley Region of Peru: Acolla, A Case Study." Ph.D. dissertation, Indiana University, 1973. (University Microfilms, Ann Arbor, Michigan, 1975.)

Hyden, Goran, and Edward Karanja. "Cooperatives and Rural Development in Kenya." In *Rural Cooperatives and Planned Change in Africa*, edited by Raymond Apthorpe, pp. 157–220. Geneva: United Nations Research Institute for Social Development, 1970.

Instituto Nacional de Promoción Industrial. *Estadística Industrial*. Lima: Ministerio de Fomento, General de Industrias, Banco Industrial del Perú, 1963.

Isbell, Billie Jean. "The Influence of Migrants upon Traditional Social and

Political Concepts: A Peruvian Case Study." In *Latin American Urban Research*, vol. 4, edited by W. A. Cornelius and F. M. Trueblood, pp. 234–262. Beverly Hills, California: Sage Publications, 1974.

————. "Kuyoq—Those Who Love Me: An Analysis of Andean Kinship and Reciprocity in a Ritual Context." In *Andean Kinship and Marriage*, edited by Ralph Bolton and Enrique Mayer. Washington, D.C.: American Anthropological Association, 1977.

Jachanowitz, A. "La instalación metalúrgica de La Oroya." *Boletín Oficial de Minas y Petroleo* (Lima), no. 3.

Kapsoli, W. *Los movimientos campesinos en Cerro de Pasco: 1880–1963*. Lima: Universidad Nacional Mayor de San Marcos, 1972.

————. *El campesinado peruano: 1919–1930*. Lima: Seminario de Historia Rural-Andina, Universidad Nacional Mayor de San Marcos, 1972.

Kay, Cristóbal. "The Comparative Development of the European Manorial System and the Latin American Hacienda System." *Journal of Peasant Studies* 2, no. 1 (October 1974): 69–98.

Keatinge, Elsie B. "Latin American Peasant Corporate Communities: Potentials for Mobilization and Political Integration." *Journal of Anthropological Research* 29 (1973): 37–58.

Keith, Robert G.; Fernando Fuenzalida; José Matos Mar; Julio Cotler; and Giorgio Alberti. *La hacienda, la comunidad y el campesino en el Perú*. Lima: Instituto de Estudios Peruanos, 1970.

Klarén, Peter F. *Modernization, Dislocation and Aprismo: Origins of the Peruvian Aprista Party, 1870–1932*. Austin and London: University of Texas Press, 1973.

Laclau, Ernesto. "Feudalism and Capitalism in Latin America." *New Left Review* 67 (May–June 1971): 19–38.

Laite, Julian. "Trade Union and Political Organization among Miners in the Peruvian Sierra." Mimeographed. Department of Sociology, The University of Manchester, 1975.

Landsberger, Henry A. "The Labor Elite: Is It Revolutionary?" In *Elites in Latin America*, edited by S. M. Lipset and A. Solari, pp. 256–300. New York: Oxford University Press, 1967.

Larson, Magali Sarfatti, and Arlene Eisen Bergman. *Social Stratification in Peru*. Berkeley: Institute of International Studies, University of California, 1969.

Latin Project. *Training the Rio Mantaro*. Basle/Lima: 1968.

Lenin, V. I. *The Development of Capitalism in Russia*. Moscow: Progress Publishers, 1967.

Lipsky, Michael. "Protest as a Political Resource." *American Political Science Review* 62, no. 4 (1968): 1144–1158.

Long, Norman. "Commerce and Kinship in Highland Peru." In *Andean Kinship and Marriage*, edited by Ralph Bolton and Enrique Mayer. Washington, D.C.: American Anthropological Association, 1977.

————. "Cooperative Enterprise and Rural Development in Tanzania." In *Rural Cooperatives and Planned Change in Africa*, edited by Raymond Apthorpe, pp. 333–361. Geneva: United Nations Research Institute for Social Development, 1970.

————. "Multiple Enterprise in the Central Highlands of Peru." In *Social Relations of Confidence in Enterprise*, edited by Arnold Strikon and Sidney M. Greenfield. Albuquerque: University of New Mexico Press, 1978.

————. "The Role of Regional Associations in Peru." In *The Process of Urbanization*, edited by M. Drake et al., pp. 173–191. Bletchley, England: The Open University Press, 1973.

————. "Structural Dependency, Modes of Production and Economic Brokerage in Rural Peru." In *Beyond the Sociology of Development*, edited by Ivar Oxaal, Tony Barnett, and David Booth. London: Routledge and Kegan Paul, 1975.

————, and David Winder. "From Peasant Community to Production Cooperative: An Analysis of Recent Government Policy in Peru." *Journal of Development Studies* 12, no. 1 (October 1975): 75–94.

Lowenthal, Abraham F., ed. *The Peruvian Experiment*. Princeton and London: Princeton University Press, 1975.

Luxemburg, Rosa. *The Accumulation of Capital*. London: Routledge and Kegan Paul, 1951.

Maguire, G. A. *Towards "Uhuru" in Tanzania*. London: Cambridge University Press, 1969.

Malpica, Carlos. *Los dueños del Perú*. Lima: Ediciones Ensayos Sociales, 1964.

Mangin, William. "The Role of Regional Associations in the Adaptation of Rural Migrants to Cities in Peru." *Sociologus* 9 (1959): 23–36. Reprinted in *Contemporary Customs and Societies of Latin America*, edited by D. B. Heath and R. W. Adams, pp. 311–323. New York: Random House, 1959.

Manrique P., Rafael. "La transformación de una empresa industrial textil del sistema capitalista al sistema cooperativo." Thesis, Universidad Nacional Mayor de San Marcos, Lima, 1972.

Mariátegui, José Carlos. *Seven Interpretive Essays on Peruvian Reality*. Translated by Marjory Urquidi. Austin and London: University of Texas Press, 1971.

Martínez-Alier, Juan. *Los huacchilleros del Perú*. Lima-Paris: Instituto de Estudios Peruanos–Rueda Ibérica, 1973.

Matos Mar, José. "Migration and Urbanization—The 'Barriadas' of Lima: An Example of Integration into Urban Life." In *Urbanization in Latin America*, edited by Philip Hauser, pp. 170–190. Liege, Belgium: UNESCO.

————, et al. *Dominación y cambios en el Perú rural*. Lima: Instituto de Estudios Peruanos, 1969.

Maynard, Eileen A. "The Pattern of Community Service Development in Selected Communities of the Mantaro Valley, Peru." *Socio-Economic Development of Andean Communities*, Report No. 3. Ithaca: Department of Anthropology, Peru Project, Cornell University, 1964.

Medina, Rubens. *Agrarian Reform Legislation in Peru*. Land Tenure Center Monograph No. 73. Madison: Land Tenure Center, University of Wisconsin, 1970.

Meillassoux, Claude. "The Social Organization of the Peasantry." *The Journal of Peasant Studies* 1, no. 1 (October 1973): 81–90.

Mejía, José M., and Rosa S. Díaz. *Sindicalismo y reforma agraria en el valle de Chancay*. Lima: Instituto de Estudios Peruanos, 1975.

Metcalf, David. *The Economics of Agriculture*. Harmondsworth, England: Penguin Books, 1969.

Mintz, Sidney W. "A Note on the Definition of Peasantries." *The Journal of Peasant Studies* 1, no. 1 (1973): 91–106.

————. "The Rural Proletariat and the Problem of Rural Proletarian Consciousness." *The Journal of Peasant Studies* 1, no. 3 (April 1974): 304–306.

Montoya, Rodrigo. *A propósito del carácter predominantemente capitalista de la economía peruana actual.* Lima: Editorial Teoría y Realidad, 1970.

―――, et al. *La Sais Cahuide y sus contradicciones.* Lima: Universidad Nacional Mayor de San Marcos, 1974.

Moore, Wilbert E., and Arnold S. Feldman, eds. *Labor Commitment and Social Change in Developing Areas.* New York: Social Science Research Council, 1960.

Mostajo, F. *Algunas ideas sobre la cuestión obrera (contrato de enganche).* Arequipa, Perú: Universidad de Arequipa, 1913.

Murra, John. "An Aymara Kingdom in 1567." *Ethnohistory* 15, no. 2 (1968): 115–151.

―――. "El 'control vertical' de un máximo de pisos ecológicos en la economía de las sociedades Andinas." In Íñigo Ortiz de Zúñiga, *Visita de la provincia de León de Huánuco* (1562), vol. 2. 1972. Reprinted in John Murra, *Formaciones económicas y políticas del mundo andino,* pp. 59–116. Lima: Instituto de Estudios Peruanos, 1975.

―――. *Formaciones económicas y políticas del mundo andino.* Lima: Instituto de Estudios Peruanos, 1975.

Nash, Manning. "The Social Context of Economic Choice in a Small Society." In *Economic Anthropology,* edited by E. E. Le Clair, Jr., and H. K. Schneider, pp. 311–321. New York: Holt, Rinehart and Winston, 1968.

Neira Samañez, Hugo. *Cuzco, tierra o muerte.* Lima: Populibros Peruanos, 1964.

―――. *Los Andes, tierra o muerte.* Santiago: Editorial ZYX, 1968.

Nieto, E. *Recopilación de leyes y decretos desde la independencia.* Lima, 1864.

Noriega, A. "El enganche en la minería en el Perú." *Boletín de Minas,* nos. 4–6.

Núñez del Prado, Óscar. *Kuyo Chico: Applied Anthropology in an Indian Community.* Chicago and London: University of Chicago Press, 1973.

O'Brien, J. Philip. "A Critique of Latin American Theories of Dependency." In *Beyond the Sociology of Development,* edited by Ivar Oxaal, Tony Barnett, and David Booth. London: Routledge and Kegan Paul, 1975.

Oficina Nacional de Estadística y Censos. *Población del Perú: Resultados provisionales del censo de 1972.* Lima, 1973.

Ogura, T., ed. *Agricultural Development in Modern Japan.* Tokyo: Fuji Publishing Co., 1970.

Ordaya, E. Teogonio. *Chupaca: Estudio monográfico.* Huancayo, Peru, 1957.

Ortiz, Sutti. "Reflections on the Concept of 'Peasant Culture' and Peasant 'Cognitive Systems.'" In *Peasants and Peasant Societies,* edited by Teodor Shanin, pp. 322–336. Harmondsworth, England: Penguin Books, 1971.

Padilla, D. Norberto. *El Peruano,* July-October 1874. Cited in Ricardo Tello Devotto, *Historia de la provincia de Huancayo,* pp. 50–53. Huancayo, Peru: Casa de la Cultura de Junín, 1971.

Petras, James, and Hugo M. Zemelman. *Peasants in Revolt: A Chilean Case Study, 1965–1971.* Austin and London: University of Texas Press, 1972.

Piel, Jean. "Notas históricas sobre la evolución y la permanencia de las estructuras de dominación interna y externa en la sociedad peruana." *Revista del Museo Nacional* (Lima) 35 (1967–1968): 188–210.

―――. "The Place of the Peasantry in the National Life of Peru in the Nineteenth Century." *Past and Present* no. 46 (February 1970): 108–133.

Pike, F. B. *The Modern History of Peru.* London: Weidenfeld and Nicolson, 1967.

Preobrazhensky, E. *The New Economics.* Oxford: Clarendon Press, 1965.

Quijano, Aníbal. "Contemporary Peasant Movements." In *Elites in Latin America,* edited by S. M. Lipset and A. Solari. New York: Oxford University Press, 1967.

———. "Imperialismo y capitalismo de estado." *Sociedad y Política* (Lima) no. 1 (June 1972).

———. "The Marginal Role of the Economy and the Marginalised Labour Force." *Economy and Society* 3, no. 4 (November 1974): 393–428.

———. "Redefinición de la dependencia y proceso de marginalización en América Latina." In *Populismo, marginalización y dependencia,* edited by Francisco Weffort and Aníbal Quijano, pp. 171–329. San José, Costa Rica: Editorial Universitaria Centro-Americana, EDUCA, 1973.

———. "Tendencies in Peruvian Development and Class Structure." In *Latin America: Reform or Revolution?* edited by J. Petras and M. Zeitling. Greenwich: Fawcett, 1968.

Roberts, Bryan R. "Center and Periphery in the Development Process: The Case of Peru." In *Latin American Urban Research,* vol. 5, edited by W. A. Cornelius and F. M. Trueblood, pp. 77–106. Beverly Hills, California: Sage Publications, 1975.

———. "The Interrelationships of City and Provinces in Peru and Guatemala." In *Latin American Urban Research,* vol. 4, pp. 207–236. Beverly Hills, California: Sage Publications, 1974.

———. "Migración urbana y cambio en la organización provincial en la sierra central de Perú." *Ethnica: Revista de Antropología* (Barcelona) 6 (1973): 237–261.

———. "The Social History of a Provincial Town: Huancayo, 1890–1972." In *Social and Economic Change in Modern Peru,* edited by R. Miller, C. T. Smith, and J. Fisher. Liverpool: Centre for Latin American Studies Monograph Series, 1976.

Rogers, Everett. *Modernization among Peasants: The Impact of Communications.* New York: Holt, Rinehart and Winston, 1969.

Romero, Emilio. *Historia económica del Perú.* Lima: Imprenta Torres Aguirre, 1949.

Rowe, John H. "Inca Culture at the Time of the Spanish Conquest." In *Handbook of South American Indians,* edited by J. Steward, pp. 183–330. Washington, D.C.: Smithsonian Institution, 1946.

———. "The Incas Under Spanish Colonial Institutions." *Hispanic American Historical Review* 37, no. 2 (1957): 155–199.

Rubel, Arthur, and Harriet J. Kupferer. "Perspectives on the Atomistic-Type Society: Introduction." *Human Organization* 27, no. 3 (1973): 189–190.

Sabogal-Wiesse, José R. "Gamonalismo en los Andes." Paper presented at symposium, "Landlord and Peasant in Latin America and the Caribbean." Cambridge: Cambridge University, December 1972.

Samaniego, Carlos. "Location, Social Differentiation and Peasant Movements in the Central Sierra of Peru." Ph.D. dissertation, University of Manchester, 1974.

Saul, John S. "Marketing Cooperatives in a Developing Country: The Tanzanian Case." In *Two Blades of Grass: Rural Cooperatives in Agricultural*

Modernization, edited by Peter Worsley, pp. 347–370. Manchester: Manchester University Press, 1971.

Schaedel, Richard. *Plan regional para el desarrollo del sur del Perú*, vol. 5. Lima: Informe, Los Recursos Humanos del Departamento de Puno, 1959.

Schelling, Thomas. *The Strategy of Conflict*. Cambridge, Massachusetts: Harvard University Press, 1960.

Scott, Christopher. "Agrarian Reform, Accumulation and the Role of the State: The Case of Peru." In *Dépendance et Structure de Classes en Amérique Latine*, IV Seminaire Latino-Americain, CETIH (AFJK), October 1972.

———. "Peasants, Proletarianization and the Articulation of Modes of Production: The Case of Sugar-cane Cutters in Northern Peru, 1940–1969." *The Journal of Peasant Studies* 3, no. 3 (1976): 321–342.

Scott, Robert E. *Latin American Modernization Problems*. Urbana Chicago, London: University of Illinois Press, 1973.

Shanin, Teodor. *The Awkward Class*. London: Oxford University Press, 1972.

———. "The Nature and Logic of the Peasant Economy: A Generalization." *The Journal of Peasant Studies* 1, no. 1 (1973): 63–80.

———, ed. *Peasants and Peasant Societies*. Harmondsworth, England: Penguin Books, 1971.

Shickele, R. *Agrarian Revolution and Economic Progress*. New York: Praeger, 1968.

Skrubeltrang, F. *Agricultural Development and Rural Reform in Denmark*. Rome: Food and Agricultural Organization, United Nations, 1953.

Slater, David. "Underdevelopment and Spatial Inequality: Approaches to the Problems of Regional Planning in the Third World." *Progress in Planning* 4, part 2 (1975): 97–167.

Smith, Gavin A. "Internal Migration and Economic Activity: Some Case Studies." Centre for Developing Area Studies Working Papers, No. 14. Montreal: McGill University, 1975.

———. "The Social Bases of Peasant Political Activity: The Case of the Huasicanchinos of Central Peru." Ph.D. dissertation, University of Sussex, 1975.

Soares, G. A. O. "The New Industrialization and the Brazilian Political System." In *Latin America: Reform or Revolution*, edited by J. Petras and M. Zeitlin. Greenwich: Fawcett, 1968.

Solano Sáez, Juan. "Un estudio caso de la Sociedad Agrícola Pucará." Thesis, Universidad Nacional del Centro del Perú, Huancayo, 1973.

Spalding, Karen. "Class Structures in the Southern Peruvian Highlands, 1750–1920." In *Economía y sociedad en el Perú moderno*, vol. 2, edited by Heraclio Bonilla. Lima: Universidad del Pacífico, 1975.

———. "Hacienda-Village Relationships in Andean Society to 1830." In *Economía y sociedad en el Perú moderno*, vol. 2, edited by Heraclio Bonilla. Lima: Universidad del Pacífico, 1975.

Spiro, Melford E. *Kibbutz: Venture in Utopia*. New York: Schocken, 1970.

Stavenhagen, Rodolfo. "Classes, Colonialism and Acculturation." *Studies in Comparative International Development* 1, no. 6 (1965): 53–77.

Stein, William W. *Countrymen and Townsmen in the Callejón de Huaylas, Peru: Two Views of Andean Social Structure*. Special Studies Series, Council on International Studies. New York: State University of New York at Buffalo, 1974.

Stewart, Watt. *Henry Meiggs, Yankee Pizarro*. New York: AMS Press, 1946.

Stirling, Paul. *A Turkish Village*. London: Wiedenfeld and Nicolson, 1965.

Sulmont, Denis. *Mining Bibliography*. Lima: Pontificia Universidad Católica, 1971.

Tello Devotto, Ricardo. *Historia de la provincia de Huancayo*. Huancayo, Peru: Casa de la Cultura de Junín, 1971.

Tschopik, Harry. *Highland Communities of Central Peru*. Washington: Institute of Social Anthropology, Smithsonian Institution, 1947.

Tullis, F. Lamond. *Lord and Peasant in Peru: A Paradigm of Political and Social Change*. Cambridge, Massachusetts: Harvard University Press, 1970.

Vega, Garcilaso de la. *First Part of the "Royal Commentaries of the Incas."* Edited by Clements Markham. Vols. 41, 45. London: Hakluyt Society, 1869.

Webb, Richard. "Government Policy and Distribution of Income in Peru, 1963–1973." Discussion Paper No. 39, Research Program in Economic Development. Princeton: Woodrow Wilson School of Public and International Affairs, 1974.

Webster, Steven S. "Native Pastoralism in the South Andes." *Ethnology* 12 (1973): 115–133.

Whyte, William F., and Lawrence K. Williams. *Toward an Integrated Theory of Development*. Ithaca: New York School of Industrial and Labor Relations, 1968.

Wilkie, Raymond. *San Miguel: A Mexican Collective Ejido*. Stanford, California: Stanford University Press, 1971.

Winder, David. "The Effect of the 1970 Reform on the Peasant Communities and on the Community Development Process in an Area of Peru." M. Ed. thesis, University of Manchester, 1974.

Wolf, Eric R. "Aspects of Group Relations in a Complex Society: Mexico." *American Anthropologist* 58, no. 6 (1956): 1065–1078.

———. *Peasants*. Englewood Cliffs, New Jersey: Prentice-Hall, 1966.

———. "Types of Latin American Peasantry: A Preliminary Discussion." *American Anthropologist* 57, no. 3 (1955): 452–471.

Wolpe, Harold: "The Theory of Internal Colonialism: The South African Case." In *Beyond the Sociology of Development*, edited by Ivar Oxaal, Tony Barnett, and David Booth. London: Routledge and Kegan Paul, 1975.

Worsley, Peter, ed. *Two Blades of Grass: Rural Cooperatives in Agricultural Modernization*. Manchester: Manchester University Press, 1971.

Yepes, Ernesto. *Peru, 1820–1920: Un siglo de desarrollo capitalista*. Lima: Instituto de Estudios Peruanos, 1972.

———. "Some Aspects of Recent Peruvian Socio-economic History." Ph.D. dissertation, University of Manchester, 1974.

Young, Frank W. "A Proposal for Cooperative Crosscultural Research on Intervillage Systems." *Human Organization* 25, no. 1 (Spring 1966): 46–50.

Zaldívar, Ramón. "Agrarian Reform and Military Reformism in Peru." In *Agrarian Reform and Agrarian Reformism*, edited by D. Lehmann. London: Faber and Faber, 1974.

Index

Acolla, 18, 313

Adams, Richard N.: criticisms of community study approach, 18; on Muquiyauyo, 17–18, 27–28

Administrative units in Peru, 24, 26, 48, 56, 211, 218

Agrarian reform, 323; and agrarian debt, 244; attitudes of villagers to, 176, 180, 186, 188, 204; government policy on, 184, 255, 261 n. 1; of military junta, 209, 225–226, 240 n. 49, 241–246; in political campaigns of 1961 and 1963, 170–171; and problems of implementation at village level, 233–234, 242–243, 291

Agrarian Society of Pucará, 193

Agriculture: in nineteenth-century Mantaro region, 29, 49; productivity of, 30; risks in, 174; types of, in Peru, 12

Agromining economy, 321, 323; and community organization, 214; and foodstuff production, 59

Ahuac, 53–56, 59–62, 313; land ownership in, 54; political struggles in, 56, 59–60, 254; population of, in 1876, 53

Alavi, Hamza: on crosscutting ties among peasantry, 320

Alberti, Giorgio, and Sánchez, Rodrigo: on changes in village organization and politics in the Mantaro area, 24

Alers-Montalvo, Manuel: on Pucará, 195

Andean socio-cultural patterns: concept of, 14

Anexo (sub-district), 48

Applied anthropology: 299–300; criticisms of, 304

APRA (American Popular Revolutionary Alliance): 148, 168, 169–170, 323; activities in Mantaro region, 66, 90, 148, 168, 282; bases of support, 5, 93, 148–149, 169; in textiles, 148–149

Arguedas, José María: on "free" peasantry, 18; on Mantaro Valley communities, 18, 27; on patterns of land tenure, 211–212

Ayllu (localized corporate grouping), 25, 28, 210, 212, 213, 237 n. 5, 309

Barrio: as basis for village organization, 66, 108, 110, 120, 195, 218, 223

Belaúnde Terry, Fernando, 168, 171, 176, 183–184; rural development programs of, 270–271, 324

Bloch, Marc: on feudal village, 165

Bolívar, Simón: 1824 decrees of, 212–213

Bradby, Barbara: on non-capitalist forms of production, 303

Brokers, political, at village level, 213, 299

Bustamante y Rivero, José Luis, 90, 148

Cacchi, 8, 38, 62, 215, 249–255, 310

Cáceres, Andrés, 52, 55–56
Callejón de Huaylas, 20–21
Capital: role of foreign, in region,
131, 146
Capitalism: centralizing tendencies
of, 324; dependent, 147, 321–325;
expansion of, in Mantaro region,
4–5, 48, 59, 76, 78; industrial, in
Huancayo, 143–146, 153; as limit
on agrarian reform, 236–237, 261;
limits on expansion of, 304; and
persistence of non-capitalist
forms, 302–303; stages in penetration of, 304, 321–325
Castillo, Hernán: on village development, 21–22
Castro Pozo, Hildebrando: on the
Indian community, 15, 313; on
Muquiyauyo, 115
Cerro de Pasco Copper Corporation,
73–95 passim; crises of, 82, 111–
112; disputes of, with comunidades, 81, 84, 88–89, 92; formation of, 79, 83; haciendas of, 5–6,
29, 241; increase in output of, 80;
nationalist opposition to, 85–86;
reason for purchase of haciendas
by, 81, 87, 90, 93–94; smelter of,
36
Chaplin, David: on Lima textile industry, 131–132
Chaquicocha: compared with valley
villages, 21
Chilean war: 46; impact of, on Mantaro region, 29, 52, 166
Cholo: concept of, 19, 134
Chupaca, 26, 45, 69; dominant position of, 51, 57; as educational center, 8, 251; independent farmers
of, 65; in late nineteenth century,
48–49; as market center, 192; politics in, 66–67, 282; project to
create province of, 56
Class: formation of, among peasantry, 36, 301
Cofradía system, 26, 212, 237 n. 11,
312–313; sale of lands of, 217; village interest in lands of, 60–61,
65–67, 103, 194, 215–216, 312
Comas, 272, 278–279
Community institutions: conflicts

over, 192, 194, 197–198, 232, 249;
organization of, in Mantaro region, 57, 106–107, 179, 192, 194,
197–198, 232, 249; role of, in local
differentiation, 314. SEE ALSO
Comuneros, Comunidad, Comunidad indígena, Faena, Peasant
community
Compañía Mercantil de la Oroya:
78, 81, 93
Comuneros: 212, 226; attitudes of,
toward comunidad, 228; characteristics of, in villages, 117, 227–
232, 258, 285; cooperation among,
105, 219, 220
Comunidad (community): campesina, 306; closed corporate, 298;
concept of, 17, 74, 84, 236, 246,
299–300; differentiation within,
92, 219; economic activities of,
75–76, 112, 218; history of, in
Peru, 210–214, 224–225; individualization of, 218, 224, 260; industrial, 156; instrumental use of,
77, 81, 87–88, 91, 101, 122–123,
217, 219, 321; landholdings of, 26,
28, 85, 102–103, 111, 194; leaders
of, 123; relation of, to capitalist
expansion, 124, 209–210; relation
of, to state, 209, 298, 314; role of,
in local development, 4, 15, 22,
68, 122, 124, 214–224, 228. SEE
ALSO Community institutions,
Comuneros, Comunidad indígena,
Peasant community
Comunidad indígena, 211–214, 314;
difference between, and el común,
26, 101–103; and economic
change, 15, 58; ethnic connotation of, 57, 103, 225; legal recognition of, in villages, 38 n. 4, 46,
58, 111, 166, 194, 214–216, 246,
314; number of, in Peru, 4, 214;
relation of, to district council,
111, 218, 229; relation of, to large
estates, 63, 167, 215, 246; use of,
by exterior agents, 58, 315, 322.
SEE ALSO Community institutions,
Comuneros, Comunidad, Peasant
community
Concepción (province), 8–10

Varayoq (Indian council), 27
Velasco Alvarado, Juan, 209. See
    also Military government
Verticality. See Ecological levels
Vicos project, 20–21, 299
Villages in Mantaro region, 180,
    207, 246, 252, 316–318, 320–321,
    323–324; economic characteristics
    of, in highlands (puma), 46, 49,
    57, 62, 241–242, 245, 247–249, 260;
    economic characteristics of, in val-
    ley, 58, 132–135, 140–141, 167;
    formal associations within, 60, 66–
    67; independence movements
    within, 215, 246–247, 249; inter-
    village systems of, 22–23; leader-

ship within, 64–65, 122, 202, 282–
    284, 286–287. See also Cacchi,
    Huasicancha, Matahuasi, Muqui-
    yauyo, Pucará, Sicaya

Wolf, Eric: on closed corporate
    community, 298
Wool: as export, 19, 76, 242; and
    the textile industry, 137

Yanacancha, 62–64, 168–169, 182,
    249, 254, 258–259; internal dif-
    ferentiation in, 50, 52; overgraz-
    ing in, 62, 252
Young, Frank: on intervillage sys-
    tems, 32